*Sergei Zubatov and
Revolutionary Marxism*

# Sergei Zubatov and Revolutionary Marxism

## THE STRUGGLE FOR THE WORKING CLASS IN TSARIST RUSSIA

### Jeremiah Schneiderman

Cornell University Press

ITHACA AND LONDON

HD
8526
.S32

Cornell University Press gratefully acknowledges a grant from the Andrew J.
Mellon Foundation that aided in bringing this book to publication.

First published 1976 by Cornell University Press.
Published in the United Kingdom by Cornell University Press Ltd., 2-4 Brook
Street, London W1Y 1AA.

International Standard Book Number 0-8014-0876-8
Library of Congress Catalog Card Number 75-27881
Printed in the United States of America
*Librarians: Library of Congress cataloging information
appears on the last page of the book.*

*For my parents and Aunt Mary*

# Contents

# Illustrations

# Preface

At the turn of the century Sergei Zubatov, a dedicated monarchist, established a remarkable record in police counterintelligence. He was chief of the Moscow Okhrana, the security police, from 1896 to 1902, and as he ferreted out the clandestine networks of the revolutionary parties, he became aware of the needs of the new industrial working class and the attempts of the socialists to win its allegiance.

Challenging the traditional government view held by the Ministry of Finance, Zubatov initiated a labor program, commonly called the Zubatovshchina, which recognized the workers' need to organize and which became the prevailing tsarist labor policy during these years. It is uniquely significant, for it interacted with the two other decisive elements in prerevolutionary labor history in Russia: the Social Democrats' response to this policy and the response of the working class to the forces competing for its loyalty at a crucial time.

The reflection of the Zubatovshchina could be seen in industrial centers other than those studied here. The Social Democrats from the first recognized its significance and the grave danger it posed to their movement, and they attacked it. In studying the social-democratic response, it is necessary to take into account the controversies among the émigré ideologues and the differences between the émigré centers and the local social-democratic committees in those cities where the Zubatovshchina was implanted, as well as the disputes within the local committees and between the committees and their working class followers, the last reflecting the alienation between worker and intelligentsia. Russian social democracy was then in its formative stage, with many important tactical and theoretical problems unresolved. Only at the party's second congress, in the summer of 1903, when the Zubatovshchina was already in decline, did it enunciate a tactical position toward the Zubatov unions which challenged them for the leadership of the working class. The socialists' overweening optimism that the Zubatovshchina bore the seeds of its own destruction and their concentration on programmatic and organizational problems may explain the tardiness. In this study the social-democratic Jewish Labor Bund is treated separately from Russian social democracy, for the Zubatovshchina in the western provinces was aimed at undermining the Bund's hold over the Jewish artisans of the Pale.

I began the research for this work at the University of California at Berkeley and continued while I was an exchange student at Leningrad University, sponsored by the Inter-University Committee on Travel Grants. The Ford Foundation and the Research Foundation of the State University of New York funded additional study. Further research in the Soviet Union and in Paris was supported by a grant from the Penrose Fund of the American Philosophical Society, for which I am especially thankful.

I am grateful to librarians at the University of California at Berkeley, Columbia University, the University of Illinois at Urbana-Champaign, Vassar College, the New York Public Library, the Jewish Theological Seminary, and the YIVO Institute for Jewish Research. In England I received permission to use the libraries of the University of London, the London School of Slavonic and East European Studies, and the British Museum.

Special thanks are due to Julia Kamermacher of the Menshevik Project at Columbia University for use of the Project's research materials; to the Administrative Committee and Lev F. Magerovsky, Curator, for permission to use the Archive of Russian and East European History and Culture at Columbia University; and to the administration of Yale University Library for permission to study the Aleksandr Ivanovich Spiridovich Papers. Hillel Kempinski and J. S. Hertz of the Bund Archives in New York generously provided relevant photographs and other materials from the Archives and discussed with me at length various aspects of the Bund's relations with the Zubatovshchina. The French government gave permission to use the valuable ambassadorial and consular reports from Russia found in the archives of the Ministry of Foreign Affairs at the Quai d'Orsay. Photographs 1–10 originally appeared in *Al'manakh sovremennykh russkikh gosudarstvennykh deiatelei* (St. Petersburg, 1897). No photograph of Zubatov has ever been published, nor have I been able to locate an unpublished one.

Soviet librarians and bibliographers were a model of cooperation and readily gave their time and assistance. The same was not true of the Soviet authorities, who during both sojourns in the Soviet Union denied me access to the archives.

The study has benefited from criticisms and suggestions of fellow scholars. Parts or all of the manuscript have been read by Nicholas Riasanovsky, Martin Malia, Reinhard Bendix, Robert Johnson, Harvey Richman, Hans Rogger, Theodore H. Von Laue, Allan K. Wildman, and George L. Yaney. Solomon Schwarz read the chapters on the Minsk Zubatovshchina; I am very grateful for his warm encouragement.

Celia M. Coulter, Mary Jane Sherwig, and Linda Pfeiffer of the library staff at the State University College at New Paltz graciously fulfilled a multitude of requests for research materials. Alfred H. Marks scrutinized the manuscript and suggested many changes that improved its style and organization.

Parts of this book are drawn from material in my article "From the Files of the Moscow Gendarme Corps: A Lecture on Combatting Revolution," *Canadian Slavic Studies*, 2 (1968), 86–99, by permission of the journal.

A note about dating and transliteration: Dates are given in the old style according to the Julian calendar used in prerevolutionary Russia. In the twentieth century the Julian calendar was thirteen days behind the Gregorian calendar used in the West. In citations of French and American diplomatic correspondence in the notes, the letters n.s. (new style) have been appended to the dates to indicate the use of the Gregorian calendar in the dispatches. The Library of Congress system of transliteration has been used throughout except where common usage has dictated otherwise — e.g., Witte, rather than Vitte.

JEREMIAH SCHNIEDERMAN

*New Paltz, New York*

*Sergei Zubatov and*
*Revolutionary Marxism*

# CHAPTER 1

# The Tsarist Government and the Labor Question

During the quarter century before World War I the Russian Empire underwent major changes that brought it closer in form to the states of Western Europe. The autocracy under the duress of revolution pledged to respect civil liberties and permitted an elected parliament. A vigorous political life emerged from the underground as many political parties openly fought for election. The agrarian structure of society based on peasant and landlord, traditional in Russia for a millennium, was altered to accommodate new classes. The most fundamental change, disrupting society and state in its impact and raising unprecedented social problems, was the intensive industrialization that occurred in Russia more than a half century after it first flourished in Western Europe.

In the 1890's Russia experienced a great industrial upsurge stimulated and shaped by government policy, its chief architect being Sergei Witte, Minister of Finance from 1892 to 1903. Witte's conservative budgetary policies and monetary reforms, which stabilized the currency on the gold standard, instilled confidence in Russia's financial soundness among investors abroad. Foreign capital began to occupy a significant place in the capitalization of Russian industry.[1] Although the average annual rate of industrial growth from 1860 to 1913 was 5 per cent, in the 1890's it reached 8 per cent, the highest for any decade.[2] Railroad construction was the main stimulant to the industrial growth. The railway network,

1. John P. McKay, *Pioneers for Profit* (Chicago and London, 1970).
2. Raymond W. Goldsmith, "The Economic Growth of Tsarist Russia, 1860–1913," *Economic Development and Cultural Change*, 9 (1961), 442; Alexander Gerschenkron, "The Rate of Industrial Growth in Russia since 1885," *Journal of Economic History*, supplement 7 (1947), pp. 146, 150.

including the vast but incomplete Siberian line, doubled during the decade. Railroads widened the market for industrial products and brought the produce of previously untapped geographic regions into the national economy. The chief beneficiary of the economic activity was heavy industry, notably machine building and the metallurgical and fuel industries.

Fundamental to the great surge forward of Russian industrial power was vastly enlarged output of iron, steel, and oil in the southern Ukraine and Caucasus. Between 1895 and 1900 Russian iron and steel production doubled, with the southern industrial region becoming responsible for half of the output. Even more striking was exploitation of the rich Baku oil fields, which in 1900 supplied over 95 per cent of Russian oil and attained world prominence, surpassing American output.

Statistics confirm substantial growth in all phases of economic life that are barometers of modern industrialization. Between 1887 and 1897 the number of factories increased by 26.3 per cent to a total of 39,000, and the total value of production doubled; 40 per cent of Russian factories existing in 1900 had been founded in the 1890's.[3] Intensive application of machine technology became widespread. In absolute value of production the textile industry held the leadership, closely followed by heavy industry.

In Russia, as elsewhere, industrial growth accelerated urbanization, although it was less pronounced than in Western Europe. While the total population of the empire increased 58 per cent from 1863 to 1897, urban population doubled. The census of 1897 reported forty-four cities with a population of more than 50,000; the urban population, less than 6 per cent on the eve of emancipation, was calculated at 16.8 million, or 13.4 per cent of the entire nation.[4] Despite the drift from the countryside to the city, urbanization was much less pronounced than in Western Europe.

3. Peter I. Lyashchenko, *History of the National Economy of Russia to the 1917 Revolution* (New York, 1949), p. 526; A. G. Rashin, *Formirovanie rabochego klassa Rossii* (Moscow, 1958), pp. 24–25, 38–39; A. V. Pogozhev, *Uchet chislennosti i sostava rabochikh v Rossii* (St. Petersburg, 1906), p. 76.
4. Warren W. Eason, "Population Changes," in Cyril E. Black, ed., *The Transformation of Russian Society* (Cambridge, Mass., 1960), pp. 73, 82; I. F. Rybakov, "Dinamika gorodskogo naseleniia Rossii vo vtoroi polovine XIX veka," Leningradskii ordena Lenina gosudarstvennyi universitet imeni A. A. Zhdanova, *Uchenye zapiski,* no. 288, Seriia ekonomicheskikh nauk, pt. 2 (1959), p. 205; Lyashchenko, p. 504.

The industrial boom of the 1890's greatly increased the ranks of the industrial proletariat. Many peasants sought seasonal employment in towns, as evidenced by the ever increasing number of short-term passports approved by the *mir* (village community). Emancipation of certain categories of laborers without land, including former household domestics and mine and mill workers, created a potential industrial proletariat of considerable size; their number, together with peasants who opted at the time of emancipation to receive minute landholdings unencumbered by redemption payments, reached four million. Such peasants, in particular, requested extended leave from their villages to work in industry; the average number of annual long-term passports, 60,000 during the decade following emancipation, reached two million in the 1890's. Official statistics, frequently criticized for being grossly incomplete, record the Russian factory work force in 1897 at over two million, a 60 per cent increase in the decade from 1887.[5]

The economic and political significance of the Russian proletariat far outweighed its relative size. Factory and railway workers, estimated at but 2 per cent of the empire's population, were concentrated in large-scale industry in a small number of geographic regions. Russian political centers were also factory cities; an economist in 1898 observed that "the concentration of Russian industry and the industrial development of such districts as the Moscow and Petersburg suburbs greatly increase the social and political significance of the one-sided development of a factory culture."[6] The Russian factory system had a long tradition of large-scale establishments, the overwhelming majority of factories employing 500 or more workers in 1900 having been founded prior to 1861. In 1903, 31.8 per cent of the 1.6 million workers under factory inspector surveillance (that is, in factories with a certain minimum number of workers) were employed in the 1.5 per cent of the enterprises with more than a thousand workers; during the same year the average number of workers at each factory surveyed by the inspectors reached 108. The proportion of factories employing 500 or more workers was greater than in several of the most highly industrialized states of Western Europe, including

5. Rashin, p. 23.
6. Pogozhev, pp. x–xi.

Germany and Belgium.[7] The vast majority of factory workers were employed in the textile and metal-processing industries, which between them accounted for more than three-quarters of those at work in large-scale factories.

Among the radical intelligentsia, deeply divided over Russia's future economic development, the character of the industrial worker and the extent of his physical and emotional ties with the land were hotly disputed. Those who believed that Russia was entering the capitalist stage maintained that an industrial working class existed in Russia for which village life was a thing of the past. This was the conclusion reached as early as 1874 by a prominent statistician, Iu. E. Ianson, after a study of factory life:

> The widespread opinion that we supposedly do not have a class of factory workers is positively untrue.... It appears that among us there are workers who have lived for decades in the factories; they send for their wives and families from their native place and gravitate to the villages only because they are listed as members of rural communities, and they pay obligations placed upon them according to the apportionment by the community; besides this, we know that more than one generation of factory workers grew up and went along the road of its fathers in our Petersburg factories.[8]

Ianson was expressing a minority viewpoint; not until the 1890's, when a relatively large proletariat emerged, could such views become convincing. Further investigation confirmed the existence of a considerable working class divorced from the land and employed year-round in factories. E. M. Dement'ev's study of the working class in Moscow *guberniia* (province) in 1884–1885, published in 1893, concluded that a special class of factory workers already existed. Though frequently reckoned as peasants, they actually constituted a landless proletariat possessing the most tenuous ties with village life, to which they felt alien. Half those investigated by Dement'ev had broken ties altogether with their native villages; over half were second generation factory workers.[9]

7. *Ibid.*, pp. xv–xvi, xxi; Ministerstvo Torgovli i Promyshlennosti, Otdel promyshlennosti, *Svod otchetov fabrichnykh inspektorov za 1903 god* (St. Petersburg, 1906), pp. i, iii.

8. Quoted in Rybakov, pp. 208–9.

9. Reported in D. Kol'tsov, ''Rabochie v 1890–1904 gg.,'' in *Obshchestvennoe dvizhenie v Rossii v nachale XX-go veka,* ed. L. Martov, P. Maslov, and A. Potresov (St. Petersburg, 1909), I, 183; V. Zel'tser, ''Promyshlennaia revoliutsiia v Rossii,'' *Bor'ba klassov,* Sept. 1934, p. 85.

Russia thus had a factory proletariat in the making as it entered the twentieth century.

Yet Russia at the end of the nineteenth century remained predominantly agrarian. The country was overwhelmingly peasant; justifiably, peasant problems were the center of government concern. Industry, despite recent progress, was in an early stage. Western European experience gave cause for concern, nevertheless, for precisely during this stage sharp class conflict erupted. There was no reason to expect that Russia would avoid the social and economic dislocation and class antagonism which attended the coming of the industrial revolution elsewhere. In its favor the Russian government could draw upon a century of Western European experience in resolving these problems. During the first half of the nineteenth century, when the economic philosophy of laissez faire prevailed, the European states refused labor reforms and prohibited mass labor organizations and strikes. This position was reversed in the second half of the century, when such staunch conservatives as Disraeli and Bismarck, convinced that with labor reforms the working class would cease to threaten the social and political structure, led the way in enacting factory legislation.

The Russian working class brought the monarchy to its knees in 1905 and toppled it in 1917. Yet in the decade before the revolution of 1905 the government could have evolved a labor policy capable of satisfying the working class. The factory workers, fundamentally loyal to the throne, were discontented with working and living conditions, protesting through spontaneous economic strikes of a generally peaceful nature. Whether the proletariat would continue to confine itself to economic protest or would take the road of political action and revolution depended on the government's response to its basic needs and demands. Failure to act positively would put in question the compatibility of the labor movement with the further existence of the tsarist autocracy.

Traditional Views of the Labor Question

In the nineteenth century both society and government viewed the peasant question as Russia's most pressing social problem. The existence of a "labor question"—that is, the recognition of a European-style industrial proletariat distinct from the peasantry and with separate interests and concerns—was not generally admitted by Russian society. Some academicians, journalists, and officials in the 1860's foresaw and welcomed industrialization and advocated timely measures to prevent the Russian proletariat from undergoing the suffering borne by European industrial laborers. Others feared that industrialization would undermine the traditional rural basis of Russian life and foster the creation of an impoverished European-style proletariat out of uprooted peasants.[10] For the remainder of the century broad segments of public opinion, from the Narodniki (Populists), Russia's agrarian socialists, on the left, to the conservative gentry on the right, clung to an antiquated theory regarding the nature of Russian life and history and were reluctant to acknowledge and opposed the emergence of an industrial proletariat.

Belief that the foundations and historical evolution of Russian life were unique runs through much of Russian nineteenth-century thought. Descriptive analyses of political and economic life were combined with national prejudice and chauvinism as the basis of a philosophy stressing Russia's divergence from Europe as a positive good. Western Europe was disdained for its frequent political upheavals attributed to bitter class antagonisms engendered by industrialization. In contrast, Russia was extolled as an inherently agrarian land free of social conflict, in which all were united by bonds of loyalty to Tsar and Fatherland. The basis of Russian life therefore had to be protected from the intrusion of alien ways; foreign borrowings could lead only to social strife. These currents of thought can be traced to the reign of Alexander I (1801–1825), when agrarian opponents of protectionism and industrialization attacked the evils associated with the factory system by contrasting the alleged well-being of the Russian serf with the burdensome lot of the factory worker in the West.[11]

During the rule of Nicholas I (1825–1855) the government glorified Russian life and history in its doctrine of Official Nationality, which contrasted the "peaceful and calm fatherland" with the "restless and turbulent West."[12] Class struggle and revolution, it

10. Reginald E. Zelnik, *Labor and Society in Tsarist Russia* (Stanford, 1971), ch. 3.
11. P. A. Buryshkin, *Moskva kupecheskaia* (New York, 1954), pp. 38–40.
12. Nicholas V. Riasanovsky, *Nicholas I and Official Nationality in Russia, 1825–1855* (Berkeley and Los Angeles, 1959), p. 137. These views were shared by the Third Section, the omnipotent secret police created in the reign of Nicholas I. Sidney Monas, *The Third Section* (Cambridge, Mass., 1961), p. 277.

insisted, would remain alien to Russia. The government was, however, sensitive to the potential danger to the state posed by the small but growing number of factory workers; a report to the tsar in 1848 recommended limiting the number of factories in each city to preclude the exploitation of disgruntled propertyless workers by antisocial elements.[13]

The Slavophile ideology that flourished in the reign of Nicholas I shared with Official Nationality an antipathy for Western capitalist society. The Slavophiles, with their reverence for the pre-Petrine Russian past, regarded the simple peasant as the embodiment of ancient Russian moral virtues and the peasant collective, the *mir*, as expressing the social nature of the Russian people. Idealizers of peasant virtues, the Slavophiles hoped to forestall forever the growth of a proletariat.[14]

Indifference or opposition to industrialization was also expressed by the radical intelligentsia, whose major concern was with the welfare of the peasantry during most of the nineteenth century.[15] The belief that the *mir*, or commune, represented a primitive form of socialism was an article of faith among the Narodniki. Through the commune, with its economic equality based on periodic redistribution of land, Russia could attain a socialist society and avoid capitalism, toward which the pre-Marxist radical intelligentsia felt an almost universal revulsion. In the 1880's these assumptions of Russia's agrarian future were challenged for the first time by Marxist critics, causing the Narodniki to defend their theories more cogently. Capitalism, the Narodniki insisted, had still not penetrated Russia, and there was every hope that it could be avoided in the future. In their eyes the Russian factory worker remained a village peasant with strong ties to his rural community; even when driven by economic necessity to work in urban industry he would return periodically to his village, where he had land and shelter. Russia thus had no permanent industrial proletariat, as in

13. M. Tugan-Baranovskii, *Russkaia fabrika v proshlom i nastoiashchem*, 2d ed. (St. Petersburg, 1900), p. 179.

14. *Ibid.*, pp. 284–87; Nicholas V. Riasanovsky, *Russia and the West in the Teaching of the Slavophiles* (Cambridge, Mass., 1952), pp. 133–35, 146–47. Several Slavophiles supported Russia's industrialization (William L. Blackwell, *The Beginnings of Russian Industrialization, 1800–1860* [Princeton, 1968], pp. 146–47).

15. Alexander Gerschenkron, "The Problem of Economic Development in Russian Intellectual History of the Nineteenth Century," in Ernest J. Simmons, ed., *Continuity and Change in Russian and Soviet Thought* (Cambridge, Mass., 1955), pp. 11–39.

Europe, but merely seasonal workers whose economic and personal ties remained with their native village. Nor did Russia possess sufficient industry, it was held, to raise apprehension about the advent of capitalism and industrialization. Only through artificial stimulation—meaning the imposition from above of industrialization on the Western European model—could Russia enter the capitalistic stage.[16]

These ideas are of more than purely abstract interest, for they became an article of faith even for many in the higher bureaucracy, as well as for academicians, and prominent members of the industrial community. The allegation that neither a labor question nor industrial class conflict existed in Russia was often heard from proponents of laissez faire in labor relations. Academician V. P. Bezobrazov, for example, in a semiofficial report published at the end of the 1880's, warned that government interference in factory affairs would end pristine relations between employer and worker and lead to strife.[17] Opponents of factory legislation feared that its enactment would artificially create a distinct labor class. The history of the workmen's compensation law is a case in point. In opposing the measure in the State Council in 1893, K. P. Pobedonostsev, the influential Procurator of the Holy Synod, lashed out at the government for proposing laws of a socialist character, charging that it apparently wished to make a proletariat of the Russian factory workers, who, properly speaking, were cultivators of the soil and never had broken their ties with the land. Pobedonostsev's influence was sufficient to have the bill shelved, although it allegedly had the approval of the Emperor.[18] Similar arguments

16. On the history of Populism and the Populist-Marxist debate see Franco Venturi, *Roots of Revolution* (London, 1960); Solomon M. Schwarz, "Populism and Early Russian Marxism on Ways of Economic Development of Russia (the 1880's and 1890's)," in Simmons, pp. 40–62; Theodore H. Von Laue, "Russian Peasants in the Factory, 1892–1904," *Journal of Economic History,* 21 (1961), 61–80.

17. Cited in I. I. Ianzhul, *Iz vospominanii i perepiski fabrichnago inspektora pervago prizyva* (St. Petersburg, 1907), p. 4.

18. In his writings and in his later official testimony Witte referred to this incident as evidence of the impediments placed before the Ministry of Finance in evolving a solution to the "labor question" through legislative means. *Otchet po deloproizvodstvu gosudarstvennago soveta za sessiiu 1902–1903 g.g.* (St. Petersburg, 1904), II, 133, 139; *Gosudarstvennyi Sovet, Stenograficheskie otchety, 1911–12 gody* (St. Petersburg, 1912), p. 3402; *Rabochii vopros v komissii V. N. Kokovtsova v 1905 g.* (Moscow, 1926), p. 21; S. Iu. Witte, *Vospominaniia* (Moscow, 1960), I, 366–69; *Gosudarstvennyi Sovet, Stenograficheskie otchety, 1909–10 gody* (St. Petersburg, 1910), pp. 2643–44.

were used against the bill when it was reintroduced in 1903.[19] These views, commonly held in industrial circles, were expressed in the reports of the Moscow and St. Petersburg manufacturers at a special legislative conference called in 1903 by the Ministry of Finance. The essence of their argument was best summarized by an opponent:

> In Russia a large part of the factory workers has not given up ties with the village and is not isolated into a special class as in the West. It is apparent that if there are no special factory workers but only peasants who temporarily go to seasonal work for the sake of subsidiary earnings and who maintain a lively link with the village, then there cannot be any question about the isolation of their way of life (or) special interests and consequently about legislative initiative especially for them.[20]

Official pronouncements, statements by prominent industrialists, and newspaper editorials frequently asserted with confidence that relations between Russian workers and their employers retained a patriarchal character similar to that between peasant and landlord and were devoid of class conflict as in the West. This rosy view of labor relations died hard among extreme conservatives and was heard long after reality in the form of a large and militant labor movement had proven it untenable.[21]

## Early Labor Legislation

The Russian government in 1890 had a relatively creditable record of achievement in labor legislation, considering the country's level of industrial development. A tradition of deep involvement in economic matters unhampered by an entrenched philosophy of laissez faire, an acute sensitivity to any threat to order, and an interest in the general well-being of its people impelled the Russian government to regulate labor relations. To this end support came from those who were visibly aware of the condition of the factory working class, including police officials, factory inspectors, and a segment of industrial management. Most telling of all, the emergence in the last quarter of the nineteenth century of a vociferous labor movement intermittently bursting the bounds of

19. *Otchet . . . za sessiiu 1902–1903 g.g.,* II, 142.

20. *Zakonodatel'nye materialy k zakonu o starostakh v promyshlennykh predpriiatiiakh* (Stuttgart, 1903), p. 26.

21. See the testimony of S. P. Glezmer before the State Council on May 7, 1910, *Gosudarstvennyi Sovet, 1909–10 gody,* pp. 2645–46.

legality in large-scale strikes, caused the government to hasten investigation of factory working conditions and eradicate the most blatant abuses.

Large-scale factory strikes in the 1870's and early 1880's, capped by the strike of six thousand workers at the giant Morozov plant in Orekhovo-Zuevo in 1885, were a phenomenon new to Russia and drew the government's attention to the labor problem. In such cases the government promptly responded with repressive measures; subsequent investigation frequently revealed shocking working conditions and the exploitation of labor as the underlying causes of unrest. Flagrant abuses by factory administrations were not a private matter to which the government could be indifferent when they led to major strikes and disorders; thus official investigations of strikes were often a prelude to corrective legislation. These first strikes foreshadowed unrest on a far larger scale and indicated that the comparative smallness of the factory population did not make Russia immune to factory disorder and class conflict. Moreover, poor working conditions and an extremely low standard of living made the workers susceptible to antigovernment propaganda. A Petersburg police official noted in 1884 that there already existed an urban proletariat different in outlook from the peasantry and open to "all kinds of false doctrine." Contact between urban workers and village peasants, he warned, might lead to a dangerous situation, for "the corrupted workers may in time spread this infection even among the agricultural population."[22]

In the 1880's the government introduced a series of measures designed to eliminate certain iniquitous factory practices and established mechanisms to insure the measures were implemented. The first of these, a law of June 1, 1882, prohibited factory labor for children under the age of twelve, restricted the hours of work for juveniles, and created a staff of factory inspectors. During the next three years labor legislation was broadened to include compulsory education of factory juveniles and prohibition of night work for women and juveniles in certain branches of the large textile industry.

Considerations of order were prominent in the promulgation on June 3, 1886, of a law, restricting the factory owner's previously

---

22. Quoted in Reinhard Bendix, *Work and Authority in Industry* (New York and London, 1956), p. 188.

unlimited freedom in relations with his employees. The new measure outlawed the most blatant factory malpractices and placed limitations upon factory administrations in the assessment of fines, the payment of wages, and the conditions under which employees could be discharged. The corps of factory inspectors was given the thankless task of enforcing these rules in the face of opposition by the factory administrations.

## Government Intervention and the Labor Question

By the end of the nineteenth century, labor relations in many Western European countries had changed more favorably for the working class, the law having sanctioned trade unions and strikes; in Russia such legislation was judged "not corresponding to the conditions of our state order."[23] The Russian government was willing to intervene in relations between capital and labor only to eliminate blatant abuses and restrict the arbitrary power of factory management. State regulation of hours and wages, which had been enacted for serf workers in state-owned industry in the eighteenth century, was considered inappropriate in an economy in which private ownership was predominant. Indeed the government in its anxiety for public order legislated against all forms of collective activity and association by workers. Here it acted in conformity with its general policy toward society; voluntary associations and group activity were tightly restricted or prohibited, with little distinction made in this regard between supporters and opponents of the monarchy. Public initiative was equated with potential sedition. Organizations without official approval of their statutes were treated as illegal societies, so that, in practice, only the most politically innocuous benevolent organizations were authorized.

The Russian worker at the turn of the century had fewer legal rights than workers in the West and was more limited in his means of exerting pressure to attain his ends. He lacked political freedoms, parliamentary representation, and certain basic civil rights; moveover, the law was so weighted to the advantage of the employer that peaceful measures for the outlet of labor discontent were closed to him.

23. See the discussion in the State Council of the proposed law to limit working hours for factory workers: *Otchet po deloproizvodstvu gosudarstvennago soveta za sessiiu 1896–1897 g.g.* (St. Petersburg, 1897), p. 194.

For one thing, the government tended to consider a premeditated strike or a simple work stoppage before termination of a contract a violation of criminal law. By the law code of 1845 both instigators and participants in strikes were subject to imprisonment. A supplement to the code in 1874 punished those who joined together to "incite hostility between owners and workers" with either exile to Siberia and deprivation of rights, or imprisonment.[24] The law of June 3, 1886, which protected workers from the abuses of management, reflected the duality of reform and repression that so often marked tsarist labor legislation. Harsher penalties were set for premature breach of contract; a prison sentence of four to eight months was prescribed for leaders of a strike, two to four months was levied for willful absenteeism after a preliminary warning to resume work had been given. Criminal penalties failed to halt departure of many factory workers for seasonal labor in their native villages before the terminal contractual date; this legal infraction was by far the most frequent source of complaint lodged by management with the factory inspectors.[25]

While the law dealt with the worker's breach of contract as a criminal misdemeanor it treated a similar infraction by management as a mere civil breach of contract. Factory inspectors often commented critically upon this inequity. In the words of one inspector the legal imbalance "only embitters the workers, and places the government organs, in the latter's eyes, in the extremely false position of one-sided defense of the employer's interest."[26]

The workers were not in a practical position to take legal action

24. L. Martov, "Razvitie krupnoi promyshlennosti i rabochee dvizhenie do 1892 g." in *Istoriia Rossii v XIX veke* (St. Petersburg, 1907–1911), VI, 136; V. Grinevich [M. G. Kogan], *Professional'noe dvizhenie rabochikh v Rossii* (St. Petersburg, 1908), p. 7; Tugan-Baranovskii, p. 176.

25. The Moscow *okrug* (region) factory inspector reported in 1902: "From the circumstance that the number of cases of unwarranted departures from work by no means decreases with the course of time, despite the application of the penalty established by article 51⁴ of the Penal Code, one can conclude this article is useless as a measure of a preventive character; with regard to its moral significance one can consider it openly harmful, since establishing criminal responsibility for the worker for a civil transgression of the law, to which the employer is not subject, creates an inequality before the law of the right of the parties who conclude a hiring contract" (Ministerstvo Finansov, Otdel promyshlennosti, *Svod otchetov . . . za 1902 god* [St. Petersburg, 1904], p. xviii). In 1901 more than 3,000 such complaints were directed by management to the factory inspectors, constituting more than three-quarters of the total of all types of complaints received by the inspectors against the workers (*Svod otchetov . . . za 1901 god* [St. Petersburg, 1903], p. ix).

if they were discharged before their contract expired or when malpractices, condemned by the law of 1886, continued.[27] The factory management usually took advantage of this impotence, and the worker concerned with making a living had either to remain silent or face dismissal. For example, the worker had the right in case of a breach of contract either to appeal to the courts or to dissolve the contract. Rarely, however, did the case reach the courts, for a successful judgment involved the award of an insignificant sum and the risk of the loss of job. Consequently, one inspector noted, "in the majority of cases the worker does not wish at all to take advantage of the right of annulling the contract, but on the contrary wishes to continue work."[28] The patent inadequacy of the law led factory inspectors to urge that the factory administration be held criminally responsible, a step the government refused to take.[29]

The average factory worker had little knowledge of the terms of labor legislation; many were unaware even of the existence of the laws. Provoked by arbitrary treatment and burdensome labor conditions, they often complained to the factory inspector about matters beyond his legal competency to rectify. Informal representations by the inspector on the workers' behalf were bound to be futile, for the factory administration knew it need not make concessions. In due course the management would dismiss employees who had petitioned for improvements, discouraging others from following their example.

26. Quoted from a regional inspector's report for 1903. I. Kh. Ozerov, *Politika po rabochemu voprosu v Rossii za poslednie gody* (Moscow, 1906), p. 155.

27. The chief causes of complaints made by the workers against their employers included incorrect calculation and lowering of wages, nonpayment or withholding of wages, and dismissal before termination of the contract (*Svod otchetov . . . za 1903 god,* p.vii). The helpless position of the worker whose wages were illegally withheld or delayed by the factory administration was noted with sympathy in the report of a senior factory inspector of Moscow *guberniia* in 1901: "The . . . delay [in payment] of wages places the worker in such a burdensome position that he either must reconcile himself to it, since the factory inspector is not in a position to help him, or take his complaint to court and lose his job and often for a long time remain without wages" (*Svod otchetov za 1901 god,* p. xii). The factory inspector of the St. Petersburg *okrug* likewise reported that year that "in the majority of such cases" for the average worker to turn to the courts for redress was "either an extremely difficult matter or even often completely impossible" (*ibid.*).

28. *Svod otchetov . . . za 1902 god,* p. xvi.

29. D. S. Sipiagin, the Minister of Interior, in 1901 suggested criminal responsibility for factory owners who arbitrarily terminated the hiring contract before its legal date of expiration, but Witte opposed (Ozerov, pp. 140, 142–43).

In moments of desperation the factory workers appealed for the aid of the government; occasionally they petitioned the higher authorities, such as members of the imperial family, or the tsar himself, as on that famous Sunday in January 1905, when a march to the Winter Palace touched off a revolution. Trust in the government's benevolence and responsiveness to the needs of the workers once it became acquainted with their sufferings, lingered on among the workers despite government reluctance to become a party to labor relations.[30]

When Russia entered the 1890's the government's basic policy was to leave terms and conditions of labor to the free play of the contracting parties. State intervention went no further than limiting the employment of women and children, abolishing flagrant abuses, and establishing a corps of factory inspectors. Though informed bureaucrats were often distributed by deplorable factory working conditions, the autocracy generally maintained a hands-off attitude in times of industrial peace; when industrial disturbances broke out it acted decisively through either repression or the introduction of palliative reforms, for above all the autocracy was sensitive to any threat to its security.

## Witte and the Labor Question

When Witte was appointed Minister of Finance in 1892 the labor question was not regarded as an acute issue demanding serious government attention. The previous year a famine of great proportions had drawn the sympathies of society to the plight of the impoverished peasantry and rekindled interest in the peasant question. Witte's own unrestrained optimism about the state of labor relations in Russia is most clearly expressed in a secret circular of December 5, 1895, to members of the factory inspectorate:

In our industry a patriarchal tradition of relations between owners and workers predominates. This patriarchy in many cases is expressed in the

---

30. A petition of striking cotton-mill workers addressed to the heir to the throne, the future Alexander III, in 1878, coupled a naive expression of loyalty with a threat of working-class activism: "We turn to You as to a father. If our just demands will not be fulfilled we will then know that there is no one for us to have confidence in, that no one intercedes for us, and that we must rely on ourselves and our own hands" (Martov, p. 124; V. Sviatlovskii, *Professional'noe dvizhenie v Rossii* [St. Petersburg, 1907], p. 8).

solicitude of the factory owner for the needs of the workers and employees at his factory, in care about the preservation of harmony and accord, in simplicity and justice in mutual relations. When at the basis of such relations lies the rule of moral and Christian feeling, recourse to the application of written law and compulsion is not necessary.[31]

Witte greatly altered these views during his term of office, but not his belief in Russia's capacity to avoid class conflict and a militant proletariat. In a series of lectures prepared for the Grand Duke Mikhail Aleksandrovich from 1900 to 1902, Witte argued that state intervention to safeguard the working class through labor legislation had been necessitated by malpractices of the factory owners during the early stages of rapid industrialization. Russia could make use of Western Europe's accumulated experience and take appropriate measures for the harmonious development of all its forces. "It is easier for Russia to act also because the state path is marked out by a single Will above the struggle of parties and private interests."[32]

Precisely a year and a day after the issuance of his circular of December 5, 1895, denying the need for labor legislation, Witte petitioned the tsar to convoke a special state conference to draft legislation establishing a maximum workday for factory workers.[33] This was not Witte's sole legislative initiative in the labor field. Before his discharge from office in 1903 he had successfully obtained the passage of legislation providing workmen's compensation and the election of factory elders, and drafted bills that would have ended criminal responsibility for contractual violations and legalized peacefully conducted strikes.[34] In testimony before the Committee of Ministers in January 1905, when an unprecedented wave of labor unrest was sweeping the country, Witte blamed conservative opponents for blocking labor legislation proposed by the Ministry of Finance. Opponents of government intervention, he charged, had based their position on the view "which existed at

31. *Rabochee dvizhenie v Rossii v XIX veke*, ed. L. M. Ivanov (Leningrad, 1961), IV, pt. 1, p. 824.
32. S. Iu. Witte, *Konspekt lektsii o narodnom i gosudarstvennom khoziaistve*, 2d ed. (St. Petersburg, 1912), p. 166.
33. Ministerstvo Finansov, Otdel promyshlennosti, *Materialy po izdaniiu zakona 2 iiunia 1897 goda* (St. Petersburg, 1905), p. 6.
34. *Otchet . . . za sessiiu 1902–1903 g. g.*, II, 187–211; *Zakonodatel'nye materialy*, pp. 5–15; *Russkii zakon i rabochii* (Stuttgart, 1902), pp. 1–28.

that time about the essence of the labor question in Russia, that conditions of factory life in our country and the West are completely different in themselves," an opinion in truth Witte himself had long shared.[35]

What had motivated Witte to alter his original position and become a proponent of factory legislation? The primary cause was the emergence of a vigorous labor movement pressing economic demands in much the same manner as in Western Europe. Witte's tenure at the Ministry of Finance coincided with a sharp rise in the number of strikes and street demonstrations involving workers, culminating in the massive strikes in the Ukraine and Caucasus during the summer of 1903. The labor movement had burst the bonds of patriarchal factory relations, making government action imperative. But there were more personal considerations. The majority of Witte's labor proposals were introduced in his last years in office. During the previous years, to Witte's chagrin, the Ministry of Interior became deeply involved in labor relations, taking administrative action in matters long considered by the Ministry of Finance within its own domain. Thus Witte's legislative proposals were in large part in reaction to measures taken by a rival ministry and designed to retain the Finance Ministry's hegemony over factory affairs.

The turning point in Witte's labor policy came during the great Petersburg textile strikes of 1896 and 1897, which rekindled official concern and investigation of the labor problem. Not since the mid-1880's had government officials regularly met to discuss the state of industrial conditions; in contrast, during the six years following 1897, numerous on-the-spot investigations of labor conditions were conducted by high government officials, several interdepartmental conferences were convened to discuss labor problems, and a variety of solutions were put forward for mitigating industrial strife.

The St. Petersburg textile strikes were unprecedented for Russia in their magnitude and in the solidarity that the working class displayed. More than 30,000 went on strike, demanding a shorter workday. Clearly, the Petersburg government could not be impassive to a mass movement on its own doorstep, despite the workers' peaceful deportment and purely economic demands.

35. *Rabochii vopros v komissii V. N. Kokovtsova,* p. 21.

During the strikes Witte's labor policies were found unworkable and his views on the nature of Russian industrial relations were proved illusory. Consequently, inconsistency and arbitrariness characterized his handling of the strikes. It had been Witte's conviction that the government's initial goal at the outbreak of a strike should be to seek the immediate resumption of work.[36] To allow concessions to be extracted through coercion would only strengthen the worker's belief in the efficacy of strikes, encourage work stoppages elsewhere, and lead to a decline in the respect for law and the sanctity of contractual relations. The factory inspectors were thus enjoined to make clear to the workers that the government would not permit their retaining economic benefits derived from illegal strikes even if the factory owners had been willing to make concessions.[37]

The Ministry of Finance rigidly adhered to this policy throughout the first year of the Petersburg strikes. The St. Petersburg manufacturers had been disposed to introduce a shorter working day if legislation would follow normalizing the working day throughout Russian industry. Witte, however, stubbornly opposed any concessions at the time, describing them as "impossible and dangerous."[38] In a special declaration addressed to the textile workers on June 15, 1896, he condemned the strike as illegal while vaguely promising that the tsarist government would look after those who "carry out their duties according to the law and live by the truth of God."[39] A combination of police repression and assurances that strike demands would be seriously considered after resumption of work brought a temporary end to the strike. By January of the following year, however, the workers lost patience with unfulfilled promises and renewed the strike. This time many factory owners instituted a shorter workday on their own initiative. Witte could no longer hold the line; the government reluctantly announced that legislation establishing a maximum working day was in preparation. By mid-May an eleven-and-a-half-hour workday was standard in all Petersburg textile plants; the following month the same norm was legally established for the entire country.

36. Ozerov, pp. 25–26.
37. *Rabochee dvizhenie*, IV, pt. 1, p. 825.
38. Ozerov, p. 34; *Rabochee dvizhenie*, IV, pt. 1, p. 839.
39. *Rabochee dvizhenie*, IV, pt. 1, pp. 841–42.

In drafting the law of June 2, 1897, as with other labor legislation, the tsarist government deemed it unwise and unnecessary to consult public opinion or the workers themselves. Ministry of Interior orders from 1895 to 1897 had placed a blanket prohibition against discussion in print of factory disorders and strikes, industrial relations, or factory wages and hours. The general public had been informed of the 1896 Petersburg strike only after it had ended, when an official version of the events was published.[40] Shielded from the pressure of public opinion, government officials were free to reach a tentative agreement on the basic outlines of the proposed law. At this point opinion was sought from representatives of the factory owners, adjustments were made, and the bill sent on for higher approval.

## The Ministry of Interior and the Labor Question

The interests of the Ministry of Interior were vigorously represented in the preliminary conference that drafted the new law on working hours. Its participation was in reaction to the recent deterioration in labor relations, which escalated into street disorders and required police intervention.[41] The ministry, however, did not limit its concern to the maintenance of public order. Voicing sharp criticism of extremely low factory wages and of management's general neglect of the workers and lack of interest in improving working conditions, it called for enough real benefits to the workers to convince them that the government was a just protector of their interests and responsive to their needs. Such a solution would bring the working class and government into closer rapport, engender mutual confidence, and benefit both. S. G. Shcheglovitov, vice-director of the ministry's economic department, for example, urged the conference to be mindful that "the intervention of the

40. L. Martov, "Razvitie promyshlennosti i rabochee dvizhenie s 1893 do 1903 g.," in *Istoriia Rossii v XIX veke*, VIII, 75; L. P. Men'shchikov, *Okhrana i revoliutsiia* (Moscow, 1928), II, no. 1, p. 10. The censorship equally applied to the most conservative newspapers; the case of *Novoe vremia* (New Times) in 1901, for example, is described in A. S. Suvorin, *Dnevnik A. S. Suvorina* (Moscow-Petrograd, 1923), p. 259; A. V. Bogdanovich, *Tri poslednikh samoderzhtsa* (Moscow-Leningrad, 1924), pp. 260–61. The Ministry of Finance opposed the publication of its circulars to the factory inspectors (Ozerov, p. 112).

41. See the testimony of S. G. Shcheglovitov, vice-director of the economic department of the Ministry of Interior, in *Tainye dokumenty ot nosiashchiesia k zakonu 2-go iiunia 1897 goda* (Geneva, 1898), p. 19.

government must have such a character that the workers would see in the government their defender and protector and because of this would be imbued with the conviction that they could attain an improvement in their position not through strikes but must await it from the government authorities."[42]

The Ministry of Interior, however, evinced no optimism that a shorter workday would bring an end to the rash of labor disorders. On August 12, 1897, scarcely two months after the new law on factory hours had gone into effect, the ministry in a long and detailed circular addressed to provincial governors and police officials presented its conclusions on the causes of the St. Petersburg strikes. They originated, it declared, in the poor working conditions in the St. Petersburg factories, as investigation by the ministry had found; the disciplined unity of the strikers and the rapid spread of the movement to other cities, characteristics which distinguished the strikes from previous labor disturbances, were attributed to the involvement of outside revolutionary elements. The circular continued with detailed instructions for preventing further labor disorders. Ministerial recognition that the strikes were grounded in the economic grievances of the workers found expression in the assignment of broader authority to the police in factory affairs; the implication of political agitators in protracted strikes led to a recommendation that repressive measures be taken when prompt settlement of a strike could not be reached. Factory inspectors, gendarmes, and other local officials involved in labor matters were exhorted to intensify surveillance of factory life and to forewarn the ministry of labor unrest. On occasion, however, order might be better preserved through concessions rather than repression. In a recommendation bound to antagonize the Ministry of Finance, the circular called upon the police to intervene in strikes with a view to "eliminating, as far as possible, causes for dissatisfaction in those cases where the workers have good reason to complain of the oppression or injustice of the factory owners or the factory

42. *Ibid.*, p. 28. Shcheglovitov, in his testimony, likewise stated: "If the workers will become convinced that the government, having published [this] law, achieved favorable conditions for the workers, they will look upon it as their defender and protector, but if the new law will not leave that impression, the workers will be inclined toward anti-government suggestions" (*ibid.*, p. 21). The need for the government to take measures that would psychologically dispose the worker to look upon it as his friend and protector was basic to the views of Sergei Zubatov.

administration."[43] This recommendation, broadly interpreted, led in practice to expanded police intervention in factory affairs; police officers used it as authorization for violating the factory inspector's jurisdiction.

The remainder of the circular spelled out procedures for terminating a strike. The factory inspector and other responsible officials were first to examine the causes and endeavor to bring the parties to an amicable settlement. Should these efforts fail the strikers were to be given a definite time limit in which to return to work, after which they were to be banished without delay to their native villages. Arrest and banishment under police surveillance to a far distant province was recommended as punishment for strikers who prevented others from renewing work.[44]

The Ministry of Finance was always on guard against interference into areas within its jurisdiction. Witte was therefore irked by the circular of August 12 and used his influence in an attempt to have it revoked. In particular he was loath to have the police granted investigatory and mediative powers rightfully belonging to the factory inspectorate under his jurisdiction. On October 31 he wrote to I. L. Goremykin, the Minister of Interior, criticizing the terms of the circular and protesting its issuance without prior consent of the Minister of Finance, as called for in the Industrial Code.[45] But Goremykin stood his ground; he declared that the circular was necessary to maintain public order after the discovery of secret revolutionary groups active among the factory workers. In vain Witte again protested against the arbitrary action of the Ministry of Interior, accusing it of wrongfully assuming each strike to be a serious matter of state significance; the circular of August 12, 1897,

---

43. *Rabochee dvizhenie*, IV, pt. 1, p. 830; Ozerov, p. 31.

44. The circular is published verbatim in *Rabochee dvizhenie*, IV, pt. 1, pp. 828–31, and summarized in Ozerov, pp. 29–33. N. M. Tseimern, governor of Vladimir province, wrote favorably of the circular in his yearly report for 1898, claiming that it permitted the authorities to deal directly with factory agitators who were difficult to prosecute successfully in the courts. Banishment under police surveillance, moreover, was a greater deterrent to factory agitation than the sentences handed down by the courts ("Iz istorii bor'by samoderzhaviia s rabochim dvizheniem," *Krasnyi arkhiv*, 1935, no. 1 (68), p. 155). Administrative arrest and banishment of strike leaders on orders of the local governor had been practiced since 1870, when a secret circular of the Ministry of Interior recommended such a course (Zelnik, pp. 363–64).

45. Ozerov, pp. 33–34; A. Morskoi [Vladimir von Shtein], *Zubatovshchina* (Moscow, 1913), pp. 24–26.

was still in force when the revolution of 1905 overtook the country.[46]

## Interministerial Rivalry

The interministerial dispute over initiative in factory affairs was not new. By the turn of the century the ministries had disagreed about jurisdiction over the factory inspectorate, the inspector's rightful authority and his relations with the local representatives of the Ministry of Interior, the degree of police intervention in labor disputes, and the areas and limits of further labor legislation. These questions were often referred to special interministerial conferences charged with the demarcation and definition of authority. All too often, however, conference decisions were ignored in practice by local officials if they could count on sufficient protection from higher authorities. The result was confusion and the simultaneous application of mutually contradictory policies.[47]

The factory inspectorate was a subject of interministerial dispute from its foundation. The Ministry of Interior wanted the police nature of the inspector's duties strengthened by having him subordinated to the local provincial authorities responsible for order. The factory owners, who vehemently opposed the transfer of the inspectorate from the Ministry of Finance, which was favorable to industrial interests, successfully pressured the Ministry of Finance in the 1880's to abandon plans to shift the inspectorate to its rival ministry. The dispute did not rest there; in 1903 the Ministry of Interior gained a partial victory when the inspectors were subordinated to the provincial authorities. The following year it once again attempted to wrest control over the inspectorate from the Ministry of Finance, but failed.[48]

With the intensification of labor unrest in the 1890's both the police responsibilities of the inspectorate and the intervention of the police in factory matters greatly increased, until the lines of authority between the police official and the inspector in labor affairs became blurred in practice.[49] The Ministry of Finance or-

---

46. Morskoi, pp. 26–29; *Russkii zakon i rabochii*, pp. 15–16; *Rabochii vopros v komissii V. N. Kokovtsova*, pp. 15–16.

47. V. N. Kokovtsov, *Out of My Past* (Stanford, 1935), p. 32; V. I. Gurko, *Features and Figures of the Past* (Stanford, 1939), p. 32.

48. Ozerov, pp. 166–68; Ianzhul, p. 203; Tugan-Baranovskii, pp. 416–18; P. A. Berlin, *Russkaia burzhuaziia v staroe i novoe vremia* (Moscow, 1922), p. 128.

49. Ozerov, pp. 37, 113.

dered factory inspectors to inform the police of labor unrest or revolutionary agitation inside the plants even while it zealously guarded the inspector's legal authority from police intrusion. In a circular to the factory inspectorate of March 12, 1898, the ministry criticized the growing practice of police officials to investigate causes of labor unrest "not only without the participation of the factory inspectorate, but even without its knowledge."[50] The Ministry of Interior stood its ground; the following month Goremykin issued a circular ordering police authorities to concern themselves with preventing factory conflicts. Witte could not let the issue rest; on April 10 he recommended to the tsar that a special interministerial conference render a more precise definition of the respective authority in factory affairs of the two ministries.[51]

In his report to the tsar, Witte mentioned accumulating evidence of police intervention in labor disputes beyond the limits authorized by law. The factory inspector, equipped with first-hand technical knowledge of each individual case, was best equipped to effect harmony in labor relations. Disregard of the inspector during the investigation of labor disturbances would lead to the destruction of his moral authority and standing among the workers; to satisfy summarily illegal labor demands, as Witte charged the police with doing, "can only instill in the workers the conviction, assiduously developed and strengthened by agitators, that their wishes are to be realized not when legal and just, but when they are expressed by a group."[52]

The decisions of the interministerial conference convened on July 15, 1898, under the chairmanship of K. P. Pobedonostsev supported the position of the Ministry of Finance. The authority of the factory inspector was confirmed and the position of the Ministry of Interior sharply criticized. The conference came down particularly heavily on the police, which it held was erroneously "inclined to consider any manifestation of a discontented frame of mind among the factory workers, from whatever cause it arose, as the beginning of a disorder, which not only gives it the right, but even places upon it the obligation, to intervene in the analysis of the causes for dissatisfaction and to take measures for its removal, whereas,

---

50. Martov, in *Istoriia Rossii v XIX veke,* VIII, 96.
51. *Ibid.* Witte's report is in Morskoi, pp. 37–42.
52. Morskoi, p. 41.

according to the Industrial Code, the factory inspector is completely responsible for this."[53] The law in force defining respective rights and obligations of the police, the provincial authorities, and the inspector in factory matters was judged sufficiently clear; the two ministries were instructed to issue a joint circular to subordinate agencies reiterating the respective sphere of authority of each in factory affairs.[54] The issue did not end there, however, for growing agitation by the workers strained the self control of officials responsible for law and order; members of the Ministry of Interior never ceased to be attentive and involved with factory life.

In the interest of order, the Ministry of Interior urged that the factory inspector be authorized to participate more actively in determination of wage rates; in cases where the local pay scale was unusually low, he should have the authority to pressure the factory management to raise it to the norm.[55] The recommendation was made in the Committee of Ministers in December 1897 by the governor of Vladimir province, who suggested that the factory inspectorate should act with the knowledge and agreement of the administrative authorities in the confirmation of wage rates, since variations in wage scales were a source of disturbance among the workers.[56]

Witte, opposed in principle to government intrusion into contractual bargaining, rejected the proposal to expand the inspector's competence. In his eyes the entrance of administrative officials into the delicate area of contractual negotiations would open a Pandora's box; the authorities, lacking the necessary technical knowledge to determine wage rates, would be guided by considerations of order rather than the financial health of the factory. The result would be a heavy blow to the well-being of Russian industry upon which the economic and political strength of the country increasingly depended.[57] In reply, Goremykin, on behalf of the Ministry of

53. *Ibid.*, p. 44.

54. The circular was issued on September 4, 1898; *ibid.*, pp. 42, 44–45; *Rabochii vopros v komissii V. N. Kokovtsova*, p. 7; Ozerov, p. 171.

55. *Tainye dokumenty*, p. 25.

56. *Svod vysochaishikh otmetok po vsepoddanneishim otchetam za 1896 g. general-gubernatorov, gubernatorov, voennykh gubernatorov i gradonachal'nikov* (St. Petersburg, 1898), p. 121.

57. Theodore H. Von Laue, "The Industrialization of Russia in the Writings of Sergej Witte," *ASEER*, 10 (1951), 181. See Witte's statement in the Committee of Ministers in March 1900: *Svod vysochaishikh otmetok... za 1898 g.* (St. Petersburg,

Interior, emphasized the relationship between low wage rates and labor unrest and the unwillingness of factory managers to accept advice from either the inspector or provincial authorities, secure in the knowledge that they were not obliged to do so by law.

The decision of the Committee of Ministers gave Witte a partial victory. Establishment of wage norms was judged not to be the rightful domain of government authorities; the setting of wage rates "would radically shake the freedom of the contractual principle," a freedom the committee was not about to end.[58] Neither the inspector nor provincial authorities had the right to demand changes in contracted wage rates. Goremykin did, however, find some little solace in the committee's decisions. If wage rates were established at levels unsatisfactory to the workers and labor disturbances appeared imminent, and if the inspector, after informal talks with the factory management, was unable to obtain their increase, he was to inform the provincial administration, which could then bring influence to bear within the limits prescribed by law.[59]

The Ministry of Interior also pressed for installation of a large police staff in factory centers to insure the immediate investigation of labor disorders and the rooting out of revolutionary agitators. Such a recommendation had been made by Lt. Gen. A. I. Panteleev in 1898, after an investigation of factory disorders; it gained the support of several governors and, of greater weight, the tsar.[60] The ministry won a measure of victory when on February 1, 1899, a special factory police force was legally established, its numbers to depend on the size of the working class in each area.

---

1901), p. 39. He admitted that factory inspectors had sometimes exceeded their authority and used pressure to have the factory administration agree to higher wage rates or had requested the local governor use his influence. He weakly defended the practice on grounds the inspector's action was of a personal character and bore no official basis (*Svod vysochaishikh otmetok . . . za 1896 g.*, p. 122

58. *Svod vysochaishikh otmetok . . . za 1896 g.*, p. 125.

59. *Ibid.*, pp. 125–26.

60. "K istorii rabochego dvizheniia 90-kh g.g.," *Ivanovo-Voznesenskii gubernskii ezhegodnik na 1921 god*, pp. 113–14. Years later General Panteleev discussed his findings in the State Council (*Gosudarstvennyi Sovet, 1911–12 gody*, pp. 3544–45). On the proposal to establish a special factory police, made by Prince Urusov, governor of Vladimir *guberniia*, to the Committee of Ministers on December 15, 1898, the tsar commented: "The most prompt formation of such a police is urgently necessary." A week earlier he had approved a report of Prince Sviatopolk-Mirskii embodying a similar proposal (*Svod vysochaishikh otmetok . . . za 1897 g.* [St. Petersburg, 1899], pp. 16, 24.)

The new law however was not entirely innovative. Since 1878 the police had had free access into the factories with the right to search the premises and make arrests. Two years later factory owners were given permission to establish special police details within the factory grounds; from that time the practice of either hiring private police at their own expense, or paying the police or gendarme office to maintain secret informers inside the plant, became fairly common.[61] Moreover, when factory disorders appeared imminent, the factory directors would usually petition the Ministry of Interior to have troops quartered close to the factory gate as a warning or hire such troops out of their own pockets.[62]

The installation of police officials inside the factory premises on a regular basis was opposed by Witte as tending to undermine the authority of the factory administration among its own workers. A minor misunderstanding between management and labor might seem a disorder to the police, whose intervention was sure to aggravate the situation.[63] In practice the factory police did alienate the workers. Dmitrii Sipiagin, the Minister of Interior from 1899 to 1902, found during a personal tour of major industrial regions in the summer of 1901 that the workers looked upon the corps of factory police as guards, who supported the interests of management.[64]

## The Ministry of Interior and Labor Reforms

By the turn of the century the highest officials of the Ministry of Interior had concluded that force and repression, while necessary to combat labor disorders, were by themselves inadequate to end the discontent among the working class. Officials at every level of the ministry—police officers, governors, and the minister himself—had urged a comprehensive program of improving factory conditions to

61. Martov, in *Istoriia Rossii v XIX veke*, VI, 136. In 1898 the Ministry of Interior reported that since 1880 some 732 police officers had been employed at private expense, of which 572 were at factories (Ozerov, p. 160). The number of police maintained at private expense notably increased in the last years of the 1890's in reaction to factory disorders.

62. *Rabochee dvizhenie*, IV, pt. 1, p. 848; Ozerov, pp. 99–100. For Witte's opposition to this practice see Ozerov, p. 177. In 1898 a mounted detachment of Astrakhan Cossack troops was hired by factory owners in the important industrial center of Ivanovo-Voznesensk, eliciting the tsar's comment that the practice was "a good example for other factory districts" (*Svod vysochaishikh otmetok . . . za 1899 g.*, p. 11).

63. Ozerov, pp. 142, 162. These views were expressed in a letter to Sipiagin of April 11, 1901.

64. Ozerov, pp. 135, 141, 177.

be carried out at the expense of the factory management.[65] Official reports of the causes of labor disorders, made on the basis of first-hand investigation, bluntly criticized the factory owners' exploitation of the workers and called upon the government to ensure that workers were provided with a living wage and tolerable working conditions. The reports, taken together, are a valuable primary source of information on labor conditions in tsarist Russia at the end of the nineteenth century.

In March 1898, General Panteleev was commissioned by the Ministry of Interior to investigate the causes of recent strikes in the key industrial provinces of central Russia. Based on interviews with those intimately involved in factory affairs—responsible members of the local administration, officials of the procurator's office, factory managers, inspectors, and workers (including some in prison for labor disorders)—Panteleev's report censured the factory owners and recommended radical changes to raise living and working standards for the workers, which were found to differ widely from factory to factory. In some cases patriarchal conditions were a reality: a rudimentary formal education and suitable lodgings were provided for the workers; sanitation and wages were deemed satisfactory.[66] But this was not the rule; the state of Russian factory life was "in general a very sad one," with overcrowded and unhealthy lodgings, poor hygienic conditions, and few educational facilities for the worker and his children. Such an environment bred drunkenness and other excesses. Here Panteleev located the cause of labor unrest: "In the exploitation of the workers by the

65. The police in the early 1870's had already made such proposals (Zelnik, pp. 374, 376). N. Kh. Bunge, Minister of Finance from 1882 to 1886, recommended profit sharing for the workers to undermine the appeal of socialism and strengthen the ties between owners and workers (L. E. Shepelev, "Kopartnership i russkaia burzhuaziia," in *Rabochii klass i rabochee dvizhenie v Rossii 1861–1917* [Moscow, 1966], pp. 289–90).

66. A Soviet specialist on the tsarist labor movement maintains that factory owners in the central industrial region in the 1880's and 1890's began to provide services for their workers within the factory walls, including medical aid (hospitals, lying-in facilities, and casualty wards), schools for workers and kindergartens for their children, almshouses, and social insurance for illness and old age. In 1900 these services cost the factory owners 13.2 million rubles, or around 5 per cent of the total wages paid to the workers. It is alleged that the paternalism of the factory owner made the workers dependent on the factory and accounts for their lack of interest and opposition to an experiment of the Zubatov type (L. M. Ivanov, "Samoderzhavie i rabochii klass," *Voprosy istorii*, June 1968, pp. 46–48).

manufacturers, when the latter, making a huge profit, pay the labor force little and besides, with rare exceptions, almost do nothing for the improvement of the way of life of the workers and their families, chiefly lie the causes of the agitation and strikes, which are recurring more and more frequently."[67] Embittered by exploitation, many workers yielded to anti-government propaganda.

Panteleev boldly recommended that the government compel the factory owners to introduce a comprehensive welfare program to eliminate "the incredible situation in which care for the life and health of the workers was left to the personal discretion of the factory owners to carry out."[68] Besides raising wages, which was the first order of business, the factory administration should provide comfortable lodgings, hospital and other medical facilities, an almshouse, food stores, public baths, and pension funds. The establishment of factory schools, as well as reading rooms and tearooms for relaxation, would have a positive effect in raising the moral and cultural level of the workers. Panteleev's general contention had the support of Nicholas II, who agreed with the assertion made by the governor of Moscow province before the Committee of Ministers in 1899 that improvement in the life of the workers would be one of the most efficacious means of combatting factory disorders.[69]

Panteleev's conclusions and general recommendations were seconded in the annual reports of several provincial governors. Count Shuvalov, Odessa city governor, in a report delivered in 1899, stressed the need to broaden educational and intellectual opportunities for the working class through the opening of additional reading rooms and libraries, the organization of popular lectures, and the free distribution of "books which open to the curious mind of the worker an incomparably wider horizon than illegal literature gives."[70] Prince P. D. Sviatopolk-Mirskii, governor of Ekaterinoslav province, in a report discussed in the Committee of Ministers the following year inveighed against malpractices perpetrated by factory owners in the pursuit of maximum profits

---

67. "K istorii rabochego dvizheniia 90-kh g.g.," p. 112; see also his comments in 1912: *Gosudarstvennyi Sovet, 1911–12 gody*, p. 3545.
68. *Gosudarstvennyi Sovet, ibid.*
69. *Svod vysochaishikh otmetok ... za 1897 g.*, p. 56; "K istorii rabochego dvizheniia 90-kh g.g.," pp. 112–13.
70. Ozerov, p. 134.

and received the endorsement of the tsar, who commented that "such highhandedness by the factory owners must not be tolerated."[71] A. G. Bulygin, the governor of Moscow province, in a report of March 1901, followed Shuvalov in stressing the need for greater moral training and intellectual opportunities for the worker, insisting on the "obligatory establishment" of schools and moral-religious lectures within the factory, strict prosecution of the prevailing evil of drunkenness, and improvement of family lodgings.[72]

Two other reports demand attention because of the high official standing of their authors. The first was prepared in 1901 by Sviatopolk-Mirskii, then Assistant Minister of Interior and chief of gendarmes, after personal investigation of disorders in St. Petersburg that summer. The evidence Mirskii uncovered pointed to revolutionary agitation over poor labor conditions as the causal factor. If the government was to compete on favorable terms against political agitators for the minds of the workers, he maintained, it had to satisfy their thirst for reading materials, otherwise illegal publications would do so. Libraries and a government-sponsored newspaper devoted solely to news of factory life were needed as legal counterweights to radical literature. Factory workers should be provided with state insurance and permitted to choose representatives to discuss their needs with their employers; the establishment of consumer cooperatives, savings banks, and elementary schools in the factories should be encouraged. Mirskii's recommendations, like so many others eminating from the Ministry of Interior, combined paternalism with considerations of order. Thus special lodgings, which could reduce labor turnover by providing a more personally satisfying environment, would also facilitate police surveillance.[73]

Shortly after Sviatopolk-Mirskii's investigation, D. S. Sipiagin, the Minister of Interior, toured the major industrial provinces to examine both working conditions and the state of factory surveillance by local organs of government. Sipiagin's recommendations

---

71. *Svod vysochaishikh otmetok . . . za 1898 g.*, p. 40.

72. *Svod vysochaishikh otmetok . . . za 1899 g.*, p. 25. Two years earlier, before the same Committee of Ministers, Bulygin had urged improvements in the life of the workers and elimination of factory abuses as means of preventing factory disorders (*Svod vysochaishikh otmetok . . . za 1897 g.*, p. 56).

73.    Sviatopolk-Mirskii's report to the tsar is found in "Rabochee dvizhenie na zavodakh Peterburga v mae 1901 g.," *Krasnyi arkhiv*, 1936, no. 3(76), pp. 52–66.

were similar to those of subordinate officials: labor difficulties could best be avoided through more extensive government tutelage of the working class and tighter factory surveillance. Passive neutrality was a dangerous and undesirable position; the government "cannot in any respect leave the working class to the arbitrary rule of the blind performance of economic phenomena, but is obliged to take solidly and firmly into its hands all threads in directing the vital interests of these layers of the population, and make them feel to a full degree its firm, but completely impartial and just tutelage." Above all, Sipiagin was mindful of retaining the allegiance of the proletariat to the autocracy and to the prevailing social and economic order: "It is necessary to take measures to form among the working class a stable and conservative element, which would be a buttress of the existing social system."[74] Sipiagin, to this end, recommended measures to advance the material security of the worker, including savings banks and insurance as well as the eventual introduction of profit. Using reasoning later advanced by Stolypin, Sipiagin urged that factory workers be encouraged to become individual proprietors of small-scale farmsteads in the expectation that the working class would thereby acquire a stake in the existing order.

Witte did not concur with the Ministry of Interior's explanations of labor unrest or recommendations for preventing it. Professional interest as well as personal outlook strengthened his conviction that the financial soundness of the factory enterprise had priority over what he viewed to be the irrational demands of the working class. In contrast to officials of the Ministry of Interior, who felt the autocracy had to compete with the revolutionaries for the mind and heart of the worker, Witte believed government measures should be formulated within the framework of general state interests, irrespective of their possible impact on the workers.[75] Nor did Witte believe that exploitation by the factory administration lay at the

---

74. Ozerov, p. 138.

75. Witte's reply to Sipiagin's report in 1901 (Ozerov, pp. 179–80). Witte later held (before the State Council in April 1912, long after he had any responsibility in the matter) that the government could never entirely free itself of solicitude about the factory workers, for considerations of public order would require the concern of the state. To maintain order among the workers the government had to be ready to use force when necessary; on the other hand, it had to show paternal concern for the weak (*Gosudarstvennyi Sovet, 1911–12 gody,* p. 3401).

base of labor unrest. At varying times he attributed it to dissatis-faction inherent in human nature, the criminal propaganda of revolutionary agitators, and the ignorance of the average worker about the complex technical aspects of industrial life.[76]

Witte was generally successful in thwarting the labor proposals of the Ministry of Interior by channeling them to ministerial conferences, where he could usually expect support. The special conference chaired by Pobedonostsev, for example, questioned Panteleev's observations about oppressive factory conditions and rejected his recommendations for immediate measures to raise the material, educational, and sanitary standards of factory life: "With a significant majority of the rural population in poverty, it is hardly possible to recognize the arbitrary conclusion that the factory workers are found in such a burdensome position, that the taking of immediate extraordinary measures for the improvement of their way of life is required."[77] The peasant question retained its priority.

Witte also sought to frustrate Sipiagin's proposal for factory housing and expansion of the factory inspector's duties in the areas of contractual disputes, fines, and contract negotiations. Sipiagin's report had brought the interministerial dispute to a head, for on December 16, 1901, the tsar, having read it, remarked that it would be "very desirable that measures now be taken for the proper settlement of the questions outlined here"; eleven days later an imperial rescript was issued calling for a special ministerial con-ference to consider the reported recommendations of Sviatopolk-Mirskii and Sipiagin.[78]

The conference, which met in March 1902 and included the Grand Duke Sergei Aleksandrovich, governor-general of Moscow, reached decisions which either ministry could interpret favorably. The group agreed on the immediate need for further factory legislation to improve working conditions and approved, within the limits of the law in force, "measures of an administrative character to eliminate those conditions, which create the opportunity of more or less well-grounded causes for displeasure accumulating among the laboring masses." The conference also approved "the basic thought of the Minister of Interior about the desirability of active interference

76. Ozerov, p. 189; Morskoi, p. 40; Ministersvo Finansov, *Materialy po izdaniiu zakona 2 iiunia 1897 goda,* p. 86.

77. Ozerov, p. 153.

78. Morskoi, p. 87.

of government authorities in the regulation of the mode of life of the working population, and concentration in its hands, so far as possible, of all the threads which control the vital interest of these strata of the population."[79] As in the past, however, Witte was able to withstand attempts to restrict the freedom of contract; the conference went on record against permitting the factory inspector to change wage rates or other terms of the contract.

Witte, however, did support proposals to allow the factory workers to choose elders, or *starosty*, to represent their interests before the factory administration. The proposal was incorporated in a bill that had the support of a broad majority in the State Council, including V. K. Plehve, the new Minister of Interior, and was signed into law in June 1903.[80] The new law, intended to improve the machinery by which both government and factory owners would be apprised of worker demands, failed to initiate an era of industrial peace. For one thing, it did not mandate the choosing of factory elders; permission from the factory owner was necessary for their election.

In announcing approval of the bill during debate in the State Council, Witte reassured conservatives with the timeworn cliché that "the labor question in our country, of course, is still far from the situation in Western Europe." Yet Witte appeared to be a proponent of further factory legislation, for he declared that "a whole series of measures" was being planned by the government.[81] Beyond the abolition of criminal responsibility for contractual violations and the legalization of peacefully conducted strikes, we know little of what Witte had planned, for in mid-August of 1903, two months after the law on factory elders went into effect, he was abruptly dismissed as Minister of Finance.

In the crucial year and a half following Witte's removal no further labor legislation was enacted. When, however, in the bloody days of January 1905 the safety of the autocracy appeared threatened by an aroused working class, recriminations and accusations flew

79. *Ibid.*, p. 88; A. F. Vovchik, *Politika tsarizma po rabochemu voprosu v predrevoliutsionnyi period (1895–1904)* (Lvov, 1964), p. 94.

80. *Zakonodatel'nye materialy,* pp. 1–2; *Otchet...za sessiiu 1902–1903 g.g.,* II, 205, 211; I. I. Shelymagin, *Zakonodatel'stvo o fabrichno-zavodskom trude v Rossii, 1900–1917* (Moscow, 1952), p. 51.

81. *Zakonodatel'nye materialy,* pp. 35–36; *Otchet...za sessiiu 1902–1903 g.g.,* II, 193–94.

between the ministries as to where blame should be properly laid for failure to resolve the labor question. The dispute engendered a partisan battle of words in conference reports and memoir literature. The most thoroughgoing defense of the Ministry of Finance is found in a report to the tsar on January 19, 1905, by V. N. Kokovtsov, then its chief minister. Kokovtsov charged the Ministry of Interior with having prevented a peaceful resolution of the labor problem by its arbitrary interference and a policy which vacillated between repression and concessions during labor disputes; he also accused the ministry of hindering enactment of factory laws planned by the Ministry of Finance, interfering with the duties of the factory inspector, and fostering and protecting illegal labor unions.[82] Yet the same Kokovtsov subscribed to the popular belief that government authorities, and particularly the Ministry of Finance, were always receptive to the needs and demands of the industrial estate and deaf to those of the working class:

Attention is turned to the fact that up to now the government authorities always willingly turned for assistance to representatives of industry for elucidation of their needs, which they present either in the form of individual petitions or reports, or in the form of the establishment of various types of consultative institutions on questions of trade and industry, stock exchange committees, [or] conferences and councils. In this regard, as you know, there never arose any difficulties, and the finance department always went to meet this halfway, which is well known to you all. But, on the other hand, the workers did not have such an opportunity to express their needs; therefore the government might be completely and deservedly reproached if the consideration given to the employers was not given to those who are hired.[83]

Critics of Ministry of Finance policies pointed to its long-standing denial of the existence of a labor question, its unwillingness to consider the psychological needs of the factory worker, and its partisanship toward the industrial community; they also accused it of being motivated, like its rival ministry, by demands of order.[84] Other critics censured the entire government for approaching the

82. Kokovtsov's report is in *Rabochii vopros v komissii V. N. Kokovtsova*, pp. 1–17. It includes one of the most thorough attacks on the Zubatovshchina by the Ministry of Finance (pp. 2–6, 11–12).
83. *Ibid.*, p. 197.
84. Ozerov, pp. 116–17; A. I. Spiridovich, "Pri tsarskom rezhime," *Arkhiv russkoi revoliutsii*, 15 (1924), 149.

labor problem piecemeal rather than attacking it as a whole with an interrelated series of measures.[85]

Tsarist Labor Policy in Perspective

The labor proposals of the Ministry of Interior foresaw governmental guardianship of the working class; the legislation that did emerge during the years 1897–1903 reflects only a small part of the plans conceived by the two responsible ministries to lay the rising labor question to rest. The most fundamental right of labor— that is, the right to unite and establish labor unions for the pursuit of common needs—the government denied to the worker, for this right would have entailed additional freedoms which it was unwilling to grant other sections of the population. A report of the St. Petersburg Society for Assistance to the Improvement and Development of Manufacturing Industry put the issue succinctly in 1905: "Freedom of unions presupposes freedom to assemble and to strike, freedom to discuss questions in the press, that is, freedom of the press, presupposes personal inviolability and, in connection with this, the sanctity of the home."[86]

The government by the turn of the century was cognizant of the steady rise and inherent danger of the labor movement without feeling the immediacy or priority of the problem. The proletariat was still a very small part of the population; other, seemingly more pressing, matters competed for the government's attention. During the crucial years from 1898 to 1903 there was deep unrest among all sections of the population. The broad spectrum of political parties that emerged in 1905 had its origin in these years. The Social Democrats and the Socialist Revolutionaries formed nationwide parties to advance the causes of the proletariat and the peasantry respectively; the liberal-democratic intelligentsia likewise began to organize; the Zemstvo leaders grew bolder in their agitation for reforms. A rash of student disturbances and demonstrations, a revival of terrorism against high government functionaries, unrest among the non-Russian nationalities in Finland and the Caucasus, and, finally, a renewed outbreak of peasant disorders after a decade

85. *Rabochii vopros v komissii V. N. Kokovtsova,* p. 61; *Gosudarstvennyi Sovet, 1909–10 gody,* pp. 2628–29, 2691–92, 2718. Witte agreed with the criticism in the State Council that Russian labor legislation had lacked direction (*ibid.,* p. 2736).
86. *Rabochii vopros v komissii V. N. Kokovtsova,* p. 62.

of relative calm, gave warning of the revolutionary events to come.

The political significance of the working class far exceeded its relative numbers, as the revolution of 1905 demonstrated. In the years preceding that revolution, when government labor policy was characterized by hesitancy and contradictions, an experiment was undertaken in several important cities aiming at administrative organization and control of the labor movement. The Zubatovshchina, named for the Moscow Okhrana chief who conceived the plan, sought by extra legal administrative means to secure the loyalty of the working class to the monarchy at a time when revolutionary groups were intensifying efforts to channel the discontent of the workers against the government and the economic and social order. Police socialism, the misnomer commonly used to describe the Zubatov movement, has been justifiably considered "the last major government experiment to cope with the problem of labor unrest before 1905;"[87] its origins, development, and fate can be properly understood only against the background of the interministerial labor dispute, and the ideas and program of its creator.

87. Gaston V. Rimlinger, "Autocracy and the Factory Order in Early Russian Industrialization," *Journal of Economic History,* 20 (1960), 89.

# CHAPTER 2

# Sergei Zubatov:
# Career and Ideology

Sergei Vasilevich Zubatov was born in 1863 or 1864 in Moscow, where he was to spend most of his life.[1] Concerning his family background and boyhood we have scant information. His father managed an apartment house on Tverskoi Boulevard in the center of Moscow; little else is known about his parents. V. N. Morozov, a member of the revolutionary Narodnaia Volia (People's Will), a visitor to the Zubatov household on several occasions and our only source of information about the early youth of Sergei, noted Zubatov's seriousness as reflected in his devotion to intellectual pursuits and predilection for the progressive literature of the time.[2]

The years during which Zubatov attended a Moscow gymnasium were crucial ones for Russia and for Zubatov's future career. In March 1881, a year after he entered the gymnasium, the terrorists of Narodnaia Volia assassinated Alexander II, the Tsar Liberator. The assassination did not spell the end of the autocracy, as the revolutionaries had envisioned; indeed repression and an un-compromising spirit against reform were dominant during the next two decades.

Shortly after the assassination, clandestine circles were formed at the Moscow gymnasia to study the writings of the nihilist D. I. Pisarev. Zubatov was caught up in this activity, became a disciple of Pisarev, and while in the sixth class of his gymnasium formed and

1. The date of 1863 is given in an anonymous entry, "Zubatov," *Malaia sovetskaia entsiklopediia*, 2d ed., IV (1935), 571; the latter date is given by D. Zaslavskii, "Zubatov," *Bol'shaia sovetskaia entsiklopediia*, XXVII (1933), 267; also "Zubatov," *Sovetskaia istoricheskaia entsiklopediia*, V (1964), 710.

2. Morozov's information is found in K. Tereshkovich, *Moskovskaia revoliutsionnaia molodezh' 80–kh godov i S. V. Zubatov* (Moscow, 1928), pp. 4, 18.

led a circle of fellow students.[3] His natural talents as a speaker and propagandist, qualities which later served him well in his police career, attracted many students to his circle. Soon he made contact with revolutionary circles outside the gymnasium, aided by his friendship with Morozov, an established revolutionary.

For reasons that are uncertain, Zubatov's formal education was terminated by his removal from the gymnasium before he was to graduate.[4] After working for a time in a postal-telegraph office, he renewed his contacts with radical students as manager of a bookstore owned by Aleksandra Nikolaevna Mikhina, his future wife. The bookstore, in the heart of Moscow, soon acquired a reputation among students for its sale of cheap books, particularly those banned by the censor.[5]

There Zubatov extended his acquaintance with the Moscow Narodnovoltsy, some of whom had invested in the store and supplied it with books. In 1882, M. R. Gotz, the leader of a circle of students studying the works of Pisarev and Mikhailovskii, became acquainted with Zubatov, who led a circle of his own studying political economy.[6] Gotz's memoirs provide the only insight into Zubatov's outlook in his youth. At one of their meetings Zubatov

---

3. K. Tereshkovich, "Moskovskaia molodezh' 80-kh godov i Sergei Zubatov," *Minuvshie gody*, 1908, no. 5–6, pp. 207–8.

4. Zubatov, in a letter of November 22, 1906, blamed his father, who was annoyed at his friendship with students involved in conspiratorial activities (B. P. Koz'min, ed.), *S. V. Zubatov i ego korrespondenty* [Moscow-Leningrad, 1928], p. 54). Tereshkovich, who knew Zubatov at the gymnasium, doubted the truth of this story and maintained in his 1928 brochure that Zubatov's conspiratorial activities came to the attention of the authorities, who thereupon expelled him for political unreliability. This opinion was widely circulated in the revolutionary press. Yet Tereshkovich's article "Moskovskaia" (p. 208) lends credence to Zubatov's version. According to Tereshkovich, the widespread conspiratorial student movement in the Moscow schools after the assassination of Alexander II was a cause of deep concern to the parents, who frequently met to consider how to end it. Probably Zubatov's father participated in these discussions and decided to remove his son from the gymnasium to shelter him from a radical environment and eventual arrest. A. I. Spiridovich, a close colleague of Zubatov in the Okhrana, held that Zubatov's friendship with Jewish youths led to conflict with his father and withdrawal from school (*Mladorosskaia iskra*, Nov. 15, 1933).

5. Tereshkovich, "Moskovskaia," pp. 208–9; A. A. Kizevetter, *Na rubezhe dvukh stoletii* (Prague, 1929), p. 18; *Mladorosskaia iskra*, Nov. 15, 1933.

6. M. R. Gotz, "S. V. Zubatov," *Byloe*, Sept. 1906, pp. 63–64. Gotz subsequently played a notable role in the revolutionary movement. He was among the founders of the Socialist Revolutionary Party, became the representative outside of Russia of its terrorist arm, the "Battle Organization," and served on the staff of the party's organ, *Revoliutsionnaia Rossiia*.

read a paper of his own composition on the subject of morality: "Everything in this theory," reports Gotz "was based on the application of a strong will, which demanded the completely conscious performance of a whole series of abominations. The person carrying out these abominations would have to have a complete understanding of their significance, but go against the adopted moral ideas and thereby exercise his 'will.' "[7]

Disagreements between Zubatov and Gotz soon appeared but did not lead at once to complete estrangement; during the next four years, while Gotz and his circle were drawn ever closer to the Moscow Narodnaia Volia, they were dependent on Zubatov's store for illegal books. During these years the Moscow intelligentsia never questioned Zubatov's political reliability, and they continued to patronize the bookstore.

## Zubatov's Career in the Okhrana

The exact moment when Zubatov began to cooperate with the Moscow secret police is still uncertain. Some contemporaries have dated his earliest such activities as 1883–1884, with his more significant contributions in disrupting Moscow revolutionary circles commencing in 1886.[8] The arrest in March 1886 of a circle of Moscow Narodnovoltsy has been attributed to information he supplied to the police; Zubatov, however, denied any implication in the case and placed the date of his first encounter with the police in June 1886, when he was arrested in connection with the activities of the bookstore.[9] From this time forward he worked closely with the

7. *Ibid.*, p. 65. The evidence available about Zubatov's youth does not sustain Kyril Tidmarsh's thesis that "one should already from early childhood discern in him the makings of a fanatical counter-revolutionary" (Tidmarsh, "The Zubatov Idea," *ASEER*, 19 [1960], 340). This article should be used with caution because of its factual errors and questionable interpretations. Gotz, in his memoirs, is unable to explain why he did not develop a close friendship with Zubatov or why they soon separated. In his letter dated November 22, 1906, Zubatov maintained that the separation was due to mutually irreconcilable natures, jealousy over leadership of a circle, theoretical differences, and the fact that, in contrast to Gotz, he was at the time "a follower of Pisarev, a cultural worker-idealist *(kul'turnik-idealist)*" (Koz'min, pp. 52–53).

8. Gotz, pp. 65–66; Tereshkovich, *Moskovskaia*, p. 18; *Listok "Rabochago dela,"* no. 5 (Jan. 1901), p. 3; *Osvobozhdenie*, no. 22 (May 8, 1903). Evidence does not support Witte's statement in October 1903 that Zubatov was arrested on political charges as early as 1881 (A. M. Kuropatkin, "Dnevnik A. M. Kuropatkina," *Krasnyi arkhiv*, 1922, no. 2, p. 81).

9. Gotz, p. 66; Zubatov's letter of Nov. 22, 1906 (Koz'min, pp. 52–53). Leonid Men'shchikov, a member of an illegal circle led by Zubatov in the second half of the

Moscow Okhrana (security police), although not openly, for Zubatov still retained the confidence of a number of revolutionary acquaintances and had contacts with the radical student youth. The seizure of the clandestine printing presses of the Moscow Narodnovoltsy in the fall of 1886 and the arrest of radical student leaders at the Petrovskii Academy at about the same time are alleged to have been due to information he provided.[10] Unconfirmed rumors that Zubatov was in the service of the secret police began circulating among revolutionary circles; during 1887 the charge was made openly, and it directly reached Zubatov.[11]

Services to the Moscow Okhrana as an informant thus could not continue indefinitely, and Zubatov soon formally entered its official world, where he rapidly made a brilliant career.[12] The Okhrana was then in its infancy and had not yet attained the pre-eminent reputation for counterrevolutionary investigation and detection it later acquired. The assassination of Alexander II had led to the promulgation in August 1881 of a Statute about Measures for Safeguarding the State Order and Public Tranquillity, giving extraordinary powers to the police and local authorities to eradicate the revolutionary movement. Concurrently there was established

---

1880's, alleges that Zubatov betrayed the circle to the police (B. I. Gorev, "Leonid Men'shchikov," *Katorga i ssylka*, 1924, no. 10, p. 132).

10. Zubatov's complicity in these and other cases in 1886–1887 is discussed in *Osvobozhdenie*, no. 22 (May 8, 1903); Tereshkovich, *Moskovskaia*, pp. 9–10; Gotz, pp. 66–67; Men'shchikov, *Okhrana i revoliutsiia*, I, 20–27.

11. *Osvobozhdenie*, no. 22; Men'shchikov, I, 25–28. Viktor Gol'tsev, a well-known publicist and editor, in 1887 was warned by an acquaintance in prison that Zubatov, whom Gol'tsev had known for over a year, was a police informer. When Zubatov directly accused Gol'tsev of circulating the rumor, the latter admitted he had done so and affirmed his belief in its validity (V. Gol'tsev, "Pervyi arest," *Russkaia mysl'*, Nov. 1906, p. 117). In a letter of November 27, 1906, Zubatov stated that on his visit to Gol'tsev's apartment the latter denied he was spreading tales of Zubatov's alleged counterrevolutionary activities (Koz'min, pp. 57–58). The intelligentsia by this time had also begun to doubt the reliability of the bookstore as a place for acquiring illegal books, since several revolutionaries had been arrested there (Kizevetter, p. 18). Despite the rumors Zubatov retained for some time the confidence of many revolutionaries, who found it difficult to believe the accusations (Tereshkovich, *Moskovskaia*, p. 14; Gotz, p. 67).

12. When Zubatov retired in October 1903, he mentioned fifteen years of service; thus his formal entrance into the Okhrana would have been in 1888 ("K istorii Zubatovshchiny," *Byloe*, July 1917, p. 97). Mikhail Afanas'ev, who was closely associated with Zubatov in Moscow, told Lev Tikhomirov in January 1904 that Zubatov had been deprived of a pension after seventeen years of service; this would place his entrance into the Okhrana at 1886 (Tikhomirov, "25 let nazad," *Krasnyi arkhiv*, 1930, no. 1 [38], p. 24).

in St. Petersburg, Moscow, and Warsaw, major centers of revolutionary activity, a Section for Safeguarding of State Order and Public Tranquillity, known also under the name of Security Section *(okhrannoe otdelenie)*, or more popularly, the Okhrana. It was subordinate to the Department of Police and ultimately to the Minister of Interior and was assigned the vital task of directing intelligence work against political crimes and revolutionary groups, supplementing but not supplanting the gendarme corps.[13]

In the mid-1890's the Moscow branch of the Okhrana assumed the leadership of the counterrevolutionary police. As reward for repeated success in rooting out hidden centers of sedition, it was authorized to extend its investigatory jurisdiction far beyond Moscow. Its achievements were attributed principally to the single-minded capacity for work, general ability, and unrivaled knowledge of the revolutionary movement that Zubatov brought into the Moscow Okhrana and for which he was rewarded with appointment as assistant chief.

When Zubatov began his official career, police intelligence had not progressed from the days when the main threat to the autocracy came from a small band of dedicated revolutionaries in Narodnaia Volia. The challenge to the Okhrana in the 1890's was more demanding. The resurgent revolutionary movement had a wider following and a broader network than in the past, along with a more unified and centralized leadership and greatly improved conspiratorial methods. The ranks of the police showed little awareness of the urgency to update investigatory methods and still less comprehension of the political ideologies of the revolutionary groups.

Zubatov's first innovation was the introduction of modern police techniques, including photographic files and systematic registration of all political suspects. New recruits had to undergo special training in the techniques of conspiratorial work and education in the political doctrines of the revolutionary parties. A training school was established within the Moscow Okhrana to prepare a cadre of police agents equipped with an intimate knowledge of the history and literature of the revolutionary movement and thus better acquainted

13. Marc Szeftel, "Personal Inviolability in the Legislation of the Russian Absolute Monarchy," *ASEER*, 17 (1958), 14–18; A. A. Lopukhin, *Nastoiashchee i budushchee russkoi politsii* (Moscow, 1907), pp. 28–30; *Bol'shaia sovetskaia entsiklopediia*, XLIII (1939), 706.

with the operations and ideology of their adversaries. From the ranks of the school Zubatov organized a special group of reliable counterintelligence agents known as the "flying squadron," whose very designation indicated its readiness for assignments anywhere the enemy was active.[14]

Zubatov was pessimistic, however, that police methods could completely destroy political opposition. His youthful infatuation with revolutionary ideas had taught him that "an oppositional attitude toward the authorities or even revolutionary intentions cannot be destroyed"; all that the government could and must do was to keep abreast of the direction of the revolutionary movement. With the growth of centrally controlled networks of secret revolutionary groups the aim of the security organs should be directed not at the periphery but at the very heart of the movement: "One must strike blows at the centers, avoiding mass arrests. To seize the printing presses from the secret organizations, to arrest their whole technical and administrative apparatus, to arrest the local central board—this means to smash also the whole periphery. Mass arrests of the periphery signifies an incorrect organization of intelligence matters."[15]

The capture of the revolutionary centers, however, did not bring the movement to a standstill, for the revolutionary cause had an inexhaustible capacity to survive. To seek out those who remained at large a number of those arrested were released under strict and secret surveillance for "breeding purposes." In this manner the police could be continually informed of each new revolutionary cell.[16]

The rapidity with which the Moscow Okhrana succeeded in uncovering the many-headed hydra of revolution enhanced its standing with Petersburg officialdom; it also led to enmity, not unmixed with jealousy, on the part of the gendarmery, the older

---

14. Men'shchikov, I, 110; P. P. Zavarzin, *Rabota tainoi politsii* (Paris, 1924), p. 69; Maurice Laporte, *Histoire de l'Okhrana* (Paris, 1935), p. 53; A. T. Vassilyev, *The Ochrana* (Philadelphia and London, 1930), p. 60; I. V. Alekseev, *Istoriia odnogo provokatora* (Moscow, 1925), p. 61; Spiridovich, "Pri tsarskom rezhime," p. 150; Gurko, p. 116. On the "flying squadron" and its activities see: L. A. Rataev, "Iz perepiski okhrannikov," *Golos minuvshago*, June 1922, p. 51; P. P. Zavarzin, *Zhandarmy i revoliutsionery* (Paris, 1930), pp. 42–43; I. V. Alekseev, *Provokator Anna Serebriakova* (Moscow, 1932), pp. 11, 122.

15. Zavarzin, *Zhandarmy*, pp. 56–57.

16. Men'shchikov, I, 213.

security organ. Many gendarme officers with long and distinguished service records were either unwilling or unable to understand the new tactics and conspiratorial methods of the political underground. Above all, they resented the intervention of Okhrana officers sent from Moscow to investigate cases they thought were within their own competency.[17] Beginning in 1893, Zubatov later wrote, he "already acted in complete union with the department [of police], chasing throughout all Russia, fighting with the 'reds' and quarreling with the 'blues' [the gendarmes], the lazybones."[18] The most consistent and bitter criticism of his person and program, including measures to deal with the labor problem, came from highly placed officers of the "blues."

The new methods of counterrevolutionary detection paid handsome dividends in the early 1890's in the disclosure and arrest of a goodly number of political groups of varying ideologies. It did not take Petersburg officials long to realize that Zubatov was largely responsible for the rise to pre-eminence of the Moscow Okhrana and its "flying squadron" of special agents. In 1895, Zubatov was summoned to St. Petersburg to report to the Minister of Interior on the growing liberal movement and serve in attendance at the imperial reception following the coronation of Nicholas II.[19] The following year Goremykin, the Minister of Interior, sent personal congratulations to Zubatov for his part in the detection of the Narodnovoltsy printing press in St. Petersburg.[20] It was thus not unexpected when in 1896 Zubatov was appointed chief of the Moscow Okhrana.[21] At the age of thirty-two he now bore the heavy responsibility of protecting the monarchy from its revolutionary enemies.

17. Zavarzin, *Rabota,* p. 71. Also see the memoirs of two gendarme chiefs, bitter opponents of Zubatov and his plans: A. V. Gerasimov, *Tsarisme et Terrorisme* (Paris, 1934); V. D. Novitskii, *Iz vospominanii zhandarma* (Leningrad, 1929).

18. Zubatov to V. Burtsev, Dec. 18, 1906 (Koz'min, p. 70).

19. Laporte, pp. 12–13. Laporte's book is allegedly based on study of police documents. However, his is the only reference to Zubatov's presence at the coronation in the historical literature and has yet to be confirmed.

20. S. Zvolianskii to Zubatov, July 3, 1896 (Koz'min, p. 26).

21. *Delo A. A. Lopukhina v osobom prisutsvii pravitel'stvuiushchago senata* (St. Petersburg, 1910), p. 39; Zavarzin, *Zhandarmy,* p. 54. Zubatov was given credit for thwarting an attempt to assassinate Nicholas II at around the time of the coronation (*Mladorosskaia iskra,* Nov. 15, 1933). Zubatov's critics have attributed his promotion to intrigue against his superior, Berdiaev; *Iskra,* no. 1 (Dec. 1900); *Osvobozhdenie,* no. 22 (May 8, 1903); *Revoliutsionnaia Rossiia,* no. 4 (Feb. 1902).

## Zubatov as a Monarchist

Zubatov's meteoric rise to chief of the Moscow Okhrana within a single decade led some of his critics within and without the government to consider him an unscrupulous careerist. Those who worked closest with him describe Zubatov as having a zealous and passionate devotion to work; in appearance and mannerism he resembled the typical intellectual of his time.[22] He was remarkably well read in contemporary social and political thought, particularly the history of the revolutionary movement abroad. His all-consuming passion for combating the revolution was carried well beyond the call of duty and at once set him apart from his more prosaic co-workers. For Zubatov was that rare type of individual, then more often found among the revolutionary intelligentsia, whose active work is but a reflection of some inner faith or abstract idea that has captured his entire being. Along his chosen path he had not merely been transformed from radical youth to government official; more important, he had undergone an emotional and ideological reformation which stamped him a fanatical monarchist, a mold into which he endeavored to shape those he trained. Fanaticism and utter conviction in the righteousness of his cause, Zubatov believed, sustained the revolutionary in the worst adversity; fanaticism in the cause of the autocracy must permeate the thoughts of the police officer and thus give him that inner strength necessary to meet the enemy on equal terms.[23]

Zubatov never tired of preaching faith in monarchism to the monarchists about him in the bureaucratic world. "I am a unique monarchist in my own way and therefore deeply believing," Zubatov once wrote, a view confirmed by his closest associates; his devotion to the monarchic cause never wavered to his death.[24] The "idea of a pure monarchy," unrestricted in its powers, was not for him a mere abstraction but something which he "warmly defended

22. Zavarzin, *Zhandarmy,* pp. 54–55; Spiridovich, "Pri tsarskom rezhime," pp. 118, 123–24; *Mladorosskaia iskra,* Nov. 15, 1933. No photograph of Zubatov has ever appeared. Descriptions of his physical appearance are found in the works of Spiridovich.

23. Spiridovich, "Pri tsarskom rezhime," p. 124; D. N. Liubimov, "Russkaia smuta nachala deviatisotykh godov 1902–1906. Po vospominaniiam, lichnym zapiskam i dokumentam" (manuscript in the Archive of Russian and East European History and Culture at Columbia University, n. d.), p. 24; Jeremiah Schneiderman, trans., "From the Files of the Moscow Gendarme Corps," *Canadian Slavic Studies,* 2 (1968), 86–99.

24. Zubatov to Burtsev, March 21, 1908 (Koz'min, p. 90).

... in practice"; all his subsequent schemes for coping with the social and economic problems of the time started with that underlying principle.[25] Monarchy as a political institution, he asserted, had been popularly recognized for over a millennium for its universal beneficence and for its defense of the weak and downtrodden, the sole force working for the common good. The Russian monarchy was "in a position to satisfy ultimate ends—to meet the needs and requirements of the average person"; indeed it could "give the country all those blessings which the West enjoys, owing to its complete independence from governmental and public parties—and even much more than that."[26]

Zubatov's ideas were in the traditional mold of monarchic conservatism, with its stress on obedience to church and ruler; his originality among Russian monarchists lay in his acute perception of new social forces and his ability to devise programs to incorporate them into the existing order without weakening the monarchy. History, he held, does not stand still, and new economic and social forces alter the tasks of the autocracy. Zubatov and his close associates dedicated themselves to these tasks, devoting their energies "not so much to the statics of the autocracy as to its dynamics."[27] At the end of the nineteenth century, with the appearance of the working class on the historical stage and the development of class struggle, this meant a monarchy working to maintain social peace through a just, impartial, supraclass reconciliation and equilibrium of social forces. The monarchy could not stand aloof and cut itself off from the problems of the time; its unique position was justified by the very function it served, blending society into something more than the classes and groups of which the nation was composed. Zubatov, in a confession of faith, declared in 1906: "I myself believed and believe that, correctly understood, the monarchic idea is able to give the country all that is necessary by unbinding the social forces ... without, at the same time, bloodshed and other abominations."[28]

Zubatov was intensely interested in the meaning and basic nature of Russian history. To him the Russian way was monarchic,

25. *Ibid.; Mladorosskaia iskra,* Nov. 15, 1933.
26. A. P. Korelin, "Krakh ideologii 'politseiskogo sotsializma' v tsarskoi Rossii," *Istoricheskie zapiski,* 92 (1973), 112.
27. Zubatov to Burtsev, Dec. 18, 1906 (Koz'min, p. 72).
28. Zubatov to Burtsev, Dec. 12, 1906 (*ibid.,* p. 64).

embodied in the formula "Tsar and People—an inseparable unity."[29] Russia's progress, civilization, and prosperity stemmed from the autocracy, which incarnated the national will and was the sole form of rule natural to the country. "Without a Tsar there cannot be a Russia. . . . The happiness and greatness of Russia is in its sovereigns and their work."[30] As a monarchist, then, Zubatov was committed to solving the country's problems within the traditional framework of direction from above.

Yet Zubatov was not fearful, as were most conservative monarchists, of marshaling the loyal masses in the struggle against political opposition.[31] Diehard conservatives distrusted the masses and warned that once organized they could not be controlled; anarchy would be the consequence and the revolutionaries the beneficiary. Zubatov countered this argument with his own warning: to shackle the loyal majority among the masses would strengthen the position of the vocal, unified minority and eventually give it, by default, leadership over the masses. Moreover, concerned as he was with the strategy and tactics of preserving the autocracy, Zubatov was not above forming alliances with groups antipathetic to extreme conservatives, as his relations with the Russian Zionists, described elsewhere in this book, illustrate.

Zubatov's recommendations on the student question were typical of his approach; the government's handling of the problem exemplified for him the futility of mere repression as a tactic. Continual agitation among university youth at the turn of the century brought censure from the conservative press and the closure of student organizations by the government. In Zubatov's opinion, the government, by dealing with the student body as an

29. *Grazhdanin-Dnevniki*, Nov. 19, 1906; *Mladorosskaia iskra*, Nov. 15, 1933.

30. Spiridovich, "Pri tsarskom rezhime," p. 123; Zubatov's views on the subject are also found in Zavarzin, *Zhandarmy*, pp. 55–56; *Grazhdanin-Dnevniki*, Jan. 12, 1906.

31. Hans Rogger, "Reflections on Russian Conservatism: 1861–1905," *Jahrbücher für Geschichte Osteuropas*, 14 (1966), 209. I concur with Richard Pipes's description of post-1881 bureaucratic conservatism: "Characteristic of it is mistrust of society grounded in the belief that once people are given freedom they rebel and destroy. It is the attitude of functionaries who regard every manifestation of public initiative as "insubordination" that must be repressed or, if that is not possible, subverted." Pipes is wrong, however, in describing the Zubatovshchina as "the acme of this process" (Pipes, "Russian Conservatism in the Second Half of the Nineteenth Century," *Slavic Review,* 30 [1971], 128). Indeed it is precisely mistrust and fear of the proletariat by bureaucratic conservatives that Zubatov sought to dispel. He failed, however, to convince them; the bureaucratic conservatives remained staunch opponents of the Zubatovshchina.

undifferentiated mass of like-minded youths, played directly into the hands of the small revolutionary minority among them. The majority of the students were basically loyal but deprived of an opportunity to discuss their problems they fell prey to rumors circulated by radical elements and followed the political activists. The legalization of representative student assemblies, Zubatov maintained, was the sole means through which the conservative majority could recapture the leadership of the student body and isolate the radical minority.[32]

### The Growth of Russian Social Democracy

Zubatov's tenure as head of the Moscow Okhrana began at an auspicious moment in the history of the Russian revolutionary and labor movements. The dynamic industrial growth of the second half of the 1890's had been accompanied by the spontaneous outbreak and spread of labor strife. The strike movement by itself, however, was not an immediate threat to the government, for the discontent of the workers was not channeled in a political direction, but like that of the peasants was directed against the immediate source of discontent, in this case the factory owners and the working conditions they provided. What made the elemental outbursts of the working class potentially dangerous to the stability of the regime was the rise of Marxism to respectability among the intelligentsia and radical youth in the 1890's, and the possibility, eagerly pursued by the Marxists, of a fusion of the intelligentsia with the larger and more explosive force of the workers. The undeniable existence of a fairly large Russian proletariat, visibly expressing discontent with conditions through methods used by the working class of Western Europe, gave credence to the Marxist critique of the populist dogma that Russia would never undergo the capitalist stage of history. A segment of the radical intelligentsia found in the proletariat a new revolutionary hero to replace the peasantry, which despite the lavish hopes long placed in it had not proven readily susceptible to revolutionary ideas.[33]

32. S. Ainzaft, "Zubatov i studenchestvo," *Katorga i ssylka,* 1927, no. 5 (34), pp. 65–69; Robert Jean Burch, "Social Unrest in Imperial Russia: The Student Movement at Moscow University, 1887–1905" (Ph.D. dissertation, Department of History, University of Washington, 1972), pp. 140–41; Zubatov to Burtsev, Dec. 18, 1906 (Koz'min, p. 71).

33. Allan K. Wildman, "The Russian Intelligentsia of the 1890's," *ASEER,* 19

Social Democrats spent the first half of the 1890's slowly broadening the base of their movement among the radical intelligentsia and factory workers. By the mid-1890's some were impatient with the time it took revolutionary propaganda to filter from the workers' circles, where Marxism was propagated among a small number of workmen, through to the factories; Social Democrats, they urged, should turn their attention to the more significant task of giving leadership to the emerging mass labor movement. The program for the new course was set forth in the brochure *Ob agitatsii* (On Agitation), composed in 1894 by Arkady Kremer and Martov (Iulii Osipovich Tsederbaum), later noted respectively as leaders of the Jewish Labor Bund and the Menshevik wing of Russian social democracy.

Social Democrats, Kremer and Martov advised, should participate in the economically oriented strike movement by organizing the workers and aiding them in drawing up their concrete economic demands; by so doing the Social Democrats would deepen their own experience and bring the workers closer to class consciousness and an awareness of their potential strength. Implicit in the new program was the postponement of political agitation to an indefinite future when the working class, through bitter experience, had come to realize that behind the factory owner stood the power of the state, that is, when they realized that an economic struggle is also essentially a political one.[34] Although many workers in the study circles protested against the discontinuance of their education, the new course gained wide acceptance by 1895 among the socialist intelligentsia in such major centers as Moscow and Petersburg.

Guided by these new tactics the social democratic intelligentsia sought to widen contacts with the factory workers and gain their confidence. They helped to organize strike funds. During strikes they assisted in elaborating and printing the strikers' demands. Although these activities were illegal, in the words of a popular historian of Russian social democracy they went "no further than

(1960), 172–79; S. I. Mitskevich, ed., *Na zare rabochego dvizheniia v Moskve* (Moscow, 1932), p. 13; N. Baturin, *Ocherki istorii sotsial-demokratii v Rossii*, 11th ed. (Leningrad, 1926), pp. 48–49.

34. Baturin, pp. 52–53; Allan K. Wildman, *The Making of a Workers' Revolution* (Chicago and London, 1967), pp. 45–48; Martov, in *Istoriia Rossii v XIX veke*, VIII, 107; Leonard Schapiro, *The Communist Party of the Soviet Union* (New York, 1959), p. 28.

the program of trade unions in free countries;"[35] yet through these services Russian Marxists strengthened their ties with the workers and increased the possibility of leading the working class movement and directing it toward political ends.

## Zubatov, Trepov, and the Labor Question

Zubatov's youthful sojourn in the revolutionary underground and his long devotion to the study of modern revolutionary theory and tactics made him unique among police officials in understanding the causes of the unrest disturbing the peace of Russia at the turn of the century. Moreover, his immediate superiors in Moscow were attentive to his ideas and generally supported the implementation of his programs. General D. F. Trepov, who was appointed chief of police for Moscow in 1896, the year Zubatov became head of the Moscow Okhrana, became a close collaborator of Zubatov's and wielded considerable influence in Petersburg bureaucratic and court circles on his behalf.

Trepov's background and career do not foreshadow his later sympathy toward proposals to end growing social unrest by other than police methods. A son of General F. F. Trepov, former military governor of St. Petersburg, Dmitrii Feodorovich received a military education, which little prepared him to understand the socio-economic problems plaguing the monarchy to which he was completely devoted. He was willing, however, under Zubatov's tutelage, to study the problems besetting the monarchy without ever divorcing them fully from police considerations.[36]

Trepov examined in detail materials on the labor movement Zubatov compiled for him, including relevant laws and circulars. Police reports on factory unrest particularly interested him; Zubatov noted that Trepov's ruling principle, "according to conscience and with justice," led him frequently to conclude that the blame lay with

35. Baturin, p. 63.
36. Gurko, pp. 355, 624. On Trepov's background, court influence, and relations with the Grand Duke Sergei Aleksandrovich see Witte, *Vospominaniia*, II, 346–53, and L. G. Zakharova, "Krizis samoderzhaviia nakanune revoliutsii 1905 goda," *Voprosy istorii*, Aug. 1972, pp. 125, 138–39. Zubatov was pleased with Trepov's attention to his new duties: "He had only descended from [his] horse at this time and sat at home for two months reading laws and circulars. What very much surprised me was his attentive reading of proclamations, illegal brochures, etc., which I never earlier noted among any of the commanding personnel" (Zubatov to Burtsev, Dec. 18, 1906, Koz'min, p. 70).

the factory owners. Before long the two men were conducting a "re-evaluation of values" on such questions as student agitation and the labor problem. The initiative and the ideas were Zubatov's; in later years he would refer to Trepov as "my political pupil, my alter ego," a steadfast friend even after Zubatov's discharge from service.[37]

Zubatov found a second and more powerful supporter in the Grand Duke Sergei Aleksandrovich, governor-general of Moscow. The fourth son of Alexander II, the Grand Duke Sergei shared many of the characteristics of his eldest brother, Alexander III, whom he idolized. High-handed and narrow in outlook, he merited his unpopularity among liberals and ministers alike, for he ruled Moscow as an all-powerful viceroy. An uncle of Tsar Nicholas II and married to the sister of the Empress, he was an invaluable link with the court. Yet the reasons for his continual support and his spirited defense of Zubatov when the latter came under attack from bureaucratic circles remains an enigma. The Grand Duke Sergei, a notorious archconservative and outspoken anti-Semite, was determined to make Moscow a Great Russian center purified of its Jewish population. Nevertheless he persevered in upholding Zubatov's program, even though it permitted the working class to organize and brought the Jewish masses and intelligentsia into cooperation with the monarchy, actions anathema to most conservatives. One can only surmise that he trusted Trepov implicitly, and that once he adopted a course of action, critical opposition would make him more stubborn in defending his original commitment.[38]

## The Report of April 8, 1898

The spread of mass labor unrest encouraged by the Marxist intelligentsia was the immediate problem for the police authorities in the first years after Trepov's appointment. Zubatov, after

37. *Koz'min*, pp. 70–1.
38. Zakharova, pp. 124–25; E. M. Almedingen, *An Unbroken Unity* (London, 1964); A. G. Avchinnikov, *Velikii kniaz' Sergei Aleksandrovich* (Ekaterinoslav, 1915); L. M. Aizenberg, "Velikii kniaz' Sergei Aleksandrovich, Vitte i evrei-moskovskie kuptsy," *Evreiskaia starina*, 13 (1930), 88–99. The Grand Duke Sergei contributed 100,000 rubles to the Moscow Zubatovshchina and defended it before the Department of Police in May 1901 (I. A. Shmeleva, "Bor'ba moskovskikh rabochikh protiv zubatovshchiny" [Candidate of Historical Science dissertation, Moskovskii gosudarstvennyi pedagogicheskii institut imeni V. I. Lenina, 1962], pp. 127, 172). The grand duke had

considerable study and experience, prepared an analysis and recommendations. The report was edited by Trepov and sent on to the Grand Duke Sergei, signed by Trepov and dated April 8, 1898.[39] Its very first paragraph warned of the grave danger should the Marxist intelligentsia and the working class join forces:

The history of the revolutionary movement has shown that the intelligentsia by itself has insufficient forces for a struggle against the government even if by chance it is armed with explosives. Bearing this in mind, all opposition groups now applaud the social-democratic movement with the expectation that having united the workers to antigovernment undertakings, it has at its disposal such a mass force that the government must seriously take into account.[40]

A description of the new tactics set forth in *Ob agitatsii* followed, although their origin was attributed to the German Social Democratic Party. Russian Social Democrats had adopted a practical course of action in working closely with the factory masses. They had become defenders of their daily needs and their interests. Such tactics were more successful than ideological appeals of a theoretical nature in attracting the working class to the revolutionary intelligentsia. "Their tactics have given excellent results in practice: mass strikes occurred, giving sufficient satisfaction as a result to their participants." The success of the strike movement had been in part due to the blindness of the responsible government organs, which had been unwilling to undertake the guardianship of the working class and satisfy its just needs; it was necessary that the

---

an inordinate fear of the labor movement and factory disorders; this may account for his support of Zubatov's labor program (Iu. B. Solov'ev, *Samoderzhavie i dvorianstvo v kontse XIX veka* [Leningrad, 1973], pp. 138, 150, 153).

39. The report was published in full within a year of its composition in two publications of "Economism" and correctly attributed to Zubatov: *Rabochee delo*, no. 1 (April 1899), pp. 24–34; *Rabochaia mysl'*, supplement to no. 6 (April 1899), pp. 1–2.

40. *Rabochee delo*, no. 1 (April 1899), p. 24; the following quotations are from pp. 25–29. The inability of the radical intelligentsia to combat the government effectively without mass support and the government's need to take positive measures of benefit to the masses so that they would not follow the revolutionaries were basic points in Zubatov's approach to the labor problem. In a letter of September 10, 1900, discussing further government legislation on behalf of the workers, Zubatov wrote: "such a policy leaves the revolutionary staff without an army and the struggle with the government becomes a physical impossibility" (D. Zaslavskii, "Zubatov i Mania Vil'bushevich," *Byloe*, March 1918, p. 110). As Stalin later said, "The working class without a revolutionary party is an army without a general staff" (J. Stalin, "Foundations of Leninism," in *Leninism*, trans. Eden and Cedar Paul [New York, 1928], p. 163).

government in the future "sanction as reasonable the solicitations of the workers, despite all the perniciousness of this in a political regard."

The report analyzed the effect of the strike tactics upon the working class and their implications for the security of the monarchy, an analysis which might have come directly from *Ob agitatsii* or been culled from the writings of leading Russian Social Democrats of the time:

Successes gained by means of strikes have a dangerous and harmful state significance, appearing as an elemental school of political education of the workers. Success in the struggle brings to the worker faith in his strength, teaches him practical methods of struggle, prepares and draws out of the crowd able pioneers, convinces the worker in practice of the possibility and usefulness of unity and, in general, of collective actions; agitation by struggle makes him more receptive to . . . the ideas of socialism, which seemed to him until then an empty dream; owing to the local struggle [he] develops a consciousness of the solidarity of his interests with the interests of other workers, that is, a consciousness of the necessity of class struggle, for the success of which there is found greater and greater urgency for political agitation, which sets itself as goal the change of the existing state and social structure on the principles of social democracy.

The government had to end a situation in which labor unrest and agitation fed on their own success; it could effectively counter the new socialist strategy by undermining the social democratic appeal to the workers' petty needs and demands. The revolutionaries, left to themselves, were politically impotent; supported by the workers, however, they became a powerful force: "So long as the revolutionary propagandizes pure socialism one can cope with him by solely repressive measures, but when he begins to exploit to his advantage the petty shortcomings of the existing legal order, repressive measures alone are not enough, and it is necessary immediately to tear away the ground from under his feet." The inadequacy of repression to combat social democracy and the impotence of the radical intelligentsia without a mass following were constant themes in Zubatov's writings, many of which were designed to convince the higher authorities of these basic truths.

In essence, Zubatov reiterated, the revolutionary was not primarily concerned with the worker and his needs, nor with the immediate outcome of a strike, but with the tempering effect of strikes on the workers, who thereby got a taste for concerted action. "The worse, the better" was the motto of the revolutionary; "it is not in the interests of the revolutionary that the authorities care about these needs and satisfy the needy." The government thus must act to weaken mass support for the political agitator:

Naturally in order to disarm him at the very root it is necessary to reveal and indicate to the worker a legal outlet from the difficulties of his position, having in view that only the most youthful and energetic part of the crowd follows behind the agitator, but the average worker always prefers not the brilliant outcome but the quiet legal one. Broken up in that way the crowd loses all its strength, on which the agitator so hopes and depends.

The government had used two methods of combatting the influence of labor agitators: repression, that is, arrest and administrative banishment, and "the introduction of the principle of legality into the sphere of factory relations." Commitment to the latter method "demands the elimination of all willfullness on the part of the employer." Good factory laws have often gone unexecuted. Moreover, factory owners have often violated the spirit of the law while adhering to its letter, for they "often cannot reconcile themselves to the thought of equality of rights for the parties who have come to an agreement." Employers frequently vent their anger at workers who lodge a valid complaint against factory abuses by discharging them just as quickly as the law permits. The factory owner might consider himself legally justified in taking such action, but "from the political point of view such discharge [from work] appears as harmful willfullness since it disarms and embitters the worker, delivering him up as a victim to revolutionary intrigues." The government possesses sufficient means to regulate relations between factory owners and their workers and should respond to the just demands of the workers where the factory administration has acted irresponsibly.

The remainder of Zubatov's report, fully half, was imprinted with the interministerial squabble over jurisdiction in factory matters. As might be expected, Zubatov supported the stand of the Ministry of Interior and sharply criticized the factory inspectorate. Of greater interest, the report presented a spirited defense of police involvement in labor relations.

The relationship between employers and workers . . . in no way can avoid strict police surveillance.

According to the spirit of the times, when Western Europe is absorbed by the labor question, the whole interest of the revolution is concentrated in factory surroundings, and where the revolutionary settles there the state police are also obliged to be.... The more the revolutionary is busy the more the police are obliged to be interested. If lately the agitator carries on his intrigues on the basis of legality, exploiting the failings in the activity of the factory administration, then in the interests of the persistent and indefatigable creation of limits to his intrigues, the police are obliged to follow vigilantly the arrangements of factory institutions and, in general, all that has a connection with the person and practices of the workers. Such is the position of things and such is the demand of the times.

The police had been authorized by the Ministry of Interior's circular of August 12, 1897, to investigate, report and eliminate potential and actual causes of labor discontent. There could be no justification for limiting police obligations in factory affairs, as the Ministry of Finance demanded in its circular of March 12, 1898, to the factory inspectorate, for statute law granted the police exceptional jurisdiction and authority superior to that of the inspector when questions of state security were involved. The presence of the police in labor matters was made equally urgent by the inadequately small staff of factory inspectors. Their duties left little time for the more vital tasks that directly affected the workers, such as the investigation of workers' complaints and direct examination of the causes of factory disorders with a view to bringing them to an end.

Zubatov's report ended with an attack on the competence of the factory inspectors and a vindication of police intervention in the area of labor relations. The report itself was written partly to answer criticism from the Ministry of Finance of the circular of August 12, 1897; no doubt Zubatov's strong defense of the police was in part a justification of the increasingly independent action of the Moscow authorities in labor relations, action which had already drawn official protests from the Ministry of Finance.[41] The report's emphasis on the limitations of repression, its indictment of factory owners, and its call for further governmental aid to the working class supported conclusions similar to those of General Panteleev, Prince Sviatopolk-Mirskii, and other enlightened representatives of the Ministry of Interior who had studied the labor problem at first hand.

Then wherein lies the importance of Zubatov's report? It is, above

---

41. S. V. Zubatov, "Zubatovshchina," *Byloe*, Oct. 1917, pp. 161–62. On April 2, 1898, six days before the date of Zubatov's report, the Ministry of Finance was notified by one of its agents of unauthorized interference by the Moscow administration in factory labor relations (Martov, in *Istoriia Rossii v XIX veke*, VIII, 97).

all, unique among government studies of the time for its detailed analysis and understanding of the new theory and tactics of Russian social democracy to gain control of the labor movement. Without clearly defining a plan of action, the report advocated repression to isolate the revolutionaries from the working class combined with constant governmental solicitude for the workers' well-being; this dual program would both undermine the mass appeal of social democracy and eliminate the causes of labor disorders; such was the heart of Zubatov's approach to the labor question.

The report is also significant for the hearing it received among the higher authorities. General Trepov, for whom the "ideas of the report became ... an unwavering conviction, ... spoke about them and developed them everywhere, in particular in the higher circles [of government]";[42] Trepov was also instrumental in winning over the Grand Duke Sergei Aleksandrovich to Zubatov's views. Zubatov's prestige was great among his Petersburg superiors in the Department of Police, but without the encouragement and protection of Trepov and the grand duke, his labor experiments could not have begun.

Finally, the report is of more than passing academic interest because its author had the opportunity to realize his ideas in practice. Between 1898 and 1903, when the labor movement was reaching maturity and the Social Democrats were organizing on a national scale and striving to lead the working class, Zubatov's program was the only consistent labor policy emanating from government quarters. The first labor organizations to receive semiofficial approval in tsarist Russia were found under his auspices; during their short span of existence they embraced thousands of workers, primarily in Moscow, Minsk, and Odessa, but traces of similar affiliated organizations were to be found in other cities. Broad differences in the economic character of each area, the composition of the working class, and the strength and nature of the local revolutionary movement, however, justify separate treatment here of the three major cities involved. The close association between the movements in Minsk and Odessa and their relationship

42. Zubatov to Burtsev, Dec. 18, 1906 (Koz'min, p. 71). Spiridovich maintains that through his uncle, the Grand Duke Sergei Aleksandrovich, the tsar was made acquainted with the report and, as a consequence, the Moscow authorities were encouraged to go forward with Zubatov's program (*Mladorosskaia iskra*, Nov. 15, 1933).

to the downfall of Zubatov and his system dictates that we begin our study with Moscow, where elements of the Zubatovshchina survived longest.

# CHAPTER 3

# The Moscow Zubatovshchina: Background

Moscow was at the beginning of this century challenged only by St. Petersburg as the economic capital of the country. Long known as a trading center, Moscow had also become an industrial city comparable in size and influence to the major cities of Western Europe. It was the chief railway hub of the country and the natural economic focus of the central industrial region which surrounded it. In 1901 more than 286,000 of the total of 1.7 million factory workers under the factory inspectors' surveillance were employed in Moscow *guberniia*, which included the city of Moscow, making it by far the largest *guberniia* in terms of the size of its labor force.[1]

## The Moscow Working Class

Moscow entered the twentieth century as a major beneficiary of the great industrial upsurge of the 1890's. The city census of 1902 recorded a population of over a million, an increase of 400,000 in two decades, placing Moscow tenth in rank among cities of the world.[2] Textile factories surpassed by far all other industry in total production, followed by the metal and machine construction plants, whose importance had grown rapidly in the last years of the century. Moscow's industry around the turn of the century was characterized by big industrial units, some employing thousands of workers; among them were the textile plants of Emil' Tsindel (2,300) and Prokhorov-Trekhgornoi (5,300) and such metallurgical and machine construction plants as Guzhon (2,200) and Bromlei (1,200).[3]

1. *Svod otchetov fabrichnykh inspektorov za 1901 god,* p. 23.
2. Rashin, p. 353; *Moskovskiia vedomosti,* June 11, 1902.
3. P. M. Shestakov, *Rabochie na manufakture T-va "Emil' Tsindel" v Moskve* (Moscow,

The Moscow proletariat grew apace with industry. The number of factory workers increased from 67,400 in 1890 to 99,300 in 1900, to 107,800 in 1902. The greatest number (51,000 in 1902) were employed in textile plants, where women made up 40 per cent of the work force; the metal workers (that is, those engaged in metal processing, machine construction, and the production of tools and instruments, the second largest group of factory workers) comprised less than a third of that figure.[4]

There is evidence that Moscow's factory population at this time was more permanently settled than in the past; their links with their villages of origin were becoming perfunctory, if not terminated altogether. According to the city census of 1902, over a third of the factory workers had lived in Moscow more than ten years, more than half over five years.[5] Permanency of residence in the city varied from industry to industry and was greater in the metal and machine industries than among textile workers. Investigation among 4,391 male textile workers in Moscow in 1881 indicated that 42.8 per cent were sons of factory workers.[6] At the Prokhorov plant permanent year-round workers increased from 16 per cent in the 1870's to 30 per cent in 1900.[7] A study of 1,335 workers at the Tsindel plant in 1899 found that 56 per cent were of parents who at one time had been factory workers.[8]

Although many factory workers had links with their native villages through the ownership of land, these holdings were losing their significance. At the Tsindel plant 94.2 per cent of the workers were classified as peasant in origin with the vast majority retaining land allotments in their native villages. Some workers, however, only visited their villages on holidays while others had not visited their villages for several years and had leased out their allotments. A large number of others retained allotments that were so small as to appear meaningless to them. Only about one-eighth of the workers

1900), p. 2; R. Portal, *La Russie industrielle de 1880 à 1914* (Paris, 1966), pp. 63–64; Alexandre Pogogeff and Pavel Natanovich Apostol, *L'économie sociale à la section Russe* (Paris, 1900), pp. 255, 258; Ministerstvo Finansov, Otdel promyshlennosti, *Spisok fabrik i zavodov Evropeiskoi Rossii* (St. Petersburg, 1903), pp. 21, 24, 281, 287.

4. *Rabochee dvizhenie*, IV, pt. 1, p. viii; *Perepis' Moskvy 1902 goda*, vol. I, *Naselenie*, no. 2 (Moscow, 1906), pp. 6–7, 118–120.

5. *Perepis' Moskvy 1902 goda*, p. 10.

6. Rashin, p. 532.

7. S. Lapitskaia, *Byt rabochikh Trekhgornoi manufaktury* (Moscow, 1935), p. 37.

8. Shestakov, p. 24.

returned to their native villages in the summer months to work in the fields. These facts led Shestakov to conclude in his study of the Tsindel plant that "the development of a factory proletariat is scarcely subject to doubt."[9] Comparable figures are not available for the Moscow metal workers, but presumably, as in Petersburg, they formed even a more stable year-round working class than the textile workers. We might conclude that, on the whole, although the Moscow factory workers were mainly peasant in origin, with memories of a not-too-distant past spent among their native fields and villages, a stable, hereditary proletariat of considerable size was emerging.

Traditional loyalties and sentiments lingered on among the urban factory masses even when the link with the village was tenuous. The Moscow working class, overwhelmingly Great Russian, was conservative by instinct; the autocracy and the Orthodox church remained central to its fundamentalist outlook.[10]

The newcomer to the city and its factories was subjected to the social and economic dislocation that universally marked the early stages of the industrial revolution. In Moscow, in the early 1890's, long hours and low wages were accompanied by a high cost of living and sleeping quarters that gave little dignity to the workers' lives. Although average yearly wages for the quarter of a million workers in Moscow *guberniia* rose from 170 rubles in 1897 to 192 rubles in 1903, a sharp increase in the cost of food and shelter caused a decline in real wages. The cheapest room cost from six to eight rubles a month to rent; a corner of a room with a cot or bunk cost three to four rubles. Financial hardship made the workers give up even a minimum of privacy and enter those communal factory barracks made so famous in the works of Gorky.[11]

9. *Ibid.,* p. 75. At the giant Trekhgornoi plant in 1905–1906, 93.6 per cent of the workers were classified as peasants. Yet in the preceding years only 100 to 200 (4 to 8 per cent) left for their village in the summer months, a figure somewhat larger than in the fall or winter months. The investigator therefore concluded that these workers neither had close ties with the land nor participated in village affairs (M. K. Rozhkov, "Trekhgornaia manufaktura ko vremeni revoliutsii 1905 goda," in *Rabochie Trekhgornoi manufaktury v 1905 godu* [Moscow, 1930], pp. 12–13).

10. O. Chaadaeva, "Rabochie trekhgornoi manufaktury v revoliutsii 1905 goda," in *Rabochie Trekhgornoi manufaktury,* pp. 30–31; David Lane, *The Roots of Russian Communism* (Assen, 1969), p. 117.

11. *V staroi Moskve,* ed. L. Nikulin and G. Ryklin (Moscow, 1939), pp. 194–95. Many Moscow workers left their families in their native village because the rent for family apartments was exorbitant *(Torgovo-promyshlennaia gazeta,* Oct. 4, 1901).

## Rise and Decline of Moscow Social Democracy, 1890-1905

Strikes in Moscow, as elsewhere in Russia in the mid-1890's, were economically motivated; better working and living conditions, not political rights and revolution, were demanded.[12] The machine construction and metal workers—who were more highly skilled, better paid, and more literate than the textile workers—led the way with a series of strikes during the summers of 1895 and 1896. By the end of 1896 a ten-hour day had been won in several large machine factories and railway shops, although most Moscow factories continued to enforce longer hours. The strike movement spread to other plants in 1897 and sometimes included demands for a nine-hour day.[13] The Moscow strikes of the mid-1890's, largely led by workers and inspired by the Petersburg strike movement, came as a revelation to the intelligentsia; henceforward Moscow social democracy would direct its energy toward leading the working class.[14]

The student youth and the intelligentsia were first attracted in significant numbers to Marxist doctrine in the 1890's although Marxism was not unknown among Moscow intellectual circles a decade earlier.[15] During 1891 and 1892 Moscow social democracy attempted to create a viable organization and disseminate Marxist ideas among students and small numbers of factory workers. In the next period of its history, 1893–1894, Moscow social democracy passed from the confines of workers' circles, with their slow propagation of socialist ideas among a handful of workers, to agitation among the factory masses. The new tactics were derived from the practical experience of the socialist movement among the Polish and Jewish workers. In August 1893, Evgenii Sponti, who had spread socialist propaganda among the Vilna artisans, moved his operation to Moscow, where he set about organizing a Marxist group for systematic propaganda among the workers.[16]

---

12. A factory inspector reported: "The chief point of dissatisfaction of the workers appeared complaints against the insecurity of existence due to extremely low wages, on the one hand, and the continually increasing expensiveness of life and the absence of tolerable living conditions in Moscow and Moscow *guberniia*, on the other hand" (*V staroi Moskve*, p. 194).

13. *Rabochee dvizhenie*, IV, pt. 1, pp. 383, 407, 409, 411–14.

14. *Ibid.*, pp. 358–59, 388–89.

15. S. I. Mitskevich, *Revoliutsionnaia Moskva* (Moscow, 1940), pp. 129–30; Vasin, pp. 15, 19–20.

16. Mitskevich, pp. 146–48; N. Ovsiannikov, ed., *Na zare rabochego dvizheniia v*

In February 1894, S. I. Mitskevich, a member of the Sponti circle, journeyed to Vilna and learned from Kremer about the agitational tactics that had been carried out for some time among the Jewish artisans of the area. Before the year was up a copy of *Ob agitatsii* reached Moscow and became the credo of the local Marxist intelligentsia.[17] The economic interests of the working class now became paramount in socialist propaganda. A leaflet distributed by Moscow Social Democrats defined the tasks of the working class in Russia as follows: "Our workers must organize funds [and] unions, must acquire a shorter workday and higher wages; they must demand to be allowed to unite in unions to discuss their affairs, to organize strikes, and to ... publish books and newspapers elucidating the position of the workers."[18] Socialist leaflets chronicled factory abuses and workers' grievances at specific factories and workshops and provided news of labor disturbances.

By the spring of 1895 Moscow Social Democrats had enlisted a fairly large following at Moscow factories; a group of two hundred gathered together that year to celebrate May Day for the first time in Moscow. Plans for a mass meeting of two thousand workers and a citywide strike were disrupted by arrests of the leaders in July and August.[19] Early in 1896, Moscow Social Democrats re-established their organization under the name of the Moscow Labor (or Workers') Union. In mid-summer the Union claimed ties with workers at fifty-five of Moscow's factories and railway shops and contacts with social-democratic groups in fifteen cities; at the International Socialist Congress held in London in June of that year it claimed a following of two thousand.[20] News of the Petersburg textile strike prompted the Union's central committee to plan a mass rally and a general strike in support of Petersburg comrades; the

---

*Moskve* (Moscow, 1919), p. 20; *Ocherki istorii moskovskoi organizatsii KPSS 1883–1965* (Moscow, 1966), p. 18; I. Vasin, *Sotsial-demokraticheskoe dvizhenie v Moskve, 1883–1901 gg.* (Moscow, 1955), p. 26.

17. Mitskevich, *Revoliutsionnaia Moskva*, p. 159; Mitskevich, ed., *Na zare rabochego dvizheniia v Moskve*, p. 21; Ovsiannikov, p. 28.

18. N. Angarskii, ed., *Doklady sots.-demokraticheskikh komitetov Vtoromu s"ezdu RSDRP* (Moscow-Leningrad, 1930), p. 144.

19. Ovsiannikov, pp. 33–37; *Rabochee dvizhenie*, IV, pt. 1, p. 397

20. The following is based on an article, "Rabochee dvizhenie v Moskve," describing Moscow social democratic activities from 1895 until January 1897, as published in *Rabotnik*, no. 3–4, (1897), and reprinted in *Rabochee dvizhenie*, IV, pt. 1, pp. 396–415.

strike, however, was cut short by the timely arrest of several key workers and the unwillingness of others to go on with the planned demonstration. In July a large part of the Union's leadership was arrested.

The weakening of the organized Marxist center little affected the older, spontaneous, and broader-based movement of the workers for economic improvements; during 1896–1897 sporadic strikes occurred throughout Moscow for better wages and hours. The Union's central committee, in a report on the history of Moscow social democracy, confessed that the failure to bring about the general strike was "understandable, for the movement was never deep at the Moscow factories." The Moscow labor movement in early 1897 was said to be characterized by "the almost complete absence of the intervention of the intelligentsia in it"; after many arrests the socialist intelligentsia had returned to "the old, narrow means of action," and thus "are powerless to lead the [labor] movement and are continually compelled to follow behind it."[21]

Moscow social democracy had now passed the peak of its early influence; during the years from 1897 to 1905 it was unable to re-establish close ties with the factory masses and thus to exert a directing influence on the Moscow labor movement. The history of Moscow social democracy in these years is one of continuous efforts and repeated failures.[22] The report delivered at the second congress of the Russian Social Democratic Labor Party by N. E. Bauman, representative of the Moscow Social Democratic Committee, painted a gloomy picture:

At a time when socialist agitation and propaganda embrace each year an ever increasing number of cities, penetrate even into the most remote provincial corners, giving rise to one or another clear sign of the growth of class consciousness among the proletariat—in Moscow, in one of the most important industrial centers, the gradual weakening and even, perhaps, complete destruction of the social-democratic influence on the laboring masses is sharply evident. At least beginning in 1898, not one fact is to be noted in revolutionary annals by which one might put together even an approximate notion of the growth of social-democratic agitation.[23]

21. *Rabochee dvizhenie*, IV, pt. 1, pp. 407, 411. See also Angarskii, p. 155; *Doklad o russkom sotsial'demokraticheskom dvizhenii mezhdunarodnomu sotsialisticheskomu kongressu v Parizhe 1900 g.* (Geneva, 1901), p. 25.

22. N. Ovsiannikov, "Osobennosti moskovskogo dvizheniia," in Ovsiannikov, p. 5; "Vospominaniia I. A. Teodorovicha," *Iskrovskii period v Moskve*, ed. O. Piatnitskii, Ts. Borovskoi, and M. Vladimirskii (Moscow-Leningrad, 1928), p. 60.

23. Nikolai Ernestovich Bauman, *Sbornik statei, vospominanii i dokumentov* (Moscow,

Since 1903 the failure of Moscow social democracy to lead the city's working class has been attributed to a variety of causes: the low cultural level of the workers; the large proportion of women among the Moscow proletariat; a high rate of turnover in the work force; the workers' peasant origin and bond with the village, which stamped them as conservative and submissive to patriarchal factory relations; the preponderance of unskilled textile workers over metal workers, who commonly formed the vanguard of revolutionary agitation; the barrackslike living quarters for factory workers, which made secret agitation difficult; finally, the industrial crisis that began in 1899 is said to have caused workers to look elsewhere for jobs, thus depriving social democracy of some of its most militant supporters.[24]

These factors alone do not account for the decline of social democracy in Moscow; great credit must be given to the Moscow Okhrana for its ability to detect even the most deeply hidden revolutionary roots while sowing dissension and weakening self-confidence among socialists still at large. Repression, however, was but part of the Moscow Okhrana's program to combat social-democratic subversion; to isolate and weaken the socialist intelligentsia it planned to gain the support and loyalty of the working class. Directing the entire program was Zubatov.

Marxism had made headway among small circles of intelligentsia in the early 1890's largely unimpeded by police interference; but mass agitation among the factory proletariat posed a more serious problem for the security police. In November 1894, the Department of Police warned the Moscow police chief of the emergence of revolutionary social democracy and its grave significance: "From

---

1937), p. 71. The report is printed in *Vtoroi s"ezd RSDRP* (Moscow, 1959), pp. 619–39, without its attribution to Bauman. Memoir literature confirms Bauman's account. Mitskevich, who participated in the Moscow social democratic movement from the beginning, later wrote: "When I arrived in Moscow in 1903 the social democratic ties and organization were weaker than in 1895!" (S. M. [Mitskevich], "Na zare rabochago dvizheniia v Moskve," in *Tekushchii moment": Sbornik* [Moscow, 1906], p. 19). Rykov, on a visit to Moscow in the summer of 1904, found the local organization disintegrating, with members of the party committee either under arrest or in hiding (Rykov, "Iz vospominanii," in Ovsiannikov, p. 154).

24. D. Kol'tsov, "Rabochie v 1890–1904 gg., "in *Obshchestvennoe dvizhenie v Rossii v nachale XX-go veka*, I, 194; *Rabochee delo*, no. 6 (April 1900), p. 70; Ovsiannikov, p. 4; Bauman, pp. 71, 85–86; "O dvizhenii sredi moskovskikh rabochikh metallistov," *Materialy po istorii professional'nogo dvizheniia v Rossii*, 1 (1924), 145; *Iskrovskii period v Moskve*, pp. 61–62; *Doklad o russkom sotsial'demokraticheskom dvizhenii*, p. 24.

information in the Department of Police it is perceived that
revolutionary propaganda of a social democratic character, recently
finding a favorable ground ... among factory workers, begins to
acquire a serious significance inside the Empire and by its strength
almost exceeds the propaganda of all the remaining revolutionary
factions."[25] A month later the Moscow Okhrana made its first
arrests among the Marxist intelligentsia in Moscow, liquidating a
circle led by Mitskevich; beginning the following summer waves of
arrests occurred, cutting short each attempt to build a permanent
Marxist center in Moscow.[26]

This success was based on the counterintelligence method
commonly known as provocation. The Moscow Okhrana became
notorious for its ability to attract collaborators and informers at all
levels of the revolutionary parties. The use of secret spies and
provocateurs was long established in Russia before Zubatov came
on the scene and perfected it, for the monarchy, ever distrustful of
public opinion and initiative, willingly accepted and encouraged
secret reports of alleged sedition from any quarter.[27] The presence of
*agents provocateurs* in their ranks did not long elude Moscow Social
Democrats; the fact that the police were able to prevent their every
attempt to restore a stable base of operations led individual Social
Democrats to fear and suspect their comrades, further fragmenting
and weakening the movement.[28] Zubatov's information on the

25. Vladimir Makaskov, "Pionery sotsialdemokratii v Moskve, " in Ovsiannikov,
p. 56.

26. Bauman (p. 80) stated that in 1899, for example, arrests took place in February,
April, May, June, October, and December. Also see the account of the Moscow labor
movement from autumn 1898 to 1900 published in *Rabochee delo*, no. 6 (April 1900),
pp. 69–72, and reprinted in *Rabochee dvizhenie*, IV, pt. 2, pp. 287–90.

27. A. I. Spiridovich, *Zapiski zhandarma* (Kharkov, 1927), p. 44; Zavarzin,
*Zhandarmy*, pp. 54–58; Sidney Monas, "The Political Police: The Dream of a Beautiful
Autocracy," in Black, p. 179.

28. Leopold Ruma and Boris Kvartsev, after their arrest in the summer of 1896,
apparently agreed to Zubatov's conditions and thereupon acted as paid police
informants. Bauman (pp. 75–79) placed great emphasis on their work in undermining the efforts of Moscow social democracy. Also see the letter of V. I. Lenin to P. B.
Aksel'rod, Aug. 4, 1901, in *Leninskii sbornik* (Moscow-Leningrad, 1925), III, 231–32.
The case of Ruma, a Belgian citizen, is of interest; in Soviet publications today he is
still labeled a provocateur, but no documentary proof of the accusation was found in
the archives either of the Moscow Okhrana or the Moscow governor-general
(Ovsiannikov, p. 72). Men'shchikov (I, 305) held that Ruma was unmoved by
Zubatov's rhetoric and that rumors alleging Ruma to be a police agent probably
emanated from Zubatov, who hoped in this fashion to sow distrust among the
socialist intelligentsia.

movements of Moscow's Social Democrats was provided by a secret informer fully trusted by the socialist intelligentsia.

## Mistress of Provocation

Anna Egorovna Serebriakova diligently served the Moscow Okhrana for over a quarter of a century until her exposure in 1909 by the journalist Vladimir Burtsev. In the early 1880's Serebriakova gained the friendship and respect of the Moscow intelligentsia. Formally employed as a newspaper editor and a translator of scholarly books, she acquired a large circle of acquaintances in the academic and literary worlds, including elements of the radical intelligentsia in Moscow and other cities. Although she was never a member of any party, a number of radical groups entrusted her with the delicate position of emissary in the revolutionary Red Cross organized to provide material help to political prisoners.[29] Serebriakova was better known as a vivacious hostess, whose apartment was open to visitors and overnight guests from the socialist intelligentsia; her "evening parties . . . had the character of a Marxist salon."[30] A visitor to her apartment might encounter Petr Struve, the pioneer Russian Marxist; Anatolii Lunacharskii, the future Soviet Commissar of Education; A. I. Elizarova, Lenin's sister; and others prominent in Moscow radical circles.[31] The Moscow Social Democratic Committee used the apartment occasionally for its meetings or as a storehouse for party literature. Zubatov had good reason to write of Serebriakova that "the Moscow Okh[rana] owes success in its greatest cases during all periods of its activity to her initiative."[32]

With the aid of Serebriakova and other secret agents Zubatov intended to weaken social democracy by concentrating first on destroying the center of the movement. Thus, during the first police

29. Letter of Zubatov, March 26, 1907, in Alekseev, *Istoriia*, pp. 26–27. Burtsev's denunciation of Serebriakova appeared in *Obshchee delo*, no. 2 (Nov. 15, 1909); Men'shchikov, I, 98.

30. The words are those of A. Lunacharskii, a frequent visitor to Serebriakov's salon in the 1890's (Alekseev, *Istoriia*, p. i).

31. *Ibid.*, p. 55.

32. Letter of Zubatov, March 26, 1907 (*ibid.*, p. 27). Her unmasking by Burtsev in 1909 apparently had a bad effect on her declining health. Largely as a result of Stolypin's appeal to the tsar in February 1911, she was granted a yearly pension for life of 1,200 rubles, which was regularly paid until the revolution of February 1917. Arrested in 1923, she was tried in an open session of the Moscow *guberniia* court in April 1926 and sentenced to seven years in prison.

raid against Moscow social democracy, factory workers who had attended Marxist meetings were generally left at liberty. This practice was terminated with the police raid of July 5, 1896, in which the majority of those arrested were workers.[33]

The change in tactics had been devised by Zubatov, who had come to realize the strategic position of the worker-intelligentsia—those factory workers "who are the connecting link between [the intelligentsia] and the workers' milieu."[34] Zubatov's deep interest in the labor movement dates from the arrests of July 1896. Through personal interrogation of political prisoners he sought out the reasons that drew individuals into the revolutionary vortex, a practice he continued throughout his Okhrana career and for which he earned the loathing of the revolutionary intelligentsia.

## Zubatov and the Art of Brainwashing

Since the early 1890's Zubatov had regularly interviewed newly arrested political prisoners with a view to persuading them to enter the Okhrana's employment. The prisoner would be confronted with overpowering and minutely detailed evidence of his activities and those of his cohorts in an effort to dispel the slightest hope that revolutionary activity, no matter how clandestine, could escape police detection and attain its ends. Zubatov coupled sympathetic assurances of understanding for the humanitarian impulse to improve the plight of the Russian masses with biting criticism of the prisoner for drawing innocent workers into conspiratorial activity where certain arrest awaited them. Far from being an enemy of the people, Zubatov asserted, the autocracy was still progressive and capable of initiating reform and acting for the welfare of its people; the militancy of the radicals, however, provoked the government to take a reactionary course, vitiating its good intentions and delaying the institution of needed reforms. In the end, therefore, the revolutionary retarded rather than promoted the welfare of the masses whose well-being was his alleged *raison d'être*. Forsaking the radical movement, the revolutionary could fulfill his ideals through cooperation with the government and support of its reformist

---

33. Men'shchikov, I, 304.
34. *Rabochee dvizhenie*, IV, pt. 1, p. 348. On the significance of the worker-intelligentsia see Richard Pipes, *Social Democracy and the St. Petersburg Labor Movement, 1885–1897* (Cambridge, Mass., 1963), pp. 3–12.

impulse.[35] With this ideological approach Zubatov opened the door for his prisoners to enter the services of the police; many voluntarily did so.

These early experiments were followed by more systematic attempts to win ideological converts among the Marxist intelligentsia; Zubatov scored his first victories among those arrested in July 1896. Equipped with a broad theoretical grasp of the revolutionary ideologies, master of applied psychology and profound observer of character, Zubatov was adept at the art of conversion through persuasion, the practice commonly known today as brainwashing.[36] And Zubatov laboriously applied his art: "whole hours, even days, over endless [cups of] tea, in tobacco smoke, he carried on his 'conversations' with the prisoners, who were led one at a time into the Okhrana, where they sat in a soft chair in the chief's cabinet and, on occasions when the disputes stretched out too long, were fed supper, which was brought from a neighboring inn at the treasury's expense."[37]

During these discussions, which bore many resemblances to the ideological bull sessions common among the radical intelligentsia, Zubatov was able to fathom his victim, size up his moral character and degree of conviction, and so adjust his line of approach to the prisoner. After his conversion the penitent was expected to make a full confession of revolutionary sins, after which he would be pardoned and set free. Upon release the convert was expected to keep the Okhrana informed of the activities of the revolutionary intelligentsia.

This clinical approach to the radical intelligentsia yielded such rich rewards that it became regular practice. Most notable were the gains made in 1900–1901, when Zubatov brought to bear all his powers of

35. Zubatov's interview with a student in 1893, *Rabochee delo*, no. 1 (April 1899), pp. 35–36. Also see Viktor Chernov, *Zapiski sotsialista-revoliutsionera* (Berlin-Petersburg-Moscow, 1922), pp. 201–16; *Iskra*, no. 48 (Sept. 15, 1903).

36. In a report Moscow Social Democrats prepared for *Iskra*, Zubatov was praised as a master psychologist for his skill in paralyzing the revolutionary idealist's feeling of self-sacrifice and diverting the prisoner's natural irritation against his interrogator, Zubatov, to other gendarmes, the procurator, prison authorities, or even other prisoners (Shmeleva, dissertation, p. 132). There is only one recorded incident of Zubatov's having used force against a prisoner: see the autobiographical sketch, "Sedoi (Litvin), Zinovii Iakovlevich," *Entsiklopedicheskii slovar' Russkogo biblio-graficheskogo instituta Granat*, 7th rev. ed. (Moscow, n.d.), XLI, 27; Mitskevich, *Revoliutionnaia Moskva*, p. 240.

37. Men'shchikov, I, 304–5; see also Spiridovich, "Pri tsarskom rezhime," p. 123.

persuasion to convince a number of Social Democrats closely associated with the Russian and Jewish labor movements that only the autocracy could bring progress to Russia's backward masses. Zubatov poured out his soul in describing his ideal of Russia, where the monarchy from its lofty heights meted out justice fairly to each social group. The Marxist tenet of class struggle, a reality in Western Europe experience, could be obviated in Russia, where class harmony would flow from the power and even-handedness of the autocracy.[38]

Zubatov invoked contemporary socialist thought to dissuade the intelligentsia from its activist revolutionary leanings. The publication of one of Eduard Bernstein's major revisionary work in a Russian translation gave Zubatov, in his own words, an "ally against the hideous Russian social democracy."[39] The writings of Bernstein, Sidney Webb, S. N. Prokopovich, and Werner Sombart on the development of the Western European trade-union movement, describing the tangible gains made by the working class through legal organization and concerted pressure, were welcomed by Zubatov as means of opening minds previously closed to the belief that advances could be made by other than revolutionary means.[40] Zubatov boasted to his superiors that he "began to give those arrested the most stunning illegal books on the labor question, since these books completely demolish all conspiratorial activity. The results are excellent. They themselves confessed to me that they illuminate a new world for them. The past is explained by their lack of education. And this education takes place in the prisons

38. According to one prisoner, Zubatov presented "a theory of a democratic people's monarchy, which stands above classes and class struggle, which mitigates class antagonisms, which establishes social peace, national welfare and the general happiness" ("Rabochee dvizhenie i zhandarmskaia politika," *Revoliutsionnaia Rossiia*, no. 5 [March 1902]); this article was written anonymously by Grigorii Gershuni, who was interrogated by Zubatov in prison. It was reprinted later under his authorship in *Sbornik statei Antonova (i dr.)* (Moscow, 1908), pp. 102–7.

39. Zubatov to the Department of Police, Oct. 30, 1900, in Zaslavskii, "Zubatov i Mania Vil'bushevich," p. 117. Apparently Bernstein's book was published on Zubatov's orders; Serebriakova translated it (V. Ignat'ev, *Bor'ba protiv zubatovshchiny v Moskve* [Moscow, 1939], p. 18).

40. Zubatov, "Zubatovshchina," p. 160. See also Zvolianskii's undated report to Plehve on Zubatov's activities in N. A. Bukhbinder, "K istorii zubatovshchiny v Moskve," *Istoriia proletariata SSSR*, 2 (1930), 170–71; A. I. Chemeriskii, "Vospominaniia o 'evreiskoi nezavisimoi rabochei partii,'" in "Novoe o zubatovshchine," *Krasnyi arkhiv*, 1922, no. 1, p. 316.

of the O[khrannoe] O[tdelenie]. What have we come to!"[41]

Passive conversion was not sufficient for Zubatov, who was planning to undermine socialist influence among the working class through labor organizations operating under his tutelage. The penitent revolutionaries could find a fitting place in the experiment; their active participation in labor societies that would bring tangible benefits to the factory workers would substantiate belief in a progressive monarchy and fulfill the desire to do something for the working people that had initially motivated them to political action. Zubatov's spell over his prisoners was extraordinary; his arguments convinced many, even seasoned revolutionaries, to convert out of conscience. Grigorii Gershuni, who underwent Zubatov's ideological training course, described its effect: "The prisoners begin to look upon themselves as persons who hold the fate of Russia in their hands and can lead the revolution in any direction at their own discretion."[42]

Zubatov's technique, so successfully applied to the intellectuals, was adjusted to win over the worker-intelligentsia, the key to the spread of socialism among the factory masses. In conversations with working-class prisoners, beginning after the arrests of July 1896, Zubatov strongly expressed his sympathy for the goals of the labor movement and alleged that the government was preparing generous labor measures; little, however, could be done to benefit the working class so long as it succumbed to the lure of socialist propaganda.

Zubatov also directed his efforts at expanding the wedge of suspicion between the workers and the Marxist intelligentsia; in his talks he endlessly iterated the thesis that the revolutionary intelligentsia was not to be trusted, for it intended to use the working class as a tool to attain goals completely opposed to those of the workers. The revolutionaries, having used the working class to seize power, would certainly thereafter forsake it. Not senseless political dreams, but his own concrete class interest were the worker's proper concern. "Your task," Zubatov lectured to the workers in his grasp, "is to study and to teach the workers a general educational knowledge, to fight against drunkenness and defend

41. Undated report of Zubatov, reprinted in "Dva dokumenta iz istorii zubatovshchiny," *Krasnyi arkhiv*, 1926, no. 6 (19), p. 211.

42. *Revoliutsionnaia Rossiia*, no. 5 (March 1902).

your economic rights; political struggle is a 'pastime for the high and mighty.'"[43] Zubatov described his approach to the worker-intelligentsia in the following terms:

At the interrogations I separate the antigovernment elements from the masses with brilliant success—I can say honestly speaking. In the Russian movement and perhaps also in the Jewish one, I am successfully convincing the public that the workers' movement is one thing, and the social democratic one is another. There a kopek is the goal — here, ideological theory. The worker must aspire to civil equality with the so-called "privileged" classes. . . . The social democrats, ignoring his immediate interests, call upon him to help the privileged classes in attaining their interests (to complete the revolution), promising every blessing to him after this. It is apparent that only the stupidity and ignorance of the workers make them unable to see this.[44]

## The Moscow Administration and the Working Class

Interrogation of the worker-intelligentsia was instructive for Zubatov; in probing to understand the causes that had drawn them into the socialist movement he learned of the factory abuses that so aggrieved the workers and gained a deeper knowledge of the actual conditions of factory life.[45] Convinced that many recent disturbances were grounded in managerial malpractices, Zubatov determined to transcend formal police authority to halt such abuses where the workers' grievances were legitimate.

The Moscow city administration had a long record of independent action in factory affairs.[46] In the late 1870's for example, a commission established by the Moscow governor-general, Prince

43. I. A. Shmeleva, "Bor'ba protiv zubatovshchiny v Moskve po vospominaniiam rabochikh," Shuiskii gosudarstvennyi pedagogicheskii institut, *Uchenye zapiski*, pt. 9 (1960), pp. 58–59. See also *Iskra*, no. 29 (Dec. 1, 1902), no. 48 (Sept. 15, 1903).

44. Undated communication from Zubatov to L. A. Rataev, chief of the Special Section of the Department of Police, in N. A. Bukhbinder, "Nezavisimaia evreiskaia rabochaia partiia," *Krasnaia letopis'*, 1922, no. 2–3, p. 208. Zubatov's pupils in the Okhrana practiced the same approach with political prisoners. See the testimony of M. A. Bagaev in *Vladimirskaia okruzhnaia organizatsiia R.S.-D.R.P.* (Vladimir, 1927), pp. 93–94. A fictionalized account of a typical conversation between a gendarme officer of the Zubatov school and a factory worker can be found in M. Gorkii, *Zhizn' Klima Samgina* (Moscow, 1934), II, 163.

45. Zubatov, pp. 159–61.

46. In 1832, for example, Prince D. V. Golitsyn, the Moscow governor-general, proposed a comprehensive plan for dealing with the complaints of both owners and workers to the Moscow Section of the Manufacturing Council. The proposal as amended by the Council was signed into law by the tsar on May 24, 1835 (Tugan-Baranovskii, pp. 169–71).

Vladimir Andreevich Golitsyn, employed specialists to prepare studies of the Moscow factories and gather information on foreign factory legislation. A set of "Rules for Owners and Workers of Factories and Plants," compiled by the commission and made obligatory for Moscow *guberniia*, defended the rights of the workers within the framework of existing legislation. The Moscow industrialists frequently disregarded these rules; without the strong support of the Moscow governor-general and the chief of police the factory inspectors would have been helpless to enforce them.[47]

The sensitivity of the Moscow administration to factory matters was, as in other industrial centers, a consequence of growing unrest among the workers; in part it was also due to awareness that poor working conditions had aroused working-class dissatisfaction and given the radical intelligentsia opportunities to incite the workers. The Moscow police therefore maintained a close check on the mood of the workers, alert for any signs of discontent, mass meetings, or illegal activities.[48] Moreover, the local administration could not long remain passive toward the factory world, for the workers, when aggrieved by frequent wrongs, were in the habit of appealing to the authorities. In a patriarchal system it is natural for the worker to seek out some higher authority for protection. The local administration, and particularly members of the Imperial family, became a court of last resort when other appeals failed. Workers from plants in the Moscow suburbs or even in neighboring provinces on occasion petitioned the Grand Duke Sergei Aleksandrovich, Moscow governor-general, for intercession on their behalf, although his response was usually negative.[49] When Trepov first became Moscow chief of police—that is, before be came under Zubatov's influence—he viewed working-class agitation for increased wages

47. Ianzhul, pp. 9–11, 15, 41, 63, 78–79.
48. Men'shchikov, II, no. 1, p. 11.
49. In April 1895 striking workers at a Iaroslav cotton mill sent representatives to the Grand Duke Sergei but were unsuccessful in obtaining his intervention. In the spring of 1896 workers on strike at the Filippov woolen mill appealed for support from both the Moscow chief of police and the Grand Duke Sergei (*Rabochee dvizhenie*, IV, pt. 1, pp. 133, 401; Martov, in *Istoriia Rossii v XIX veke*, VIII, 71). In 1897 a petition for a shorter workday bearing the signatures of one hundred workers at the Shmidt furniture plant was forwarded to the grand duke by elected representatives of the workers, but nothing came of it (S. Ainzaft, *Istoriia rabochego i professional'nogo dvizheniia derevoobdelochnikov do revoliutsii 1917 goda* [Moscow, 1928], p. 83). In January 1898 representatives of striking workers, who walked to Moscow from Bogorodsk to present their case before the grand duke, were told it was of little concern to him

and a shorter workday as disturbances of the peace that demanded police repression and arrest of the instigators.[50]

Zubatov understandably had to spend considerable time persuading his superiors to forsake what he viewed as a formalistic approach to a deep-rooted problem and to investigate factory conditions which, irrespective of the presence of outside agitators, alienated and angered the factory workers. By the fall of 1896, Trepov gave indications he had been won over to Zubatov's point of view. The police issued warnings to factory administrators to correct abuses; in one factory, which left its promises to the workers unfulfilled, Trepov commanded that this declaration be posted: "On the orders of the chief of police the workers' demands will be satisfied by January 1."[51] Thus the course of police involvement with the Moscow working-class movement was charted; administrative pressure in the name of the Moscow chief of police and governor-general to compel rectification of injustices in working conditions became a regular feature of the city's economic life during the remainder of Zubatov's days in the Okhrana. The workers were quick to perceive the new turn of events and eagerly sought the protection of the authorities as "defenders of the oppressed."[52]

## Witte and the Moscow Administration: The First Round

In its new concern for the state of factory conditions the Moscow authorities often ignored the jurisdiction of the factory inspectors. At times they conducted their own investigations into working conditions and labor conflicts, calling the attention of the inspectors to the results of their enquiries. On occasion they demanded that management make economic improvements to eliminate potential

---

(Men'shchikov, II, no. l, 93; Ozerov, p. 50). He seems to have had no compunction against the use of force against strikers; twice in the early months of 1898 he approved the dispatch of troops to factories where the owners requested that force be used to suppress strikes (Ozerov, pp. 99–100; Men'shchikov, II, no. 1, 94).

50. *Rabochee dvizhenie,* IV, pt. 1, p. 343.

51. *Ibid.,* p. 410.

52. The expression was used by a group of factory workers in a petition of grievances given to Trepov in February 1898 (Men'shchikov, II, no. 1, 97). There is a considerable body of evidence concerning police interference in individual Moscow factory disputes from 1896 onward (Morskoi, pp. 84–85; Men'shikov, II, no. 1, pp. 91–98; Iu. Milonov and M. Rakovskii, *Istoriia moskovskogo professional'nogo soiuza rabochikh-derevoobdelochnikov* [Moscow, 1928], p. 43).

causes of discontent without prompting from the workers.[53] For Trepov, the demands of order came before the niceties of the law.

Witte was not likely to let this usurpation of his authority go unchallenged. Aroused by factory inspectors' reports from Moscow protesting police interference in labor matters, Witte sought through direct and indirect methods to prohibit the practice and restore the authority of the Ministry of Finance. On the one hand, he appealed for an unequivocal statement of support from the highest authorities at an interministerial conference; on the other, he tried to arbitrate the differences directly with the Moscow administration. Both methods, however, failed to bring about substantial change, for Zubatov and Trepov were protected by the power and influence of the Grand Duke Sergei, a law unto himself in Moscow.

Matters first came to a head in the early spring of 1898.[54] On April 2, Witte received a report from a Moscow factory inspector complaining that the interference of the Moscow police in labor matters had aggravated unrest by leading the workers to conclude that the government authorities were on their side.[55] When on April 10 (two days after the date of Zubatov's report discussed in Chapter 2) Witte forwarded a report to the tsar requesting a state conference to define and delimit ministerial authority in factory affairs, he alluded to developments in Moscow detrimental to the factory inspectorate:

Thus recently disclosed cases of discontent among the workers and even strikes in some industrial establishments, especially in the central industrial region, have made clear ... that the success of the activity of the factory inspectorate, which depends chiefly on the moral authority its officials have acquired among the workers, was to a significant degree weakened by the inconsistency between its actions and directives aimed at the removal of workers' discontent, and administrative directives and pronouncements.[56]

Moreover, police and provincial authorities in some factory centers had ordered investigations of factory disturbances and had even

53. Men'shchikov, II, no. 1, pp. 91–92, 98; Morskoi, p. 30; Vovchik, pp. 134–35.

54. *Rabochii vopros v komissii V. N. Kokovtsova,* p. 3.

55. Martov, in *Istoriia Rossii v XIX veke,* VIII, 97. The previous month Witte had notified the factory inspectors, through a ministerial circular that did not specifically mention Moscow, of recent police investigations of factory disorders without the knowledge of the inspectors (*ibid.,* p. 96; *Rabochee delo,* no. 1 [April 1899]).

56. Morskoi, p. 39. In a report of June 23, 1898, responding critically to General Panteleev's recommendations, Witte obliquely protested against the interference of the Moscow administration in labor relations (Vovchik, p. 67).

attempted to eliminate causes of agitation on grounds that they possessed the authority to prevent and terminate disorders.

In essence Witte's statement was an answer to Zubatov's report of April 8, 1898, although there is no evidence Witte had read it. The conference, which met on July 15, supported Witte in upholding the prevailing laws that defined the respective authority of the police and the inspectors. Nevertheless the matter did not end to Witte's satisfaction, for the Moscow authorities continued to carry on in their accustomed manner.[57]

Over the course of two years the Ministry of Finance sent a succession of representatives to Moscow in an attempt to negotiate an agreement directly; among them were a factory inspector, A. Astaf'ev; the director of the Department of Trade and Manufacture, V. I. Kovalevskii; and the vice-director of the department, N. P. Langovoi.[58] The Assistant Minister of Finance, V. N. Kokovtsov, conferred with the Grand Duke Sergei and Trepov in June 1898, but to no avail. The police had usurped the role of the factory inspector in the surveillance of factory affairs and had no intention of abandoning its course, Kokovtsov reported to Witte. As a consequence the workers had lost confidence in the inspector's authority and were turning to the Okhrana or the chief of police whenever the inspector responded unfavorably to their complaints. The police authorities would then conduct their own investigations and forward the results to the inspector for his consideration.

Trepov justified his actions to Kokovtsov with reasoning he had learned from Zubatov. The working class would place its confidence in the authorities and forswear antigovernment elements only when the government was prepared to act promptly to right injustices and protect the workers' interests. The police were thus obliged to intervene in all cases of discontent, regardless of the cause. Workers petitions were tangible evidence of circumstances that could lead to factory disorders and thus required police investigation and expeditious measures. The Ministry of Interior had authorized police intervention in factory affairs, Trepov maintained, citing the ministerial circular of August 12, 1897.[59]

57. Morskoi, pp. 42–45.

58. *Ibid.*, pp. 82–83; Vovchik, pp. 61, 134–35; V. Ia. Laverychev, *Tsarizm i rabochii vopros v Rossii* (Moscow, 1972), p. 128.

59. Kokovtsov's report is summarized in Morskoi, pp. 32–37; Ozerov, pp. 143–44; Vovchik, p. 61. The Moscow authorities, according to Zubatov (p. 161), found

In November 1899, V. I. Kovalevskii was sent to Moscow on a mission similar to Kokovtsov's but could extract only minor concessions during negotiations that continued into the following summer. In Moscow the factory inspectors were thus unable to obtain recognition of the rightful authority assigned them in the Industrial Code. The war of attrition between Trepov and the factory inspectorate dragged on, with Trepov generally victorious.[60] In essence the dispute reflected the prolonged struggle carried on at a higher level between the Ministries of Finance and Interior.

Unable to gain his way through negotiation, Witte exerted pressure on the Ministry of Interior to discipline the Moscow administration. On May 19, 1900, he wrote to Sipiagin; if Trepov and the Moscow authorities continue to undermine the position of the factory inspectors and accede to illegal demands, Witte exaggerated, the workers might be encouraged to demand in the future the abolition of the existing order. The dispute had reached such proportions that Sipiagin agreed to the convocation of a special conference under the chairmanship of Sviatopolk-Mirskii to resolve the issue. Witte, however, gained little. Sviatopolk-Mirskii reprimanded Trepov for police interference in the jurisdiction of the inspectors but could do little to restrain him because of the backing of the Moscow governor-general.[61]

The conflict was never resolved to Witte's satisfaction. In his memoirs Witte wrote: "I supported the inspectorate, but I could not

---

authorization for their activities in two articles of the August 12 circular. Article 2 called upon the police to maintain strict surveillance of the factory workers and to eliminate disturbances when an injustice on the part of the factory administration existed. Article 5 authorized them to investigate the causes of strikes and to take measures to reach a peaceful agreement between the contending parties. For Trepov's indictment of the Ministry of Finance and the factory inspectorate see his remarks of 1905: I. Tatarov, "K istorii 'politseiskogo sotsializma,'" *Proletarskaia revoliutsiia*, May 1927, pp. 116, 118.

60. In 1901 on Trepov's insistence the senior factory inspector, Chizhov, was transferred from Moscow (Morskoi, pp. 46, 83; *Osvobozhdenie*, no. 17 [Feb. 16, 1903]; Vovchik, pp. 134–35).

61. Vovchik, pp. 135–36; Laverychev, pp. 135–36. On December 21, 1900, the Grand Duke Sergei wrote to Sipiagin, requesting another interdepartmental conference in Moscow to demarcate the functions of the inspectorate and the police. On June 20, 1901, the conference decided in favor of the Moscow administration; supervision of the Moscow Board for Factories and Metallurgical Affairs, an institution charged with matters of industrial relations, was removed from the senior factory inspector and assigned to an official under the Moscow chief of police (Laverychev, pp. 136–37, 143).

do anything substantial to destroy these undertakings," since neither Minister of Interior—Goremykin nor Sipiagin—could give orders to the Grand Duke Sergei.[62] From within this sheltered position, which even Witte, the most powerful minister, could not penetrate, Zubatov was able to transform what had been sporadic and unplanned intervention in factory matters into a systematic endeavor to organize and direct the Moscow labor movement.

## The Moscow Working Class Comes of Age

By 1900 the Moscow working class had matured to the extent that it consciously sought out means to secure itself against illness and want and aspired to general and professional education as an avenue to personal advancement and a broader awareness of life. Both legal and illegal opportunities for the workers to organize in fulfillment of these aspirations had multiplied in the 1890's. One of Zubatov's primary responsibilities was to prevent the radical intelligentsia from penetrating and subverting legally authorized institutions ostensibly established to educate the worker and improve his lot financially.

Since the 1860's, when liberal elements in society had initiated programs to improve the educational level of the working class, Sunday schools for workers had existed in the main industrial centers; twelve such schools were opened in Moscow alone during the decade ending in 1898 when the proletariat had grown so rapidly.[63] Starting in the 1860's also, the more liberal factory owners had established evening and Sunday schools at their factories to train their workers in specialized skills and to provide a rudimentary education for them and their families; by 1900 many of the largest Moscow factories had such schools.[64] Outside the factory, the

62. Witte, *Vospominaniia*, II, 217.

63. Martov, in *Istoriia Rossii v XIX veke*, VI, 138; *Prechistenskie rabochie kursy* (Moscow, 1948), p. 14; "Doklad moskovskogo delegata Veismana (Tseitlina) na II s"ezde RSDRP," in *Iskrovskii period v Moskve*, p. 55. In 1904 there were fifteen Moscow Sunday schools for adults, offering workers a primary education beginning with lessons in reading and writing (S. Bleklov, "Obrazovatel'nyia uchrezhdeniia dlia rabochikh g. Moskvy, " *Russkaia mysl'*, 1904, no. 5, pp. 127–28).

64. Bleklov, pp. 129–30, 134; Martov, in *Istoriia Rossii v XIX veke*, VI, 138; Reginald E. Zelnik, "The Sunday School Movement in Russia, 1859–1862," *Journal of Modern History*, 37 (1965), 164–65; Pogogeff and Apostol, pp. 17, 19, 24–25. A Ministry of Finance circular of June 25, 1902, maintained that since 1882, 446 general educational schools had been established in factories; 47,000 persons had attended at the expense of the factory owners (*Grazhdanin*, July 11, 1902).

Society of Popular Sobriety administered a network of tearooms and reading rooms with a view to weaning the workers away from addiction to hard drink by giving them a hangout other than the tavern in which to spend their few idle hours. Popular education modeled on university extension courses in England and the United States were offered in Moscow from the early 1890's by the Commission for the Organization of Home Readings.[65] Public lectures were presented in various parts of the city by the Moscow Commission for the Organization of Public Popular Readings, the Moscow Capital Guardianship of Popular Sobriety, and the Society for Popular Entertainment; on one Sunday afternoon in 1901, for example, thirteen lectures were offered by the Moscow Commission for the Organization of Public Popular Readings in such varied locales as the tearooms of the Society of Popular Sobriety, local museums, and several factories and railway shops.[66]

To the more intelligent and ambitious workers, the libraries and tearooms, the public lectures, and the schools opened up a whole new world beyond the factory walls and barracks. Accounts of this period by those closely acquainted with the Moscow labor movement stress the great zeal for education among the factory masses:

At this very time, the workers, especially those who finished the course of [regular] schools or industrial schools, began to exhibit a noticeable yearning for self-education: they registered in libraries, visited the city reading rooms and public lectures, subscribed by pooling their resources to liberal newspapers, ... most of all valuing in them the foreign section, in which they came across serious articles about the labor movement in the West.[67]

Thanks to these new educational opportunities, a sizable worker-intelligentsia had arrived on the scene, separated from their comrades by their learning. Their high prestige and influence among their fellow workers made their allegiance vital to those who

65. Kizevetter, p. 286.

66. *Russkiia vedomosti,* Oct. 28, 1901. The Moscow Commission for the Organization of Public Popular Readings in an account of its activities for the years 1899–1901, reported it had offered 772 religious discussions or readings and 752 general educational lectures to a combined audience of 267,724 (*ibid.,* April 25, 1902).

67. Mitshevice, ed., *Na zare rabochego dvizheniia,* p. 15; see also Shestakov, p. 60. Sviatopolk-Mirskii on his tour of Russian factories observed this thirst for learning and suggested in his report of 1901 that workers' libraries be opened ("Rabochee dvizhenie na zavodakh Peterburga," p. 63).

wanted to lead the factory masses, and created an intensive rivalry between Zubatov and the social-democratic intelligentsia for their support.[68]

The radical intelligentsia found the schools and lectures for workers, which functioned with the permission of the authorities, a readily available channel through which to reach the working class with its message of revolution. Taking notice of the workers' unfulfilled desire for education, Social Democrats in the 1890's established libraries and distributed newspapers among their working-class followers to raise their educational level and political consciousness. Some socialists, usually women, enlisted as teachers in Sunday schools. Lecture courses were slanted to stimulate the audience's interest in social and economic problems; progressive literature was distributed to working-class students, along with conventional course materials. A. Ul'ianova, Lenin's sister, recalls in her memoirs history and geography courses designed to present a progressive point of view rather than objective knowledge, and a course in political economy given in the guise of lessons in bookkeeping.[69] Even in the worst days of police repression the Sunday school teachers kept alive social-democratic contacts with the Moscow factory workers.[70]

The police realized that the Sunday schools were convenient for the propagation of revolutionary ideas and kept close watch over the courses and teachers. In January 1894, the Ministry of Interior by secret circular alerted the local authorities to widespread infiltration of the radical intelligentsia into responsible positions in public libraries, reading rooms, and workmen's schools.[71] The following March I. N. Durnovo, then Minister of Interior, wrote to the Procurator of the Holy Synod, K. P. Pobedonostsev, to alert him that lecturers in the Sunday schools under the authority and administration of the local diocesan governing body were misusing their positions. Lectures on spiritual and moralistic themes had been given a Marxist bias, which the supervisors were hardly in a

68. "There is already in Russia this "worker-intelligentsia" and we must exert every effort to expand its ranks, satisfy completely its high intellectual needs in order that from its ranks will come the leaders of the Russian social-democratic labor party," Lenin wrote at the end of 1899 (*Polnoe sobranie sochinenii*, 5th ed., IV [Moscow, 1959], 269).

69. A. Ul'ianova, "Vospominaniia," in Ovsiannikov, pp. 33, 124–25.

70. *Iskrovskii period v Moskve*, p. 57.

71. Men'shchikov, II, no. 1, pp. 49, 53.

position to detect. Durnovo singled out the Moscow Sunday schools for criticism, specifically referring to the school at the Prokhorov plant.[72]

The Moscow police were acutely aware that the libraries and schools were becoming an outlet for socialist propaganda, but they felt hampered by legal restraints from ending the practice. Conditioned to struggle against the conspiratorial revolutionary underground, the Moscow Okhrana was perturbed when the enemies of the tsarist order began openly to work through long-established, licensed nonpolitical societies.

Nor was it simple for the police to differentiate between purely instructional educational activities and those infused with socialist concepts. Routine surveillance was not likely to result in sufficient reliable information.[73] Internal infiltration could succeed where external surveillance failed. Zubatov thus assigned his agents to attend the many Sunday and factory schools, employing for this purpose factory workers who were arrested in July 1896 and had subsequently been converted and welcomed into his service.[74]

The best organized, most successful, and longest lasting of the new educational institutions were the Sunday and evening Prechistensk workers' courses. Founded by the Permanent Commission on Technical Education of the Imperial Russian Technical Society, the Prechistensk courses modestly began with a student body of some 300 workers in October 1897; a decade later there was an enrollment of 1,500 and a staff of 200. The school, established in the Prechistensk *raion* of Moscow, attracted to its free courses workers from the large factories, plants, and railway shops of the surrounding districts.[75] The Permanent Commission on

72. *Rabochee dvizhenie,* IV, pt. 1, pp. 821–24. Sviatopolk-Mirskii referred several times in his report to the infiltration of radical youths as teachers, lecturers, and librarians in the Sunday schools and other educational institutions for workers. The practice presented a danger to the government because the workers who attended the schools might be politicized and then succeed in persuading their factory comrades of their views. Most labor agitators and strike leaders of working-class origins had attended these schools where they had come under the influence of the revolutionary intelligentsia ("Rabochee dvizhenie na zavodakh Peterburga," pp. 57, 62, 65–66).

73. Men'shchikov, II, no. 1, pp. 38–45, 50–54, 61–64.

74. *Ibid.,* pp. 45–46.

75. *Prechistenskie rabochie kursy,* pp. 5–6, 13–16, 43; *Russkiia vedomosti,* Sept. 30, Oct. 18, 1901; "Prechistenskie rabochie kursy," *Bol'shaia sovetskaia entsiklopediia,* 2d ed., XXXIV (1955), 454; *Rabochii zavod "Serp i molot"* (Moscow, 1931), p. 64; *Rabochie Trekhgornoi manufaktury,* p. 107; Bleklov, p. 133.

Technical Education, besides administering the formal course offerings, organized the sale of books and pamphlets in the areas of technical and general education to the factory workers. Here was an open field for the radical intelligentsia; within a year of the school's founding illegal circles had been organized involving several of the teachers. By the early 1900's there was a literal tug of war for the minds of the worker-students: among the teaching staff were Social Democrats—both Bol'shevik and Menshevik—Socialist Revolutionaries, and liberals, each propagating their respective ideologies in the classroom.[76]

There was also renewed interest among the workers in the 1890's in independent activity and organization. The tsarist government would not tolerate labor unions but did sanction mutual-help funds when their statutes met with ministerial approval. The avowed purpose of these funds was to provide material security for the workers and their families in time of sickness, injury, or death, a type of insurance already provided by the state in several advanced industrial countries. The earliest mutual-help funds in Russia, like the Sunday schools, were founded at the time of the Great Reforms on the initiative of the intelligentsia and, in some cases, the factory owners. For the first few decades of their existence representatives of management, the higher bureaucracy, and the Imperial family were included as honorary members. Until the last decade of the century such funds were mainly found among the artisans, salesmen, miners, railway workers, and typesetters; only in the mid-1890's did the factory workers show a sustained interest in their formation.

The new funds served the same purposes but were no longer administered by the factory management; they were in the hands of the workers, to whom membership was restricted. The new inclination for organization, mainly found among the skilled workers, received its furthest development in the Kharkov Society of Mutual Help of Persons Engaged in Industrial Labor, established in 1898 for machine workers. The Kharkov Society had government approval of its statutes, which were quite liberal for their time; with 1,300 members in 1904, the society was the model for other labor organizations in Kharkov and had branches in other cities of southern Russia. Its original functions were soon expanded; the

76. *Prechistenskie rabochie kursy,* pp. 8–9, 21.

Kharkov Society became an instrument for improving the working conditions of its members, becoming in the process the closest Russian approximation to a Western European trade union in its time.[77]

Workers' funds were not alien to the purposes of the socialist intelligentsia; organizational development among the workers was always to be encouraged per se. The scope and purpose of the funds, however, were too narrowly economic for the socialists, who wanted to turn them into weapons for political and economic struggle, to steer the spontaneous movement for organization toward the establishment of strike funds, whose purpose would be to finance the cause of revolution. The socialists also intended to broaden the significance of the funds by consolidating them, first by industry and then by city. The workers, however, frequently thwarted these plans; having established the funds on their own initiative, they were often justly suspicious that the intelligentsia desired to take control for their own purposes and refused to cooperate.[78]

### Zubatov and the Moscow Workers: First Experiments

Zubatov understood that the growing number of mutual-benefit funds and consumer societies arose from the workers' increasing consciousness of the need for organization to promote their economic interests; for this reason he was willing to encourage their growth. Essentially they were not dangerous for the existing order if kept under careful supervision. The mutual-benefit society therefore became the standard form through which he encouraged the organization of the Moscow working class.

Zubatov's first encounter with mutual-help funds came on the initiative of workers: engravers employed at the largest Moscow textile mills. Socialist teachers at the factory schools had initiated a

77. On the history of mutual-help and other funds among Russian workers see Sviatlovskii, pp. 21–52; *Zhizn'*, May, 1902; Martov, in *Istoriia Rossii v XIX veke*, VI, 138–39; V. V. Sher, *Istoriia professional'nago dvizheniia rabochikh pechatnago dela v Moskve* (Moscow, 1911), pp. 73–93; F. Semenov-Bulkin, *Soiuz metallistov i departament politsii* (Leningrad, 1926), pp. 4–5. A prototype of the mutual-help societies founded in Moscow with Zubatov's encouragement is described in P. Arbekov, "Ochag zubatovshchiny: Kizil-Arvatskoe remeslennoe sobranie," *Turkmenovedenie*, Dec. 1930, pp. 24–29. On the Kharkov society see *Zhizn'*, May 1902; Martov, in *Istoriia Rossi v XIX veke*, VIII, 139; Kol'tsov, *Obshchestvennoe dvizhenie*, I, 192; P. Kolokol'nikov and S. Rapoport, eds., *1905–1907 gg. v professional'nom dvizhenii* (Moscow, 1925), p. 20.
78. *Zhizn'*, May 1902; Pipes, *Social Democracy*, pp. 28, 77–78, 90–91.

plan to found a mutual-help society among the engravers, in the hope that they could use it for their own purposes; the proposed statutes of the fund therefore reflected their imprint. Sergei Prokhorov, director of one of the largest textile mills, however, persuaded the workers to jettison sections of the statutes that contained political implications and to allow factory owners to participate in the proposed society. The revised, conservative draft was endorsed by Prokhorov and directors of four other Moscow textile mills on January 9, 1899, and forwarded to the Grand Duke Sergei with a note supporting the proposed Moscow Society of Mutual Help of Engravers as a "very desirable and useful institution."[79]

Zubatov examined the statutes, which envision a nationwide society of engravers, before they were forwarded to St. Petersburg for ministerial examination. In such cases the Okhrana was expected to investigate the true purposes of a society and the political reliability and affiliation of its initiators. In this case the investigators reported that the engravers, who suffered from occupational health hazards, sincerely desired to establish funds to assist them in cases of industrial accidents. Some organizers, however, had different goals and saw "in the organization of the society one of the means for the development of the workers' class consciousness in a socialist direction," Zubatov reported.[80] Nevertheless Zubatov did not disapprove of the society out of hand. Instead he proposed changes in the statutes that strengthened police surveillance of every aspect of the society. The Moscow authorities were expected to exercise broad control: advance approval of subjects to be discussed at its meeting was mandatory; police were to be in attendance to insure conformity with the approved agenda; the Moscow governor-general would confirm the officers nominated by the society and had the right to close it at any time.[81]

The statutes, along with Zubatov's proposed revisions, were forwarded in turn to the Ministry of Interior and the Ministry of Finance. Witte, already in conflict with the Moscow administration over police interference in labor affairs, disapproved of Zubatov's recommendations. Writing to Sipiagin, the Minister of Interior, on

79. M. Rakovskii, "Zubatov i moskovskie gravery," *Istoriia proletariata SSSR,* 2 (1930), 203.

80. Zubatov's report of March 13, 1899 (*ibid.,* p. 210).

81. Zubatov's full report is in *ibid.,* pp. 209–14.

February 15, 1900, he argued that the police had sufficient powers to deal decisively with seditious elements without receiving additional authority.[82] Witte's opposition placed Sipiagin in a dilemma. Without Witte's backing he was unwilling to approve the statutes; on the other hand, he did not dare to confront the Moscow governor-general with a firmly negative response. He resolved the dilemma in traditional bureaucratic fashion, by routing the problem back to the Moscow authorities for disposal. Having failed to receive Petersburg's sanction the Grand Duke Sergei let the matter drop, and the society of engravers never came into existence.[83] Witte had successfully thwarted the first prototype of a police-guided labor organization; a year later the Moscow authorities would move more boldly in this direction, ignoring opposition from the Minister of Finance.

Zubatov's awareness of proletarian aspirations and his desire to steer the workers onto a path free of alien elements was revealed in one other episode. In the spring of 1900 a group of workers at the Gustav List factory attending the Prechistensk evening classes requested financial support from the factory owners to open a new school for workers. Learning of the plan through one of his agents, Zubatov sought to persuade the workers to forego financial dependence on the owners and build the school solely from their own funds. If the school's administration were entirely in their hands, he reasoned, the workers would become responsible and guard against revolutionary teachings in its classes, for otherwise they would "risk losing their school, and with it their money gathered for the institution."[84] Zubatov's advice fell on deaf ears; the new school was opened with financial support from the Moscow industrialists.

Despite these setbacks Zubatov was convinced he had rightly fathomed the working-class mentality through his many long discussions with socialist intellectuals and factory workers and knew how to counteract the attraction of socialist propaganda for the worker. In a series of communications in the summer and fall of 1900 to the Department of Police, destined ultimately for Sipiagin,

82. *Ibid.*, pp. 230–31.
83. *Ibid.*, pp. 207–8. In February 1901, Sipiagin officially rejected the statutes (V. I. Novikov, "Leninskaia 'Iskra' v bor'be s zubatovshchinoi, " *Voprosy istorii*, Aug. 1974, p. 28).
84. Bukhbinder, "K istorii zubatovshchiny," p. 169.

he put forward his thoughts on this vital subject. Accompanying Zubatov's analysis of the labor question were suggestions for government implementation. Taken as a whole, they would have committed the government to a more positive labor policy on behalf of working-class interests through enforcing existing labor legislation and entrusting the factory masses with broad autonomy.

The fullest expression of Zubatov's views was presented in a communication of September 10, 1900, to the Department of Police. Here he stressed the theme he had harped upon earlier: economic needs, not political principles, were of primary concern for the workers. Specifically he recommended the abolition of criminal penalties for strikes where neither criminal nor political activity was present. More indicative of his future plans was the proposal that the workers be allowed various types of cultural societies and institutions; if they were permitted to control and direct organizations of their own financed by contributions from their hard-earned wages, they would see to it that outside subversives were prevented from penetrating and seizing power. Zubatov stressed that the concept of legality should be encouraged among the workers by permitting them to organize schools and lectures and to print special brochures and newspapers; here, in outline, was the program of working-class institutions inaugurated with his assistance the following year in Moscow and Minsk. Above all, Zubatov insisted, it was imperative that the government attract and hold the support of the working class by entrusting it with a greater degree of responsibility:

I base this on the indisputable law: for the revolutionaries the "majority" is inaccessible; wherever the masses are they will choke them. "Let well enough alone." Obtaining satisfaction from the hands of the government, why should the masses go against it and listen to chatterboxes? There is no sense. So, a little more faith in the masses; they will not betray it. We will entice them and they will be ours: "the gates of hell will not conquer them."

Zubatov concluded confidently: "If the Minister would accept all this then great good would be done (without any political concession in principle) and the revolution dealt a blow which not even the strongest repression has the power to do."[85]

On September 19, Zubatov further elaborated to the Department of Police the ideological basis of his labor program. Placing his ideas in historical perspective he maintained that since the time of the

85. Zaslavskii, p. 112.

French Revolution various groups had attempted to exploit the working class for their own interests. European rulers guided by Metternich understood the tactics of the revolutionaries and had acted vigorously against them; distrustful of the masses, however, they did nothing to satisfy their needs and paid for their inattentiveness in the revolutions of 1848. The Russian autocracy should avoid this mistake and court the masses who, despite the propaganda of the revolutionaries, were still strongly faithful to it. To "feed" this faith, to keep it alive, a policy of good deeds was imperative. Following the lines of his report of April 8, 1898, Zubatov urged the government without delay to institute measures to assuage "the masses by means of opportune and tireless government improvement of their position on the basis of their everyday needs and demands." His plan for saving the autocracy from revolution was not without its Machiavellian aspects:

> The classes nowadays are so defined and developed that even Marx devised a special theory of class struggle in place of the former one—the struggle of the government against the people. In the present situation the motto of domestic policy must be "the maintenance of the equilibrium among the classes," who look with hostility at one another. It remains for the supraclass autocracy to "divide and rule."

In the context of contemporary Russia this meant "taming the bourgeoisie and the ideologists and gaining the favor of the workers and peasants."[86]

Zubatov maintained that generally the autocracy simply reacted against the forces that opposed it and had no long-run program for retaining the loyalty of the vast majority of its subjects. Time and again he indicted the government for focusing attention on the revolutionaries and disregarding the needs of the working class. The government had not shown as much concern for the factory worker as for the peasant; it could rectify past failures by convoking a commission to draft a "Special Statute on the Organization of the Life of the Workers," containing provisions to improve the lives of the workers and their families, including protection against unemployment and exploitation by merchants.[87]

86. "Dva dokumenta iz istorii zubatovshchiny," p. 211. In a report of December 19, 1895, B. I. Witte, Odessa procurator, adumbrated Zubatov's approach to combat the revolutionary movement, urging protective legislation for the workers, mutual-help funds, and other means of satisfying the needs and interests of labor (Vovchik, pp. 108–9).

87. Zaslavskii, p. 127.

We have little evidence of how Zubatov's ideas were received in St. Petersburg, for the published materials do not reveal any response from Sipiagin. Yet there are some indications that Zubatov's plans were received warily. His many letters to his superiors on the same theme is one indication. Moreover, when in the spring of 1901 Zubatov's plans for labor societies of mutual help bore fruit, official sanction was withheld for the better part of a year by the Ministry of Interior. Only support from Trepov and the Grand Duke Sergei permitted Zubatov to nurture these societies, which Sipiagin belatedly approved on an experimental basis.

# CHAPTER 4

# The Moscow Zubatovshchina: The Early Phases

The student disorders of February 1901 were probably the immediate impetus for the founding of the Moscow labor organizations associated with Zubatov. Student agitation was endemic to Russia at the turn of the century. The educational rules tightly restrained student activity at the higher educational institutions. The students, nevertheless, emboldened by a strong corporate spirit, gained a reputation for their audacity and readiness to do battle with the armed minions of the autocracy. The Temporary Rules of July 1899, calling for arrest and military conscription of the ringleaders and stricter surveillance of the universities, aroused the students to still greater fury.

The wave of student agitation reached its height in February 1901, after the assassination of the minister of education, taking the form of street demonstrations in the main university centers. The majority of Moscow students were at first apolitical, merely favoring the revocation of the Temporary Rules and restoration of academic autonomy. The anniversary date of peasant emancipation, February 19, was made the occasion for protests against government interference in academic life. Disorders spread from Kharkov to Moscow, where they continued from February 23 to 26. Each day the crowds of students and sympathizers increased, as did the number of incidental clashes with the police. The police responded with mass arrests; the students, joined by some of the public, reacted with open demonstrations. The matter took on graver implications for the authorities when factory workers joined the demonstrations. On Sunday, February 25, thousands of students, workers, and members of the general public threw up barricades in various parts of the city and clashed with the police. The disturbances were curbed with the greatest difficulty only after Cossack troops were called out.[1]

The workers had joined the students on their own initiative, purely out of sympathy with the student cause, catching both the authorities and the Social Democrats largely unaware.[2] The authorities were disproportionately frightened by the presence of factory workers in street disorders. They assumed that the workers had acted under the influence of socialist propaganda and believed that Moscow had witnessed a political demonstration of major proportions. This spontaneous, independent action on the part of the Moscow working class, and the fear it engendered among the authorities, set in motion the events that culminated in the formation of industrywide labor organizations in Moscow dedicated to the promotion of worker education and self-help.

## The Origins of the Moscow Zubatovshchina

The origins and preliminary steps in the formation of the new labor societies, which began to function in the summer of 1901, are not fully clear. Whether Zubatov planned and directed each move from offstage, or whether there was, on the other hand, an element of spontaneous action by the workers of which he took advantage, is not clarified by Zubatov's rather inconsistent testimony.[3] The few

1. Burch, pp. 109–11; N. Chervanin, "Dvizhenie intelligentsii," in *Obshchestvennoe dvizhenie v Rossii v nachale XX-go veka*, I, 262–78; "Studencheskoe dvizhenie v 1901 g.," *Krasnyi arkhiv*, 1936, no. 2(75), pp. 84–85; *Listok "Rabochago dela*," no. 6 (April 1901), pp. 20–23; A. A. Titov, *Iz vospominanii o studencheskom dvizhenii 1901 g. Moskva* (Moscow, 1906); Ivan Kheraskov, "Reminiscences of the Moscow Students' Movement," *Russian Review*, 11 (1952), 225; Iv. Kheraskov, "Iz istorii studencheskago dvizheniia v Moskovskom Universitete (Vospominaniia uchastnika, 1897–1903)," in V. B. El'iashevich, A. A. Kizevetter, and M. M. Novikov, eds., *Moskovskii universitet, 1755–1930* (Paris, 1930), pp. 431–49; N., "Tri dnia," *Vestnik russkoi revoliutsii*, March 1905, pp. 299–314. Allan Wildman believes that street demonstrations led by students and intelligentsia in the major cities in February 1901 were a turning point in the history of Russian social democracy, encouraging Social Democrats to favor their further use as a tactic of political agitation (Wildman, *Making of a Workers' Revolution*, pp. xviii, 150, 214, 216).

2. The Moscow Social Democrats later were taken to task by party comrades for failing to take the leadership of the labor movement and incite the workers to political action during the demonstrations (Bauman, p. 80; L. S. Tseitlin, "V Moskve pered II s"ezdom RSDRP," *Katorga i ssylka*, 1934, no. 5-6, pp. 90, 100). Not all workers sympathized with student agitation; the Moscow printers looked on "with curiosity but without sympathy" (Sher, p. 143).

3. Writing in retirement in 1908, Zubatov minimized his role, holding that he had

participants who chose to disclose information about their role in the movement have done so with something less than complete candor. Contemporary newspaper and journal accounts and archival materials published by the Soviets, while greatly adding to our knowledge of the Zubatovshchina, still leave certain aspects clouded.[4] Piecing together the available information makes the following story seem most plausible.

Toward the end of 1900 or the first part of 1901, Mikhail Afanas'ev began discussions with his fellow workers at the Prokhorov plant about the establishment of a mutual-help fund for the machine-shop workers. Along with his co-worker Fedor Slepov, Afanas'ev solicited advice on the drafting of statutes for the fund from the writer Leo Tolstoy, whose home they frequently visited on Sundays. On Tolstoy's suggestion they sought the assistance of Vladimir Den of Moscow University, who proved receptive to the idea and set to work to draft the fund's statutes, using as a model those of the Kharkov Society. They similarly contacted I. I. Ianzhul, who had studied labor conditions in Russia and abroad and had been one of Russia's first factory inspectors. Ianzhul, in turn, directed them to his former student and successor as professor of financial law at Moscow University, Ivan Khristoforovich Ozerov. Ozerov was at first reluctant to cooperate, on grounds the Ministry of Finance would not approve the statutes. Shortly thereafter

---

stood in the wings, merely using his position to protect the workers, who led the entire undertaking (Zubatov to Burtsev, March 5, 1908, Koz'min, p. 86). In a report to the Department of Police in November 1901, Zubatov gave a different version: "The organization of the trade-union labor movement in Moscow, despite the apparent spontaniety of its development and the relation of accompanying events, was at all times conducted according to a strictly thought-out plan, in which it was necessary to foresee each detail, to regulate almost every step of the worker-initiators" (A. P. Korelin, "Russkii 'politseiskii sotsializm,'" *Voprosy istorii,* Oct. 1968, p. 50).

4. Ozerov in his book describes his participation in the Moscow Zubatovshchina without mentioning his personal contact with Zubatov. He is the only member of the Moscow intelligentsia who cooperated with the Zubatovshchina to have written about it. Of the officers of the Council of Workers of Mechanical Factories of the City of Moscow only Fedor Slepov, who was associated with it from its origins, has left us an account: *Russkoe delo,* June 18, 25; July 2, 9, 11, 23, 30; Aug. 13; Nov. 12, 1905. Serebriakova's testimony at her trial sheds some light on the Zubatovshchina; it is summarized in the two books by Alekseev cited in chap. 2, n. 14. Zubatov's writings on the subject include "Zubatovshchina"; "Iz nedavniago proshlago," *Vestnik Evropy,* March 1906, pp. 432–36; and several letters in Koz'min. There is an anonymous series of articles by a participant writing under the name Tovarishch Iskra, "Zapiski rabochago," *Rabochaia gazeta,* beginning with issue 39 in 1906. The author was able to locate all but issue 39 in the Leningrad Public Library.

N. K. Dmitrieva, a teacher at the Prechistensk courses, similarly approached him for assistance on behalf of the workers; this time Ozerov agreed, having learned the workers had obtained the cooperation of his colleague, Professor Den. Den and Ozerov held several meetings with the initiators of the project, to learn about working and living conditions among the machine workers so that they might adapt the statutes of the Kharkov Society to their particular needs.[5]

The completed statutes were brought to Trepov for preliminary approval in early January 1901 but were rejected.[6] The senior factory inspector, Chizhov, to whom the workers turned next, refused to resubmit the matter to Trepov, with whom he was feuding over police interference in labor affairs, and recommended that Ozerov and Den instead be sent. In their talk with Trepov, Ozerov and Den emphasized the role of mutual-help funds as an outlet for workers' discontent and in the maintenance of social peace, citing their widespread existence among English workers. Apparently Trepov was impressed with their arguments, for he gave his support and promised to seek ministerial approval of the statutes.[7]

Approval by the Moscow authorities encouraged Afanas'ev to call a meeting of factory workers to discuss the statutes and plans for the new society. The Moscow Okhrana and the chief of police "by way of an exception" approved the meeting, which took place on March 21 at a tearoom of the Society for Popular Entertainment under the chairmanship of Professor Den.[8] The group decided to prepare a new draft of the statutes, with the assistance again of Ozerov and

5. *Russkoe delo*, July 2, 1905; Men'shchikov, II, no. 2, p. 126; V. F. Pletnev, ed., *Instsenirovka* (Moscow, 1925), pp. 15, 23; Ozerov, pp. 195–96; S. Piontkovskii, ed., "Zubatovshchina i sotsial-demokratiia," *Katorga i ssylka*, 1924, no. 8, pp. 93–94. For a biographical sketch see "Ozerov, Ivan Khristoforovich," *Entsiklopedicheskii slovar' Russkogo bibliograficheskogo instituta Granat*, 7th rev. ed. (Moscow, n.d.), XXX, 528–30. At the May 27, 1901, meeting of workers thanks were expressed to Ozerov as organizer of the society, and to Ianzhul as its inspirer (Bukhbinder, "K istorii zubatovshchiny," p. 184).

6. The statutes were returned with emendations by Zubatov providing for stricter police surveillance of the Society (Shmeleva, dissertation, pp. 139–40, 175). There are many discrepancies between Slepov's and Ozerov's accounts of the origin and development of the statutes.

7. Ozerov, p. 197; *Torgovo-promyshlennaia gazeta*, March 7, 1901.

8. Piontkovskii, p. 94; *Russkoe delo*, July 9, 1905; Shmeleva, dissertation, p. 171. There is confusion over the date of the first meeting. Ozerov (p. 198) places it in May. Slepov vaguely recalls the meeting was held in March. Shmeleva gives March 27 as the date.

Den.[9] The revised statutes, framed after consultations with groups of workers, were circulating among the factory workers by the end of March in typewritten form, bearing the imprimatur of the Moscow Okhrana, which overtly gave its approval to the fledgling society; in May they were forwarded to Petersburg for approval.[10]

Those who met on March 21 were interested in assembling on a more regular basis to discuss questions of common concern to machine workers. In May, Afanas'ev and Slepov, supported by Trepov, gained permission from the Society for Popular Entertainment to use its auditorium and tearoom to hold regular Saturday meetings. The first meeting of the Moscow Society of Mutual Help of Workers in Mechanical Factories took place on Saturday, May 26, at which time Mikhail Afanas'ev was elected chairman and Fedor Slepov secretary.[11]

Afanas'ev and most other organizers and officers of the workers' societies founded in Moscow with Zubatov's support were experienced factory workers, part of that small but highly significant worker-intelligentsia. In most cases they had been drawn into Marxist circles at their shops or while attending classes and had been arrested. They knew the factory milieu and understood the psychology, outlook, and immediate interests of their fellow workers. Their record as militant labor organizers gave them, moreover, the respect and trust of their factory comrades; they spoke the language of the average worker and related to them better than did the educated intelligentsia. The rapid success of the new society in enlisting the support of the Moscow working class owed much to the fact that it was ostensibly directed by working-class leaders already popular among the factory masses as " 'sufferers' for the cause of the workers."[12]

9. *Russkoe delo,* July 9, 1905.

10. Piontkovskii, p. 94; Shmeleva, dissertation, p. 174. Zubatov to Rataev, June 4, 1901, in S. Ainzaft, *Zubatovshchina i gaponovshchina,* 4th ed. (Moscow, 1925), p. 47. In an undated letter to the Department of Police, Zubatov wrote that the workers were allowed to organize Saturday meetings beginning March 27, 1901 (Shmeleva, "Bor'ba moskovskikh rabochikh protiv zubatovshchiny," Moskovskii gosudarstvennyi pedagogicheskii institut imeni V. I. Lenina, *Uchenye zapiski,* vol. 110, Kafedra istorii SSSR, pt. 4 [1957], p. 37).

11. Ozerov, p. 197; Piontkovskii, p. 94; *Russkoe delo,* July 9, 1905. The minutes of the meeting of May 26, 1901, and those that followed were kept by the secretary, Fedor Slepov. Minutes of several meetings are found in Bukhbinder, "K istorii zubatovshchiny," pp. 181–88. Slepov indicated in his memoirs that the workers met on an irregular basis before May 26.

12. Ignat'ev, p. 16; see also Bauman, p. 83; Pletnev, pp. 15, 23, 25–26. In his report

Mikhail Afanas'ev, the chairman, had been among the workers caught in Zubatov's dragnet during the arrests of Social Democrats on July 6, 1896. By profession a modeler, or patternmaker, Afanas'ev had been employed since the early 1890's at several of the largest Moscow factories. Known to his fellow workers as a labor organizer, he had participated in Marxist circles, for which he was arrested several times. Nevertheless he continued to reside in Moscow and maintain connections with socialist circles, apparently covertly protected by the Okhrana, until he took the role as initiator and leader of the Society of Machine Workers.[13] Nikifor Krasivskii, Zubatov's principal follower and organizer among the Moscow textile workers, likewise had been arrested and imprisoned as a social-democratic agitator prominently involved in strikes. Gifted with great oratorical powers and a sharp understanding of the mind and outlook of his fellow workers, Krasivskii was able to win the unquestioned trust of large numbers of many workers, many of whom idolized him and entered the new societies under his personal influence.[14] Several other officers of the mutual-help societies, including Fedor Ignatov and P. Emelin, were also former factory workers implicated at one time or another in social-democratic agitation.[15]

Zubatov is believed to have organized his working-class converts, the future leaders of the Moscow Zubatovshchina, into educational circles or cells. Using materials gathered for him by Serebriakova,

---

of March 4, 1902, to Sipiagin, Zubatov discussed the qualities and experience his labor organizers should possess (Korelin, "Krakh ideologii," p. 116).

13. Men'shchikov, I, 304, 423; III, 69–70; S. Kanatchikov, *Iz istorii moego bytiia* (Moscow-Leningrad, 1929), I, 31–37; *Iskra*, no. 10 (Nov. 1901), no. 11 (Nov. 20, 1901); Bauman, p. 83; Pletnev, pp. 22–23, 25, 28; *Rabochee dvizhenie*, IV, pt. 2, pp. 291–94; *Russkoe delo*, July 2, 1905; Milonov and Rakovskii, p. 36; S. P. Turin, *From Peter the Great to Lenin* (London, 1935), pp. 64, 78.

14. Shmeleva, dissertation, p. 134; M. G. Golodets, ed., *Podpol'e* (Moscow-Leningrad, 1926), pp. 14, 59–60; Pletnev, pp. 15, 23, 25; Mitskevich, *Na zare rabochego dvizheniia*, p. 211; Bukhbinder, "K istorii zubatovshchiny," p. 171; *Iskra*, no. 14 (Jan. 1, 1902); "O dvizhenii," p. 133; N. M. Varnashev, "Ot nachala do kontsa s gaponovskoi organizatsiei v S.-Peterburge," *Istoriko-revoliutsionnyi sbornik*, 1 (1924), 183–84.

15. Mitskevich, *Na zare rabochego dvizheniia*, pp. 211–12; A. Gaisinovich, "Pervyi etap rabochego dvizheniia na zavode 'Serp i molot,'" *Istoriia proletariata SSSR*, 6 (1931), 163; N. A. Bukhbinder, *Zubatovshchina i rabochee dvizhenie v Rossii* (Moscow, 1926), p. 6; Men'shchikov, I, 423. It is doubtful if Slepov was ever associated with social democracy. His memoirs give no indication of such an association; moreover, his extremely conservative statements set him apart from the other leaders of the Council of Workers of Mechanical Factories of the City of Moscow.

Zubatov lectured on the history of the labor movement in Western Europe and the United States; he discussed the history, tactics, and programs of the revolutionary movement, as well as Marxist theory. He also stressed the potential benefit of a nonpolitical, evolutionary labor movement.[16]

Zubatov's supporters had a material stake in the success of the new societies; as officers they received a monthly stipend from the Okhrana.[17] This alone, however, fails to account for their deep attachment to the movement they led. Personal power and ambition no doubt motivated some; the opportunity to further working-class interests and improve the lives of the workers, who otherwise were prohibited from organizing, must have been justification enough for others. Zubatov selected his partisans well; they gave him unswerving loyalty throughout the course of his labor experiment.

Supported by the local administration and confident of eventual ministerial approval of the statutes, the leaders of the society proceeded to build a mass labor movement without awaiting formal sanction from Petersburg. With the path made smooth at each step by police assistance the machine workers made wide-ranging plans to raise living and working standards and educate themselves. They looked to the liberal intelligentsia for guidance, education, and a deeper awareness (or, as it was called at the time, "consciousness") of common working-class interests.

## The Moscow Intelligentsia Go "to the People"

The history of relations between the Moscow intelligentsia and the Society of Machine Workers reflects the larger story of tension, if not antagonism, between society and state as well as the intelligentsia's longing to do something for the people. The intelligentsia made contacts with the workers through lectures and discussions which took place on Sundays with the permission of the Moscow Okhrana and the chief of police.[18] Professor Ozerov suggested that a lecture series be inaugurated to both explicate the purposes and workings of the mutual-help fund and to educate the workers on subjects of relevance to their life and work. His

16. Spiridovich, "Pri tsarskom rezhime," p. 150; Shmeleva, Moscow *Uchenye zapiski*, p. 34; Alekseev, *Istoriia*, pp. 20, 61; Alekseev, *Provokator*, p. 134.

17. Men'shchikov, III, 71–72.

18. Bukhbinder, "K istorii zubatovshchiny," pp. 176, 182; *Russkiia vedomosti*, June 5, 1901.

suggestion coincided with the workers' own inclinations. As first announced in the newspaper *Russkiia vedomosti* (Russian Gazette) the lecture series was to be devoted to "questions related to the activity of the future society of mutual help, and also others which are closely connected with it or which turn upon the inner life of these workers."[19] The first such talk, setting the pattern for those which followed, was delivered on May 27 by A. E. Vorms of Moscow University on the topic of mutual-help funds, their nature, benefit, and history abroad.

The lectures and discussions were an immediate success among the workers. A mere fifty attended the inaugural lecture; at the fourth lecture the meeting hall, with its seating capacity of two hundred, was jammed, and many workers were turned away at the doors.[20] In July the group received permission to use the larger facilities of the Historical Museum, but by September the seating capacity of even this auditorium proved insufficient and still another, this one seating two thousand, was hired.[21]

The reason for the enthusiastic response to the lectures is clear: hitherto denied the right to assemble and discuss common interests, the Moscow workers had now found a refuge where problems and issues most closely affecting their daily lives were openly discussed. Subjects included mutual-help funds, consumer and other cooperative societies, courts of arbitration, factory sanitary conditions and their effect on the health of the workers, the advantageous pursuit of leisure time, living quarters for factory workers, the length of the factory workday, collective agreements, and factory legislation. The lecturers, moreover, gave the Moscow workers a basic education on working-class conditions abroad; the workers learned about factory legislation in Western Europe and the United States, the legal means open to workers in other states to organize, progressive factory laws in Germany, the maximum

19. *Russkiia vedomosti,* June 5, 1901. In February 1901 the eminent historian P. G. Vinogradov organized a series of lectures for the factory inspectors of Moscow *guberniia.* He was to discuss factory inspectors in England; Ozerov was scheduled to speak on consumer societies. Other speakers included P. P. Nizhegorov, A. E. Vorms, and S. N. Bulgakov. What, if any, relation these talks had with the lectures to the workers is not clear. Ozerov and Vorms participated in both lecture series (*Torgovo-promyshlennaia gazeta,* Feb. 23, 1901).

20. *Russkiia vedomosti,* June 5, 19, 24, 1901.

21. *Ibid.,* July 17, Sept. 18, Oct. 16, 1901; Zubatov to Zvolianskii, Sept. 1, 1901 (N. A. Bukhbinder, "Zubatovshchina v Moskve," *Katorga i ssylka,* 1925, no. 1, p. 110).

factory workday abroad, the role of collective agreements in labor relations in the West, the Rochedale cooperatives and workers' clubs in England, and German labor societies which with government support worked to improve the educational level of the masses.[22]

The lectures in the Historical Museum made the Moscow workers manifestly aware of the disparity in their own disfavor in legal rights and freedoms, organizational unity, and working conditions and living standards compared with workers in other lands. The lecturers were committed to improving the conditions of the factory workers within the existing political order; they never attempted to extenuate the harsh life of the workers with soothing words or advised them to accept their position passively. Nor did they exhort their audience to a heightened sense of loyalty to the throne or entreat it to maintain social peace. Instead the Moscow workers heard a realistic appraisal of their position as unenviable, one in which they were at the mercy of arbitrary powers. For example, Professor Den at a lecture in June charged that the factory contract, based on the worker's sale of his own labor, contained the roots of his exploitation: "This sale is distinguished from any other by the fact that, selling his own labor, the worker at the same time also sells the authority over his own person, by which he is usually deprived of any material security. Under such conditions various types of abuses are also possible on the part of the owner."[23] Den likewise described "the negative side of the worker's life"—that is, the precarious material position of his family in case of his illness or death, the harmful effect of long working hours on his health, and the evils associated with the employment of women and children in factories. These conditions could best be removed, Den advised, through factory legislation and the collective unity of the working class in mutual-help societies: "by the establishment of the planned Society the Moscow workers not only will set a good example to others for imitation and prepare the basis for state insurance, which is expected also in our country, but also will create in their midst the habit of common activity, a means of becoming acquainted with each other [and] unifying their now uncoordinated forces."[24] Dur-

---

22. Ozerov, p. 197. Lengthy accounts of the lectures were given in *Russkiia vedomosti* and *Torgovo-promyshlennaia gazeta*.
23. *Russkiia vedomosti*, June 19, 1901.
24. *Ibid.*

ing another lecture Professor Vorms made a more direct appeal to workers' self-interest in urging them to join mutual-help societies; a united work force, he claimed, could effect a raise in wages by hesitating to offer themselves for work.[25]

Each lecture was followed by an open discussion between the workers and the speaker on the lecture topic or other issues of interest. Here the workers could express their grievances and discuss the legal means to improve their lot. Individual workers freely complained of the humiliation of being searched upon entering and leaving the factory premises, the poor state of workers' housing, management's lack of interest in and understanding of its employees, inadequate factory sanitation and medical aid, their inability to obtain compensation for industrial accidents, the arbitrary lowering of contracted wage rates, and the undignified obeisances demanded by factory foremen.[26] In short, the sessions were a profile of labor grievances, which personal insecurity and the want of organization prevented the Moscow working class from rectifying.

The machine workers gradually recognized the price they were paying for their organizational weakness and became more receptive to the idea of institutions under their own control and direction. Among their suggestions were labor exchanges, consumer cooperatives, courts of arbitration, housing projects financed out of monthly wage contributions, and workers' councils.[27]

The lecturers, who freely gave their services, sought not merely to educate but also to learn from their audience. These contacts with the Moscow workmen were invaluable as a means of eliciting information for a projected comprehensive study of the Moscow proletariat. For this purpose, beginning with Professor Ozerov's talk on August 19, questionnaires requesting detailed information on various aspects of the worker's life began to be distributed at the meetings.[28] Beyond this academic interest in the daily lives of the workers, the intelligentsia was drawn to the mutual-help society by

25. *Torgovo-promyshlennaia gazeta*, June 3, 1901.
26. *Russkiia vedomosti*, June 12; Aug. 2, 7, 14, 21; Sept. 4; Oct. 11, 16; Nov. 4, 1901.
27. *Ibid.*, June 5, July 7, Sept. 11, Oct. 9, Nov. 6, 1901.
28. Ozerov, *Politika*, pp. 199, 201–4; *Russkiia vedomosti*, Aug. 23, 1901, p. 2; *Russkoe delo*, Supplement to No. 28, July 11, 1905. Ozerov prepared a study of workers' grievances from the questionnaires; a summary forwarded to Witte in January 1902, was published in 1906 in Ozerov's *Nuzhdy rabochago klassa v Rossii*.

the prospect that it might develop into a full-fledged labor union on the Western European model. Professor Ozerov, the most enthusiastic supporter of the society among the lecturers and the only one of them to give an account of his involvement, wrote of the lecturers' common interest in the society's development: "Our desire was that under the protection of the mutual-benefit fund would grow other European plants, that is: a bureau of juridical aid, workers' clubs, building societies, consumer societies, etc. And therefore we aimed to widen the program of the organizational meetings, aspiring to open wider horizons for the workers in the matter planned by them."[29]

The lecturers shunned political activity, assuming that the economic and other benefits of the society would inspire the workers with confidence in the possibility of attaining a better life within the existing regime. Like Zubatov, Ozerov believed the Russian labor movement would not threaten the autocracy unless the workers were continually thwarted in their efforts to unite in defense of their economic interests and lost confidence in the efficacy of legal, evolutionary means.[30]

Reports of the lectures and meetings of the machine workers appeared in the pages of *Torgovo-promyshlennaia gazeta* (Trade and Industrial Gazette), published in St. Petersburg by the Ministry of Finance, and *Russkiia vedomosti*, whose editor, V. M. Sobolevskii, was favorably impressed after attending one of the meetings.[31] Moreover, news of the talks and their great popularity with the local working class went far beyond the halls of the Historical Museum owing to the prominence of the lecturers and their wide contacts among liberal and professional circles of the city. The lecturers predominantly represented the academic and legal world; the majority, including Den, Ozerov, Vorms, A. A. Manuilov, and V. E. Ignat'ev were on the academic staff of Moscow University. Others who played a considerable part were the barrister V. G. Vilents and V. I. Anofriev, the secretary of the Moscow Consumer Societies. Several were on the governing board of the Museum of Assistance to Labor, whose facilities they hoped to use to support and broaden the activities of the Society of Machine Workers.[32]

29. Ozerov, *Politika*, p. 200.
30. *Ibid.*, pp. 216, 228.
31. *Ibid.*, p. 199.
32. On the Museum of Assistance to Labor see *Russkiia vedomosti*, Oct. 18, 1901;

The Museum of Assistance to Labor had much in common with the society. Founded by a gift of 50,000 rubles from Kh. S. Ledentsov, it began operations in early 1901, when Zubatov's followers were busy drafting the statutes of a mutual-help fund. Officially affiliated with the Moscow branch of the Imperial Russian Technical Society, the museum was based on statutes whose general aims and specific programs bore striking similarities to those drafted for the machine workers. Its general goal was "to assist in improvement of the conditions of labor and life of the laboring masses, to put into practice discoveries and inventions beneficial to the workers, to spread scientific knowledge, [and] to provide information and instructions concerning the organization of mutual-help societies";[33] these goals were to be reached through public lectures, the establishment of libraries and reading rooms, and an informational bureau for workers, among other measures.

In September the museum all but formally associated itself with the Society of Machine Workers. During his lecture of September 9, Vilents predicted the workers would receive its active support. Two weeks later the museum administration approved a series of measures of concern to the workers among them a worker-oriented periodical, publication of accounts of the lectures and discussions in the Historical Museum, a bureau for legal consultation, and organized excursions to the Moscow art galleries and museums.[34]

Vilents initiated the idea of a consultative bureau after learning of the workers' ignorance of existing factory laws and the unavailability of legal advice. The bureau was empowered to offer free legal advice and recommend other institutions that rendered legal aid. It was to be open on Sundays and holidays in the premises of the Museum of Assistance to Labor, but it was forbidden to receive petitions or draw up legal papers. Vilents enlisted ten lawyers for the project, and on October 28 the bureau opened.[35]

---

*Torgovo-promyshlennaia gazeta,* Feb. 22, 1901; A. Pogozhev, "Iz vospominanii o V. K. von-Pleve," *Vestnik Evropy,* July 1911, p. 267; I. Kh. Ozerov, "Sotsial'nyi muzei," in his *Iz zhizni truda* (Moscow, 1904), pp. 263–67. Anofriev was acting treasurer of the museum and a member of its permanent commission; Ozerov and Vilents also played a prominent role in its administration. During 1905 it became closely allied with the trade-union movement (Solomon M. Schwartz, *The Russian Revolution of 1905* [Chicago and London, 1967], p. 318; Kolokol'nikov and Rapoport, pp. 156–57; J. L. H. Keep, *The Rise of Social Democracy in Russia* [Oxford, 1963], p. 179.

33. Milonov and Rakovskii, p. 42; a slightly different statement of the museum's aims is given in Kolokol'nikov and Rapoport, pp. 155–56.

34. *Torgovo-promyshlennaia gazeta,* Oct. 4, 6, 1901.

35. *Russkiia vedomosti,* Sept. 4, 24; Oct. 29, 1901; *Torgovo-promyshlennaia gazeta,* Aug. 25, Oct. 6, 1901.

The suggestion for the periodical came from Professor Ozerov, who had inquired, after his lecture of August 17, about the reading habits of the Moscow workers; in the discussion period the workers testified to the restrictions on their access to reading materials caused by financial hardship and the insufficiency of free reading rooms. Apparently moved by their craving for knowledge and learning, Ozerov promised to do all in his power to rectify the situation.[36] On September 22, at a regular meeting of the society, Afanas'ev announced on behalf of Ozerov that the Museum of Assistance to Labor was considering a newspaper devoted to labor affairs to which the machine workers would contribute articles. The news was greeted with enthusiasm. Krasivskii, for one, sanguinely foresaw the paper as a medium to unite the Russian working class and raise its consciousness to a level of equality with the labor movement abroad. At last, he declared, the workers would have an instrument through which their voice could be heard, for they "themselves will describe their own needs [and] expose all those outrages which until now have been hidden under the thick darkness of ignorance."[37]

The museum administration decided to publish a periodical at a meeting held the same day. Ledentsov announced that he was prepared to contribute 10,000 rubles toward the new venture, and a commission consisting of Vilents, Ozerov, Manuilov, and N. A. Kablukov was established to plan the publication. But Krasivskii's prediction was premature; the project never materialized. In May 1902, the council of the Imperial Russian Technical Society withheld approval, demanding further information on the delegation of responsibility for the periodical's editorship. The following January, after reconsidering the proposal, the council for reasons that are unclear, refused to sanction the periodical.[38] The museum had also approved publication of accounts of the Sunday lectures and appointed Ozerov and Anofriev to oversee the project, but nothing apparently came of that either.[39]

The intelligentsia also failed to have the city's cultural attractions opened to the workers on a privileged basis. Ozerov had discovered that the workers were little acquainted with these pleasurable

36. *Russkiia vedomosti,* Aug. 21, 1901. On the reading habits of the Moscow workers see also Shestakov, pp. 60–68.

37. Bukhbinder, "K istorii zubatovshchiny," p. 93.

38. *Russkiia vedomosti,* Sept. 24, 1901; May 16, 1902; Jan. 28 1903; *Torgovo-promyshlennaia gazeta,* Oct. 6, 1901; Piontkovskii, p. 96.

39. *Torgovo-promyshlennaia gazeta,* Oct. 6, 1901.

aspects of urban living. The high costs of theater tickets and the reluctance of the authorities to permit special guided tours through the museums and art galleries led the workers to shun these areas of cultural life in their spare time; the unattractive state of the tearooms drove many to pass their few leisure hours either in their overcrowded living quarters or at the local tavern.[40] The workers had suggested that special theatrical performances be offered for them at popular prices on Sundays and that the galleries and museums organize guided tours.[41] Ozerov brought the suggestions to the Museum of Assistance to Labor, which established a commission expressly to petition the galleries and museums on behalf of the workers. The commission, however, made no headway; nor did two personal appeals to the director of the Moscow office of the Imperial Theater, one by Ozerov and Den and another by a group of machine workers, succeed in securing agreement for special theatrical performances.[42]

Plans for a consumer society among the machine workers were carried out more successfully, although they too ultimately ended in failure. Consumer cooperatives were a type of self-help that could bring immediate material benefits to the worker without opposition from the higher authorities. Ozerov had suggested a consumer society similar to those run by factory workers abroad to the initiators of the Society of Machine Workers in its early days.[43] The proposal was again raised at the Sunday lecture of June 23 by V. I. Anofriev, one of the mainstays of the lecture series  On Anofriev's advice the workers elected a commission to study the proposal, although several expressed doubt that the workers could make the venture a practical success. After the lecture of July 1, a commission of workers met, with the participation of Den and Anofriev, and outlined a proposed Moscow Consumers' Society of Workers in Machine Factories the following Sunday. Afanas'ev, Selpov, F. M. Ignatov, and F. L. Dolin were commissioned to seek approval of the statutes from the authorities.

40. *Russkiia vedomosti*, Aug. 21, 1901.
41. Ozerov, *Politika*, p. 207.
42. *Torgovo-promyshlennaia gazeta*, Oct. 6, 1901; *Russkiia vedomosti*, Sept. 30, Oct. 29, 30, 1901; Ozerov, *Politika*, pp. 207–10. Ozerov tried at one time to have a group of historians and artists organize museum and gallery trips for the workers (Bukhbinder, "Zubatovshchina v Moskve," p. 110).
43. Ozerov, *Politika*, p. 197. Ozerov looked to cooperative societies as a means of ending labor exploitation through their own production of finished products

Some six hundred Moscow factory and railway-shop workers indicated their desire to join even before official approval of the cooperative was announced. The high cost of food in the Moscow shops, where the workers purchased their goods on credit at a price 15 per cent higher than average elsewhere and the poor quality and high price of meals at the factory canteens explain the wide interest in a consumer society.[44]

In early October the statutes were returned with approval, and the Moscow Consumers' Society of Workers in Machine Factories formally accepted members.[45] By the time of its first general meeting, held in the Historical Museum on November 11, 970 had registered. An eleven-man administration was elected and chose F. L. Dolin as chairman. The group's aims were those usually stated by consumers' cooperatives, but Ozerov foresaw a much broader range of operations; he interpreted approval of the statutes as allowing members "under the protection of the law to organize shops, dininghalls, libraries, reading rooms, courses, [and] to gather and discuss their affairs."[46]

At the next general meeting, held in the second week of December, the membership voted by a wide margin to open cooperative stores, rather than tearooms, as favored by Slepov. The society, which at its height boasted a membership of two thousand, however, lasted less than two years. Embezzlement of funds and the lack of capable managers and business acumen, a problem some had foreseen, brought the venture to an end.[47]

## The Council and the District Meetings of Machine Workers

Beginning in the spring of 1901, the Society of Machine Workers held its business meetings at one of the tearooms or the auditorium of the Society for Popular Entertainment on Saturdays, when practical matters were debated, factory grievances discussed, and con-

---

(Ozerov, "Obshchestva potrebitelei," *Iz zhizni truda*, p. 178).

44. *Russkiia vedomosti*, June 5, 26; July 7, 13; Aug. 21, 28; Oct. 23, 1901; *Torgovo-promyshlennaia gazeta*, June 6, 1901, p. 2; July 6, 1901; *Russkoe delo*, July 9, 1905; Bukhbinder, "K istorii zubatovshchiny," p. 196.

45. *Russkiia vedomosti*, Oct. 9, 16, 1901.

46. *Ibid.*, Nov. 18, 1901.

47. *Ibid.*, Dec. 11, 1901; Mar. 3, 1902; *Russkoe delo*, July 9, 1905; *Rodnaia rech'*, May 4, 1903; Bukhbinder, "K istorii zubatovshchiny," p. 196; Pletnev, p. 17; "O dvizhenii," pp. 133–34; *Moskovskiia vedomosti*, Jan. 13, 1903.

crete proposals considered. The officers of the society dominated the proceedings, directing the discussions away from delicate issues they disapproved of and into areas they held to be of practical significance for the immediate future. At a meeting of May 26, for example, there was almost unanimous agreement to set aside as premature such "abstract questions" as overtime work and to limit discussion to areas in which the society had a reasonable chance of effecting changes.[48] The leaders rejected a suggestion, made at a meeting on July 21, to discuss with the factory inspector the question of allowing workers to arrive at work up to two hours late without being fined because it appeared to be a demand for an eight-hour day. Krasivskii felt it was premature and potentially harmful for the workers, since greater leisure might be injurious while their intellectual level was still low. Afanas'ev seconded this opinion and defended factory fines as necessary for order and discipline because "the majority of us are far from conscientious persons"; freedom for such "intellectually backward" people could be harmful.[49] A third speaker felt that failure to appear for work was just another way of going on strike; he reminded his listeners that "we, gentlemen, are going by the peaceful progressive road."[50]

Content with the conservative tenor of the regular Saturday meetings and heartened by the large influx of Moscow workers into the movement, the Moscow administration broadened the structure of the society by sanctioning district *(raion)* assemblies for machine workers throughout Moscow. These were usually held in taverns and tearooms frequented by workers of the large factories, where they discussed among themselves questions raised at the Sunday lectures. These weekly meetings, judging by their attendance, found quick popularity. Two or three hundred workers—and sometimes two to three times that number—attended.[51]

The district meetings were local organs of a citywide directorate or council *(soviet)*, which capped the edifice of the labor movement among the machine workers. The council—in full, the Council of Workers of Mechanical Factories of the City of Moscow—was initiated at the suggestion of the Moscow administration in August 1901. Afanas'ev and his supporters, with the editorial assistance of

48. Bukhbinder, "K istorii zubatovshchiny," p. 182.
49. *Ibid.*, p. 187.
50. *Ibid.*
51. *Ibid.*, p. 172; Ozerov, *Politika*, p. 205; *Russkoe delo*, July 11, 1905.

Den and Ozerov, drew up Instructions to guide the council and forwarded them for approval to the Okhrana and Trepov. Apparently Trepov was not satisfied with the draft, for on September 22 he called Afanas'ev to the offices of the Okhrana and advised revisions strengthening police surveillance of the council to preclude its subversion and increasing its powers over district assemblies.[52]

The Instructions reflect the administration's desire not to let the infant labor movement pass out of its control. The entire movement was to be managed through the council; the authorities placed greater trust in the seventeen hand-picked labor organizers on the council than in the rank and file. Formally the council was to choose its own officers, including a chairman. It could discuss the material needs of the machine workers and measures to improve their economic position, enter into "direct relations" with the lecturers, and conduct the general meetings of the society. It was also obliged to maintain strict vigilance over the district meetings. With the approval of the chief of police, the council established the agenda of the district meetings and assigned one of its officers to attend; should the district assembly deviate from its approved agenda the inspector was to report to the council, which was empowered to suspend the local assembly.[53]

Trepov approved the Instructions on October 11, 1901. The council was provided with a stamp and stationery embossed with "The Council of Workers of Mechanical Factories"—little wonder that many workers believed the society and its council functioned "on a legal basis."[54]

Thus less than six months after its inception the Moscow experiment had succeeded in fulfilling Zubatov's most exaggerated expectations. Prestigious members of the intelligentsia had consented to participate in a program of public lectures and had received overwhelmingly favorable response; a consumers' cooperative society was on its way to realization, and plans were under way for a newspaper, a library, courts of arbitration, labor exchanges, a mutual-help fund, and housing construction; district assemblies had been established throughout Moscow to accommodate the large influx of workers. Most assuring of all, the

52. Bukhbinder, "K istorii zubatovshchiny," pp. 192–93; *Russkoe delo*, July 9, 1905; Ozerov, *Politika*, p. 206.
53. Bukhbinder, "Zubatovshchina v Moskve," pp. 113–14.
54. *Russkoe delo*, July 9, 1905.

authorities, through the council, were in control of the entire movement. Moreover, Moscow workers in other professions showed great interest in organizing on a similar basis, and reports from other industrial centers told of strong interest among the workers in the Moscow Zubatovshchina.[55] The worst fears of those who opposed permitting even a minimum of independent activity among the working class appeared groundless.

Zubatov had cause for smug self-satisfaction, for through control of the council he believed he had stolen a march on the revolutionaries and had the Moscow working class within his grasp. Writing on September 20 to S. E. Zvolianskii, director of the Department of Police, Zubatov optimistically envisioned the council's domain spreading well beyond the city:

We organized a Workers' Council of seventeen persons, all our own agents. Its members, besides mutual responsibility for the whole Council, organize frequent workers' meetings on weekdays in various city districts with our knowledge as to place and hour. Things are going fine. Only a question which has been discussed at the general meeting can be a topic. The chairman of the Council designates one of its members, mainly from our friends, to be in control. . . . In short, we are in possession of the Council and have available the focus of the entire laboring masses, and thanks to this lever we can twist the whole thing. The province will send deputies to our Assemblies, and they will depart charmed.[56]

So much for the workers. But Zubatov was equally proud of his achievements in dealing with the intelligentsia. At a time when a large section of the intelligentsia was alienated from the autocracy and was increasingly attracted to socialist panaceas, Zubatov had secured the assistance of prominent figures from the Moscow intellectual world. Professor Ozerov, uninhibited in his contact with the famous Okhrana chief, symbolized for Zubatov the new rapprochement between society and state:

Yesterday was extraordinary: Professor Ozerov appeared in the [Okhrana] section. An exceptional step. In former times professors visited us only under escort. He came to receive directions in the workers' cause, to arrange joint work; he gave assurances of the lecturers' loyalty and their unfailing correctness, described the goal of their striving—the formation of social peace in trade-industrial occupations, and inquired to what degree this

55. *Russkiia vedomosti*, Aug. 19, 1901; *Iskra*, no. 10 (Nov. 1901); no. 15 (Jan. 15, 1902).
56. Bukhbinder, Zubatovshchina v Moskve," p. 111.

policy is to be firm and his sources authoritative, since, he said, retreating at a certain moment and leaving the professors isolated with the workers will create something worse than exists at present. He is fascinated to the utmost by this affair and his position in it.[57]

Zubatov patronizingly had depicted for his welcome though uninvited guest the broad significance of the Moscow labor movement and the crucial role played by the "large intelligentsia" in inculcating loyalty to the government among the workers and influencing the students to make peace with the autocracy. Ozerov, dazzled by Zubatov's delineation of the influence wielded by the lecturers and his own central position in the affair, begged the Okhrana chief to provide him with future advice and guidance and left with the firm assurance he could visit the Okhrana offices again. Zubatov concluded his description of the strange encounter with the pithy observation that "joint instructive work between the Okhrana and professors is a curious and unusual spectacle!"[58]

## First Retreat—Attack from Right and Left

The spectacle did not last for long; before the end of 1901 some of the intelligentsia reconsidered participation in the lecture program and decided to withdraw, inflicting the first major blow to Zubatov's grandiose plans. Criticism of the lectures and the lecturers had come from two sides. The radical intelligentsia at home and abroad strongly questioned any cooperation with the higher authorities and attacked the Society of Machine Workers as a perversion of a true labor organization, charging that it suited the needs of the government rather than those of the workers. The Moscow industrial community and its supporters in the higher Petersburg bureaucracy saw in the Moscow experiment the roots of sedition and a Western-style labor movement. Strange to say, these two groups, poles apart ideologically, consistently expressed a similar view: once the factory proletariat was permitted to organize it would inevitably become militant, consciously engage in class strife, and enter the arena of political action. Of the two groups the influence of the conservatives was more decisive in undermining the Zubatov experiment.

The Society of Machine Workers was most vulnerable to the

57. *Ibid.*, pp. 110–11.
58. *Ibid.*, p. 111.

criticism that it served the purposes of the Okhrana: Zubatov had chosen its leaders and the Okhrana had introduced them to Trepov and the Grand Duke Sergei, whose influence was instrumental in obtaining permission for the district meetings and the lectures; in August the Okhrana paid for Krasivskii, Afanas'ev, and Slepov to visit Kharkov to study its mutual-help society; the Okhrana had suggested the formation of the council and edited the Instructions Trepov had approved. The council's officers were regular visitors to Okhrana headquarters, where they freely used the office facilities and received advice and permission to conduct their meetings. Council officers received regular monthly stipends from the same quarter when their council duties made it impossible for them to continue at their factory jobs.[59]

The links between the society and the Okhrana did not long remain hidden. Indeed, from the start the initiators had not attempted to hide either the Okhrana's role or the support of the local administration. Afanas'ev assured the workers they could come openly to the meetings for "the police know about this."[60] These words only lent support to those who did not believe that the workers were masters of their own labor organization. Suspicious too was the presence at the lectures of Colonel Sazonov, assistant chief of the Okhrana, and his open display of friendship with Professor Ozerov.[61] Other critics alleged that the workers' meetings were a police trap to ensnare radical agitators; N. K. Dmitrieva and some of her social-democratic circle were arrested shortly after speaking out on this matter at one of the first meetings of the machine workers.[62]

Newspaper accounts of the society and the public lectures at the Historical Museum made the group a topic of dispute among the Moscow intelligentsia and the socialist émigré ideologues. Central to the discussion was the question whether the Moscow experiment was indicative of a new general course by the government in dealing with the labor question.[63] The radical intelligentsia gave little credit

59. *Russkoe delo*, July 9, 11, 1905.
60. Bukhbinder, "K istorii zubatovshchiny," pp. 182–83.
61. Piontkovskii, p. 95.
62. Shmeleva, Moscow *Uchenye zapiski*, p. 43; *Russkoe delo*, July 9, 1905. The Okhrana had known for some time through Afanas'ev that Dmitrieva, a teacher at the Prechistensk workers' courses, had organized a socialist workers' circle (Ovsiannikov, p. 135; Alekseev, *Provokator*, p. 142).
63. *Osvobozhdenie*, no. 18 (March 2, 1903).

to the initiative or spontaneous interest of the workers in the society. In general they had no faith in the undertaking, and their vague suspicions soon became allegations of police machination.[64] The council was obviously a tool of the police; why otherwise, they asked, would the authorities give the machine workers privileges denied to the working class elsewhere? Would the autocracy, which feared the labor movement, permit the workers to organize unless the entire operation was firmly controlled from behind the scenes?

Within Russia the legal press was generally sympathetic to the society and the lecture series. The censor would not have allowed it to raise disturbing questions about the Okhrana's role or the true purposes of the society. The first all-out attacks on the meetings in the Historical Museum therefore came from underground émigré publications, proscribed by officialdom but somehow reaching the Russian intelligentsia clandestinely.

The Marxist intelligentsia from the first understood Zubatov's motives and the threat his plans posed to the fusion of social democracy with the working class. In the December 1900 opening number of *Iskra*, founded in Munich by Lenin and Martov to give the fragmented Russian social democratic movement proper theoretical guidance, Zubatov's aims and tactics were subjected to lengthy analysis. An article written by Martov, ironically entitled "New Friends of the Russian Proletariat," described Zubatov's career, his use of the technique of brainwashing, and his relations with the Jewish working-class movement in the Western *krai* (region). Writing several months before the Moscow Zubatovshchina got under way, Martov prophesied that Zubatov would shortly "attempt to pervert the conscious part of the Russian proletariat." Moreover, Martov greatly feared Zubatov would succeed: "In the present position of our movement we are much less prepared for a successful struggle against the Zubatovshchina than are the Jewish workers."[65]

The Jewish Labor Bund in countering the Zubatovshchina could

---

64. Letter of Kh. P. Lunts, Nov. 1901 (Shmeleva, Moscow *Uchenye zapiski*, p. 47).

65. *Iskra*, no. 1 (Dec. 1900). The article, as all others in *Iskra*, was published anonymously. In 1925 the first fifty-two issues of *Iskra* (Dec. 1900–1903) were reprinted under the editorship of P. Lepeshinskii with the appropriate author's name attached to important articles and editorials. Shmeleva in her dissertation maintains that Martov's article became the "guiding principle" for Moscow Social Democrats in the struggle against the Zubatovshchina, although she does not give Martov credit for its authorship.

count on the solidarity of its membership and its secret press in order to warn the masses; Russian social democracy had "nothing similar" and was still lacking in unity. If Russian social democracy were not to sign its own death warrant it had to utilize all available means to raise the political consciousness of the proletariat and undermine Zubatov's policy. Echoes of Lenin's later organizational proposals, which split Russian social democracy in 1903, were to be heard in Martov's recommendation for combating the Zubatovshchina: "unite all conscious comrades and have a solid organization and strict discipline. Against the attempt to bring political perversion in the labor movement only a strongly solid, disciplined and mobile workers' party can struggle with success. Such is the first lesson given to us Russian social democrats by the history of the contemporary Zubatov adventure."[66]

Social Democrats should both encourage the growth of the elemental labor movement, which was aimed at improving living standards among the workers, and raise the political consciousness of the working class, which meant destroying the worker's blind submissiveness to the capitalist and his equally blind faith in the beneficence of the autocracy. In the light of Zubatov's tactics, "revolutionary propaganda and agitation inciting the masses on to political struggle" was an urgent necessity for revolutionary socialism.[67]

Martov's fears were realized within six months when the Society of Machine Workers was created—with the cooperation of eminent figures from Moscow intellectual society. Martov set out to breach the apparent alliance between the proletariat and the intelligentsia. In an article entitled "Bourgeois Science before the Moscow Workers" in the September 1901 issue of *Iskra,* he alternately criticized, entreated, and threatened the lecturers: Were the lectures in the Historical Museum intended to bring culture and enlightenment to the workers or merely to divert them from a revolutionary course? There was little doubt where Martov stood on the question, for he took the lecturers to task for allegedly failing to discuss the most pressing issues facing the working class—including the crucial role of strikes—and for not developing the true self-consciousness of the workers. If the intelligentsia under

66. *Ibid.*
67. *Ibid.*

conditions of legality were unable to speak openly on real issues they would be better advised to remain silent. Social democracy did not expect the bourgeois intelligentsia to share its views but did expect political tact. The lecturers must resolve in their own minds the question others were asking: Why did the Moscow authorities permit the lectures? When the workers saw the real purpose behind the talks, the lecturers would have no one to blame but themselves, Martov warned.[68]

The attack on the Society of Machine Workers emanated from the émigré centers abroad rather than from inside Russia, owing to the inability of Moscow social democracy to mount a sustained offensive against the Zubatovshchina. Frequent arrests among the leadership of the Moscow Committee of the R.S.D.R.P. sapped the confidence of those Social Democrats who managed to escape the police dragnet; contacts with the Moscow factory workers thus dwindled to a minimum. In part to repair this sad state of affairs, in part to supervise the clandestine transport of *Iskra* from abroad and its distribution throughout Russia, Nikolai E. Bauman was sent to Moscow in February 1901, as agent of the *Iskra* organization. The task was beyond Bauman's capacity.[69] The omnipresence of the Okhrana and the disintegration of the Moscow social democratic organization compelled Bauman to turn to local representatives of the rival Socialist Revolutionaries for the distribution of *Iskra*.

Bauman proved to be an uninformed and unreliable correspondent. The editors of *Iskra* surmised that the lectures in the Historical Museum were engineered by Zubatov, but Bauman, on the scene in Moscow, could provide them with no evidence. On July 28, two months after the lecture series had begun, Bauman wrote the editors that he had no clear views on the charge that Zubatov had masterminded the lectures. Indeed several of his in-

---

68. *Iskra*, no. 8 (Sept. 10, 1901). A leaflet published by the Kharkov Socialist Revolutionary organization attacked the lecturers in even stronger terms, charging the Moscow professors with working to reconcile the factory masses with the existing political order (*Iskra*, no. 11 [Nov. 20, 1901]). Lenin surprisingly had little to say at this time about the Moscow Zubatovshchina and the lectures in the Historical Museum. In *Chto delat'?*, published several months after the lectures had terminated, he scathingly attacked the intelligentsia for their participation.

69. Letters of N. E. Bauman to V. I. Lenin and to the editors of *Iskra*, May 23 (June 5), 1901, May 30 (June 12), 1901, in *Perepiska V. I. Lenina i redaktsii gazety "Iskra" s sotsial-demokraticheskimi organizatsiiami v Rossii 1900–1903 gg.* (Moscow, 1969), I, 110–11, 118–19.

formants were absolutely convinced that Zubatov did not have even the remotest connection with the lectures. "It would be very unfortunate if there appeared in the press an extreme opinion about these talks on the basis of superficial information," Bauman commented, requesting the editors of *Iskra* to refrain from attacking the lectures until he had more detailed and positive information.[70] On August 20, N. K. Krupskaia wrote to Bauman on behalf of the *Iskra* editorial board deploring his inability to provide reliable information on the Society of Machine Workers "while in the [legal] newspapers there appears information of such a nature that it is impossible for us to keep silent any longer."[71] The silence was broken by Martov's article in September.

Bauman began to campaign against the Society of Machine Workers and the lecture series once *Iskra* had denounced them.[72] In late September, however, the police arrested the leaders of the Moscow Committee of the R.S.D.R.P., dealing a setback to Bauman's plans. Little wonder then that Krupskaia, secretary of the *Iskra* organization, in separate letters to P. B. Aksel'rod and G. V. Plekhanov, colleagues on the editorial board, wrote despairingly of the weakness of social democracy in Moscow and the effectiveness of the Zubatovshchina and the lectures in corrupting the Moscow workers.[73]

The Moscow Social Democrats did succeed in the summer of 1901 in printing two clandestine broadsides aimed at Zubatov and tsarist labor policy, although the police may have confiscated them before distribution. The first attacked the Moscow academic community for accepting Zubatov's claims and deceiving the working class into

70. *Ibid.*, p. 182. Bauman again wrote in August promising information on the lectures (*ibid.*, p. 197).

71. *Ibid.*, p. 219. See also the letter of the editors of *Iskra* to Bauman around July 28 (Aug. 10), 1901, scolding him for not supplying information on the lectures in the Historical Museum (*ibid.*, p. 183).

72. The section dealing with 1901 in Bauman's report to the Second Congress of the R.S.D.R.P. was based on his personal experience (Bauman, pp. 79–82). V. P. Nogin maintained that Bauman began a campaign against the Zubatovshchina and the Moscow lecturers only in the winter of 1901, when the lectures were coming to an end (Nogin, "Vospominaniia V. P. Nogina o moskovskoi organizatsii," *Proletarskaia revoliutsiia*, Feb. 1925, p. 204).

73. N. K. Krupskaia to P. B. Aksel'rod, Oct. 23, 1901, in A. N. Potresov and B. I. Nikolaevskii, eds., *Sotsial-demokraticheskoe dvizhenie v Rossii* (Moscow-Leningrad, 1928), I, 85–86; undated letter of Krupskaia to Plekhanov, in *Gruppa "Osvobozhdenie truda,"* ed. L. G. Deich (Moscow-Leningrad, 1928), pp. 123–25.

believing that the tsarist government would voluntarily grant it concessions; in reality only through continual struggle would the working class attain its ends. The second criticized the narrowness of the goals and methods of the Society of Machine Workers. Without belittling economic struggle as a means of improving living standards or renouncing the use of mutual-help funds, it contended that political freedom (incompatible with the existence of the autocracy!) was necessary for defense of working-class interests.[74]

The barbs aimed by the revolutionary intelligentsia against the lecturers soon hit their mark. Repeated charges of cooperation with the Moscow administration and allegations of being dupes of the Okhrana embarrassed the lecturers, provoked dissension in their midst, and eventually led to the withdrawal of several of them, giving Moscow social democracy the only semblance of a victory it could claim over the Zubatovshchina.

By November 1901 it was common talk in Moscow that the Okhrana stood behind the Society of Machine Workers, using it as a bulwark against the revolutionary movement. Professor Ozerov, aware that criticism from the radical intelligentsia was disturbing his colleagues, sought a judgment on the moral worth and intellectual merits of the lecture series from an impartial and prestigious jury. P. G. Vinogradov, a renowned historian and leader of the movement for academic freedom at Moscow University, and V. Iu. Skalon, an editor of *Russkiia vedomosti*, were selected to judge the case. After several interviews and a preliminary investigation Vinogradov convoked a meeting at his apartment on December 7 to debate the issue. Several lecturers, led by Ozerov, emphasized the positive side of the talks and discounted rumors and suspicions regarding the meetings at the Historical Museum. Ranged against them were one group which wished to suspend the lectures until the statutes of the mutual-help fund were approved in Petersburg and a second group which opposed continuation altogether. The latter's charges reflected the criticism by the radical intelligentsia: the lectures had created a false picture of reality and had produced no practical results; they tended to reconcile the workers with the government; the discussion periods were a trap to ensnare the most fiery agitators among the workers; lastly, the project was producing a schism in the ranks of the working class, with the machine workers becoming a

74. Shmeleva, Moscow *Uchenye zapiski,* pp. 45–47.

government-approved privileged order compared with the vast mass of dissatisfied workers still without basic civil rights.[75]

After investigating the charges the two-man jury concluded that "these objections are not convincing."[76] The lecturers had omitted certain matters in their discussions with the workers in a desire to conform with what was legally tolerated; in truth it was surprising permission had been granted to carry on the program of lectures at all. The lectures, moreover, had beneficial practical results in providing the workers with their most essential requirement—that is, an understanding of their needs and how they could be fulfilled. Vinogradov and Skalon felt that the working class at the moment was disposed to trust the government; the government, in turn, appeared willing to go a long way toward meeting working-class needs in an effort to retain its loyalty. Finally, the jury brushed aside the charge that the lectures served as a police trap, commenting that the police surely had other means of learning the whereabouts of criminal elements.[77]

Having disposed of the indictment, Vinogradov and Skalon found a continuation of the lectures "desirable to a high degree"; "these discussions throw a large amount of light into a land of darkness, awaken consciousness, chart the path, give an impetus to attempts at self-activity and self-help. Those who set themselves the task of spreading light have hardly the right to refuse this light to people who are beginning to see clearly."[78]

They suggested two changes: the lecturers should incorporate as a separate entity with powers to manage their own affairs, select future members, and choose lecture themes; and the intelligentsia should not be permitted to take a direct part in the council, the district meetings, or the administration of the mutual-help fund. The workers should learn how to manage their own affairs; the intelligentsia could best serve them by teaching how this could be done.

The generally favorable verdict was not acceptable to all the lecturers; several, embarrassed and fearful of compromising their good name with Moscow society and the intelligentsia in general, withdrew.[79] Moreover, Professor Vinogradov, whose public

75. Ozerov, *Politika,* pp. 199, 214–19; *Osvobozhdenie,* no. 18 (March 2, 1903), no. 19 (March 19, 1903).

76. Ozerov, *Politika,* p. 219.

77. The verdict of Vinogradov and Skalon is printed verbatim in *ibid.,* pp. 219–21.

78. *Ibid.,* p. 220.

79. *Ibid.,* p. 222; *Osvobozhdenie,* no. 19 (March 19, 1903); *Iskra,* no. 16 (Feb. 1, 1902);

announcement that he would appear as a lecturer seemed to give new life to the series, failed to meet his commitment, for on December 20 he left for England. Ozerov alone among his colleagues endeavored to revive the lectures but failed; the lectures were never begun again on the old basis.[80]

The radical intelligentsia could claim but partial responsibility for bringing the lectures to a halt; the major blow came from the side of the industrial community and the Ministry of Finance. The Society of Machine Workers had not only disturbed the socialist intelligentsia, which feared the working class would become immune to its influence, but also alarmed the Moscow factory owners, who foresaw a militant revolutionary force emerging.

Conservative bureaucrats shared with the industrialists the view that factory workers should be kept ignorant about labor relations at home and abroad. In 1898 they had prohibited Professor Ianzhul from delivering a series of public lectures on the advantages of social peace between capital and labor, claiming the lectures would endanger public order.[81] The lectures in the Historical Museum similarly alarmed the Moscow industrialists, who kept abreast of developments among the machine workers through newspaper accounts and reports received from foremen whom they ordered to attend the society's meetings. In some instances they harrassed workmen known to have attended the lectures. In the factory owners' view, the workers, conditioned by years of acquaintance with illegal socialist literature, flocked to the Historical Museum out of eagerness to learn more about labor relations in Western Europe. The lectures, they maintained, were abstract and theoretical and hardly related to the existing conditions of Russian factory life.

Determined to halt the growth of the Society of Machine Workers while it was still in its infancy, the Moscow industrialists sent a deputation to Petersburg in June to petition for its closing. Witte, as could be expected, supported the Moscow businessmen, but Sipiagin for the time being defended Zubatov, and the petitioners returned home empty-handed.[82]

---

*Revoliutsionnaia Rossiia,* no. 4 (Feb. 1902); Novikov, pp. 30–31.

80. Ozerov, *Politika,* p. 222; *Russkiia vedomosti,* Nov. 8, Dec. 19, 1901; *Osvobozhdenie,* no. 19 (March 19, 1903); *Revoliutsionnaia Rossiia,* no. 4 (Feb. 1902).

81. Ozerov, *Politika,* p. 212.

82. I. Ianzhul, "Vospominaniia I. I. Ianzhula o perezhitom i vidennom," *Russkaia starina,* no. 146 (June 1911), pp. 490–95; Zubatov, "Iz nedavniago proshlago," p. 435; Ozerov, *Nuzhdy rabochago klassa,* p. 45; Shmeleva, dissertation, p. 182; *Torgovo-promyshlennaia gazeta,* Feb. 7, 1906.

Aware of the criticism from the Moscow industrial community, Zubatov spiritedly defended the society in correspondence with his Petersburg superiors. In particular, he emphasized the benefits to the existing order from labor organizations composed of thousands of enlightened and disciplined workers. With the cooperation of "liberal elements," the working class had been "torn from the hands of the revolutionaries."[83]

In the fall Zubatov visited St. Petersburg and reported on the Moscow labor movement to the Minister of Interior. Sipiagin apparently concluded that the lectures in the Historical Museum were intended merely to acquaint the workers with legal means of organization and would cease once the statutes of the society were approved.[84] Evidently Zubatov's arguments failed to quell the worst fears of his superiors, for on November 8 he was requested to prepare a full history of his "counterrevolutionary" movement.[85] It was too late, however, to save the lectures; the factory owners, allegedly alarmed by the effect of the lectures on their workmen, pressured the Petersburg authorities until Sipiagin ordered the lectures terminated.[86]

## Approval by St. Petersburg: The Revised Statutes

Although Sipiagin attempted to limit the Moscow experiment by abolishing the lecture series, the Ministry of Interior felt powerless to end it completely because of the Grand Duke Sergei's great influence among court circles; the Moscow Zubatovshchina remained very much intact. After considering the statutes of the proposed Moscow Society of Mutual Help of Workers in Mechanical Factories for nearly a year, the Petersburg authorities approved them on February 14, 1902, after making numerous alterations to weaken the society's authority and to stamp it openly with a police imprint.

83. Bukhbinder, "K istorii zubatovshchiny," p. 175. On September 1, 1901, Zubatov wrote confidently of the success of the lectures to S. E. Zvolianskii: "In a word we will give the workers to the care of the university authorities" (Bukhbinder, "Zubatovshchina v Moskve," p. 110).

84. D. S. Sipiagin to the Grand Duke Sergei Aleksandrovich, March 16, 1902 (Bukhbinder, "Zubatovshchina v Moskve," p. 124).

85. Shmeleva, Moscow *Uchenye zapiski*, p. 43; Vovchik, p. 114; Ainzaft, "Zubatov i studenchestvo," pp. 65–66. The report Zubatov prepared has not been located; his report of that date on the Jewish labor movement is published in *Krasnyi arkhiv*, 1922, no. 1, pp. 292–94.

86. The documents available do not specify when the lectures ended or whether

The statutes had originally provided for monetary benefits to members or their families in case of sickness, death, or other circumstances depriving a member of capacity to work. Funds could also be distributed in cases of involuntary unemployment.[87] The statutes as approved more narrowly restricted the eligibility requirements for unemployment compensation. The society was forbidden to grant monetary support to members who had left their jobs to find more profitable work or who had been deprived of work due to administrative measures taken against them. In all cases a certificate from the police verifying causes of unemployment was required before the society's council could approve an application for unemployment funds.[88] These changes were introduced to preclude distribution of money to labor agitators and workers on strike.

The society's entire operation was to be subjected to the close scrutiny of the local administration, which was empowered to intervene at any moment. Originally the general assembly was to elect eight members to the society's governing body; under the new arrangement the final choice was left to the Moscow chief of police, who chose eight from among the twelve nominated by the assembly. The chairman and treasurer of the assembly likewise needed the approval of the Moscow administration before they could legally take office. Decisions of the general assembly could not be acted upon without the prior approval of the Moscow administration; yearly reports of the society were to be transmitted to the Ministry of Interior through the Moscow governor-general and chief of police. The governor-general was empowered to close the society at any time at his discretion, thus ensuring that it would not develop very far along militant lines. The new statutes also

the lecturers withdrew before the order was given to end the series. The last lecture published in the newspapers was given on November 4, 1901. Zubatov, "Iz nedavniago proshlago," p. 435; Shmeleva, dissertation, p. 183; Trepov to the Grand Duke Sergei, April 19, 1902 (Ainzaft, *Zubatovshchina*, p. 66).

87. *Russkiia vedomosti*, June 10, 1901; Ozerov, *Politika*, p. 227; *Moskovskiia vedomosti*, March 2, 1902. The original statutes were summarized at length in *Torgovo-promyshlennaia gazeta*, March 7, 1901, and in *Russkiia vedomosti*, June 10, 1901. There is no certainty which of the two sets of statutes summarized in the newspapers was sent to Petersburg.

88. Ozerov, *Politika*, p. 227; *S.-Peterburgskiia vedomosti*, March 6, 1902. To the category of those ineligible as members was added "persons who are under police surveillance" (Ozerov, p. 226). For the meaning of police surveillance *(politseiskii nadzor)* in tsarist law and practice, see Szeftel, pp. 14–18.

broadened the category of candidate members, raising the question whether the society was to be exclusively run by the workers. Article 18 opened membership to police officers, factory inspectors, medical personnel, officials of the factory administration, and churchmen.[89]

The spirit and content of the revised statutes lent weight to the arguments of those who from the beginning maintained that the society was the creature of the Okhrana. Even Professor Ozerov was stunned by the degree to which the Petersburg authorities had mutilated the original statutes, and advised the workers to reject them in their new form.[90] There was also great disillusionment among some of the workers.

Ministerial approval of the statutes, however altered they may have been, was unusual; its significance should not be underestimated. In the words of a contemporary socialist critic of the Zubatovshchina, ministerial permission for the society to function was an "exceptional occurrence" for Russia: "At a time when in general all union organizations—be they of workers, peasants, or intelligentsia—were prohibited by the government in every way possible, the Moscow machine workers alone had been granted such a right."[91]

## The Moscow Workers Publicly Demonstrate Loyalty to the Crown

Five days after the statutes had been approved the Moscow workers, under the direction of the Society of Machine Workers, publicly celebrated the anniversary of peasant emancipation proclaimed by Alexander II. On February 19, 1902, the Moscow labor movement, which Zubatov had so skillfully nurtured, reached its apogee in a mass peaceful demonstration inside the Kremlin, the success of which frightened both socialists and conservatives. The socialists feared that the working class had been perverted by the purveyors of monarchical reformism into abandoning its true

89. Ozerov, *Politika*, pp. 225–28; *Osvobozhdenie*, no. 20/21 (April 18, 1903); Sviatlovskii, pp. 58–59; *S.-Peterburgskiia vedomosti*, March 6, 1902.

90. Ozerov, *Politika*, pp. 224, 227–28.

91. M. Grigor'evskii [M. G. Lunts], "Politseiskii sotsializm v Rossii," *Obrazovanie*, 15 (Jan. 1906), 198. Morskoi (p. 77) commented on the statutes in a similar fashion: "At a time when in general obstacles were placed in the way of any union-type organization be it of workers, peasants, or intelligentsia, only the mechanical workers of Moscow at the will of the royal governor-general were awarded the right of 'self-determination.'"

benefactors and leaders; for conservatives in industry and the bureaucracy the vast gathering of factory workers was an unhealthy precedent which would surely end in disorderly street demonstrations if repeated.

The Moscow authorities could hardly have chosen a more inauspicious time to demonstrate the contention that the working class could be welded into a loyal instrument of the autocracy. In late January 1902 student agitation had begun again at Moscow University, this time with a more pronounced political character.[92] On February 5, Sipiagin warned the Moscow governor-general by telegraph that street demonstrations were expected and spelled out strict preventative measures to be taken forthwith. Troops were dispatched to the large factories to isolate the workers from the students; a large rally at Moscow University on February 9 was broken up by the police and the participants arrested.[93] On that day students made two unsuccessful attempts on Trepov's life.[94] The city was tense in anticipation of imminent disorders;[95] permission for the factory workers to assemble and march en masse to the Kremlin was beyond expectation. All the more surprising was the choice of February 19, a day the revolutionary intelligentsia appropriated yearly for its own political demonstrations; in fact, since celebration of the day was prohibited, precautionary arrests were made throughout the country several days beforehand to thwart demonstrations.[96]

The celebration was scheduled by the Moscow administration as "a first test" to prove that in even such anxious times the working class could be trusted to demonstrate under the direction of its own

92. "Studencheskie volneniia v 1901–1902 gg.," *Krasnyi arkhiv*, 1938, no. 4-5 (89–90), p. 276; Kheraskov, "Reminiscences," p. 228; Spiridovich, *Zapiski zhandarma*, p. 86; Burch, pp. 121–22.

93. "Studencheskie volneniia v 1901–1902 gg.," pp. 278–83; *Times* (London), March 1, 6, 26, 1902; [F. I. Dan], *Doklad delegatsii Rossiiskoi Sots.-Dem. Rabochei Partii Amsterdamskomu Mezhdunarodnomu Sotsialisticheskomu Kongressu (14–20 avgusta 1904 g.)* (Geneva, 1904), p. 32; Martov, in *Istoriia Rossii v XIX veke*, VIII, 121; Shmeleva, Moscow *Uchenye zapiski*, p. 50. Members of the Society of Machine Workers were urged at district meetings to avoid student demonstrations. Rumors circulated throughout Moscow that demonstrators would be arrested and banished; Zubatov to Zvolianskii, Feb. 7, 1902 (Bukhbinder, "Zubatovshchina v Moskve," p. 115); *Osvobozhdenie*, no. 19 (March 19, 1903).

94. Spiridovich, *Zapiski zhandarma*, p. 94.

95. Consul Veillet-Dufrêche to Théophile Delcassé, Minister of Foreign Affairs, March 6, 1902, n.s. (France, Ministère des Affaires Etrangères, Archives Russie).

96. Grigor'evskii, p. 203; Shmeleva, Moscow *Uchenye zapiski*, p. 51.

leaders without disturbing the city's tranquillity.[97] The proposal originated with I. Sokolov, an officer of the council, at a district meeting in Januray 1902; the workers warmly responded to the suggestion, which was adopted at other district meetings.[98] Next the cooperation of the high clergy and Moscow officialdom was sought. Bishop Parfenii readily consented to officiate at the ceremonies. Through Zubatov's intervention, the Grand Duke Sergei held an audience on February 6 with a deputation from the council; both parties were reportedly moved to "songs of exultant love."[99] The celebration to honor the memory of his father was bound to please the grand duke, under whose supervision a statue of Alexander II had been erected in the Kremlin four years earlier.[100] The speech and poem delivered by Slepov on behalf of the workers visibly moved the grand duke, who praised the young labor organization and promised to support its cause.[101] From that moment preparations for the celebration in the Kremlin went on feverishly day and night, although there were still obstacles to be surmounted; agreement was necessary from the local factory owners, the Petersburg officials, and the very workers who were to participate. Several days prior to the proposed celebration, Afanas'ev and other officers of the council toured the major Moscow factories, peremptorily announcing that no work would be done on February 19. The factory directors were reluctant to comply. February 19 was not a legal holiday, and they objected to having to pay workers who might remain away on that day.

The Moscow administration upheld the demand of the council leaders; on the eve of the celebration an order to free from work all who wished to join the demonstration went out to the inspectors

97. Zubatov to Burtsev, March 5, 1908 (Koz'min, pp. 86–87); Zubatov's talk to the Moscow industrialists, July 26, 1902 (*Osvobozhdenie*, no. 8 [Oct. 2, 1902]).

98. Both Slepov and Spiridovich maintained that the initiative for the mass meeting came from the workers; *Russkoe delo*, July 23, 1905; *Mladorosskaia iskra*, Feb. 25, 1934.

99. Zubatov to Zvolianskii, Feb. 7, 1902 (Bukhbinder, "Zubatovshchina v Moskve," p. 114). In a letter to his brother, the Grand Duke Pavel Aleksandrovich, the Grand Duke Sergei mentioned the meeting and expressed doubts about the Zubatovshchina: "The affair is *very* interesting, serious—I will even say *dangerous* —double edged, but in my extreme opinion it is *necessary* at the present time" (Solov'ev, p. 158).

100. Avchinnikov, p. 30; Veillet-Dufrêche to Delcassé, March 6, 1902. n.s.

101. Bukhbinder, "Zubatovshchina v Moskve," pp. 114–15; *Russkoe delo*, July 23, 1905; *Moskovskiia vedomosti*, Feb. 7, 1902.

and the factory directors. On the morning of February 19 the factory gates were opened early as usual; in most cases the workers stayed at their places until 9:00 A.M., when they left and joined the procession headed for the Kremlin. [102]

Zubatov alone among Moscow officials appeared perfectly confident the celebration would pass without incident. Even Trepov, who had been a pillar of support for Zubatov, hesitated to sanction the gathering; on a workers' petition requesting permission for the demonstration he wrote: "Not to prevent but also not to permit." [103] Trepov "did not believe in the possibility of a peaceful outcome" to the demonstration, nor was he completely convinced that Cossacks should not be held in readiness near the Kremlin walls. [104] The Petersburg authorities were also reluctant to sanction the gathering and gave their permission at the very last moment when events had already been set in motion. [105]

The strictest precautions were taken to prevent penetration by socialist agitators. Police and members of the Society of Machine Workers stood guard at the Kremlin gates, permitting only workers to enter. Inside, patrols of trusted workers maintained order. Beginning in the early morning a throng of workers estimated at between 30,000 and 80,000—the most common estimate put their number at 50,000—quietly gathered before the statue of Alexander II. Many others were not permitted inside because of the overcrowding. At no time during the course of the ceremonies was there the "least disorder or interference" with the proceedings. [106]

---

102. Veillet-Dufrêche to Delcassé, March 6, 1902, n.s.; *S.-Peterburgskiia vedomosti,* Feb. 21, 1902; *Russkoe delo,* Feb. 5, July 23, 1905; *Osvobozhdenie,* no. 19 (March 19, 1903). Many factory owners apparently refused to obey the Grand Duke Sergei's order to close their plants. *Rabochie Trekhgornoi manufaktury,* p. 194. Critics of the Zubatovshchina maintained that compulsion and a variety of inducements were used to gain the workers' participation. *Revoliutsionnaia Rossiia,* no. 6 (May 1902); I. A. Shmeleva, "Bor'ba sotsial-demokraticheskikh organizatsii Moskvy s zubatovshchinoi," Shuiskii gosudarstvennyi pedagogicheskii institut, *Uchenye zapiski,* pt. 8 (1959), p. 145; Witte to Sipiagin, March 6, 1902 (Bukhbinder, "Zubatovshchina v Moskve," p. 119); F. Dan, *Iz istorii rabochago dvizheniia i sotsialdemokratii v Rossii 1900–1904 gg.,* 2d ed. (n.p., n.d.), p. 43.

103. Ignat'ev, p. 31.

104. Zubatov to Burtsev, March 5, 1908 (Koz'min, p. 87).

105. *Osvobozhdenie,* no. 19 (March 19, 1903). Ignat'ev (p. 31) states that preparations for the celebration were kept secret from the government.

106. *Osvobozhdenie,* no. 19; *Russkoe delo,* July 23, 1905; Veillet-Dufrêche to Delcassé, March 6, 1902 n.s.; Koz'min, p. 87. A Petersburg reporter gained access to the Kremlin only with the greatest difficulty, having been first turned away with the

The ceremonies were of a markedly religious and patriotic character. They began with services conducted by Bishop Parfenii in the Kremlin's Chudov (Miracle) Monastery in the presence of a delegation of workers and high state dignitaries from the city and province of Moscow. With the arrival of the Grand Duke Sergei, the congregation moved toward the statue of Tsar Alexander II, led by the clergy bearing holy ikons. A requiem mass was performed to the memory of the departed tsar, wreaths were laid by the workers at the base of the statue, and prayers were offered to the health of the Imperial family, followed by the playing of "God Save the Tsar." Cries of "hurrah" resounded throughout the Kremlin as thousands of caps were flung in the air in answer to the hymn and words of gratitude expressed to the workers by the grand duke. By noon the services were over and the workers slowly filed past the statue and out of the Kremlin. In the evening the celebration continued with dances and parties for the workers and their families.[107]

In any other country, solemn ceremonies honoring the memory of a deceased ruler would have aroused but passing interest; in Russia they were a minor sensation, challenging popular assumptions on the nature of the Russian working class. To the radical intelligentsia, accustomed since the mid-1890's to the militancy of labor, the conservatism of the working class and its rededication of loyalty to church and state came as a shock. Sharing the surprise were most officials charged with maintaining internal order, to whom the mass gathering seemed an open invitation to political demonstration.

This celebration was Zubatov's greatest triumph, which the revolutionary press freely, if begrudgingly, acknowledged. *Revoliutsionnaia Rossiia* (Revolutionary Russia), the organ of the Socialist Revolutionaries, for example, wrote in comment: "To a holiday which might only bear the character of a protest against the government, he [Zubatov] succeeded in imparting the aspect of unity between the workers and the government."[108] In a second article in the same organ, attributed to the terrorist Boris Savinkov, Zubatov was credited with having turned the revolutionary tide among the factory proletariat: "On those very streets, where a year ago a crowd broke

---

order: "The intelligentsia will not be allowed inside" (*S.-Peterburgskiia vedomosti*, Feb. 21, 1902).

107. *S.-Peterburgskiia vedomosti*, Feb. 21, 1902; *Russkiia vedomosti*, Feb. 20, 1902; *Moskovskiia vedomosti*, Feb. 20, 21, 1902. A fictionalized account of the festivities in the Kremlin is given in Gorkii, II, 299–314.

108. *Revoliutsionnaia Rossiia*, no. 5 (March 1902).

the grating and toppled over trolley cars, ... preparing for barricades, thousands of workers appeared who humbly celebrated February 19 before Zubatov's eyes."[109] Similar sentiments were expressed in *Zhizn'* (Life), an independent journal of social-democratic leanings published in London. Contrasting the mood of the workers assembled in the Kremlin with that of the Moscow students and factory workers during the street demonstrations of the previous February, it lamented: "now the most progressive part of these people—the machine construction workers—publicly fraternize with tsarism."[110]

The Kremlin celebration was additional proof of the impotence of Moscow social democracy and a further sign that the working class was not yet ready to cast in its lot with those out to overthrow the age-old monarchy. On February 15, *Iskra* had published with the party's blessing a proclamation signed by "A Local Organization of 'Iskra'" attacking Zubatov's tactics and the government's labor policy and calling for public demonstrations for political freedom throughout Russia on February 19. The proclamation had originated with the Moscow Social Democratic Committee, which planned to lead workers and students in a repetition of the Moscow street disorders of the previous year.[111] When the committee learned the Society of Machine Workers had appropriated the day for a patriotic manifestation, it distributed leaflets calling on the workers to boycott the Kremlin festivities. To its disappointment the workers did not heed its advice; having failed to halt the Kremlin demonstration, Moscow Social Democrats could do little but impugn and belittle the significance of the event.[112] Many skeptics who feared the consequences of a mass gathering of workers were won over by the Kremlin demonstration. Trepov returned from the ceremonies moved to tears; the Grand Duke Sergei was reported to have experi-

109. *Ibid.*, no. 31 (Sept. 1, 1903). The article, entitled "Makkiaveli okhrannago otdeleniia (Konets zubatovshchiny)," was reprinted in *Sbornik statei Antonova (i dr.)*, pp. 115–25, with Savinkov given as the author.

110. K-tsyi, "Politseiskii sotsializm i sotsialdemokratiia," *Zhizn'*, May 1902. For examples of similar statements made by Soviet writers see B. Kolesnikov, *Profsoiuzy v Rossii* (Kharkov, 1926), p. 25; M. Miliutina, "Kratkii ocherk istorii moskovskoi organizatsii," *Put' k Oktiabriu*, no. 2 (1923), p. 17.

111. *Iskra*, no. 17 (Feb. 15, 1902); P. A. Garvi, *Vospominaniia sotsialdemokrata* (New York, 1946), pp. 185–86.

112. Shmeleva, Shuia *Uchenye zapiski*, p. 145; Piontkovskii, pp. 80–81; *Iskrovskii period v Moskve*, pp. 77–78, 125–28.

enced similar feelings.[113] P. I. Rachkovskii, chief of the Russian secret service abroad, sent expressly by the Petersburg authorities to observe the Kremlin ceremonies, reported to his superiors his astonishment at the exemplary conduct of the workers.[114]

The conservative *Moskovskiia vedomosti* (Moscow Gazette) in its editorial pages rhapsodized over the Kremlin ceremonies as a magnificent display of loyalty and faith to tsar and church by the true Russian people. Continuing its support of the young Society of Machine Workers, it urged the government to avoid the labor troubles besetting Western Europe and reward the working class by energetically taking steps to improve its well-being.[115] The correspondent of *S.-Peterburgskiia vedomosti* hailed the celebration in words similar to those the socialist press used out of despair: "From a holiday of the intelligentsia, February 19 was finally turned into a holiday of the people. Without doubt this is a step on the road to declaring the great day a national holiday."[116]

Zubatov acted rapidly to apply the meaning of the Kremlin events to the entire working-class movement. A brochure, "The Significance of 19 February for the Moscow Workers," written anonymously and at Zubatov's request by Lev Tikhomirov, described the Kremlin ceremonies as a victory for the maturing national consciousness of the Russian people and a rebuff to the radical intelligentsia, which allegedly had tried in vain to disrupt the proceedings and turn the people against the autocracy.[117] To their credit the workers had revealed a growing consciousness, refusing to betray their ancient faith and true Russian loyalty to church and autocracy. The free Russian people did not wish to see their country become another France or United States, as the intelligentsia, whose roots

113. Zubatov to Burtsev, March 5, 1908 (Koz'min, p. 87); Zubatov's July 26 talk to the Moscow industrialists (*Osvobozhdenie*, no. 8 [Oct. 2, 1902]). On February 19, Trepov telegraphed the Department of Police: "The patriotic manifestation of the workers numbering up to 60 thousand took place brilliantly and in astonishing order" (Korelin, "Russkii 'politseiskii sotsializm,'" p. 42).

114. Liubimov, p. 26; Spiridovich, "Pri tsarskom rezhime," p. 151. For the reaction of a conservative to the Moscow events, see Solov'ev, p. 158.

115. *Moskovskiia vedomosti*, Feb. 26, 1902. The editorial was probably written by Lev Tikhomirov, an editor of the paper and a close collaborator of Zubatov.

116. *S.-Peterburgskiia vedomosti*, Feb. 21, 1902. Zubatov must surely have been pleased by the correspondent from *Figaro*, who concluded that the demonstration in the Kremlin "shows the power and profound respect for the monarchical regime in Russia" (quoted in *Moskovskiia vedomosti*, March 14, 1902).

117. Zubatov to Burtsev, March 5, 1908 (Koz'min, p. 87).

lay outside Russian soil, desired. The workers had refused to become enserfed to the aims of the intelligentsia and had vindicated the paternal faith shown by the Moscow grand duke and chief of police, who had granted them independent organizational activity. By their responsible behavior the Moscow workers had convinced others of their capacity and readiness to manage their own affairs, Tikhomirov concluded.[118]

Not all of the higher Petersburg authorities were so convinced. In particular there was dismay that broad newspaper coverage might have misled the public to believe the Kremlin ceremonies indicated that the government had adopted a new course in the labor question. To halt speculation a confidential circular denying such an interpretation was sent by the Chief Office on Matters of the Press of the Ministry of Interior on February 26 to all governors:

> To this completely local celebration ... some organs of the press attach the character of an important event which has very great public significance, serving as an expression of the awakening social consciousness of the working masses, and an indication of official recognition of a special class of workers among us. Such an explanation of the above-mentioned event, in essence untrue and extremely tendentious, must not by any means be permitted in the censored press. The generalization of an individual fact and the imparting to it of the character of an all-Russian event must not be allowed.[119]

February 19, then, turned out to be a hollow victory for Zubatov, who had hoped that the Moscow labor experiment would serve as a model for the entire empire. Petersburg's negative response was based on reports of the Zubatovshchina's militancy from factory inspectors, the Moscow industrialists, and the Ministry of Finance. To the critics of the Society of Machine Workers and its council, the increase in strikes in Moscow was encouraged by the local authorities. These charges led to an interministerial dispute at the highest level, in which the Grand Duke Sergei and Trepov were hard-pressed in Petersburg to defend their protégé.

## The Clergy Replaces the Intelligentsia

Unrelenting pressure from the Moscow industrial community and the Ministry of Finance eventually caused Zubatov to change

---

118. The brochure was reprinted in *Byloe*, no. 14, 1912, pp. 81–88.
119. "Iz nedalekago proshlago," *Byloe*, Feb. 1907, p. 143.

tactics in defense of his program. The abortive alliance with the intelligentsia had made him vulnerable to conservative criticism. Zubatov now sought an irreproachable ally, impregnable to criticism from Petersburg; he found it in the "spiritual intelligentsia," the clergy.[120]

Beginning with the Kremlin solemnities of February 19, 1902, Zubatov increasingly utilized the Orthodox faith and its clergy for his own ends. Traditional motifs of loyalty to altar and throne were stressed in the literature he subsidized for distribution among the workers. He also encouraged the clergy to participate in the Moscow Society of Mutual Assistance of Workers in Textile Production and a similar labor society founded in St. Petersburg.

Zubatov and his cohorts were successful in their campaign to enlist the active support of the Moscow clergy. Writing on February 2, 1902, to his Petersburg superiors, he described the local clergy as sympathetic to his labor program: "Obviously the new movement not only has been growing without being dangerous, but is the best school of monarchial education."[121] Zubatov was then planning a coordinated program of lectures for the Moscow workers under the canopy of the Orthodox church.

Public lectures by the Orthodox clergy were quite common in Moscow. During 1899 and 1900, 772 religious readings and talks were delivered by churchmen in Moscow under the auspices of the Commission for the Organization of Public Popular Readings.[122] In addition, Moscow industrialists frequently invited the clergy to their factories to conduct church services and to lecture to their workers on moral and religious themes.

The lectures for the machine workers had been too popular to be abandoned permanently by the Moscow administration. On June 16, 1902, the auditorium of the Historical Museum once again overflowed as a new series of Sunday readings and lectures for workers was inaugurated by the Moscow Society of Mutual Help of

120. "In order to save the organization formed by the efforts of the workers, there remained an appeal for the assistance of the spiritual intelligentsia, which was fulfilled" (Zubatov, "Iz nedavniago proshlago," p. 435).

121. Vovchik, p. 119.

122. *Russkiia vedomosti*, April 25, 1902; L. M. Ivanov, "Proletariat i samoderzhavie: Nekotorye voprosy ideologicheskogo vozdeistviia tsarizma na rabochikh," in *Proletariat Rossii na puti k Oktiabriu 1917 goda* (Odessa, 1967), I, 98; M. N. Belov, "Kulturnyi oblik rabochikh tsentral'noi Rossii nakanune pervoi russkoi revoliutsii," in *ibid.*, II, 138.

Workers in Mechanical Factories. Although Afanas'ev, repesenting the machine workers, and Trepov were present on the dais, the clergy were in the majority and dominated the proceedings, which took on the coloring of a religious observance. Celebrated thaumaturgical ikons were displayed to the audience, a prayer was offered by the metropolitan of Moscow, the priest Iosif Fudel spoke on the subject of "Christian Faith," and the national hymn closed the meeting. Metropolitan Vladimir addressed the gathering, announcing the inauguration of two series of weekly lectures, one devoted to religious and moral themes, the other to topics of general education. [123]

The program was under the supervision of a Commission for the Establishment of Readings for Workers, presided over by Bishop Parfenii. As first constituted, the theological section was administered by the Archimandrite Anastasii, rector of the Moscow Theological Seminary, and Iosif Fudel, a priest in the deportation prison church. The historical section was headed by V. V. Nazarevskii, chairman of the Moscow censorial committee; the section on physics by V. A. Bogdanov, director of applied physics at the Polytechnical Museum; the section on hygiene by V. E. Ignat'ev, senior lecturer at Moscow University and the only holdover from the lectures given the previous year. M. I. Struzhentsov of the Moscow Theological Seminary served as secretary to the commission. Other lecturers during the first year included the conservative historian D. I. Ilovaiskii (Byzantine history), V. I. Khitrov (Russian geography), E. V. Barsov (Russian folk literature), and the priest N. A. Liubimov (who also lectured on Russian folk literature). A. A. Tikhomirov, the rector of Moscow University, later joined the commission and lectured on zoology.

Some of Zubatov's followers, including Afanas'ev, Krasivskii, and Fedor Ignat'ev, were recruited as lecturers and remained with the program for a number of years. Lev Tikhomirov was a frequent lecturer. Financial support came from special funds assigned to the commission by the Grand Duke Sergei; in 1904 they amounted to 25,000 rubles. The lectures took place on Sundays in the Historical Museum and in church auditoriums, the latter locale being indicative of their new tenor. During the first twelve months of its

---

123. *Russkiia vedomosti*, June 17, 1902; *Moskovskiia vedomosti*, June 17, 1902; Aug. 1, 1903; *Rodnaia rech'*, June 23, 1902.

existence the commission sponsored 170 lectures for workers, of which 92 were on theology, 30 on history, 23 on physics, 11 each on folk literature and geography, and 3 on geology.[124]

Its subject matter assured the new program greater longevity than the previous lecture series. Gone were themes on the daily life of the workers and on methods of labor organization: gone, too, were the frank and intimate discussions between the intelligentsia and the working class. In their place were meetings "conducted according to a definite program, which presents in totality a systematic revelation of the basic truths of the Orthodox Christian faith and moral admonition."[125] The lectures on Russian history stressed the principles of "Orthodox faith, tsarist authority, and the strong national spirit and way of life."[126] Thus in the early days of the twentieth century, when Russia was undergoing great economic and social change, the doctrine of Official Nationality was still relied upon to maintain peace between the lower classes and the existing order.

Each meeting, which was open to all factory workers, included the singing of religious hymns by a workers' chorus and the traditional "God Save the Tsar." The first half was given over to a lecture on a religious topic, the second half to general education subjects. In the words of *Moskovskiia vedomosti*, which gave the meetings favorable publicity, "the theological readings almost come to a complete systematic course in Orthodox dogmatic theology."[127] Those who directed the readings hoped that, while avoiding general polemics, the lectures would "nevertheless become a very real means to stave off the success of anti-Church propaganda among the workers."[128] During the first three years, some twenty-five members of the Moscow clergy and teachers at the ecclesiastical schools lectured to the workers.[129]

Orthodoxy and loyalty to the throne also permeated lectures on history. Traditional values were emphasized:

124. Laverychev, p. 154; *Moskovskiia vedomosti*, June 17, Aug. 16, Oct. 27, 1902; June 17, Aug. 1, 1903; *Russkiia vedomosti*, June 17, 1902; *Russkoe delo*, July 30, 1905; *Rodnaia rech'*, Oct. 19, 1903; *V staroi Moskve*, p. 260; Ivanov, pp. 57, 91–92; L. Tikhomirov, "25 let nazad," pp. 23–24, 27, 97–98; "Iz besedy s Mariei Aristarkhovnoi Igantovoi," in Mitskevich, ed., *Na zare rabochego dvizheniia*, p. 212.

125. *Moskovskiia vedomosti*, Oct. 27, 1902.

126. Laverychev, p. 153.

127. *Moskovskiia vedomosti*, Aug. 16, 1902; see also the issues of June 25, 30, Oct. 27, 1902; *V staroi Moskve*, p. 260.

128. *Moskovskiia vedomosti*, Nov. 16, 1902; Jan. 11, 1903.

129. *V staroi Moskve*, p. 261.

clear, defined, and firm views on life, in agreement with the Russian Orthodox national ideal. Accordingly, in general, at the base of all the educational programs lies the expression of the truths of the holy Orthodox faith and the workers' acquaintance with the history of their native land, its historic destiny and contemporary situation.

Organizing readings for workers in the spirit of the primordial principles of Russian national life—devotion to the holy Orthodox faith and autocratic Tsarist authority, love of one's country and nationality—believing the object of such readings to be to raise and strengthen in the listeners Russian Orthodox national self-consciousness, the Commission, one must recognize, has adapted the organization of the readings and lectures, giving equal weight to the spiritual nature of Russian man and the life and urgent needs of the time.[130]

In essence, then, the lectures were an opiate for the people. The lectures on history, for example, were designed to arouse patriotic feelings among workers temporarily removed from their depressing environments. Enthusiastically endorsing the lectures, a reporter for *Moskovskiia vedomosti* described their effect on the workers: "These people, torn away from machines with cold, heartless steel wheels, forgetting for some hours material cares about their families, feel themselves not in the least friendless nor abandoned in the crater of the big city, which has endured thousands of lonely lives."[131]

The commission hoped that the message of the lectures would reach the more than 100,000 workers living in Moscow and its suburbs, and toward this end lectures were printed for distribution at the weekly meetings. Other brochures and pamphlets of a religious-patriotic nature, including the writings of the ultra-conservative General A. V. Bogdanovich, were also made available to the workers.[132]

Moscow conservative society heartily approved the new program. On the stage of the auditorium, lending the weight of their authority and prestige to the lectures, appeared honored guests conspicuous by their frock coats, military uniforms, and silk cassocks.[133] A set of "Temporary Rules on the Organization of the Readings" received the approval of the Minister of Interior. In May 1903, Tsar Nicholas wrote to Bishop Parfenii that he was "very happy" at the success of

130. *Moskovskiia vedomosti*, Aug. 21, 1903.
131. *Ibid.*, July 11, 1902.
132. *Ibid.*, Oct. 29, 1902; Jan. 21, June 17, Aug. 1, 1903; *Russkiia vedomosti*, Aug. 26, 1902.
133. *Moskovskiia vedomosti*, July 11, Oct. 21, 1902.

the lectures and hoped "that the readings, which are conducted under the canopy of the holy Church and with the participation of its servants, will also have such success henceforward."[134] Little wonder that the conservative press gave wide coverage and unstinting editorial praise to the lecture series.

The popularity of the lectures among the Moscow workers is difficult to assess, although there are some indications that interest in them dropped off sharply in time. The first few meetings were fully attended; a report on the lectures in the Historical Museum during the first year maintained that from 500 to 700 workers attended each meeting.[135] A large proportion of the audience was composed of women, a group whose role in the Moscow Zubatovshchina was otherwise not noted.[136]

The lectures begun under Zubatov's prompting continued until the outbreak of World War I. Undoubtedly the monarchy supported them as a platform to propagandize its ideals among the factory masses. A Soviet historian surveying the institutions and organizations the monarchy used to influence the working class ideologically during the reigns of Alexander III and Nicholas II concluded that these lectures were the "most militant" in the struggle against social democracy.[137]

The lecture series reflected Zubatov's move toward traditional Russian conservatism. The Moscow machine workers' council had become too militant for the Petersburg authorities and was forced to terminate its advocatory role on behalf of working-class demands. The Guzhon affair was the turning point in the council's history.

134. *V staroi Moskve*, p. 260; *Moskovskiia vedomosti*, May 6, 1903.

135. *Moskovskiia vedomosti*, June 17, 1903. At the other two auditoriums where lectures were conducted, attendance varied from 200 to 500 and from 300 to 600 respectively. More than 700 workers attended the meeting of June 23, 1902. It was reported in October 1902 that the meetings were popular and attended by overflow crowds. Two hundred and fifty workers attended a meeting in the Historical Museum in the spring of 1907 to hear Lev Tikhomirov lecture on socialism. Slepov maintained that the workers were little interested in the new lecture series because of its almost exclusively religious character (*Moskovskiia vedomosti*, June 25, Oct. 27, 1902; Tikhomirov, p. 98; *Russkoe delo*, July 30, 1905).

136. *Moskovskiia vedomosti*, July 1, 15, 1902.

137. Ivanov, p. 91. After 1905 the lectures reverted to themes like the labor movement in Western Europe and emphasized opposition to the use of force by the working class (*Torgovo-promyshlennaia gazeta*, March 10, 1906).

# CHAPTER 5

# The Guzhon Affair

The lectures given by the intelligentsia in the summer and fall of 1901 had been of practical interest to the machine workers. Gathering at district meetings in their local pubs and tearooms, they debated a wide range of subjects that touched their lives and at times endorsed proposals for factory legislation. In September 1901, for example, workers at a district meeting considered proposals to shorten the workday, intending to make a recommendation on the issue to the general assembly of machine workers; in October a petition on behalf of a shorter workday was circulated among the workers.[1]

Council officials attending the district meetings did not always encourage restraint. At times their speeches even bore strong anticapitalist overtones, ingrained in long years of activity as labor organizers and associations with social democracy. Sharp words against the capitalist class naturally appealed to the workers while reassuring them that the officers were not lackeys of the factory owners. Krasivskii, for one, often spoke of the antagonism between capital and labor. "Our factory owners are at present a force; they hold us in [their] hands, but organizing into a fraternal society we also will be strong and can overcome them," he boldly told a meeting of machine workers in September 1901.[2] On other occasions he sharply attacked the capitalists as "bloodsuckers" and dwelt on the natural disharmony between labor and capital, citing in support that "great scholar Karl Marx, who dedicated all of his life to

1. Ainzaft, *Zubatovshchina*, p. 52. Afanas'ev strongly opposed the petition; Bukhbinder, "K istorii zubatovshchiny," p. 177.
2. Bukhbinder, *ibid.*, p. 196; see also Sher, p. 134; *Iskra*, no. 32 (Jan. 15, 1903); Golodets, p. 59.

the workers."[3] Slepov, the most conservative officer of the council in terms of his allegiance to the ideology of Official Nationality, was guilty of inciting the workers by false statements. According to Slepov the government intended to establish an eight-hour day and turn the factories over to the workers; reports that the government would give the workers capital to take over the factories was seriously discussed by the workers at the Prokhorov plant.[4]

The officers of the council could boast of the Grand Duke Sergei's support, which apparently guaranteed their followers they could with impunity bring economic pressure to bear on their employers. As a consequence during the first four months of 1902 the Moscow labor movement under the tutelage of the workers' council took on a new militancy. The district meetings became an outlet for specific complaints and charges against the administrations of factories and railway shops. Petitions bearing particulars of abuses and malpractices were drawn up by the workers and brought to the council for forwarding to the factory inspector; since the inspectors were under orders from the Ministry of Finance not to accept petitions from the council, they were sent instead to Trepov's office. Complaints listed unsanitary toilet facilities, arbitrary lowering of piece-rates, lengthening of the workday without additional compensation, and fraudulent computation of the contracted wage.[5]

Trepov it will be recalled, had exerted the pressure of his office to enforce observance of the factory laws; under the prodding of the council he once again took up the cudgels in defense of the Moscow working class. Aware that the council had Trepov's approval, some factory owners took the line of least resistance and complied with

3. Varnashev, pp. 183–84. At a meeting of workers associated with the council a speaker was quoted as saying: "We have two enemies—our bloodsuckers—the capitalists and the revolutionaries, who for their own advantage confuse you, trying to take advantage of your economic oppression. But you also have two friends—objective science and the tsarist government. Direct your blows at these our true oppressors, and the government will take care that your struggle against them will be successful" (*Rabochaia mysl'*, no. 14 [Jan. 1902]).

4. *Rabochie Trekhgornoi manufaktury*, pp. 32, 161; *Iskra*, no. 19 (April 1, 1902); Piontkovskii, p. 98; *Russkoe delo*, March 19, 1905. It was alleged that during the ceremonies in the Kremlin on February 19, 1902, Slepov addressed the workers as follows: "The government promises you an eight hour day. It will in due course take all the factories into its hands and give them to you. For this a constitution is not necessary—on the contrary only the autocratic government can do it; the intelligentsia needs a constitution but you do not" (Baturin, p. 75).

5. Ainzaft *Zubatovshchina*, pp. 53–54, 64; Bukhbinder, *Zubatovshchina*, pp. 9–10; *Torgovo-promyshlennaia gazeta*, Feb. 14, 1906; Ozerov, *Politika*, p. 206.

the workers' demands. Physical search of employees entering and leaving the plant—a practice deeply resented by the workers—was ended at several of the large Moscow factories; at some plants concessions were made in wages and hours.[6] The Moscow workers surely appreciated these gains, for at the time Russian industry was undergoing an economic crisis resulting in unemployment and lower wages.

The Okhrana under Zubatov made it a practice to have an officer on duty on Sunday afternoons to whom the workers could bring petitions and complaints and with whom they could consult on their legal rights. Then, with competent legal advice available from a corps of lawyers headed by Vilents, the workers were encouraged to take the slow legal road through the courts for the redress of their grievances. The number of collective grievances reached extreme proportions in the first three months of 1902; during the next two to three years the Moscow courts were jammed with suits against the factory owners.[7]

The annual reports of the factory inspectors chronicled a precipitous rise in formal grievances filed by the Moscow workers, indicating to the inspectors a worsening of labor relations in Moscow. During 1902 the number of industrial enterprises against which collective labor complaints were filed rose by 10.6 per cent over the preceding year, the greatest increase occurring in Moscow *guberniia*, where they increased 47.6 per cent, from 813 to 1,200. The percentage of collective complaints judged by the inspectors to be without validity also rose; only 37.5 per cent of the workers' complaints processed by the factory inspectors in Moscow *guberniia* during 1902 proved to be substantiated, as against 72 per cent the previous year.[8] The inspectors' reports for 1902 implicitly blamed the Moscow administration for the increasing number of unjustified grievances lodged by the workers: "All these unfavorable circumstances coincide with a certain movement among the workers in

6. Bukhbinder, *Zubatovshchina*, p. 10; Bukhbinder, "Zubatovshchina v Moskve," pp. 100–101; Shmeleva, Moscow *Uchenye zapiski*, p. 39; Semenov-Bulkin, pp. 9–10; *Russkiia vedomosti*, June 14, 1902; *Torgovo-promyshlennaia gazeta*, July 17, 1901.

7. *Rabochii vopros v komissii V. N. Kokovtsova*, p. 193; Ozerov, *Politika*, p. 234. The most common causes of complaint were harsh treatment by the foremen and the computation of piecework payments on occasions when the owner either withheld materials or gave the workers faulty ones to work on (*Russkiia vedomosti*, March 2, 1902).

8. *Svod otchetov fabrichnykh inspektorov za 1902 god*, pp. xiii, xv.

the course of the current year, which most sharply came to light in Moscow *guberniia* and apparently was the cause for the outbreak of a whole series of similar demands, which had not existed earlier and [were] not always well-grounded, made by the workers to the management of industrial establishments."[9]

There was, however, foundation in fact, investigation revealed, for charges of cruel treatment and physical beatings inflicted by members of the factory administration. In Moscow *guberniia* in 1902, 2,098 such cases were reported, of which 95 per cent proved to be well-grounded, as against 56 per cent the previous year. From these facts the Moscow *okrug* (district) inspector drew the following inference: "The comparison of such a significant increase of complaints of cruel treatment in Moscow *guberniia* with the increase in the degree of their validity leads to the likely conclusion that the workers, under the influence of the above-mentioned movement, have become more strict with regard to the conduct of managers of enterprises and owners and begun to lodge complaints against actions which in former times they disregarded."[10]

The council's new function of promoting the economic interests of its membership and its attendant close ties with the Moscow chief of police were spelled out in a new set of draft statutes for the Society of Machine Workers forwarded to Trepov for approval some time in early 1902. Here the council's goals and functions were considerably broader than those set forth in the Instructions Trepov had approved the previous fall. Most crucial were the articles making the council a party to labor disputes; although inconsistent and restrictive, they nevertheless would have incurred the wrath of the Moscow industrialists and the factory inspectors. Some concession was made, however, to conservative opinion. Whenever the council, in pursuit of its goals, impinged upon the interests of the factory owners it was required to act "with the voluntary agreement of the latter, and without adverse effects on the flourishing of industrial enterprise," a clause no doubt added with the thought of appeasing the Ministry of Finance.[11]

No such consideration impeded the council's power to investigate factory disputes; according to articles 11 and 12, it was "obliged on demand of the Moscow chief of police to assist the [Moscow]

9. *Ibid.*, p. xv.
10. *Ibid.*, p. xviii.
11. Morskoi, p. 73.

administration in the elucidation and settling by peaceful and legal means of misunderstandings which arise between workers and owners at factories and plants," dispatching its officers to the scene of labor disputes for this purpose.[12] With the agreement of the factory owner the council could "enter into relations with the administration of factories and plants to bring about a mutual settlement of all misunderstandings which have risen between the workers and owners."[13] The wording of the statutes left it unclear whether the council at such times was to negotiate in a disinterested fashion between capital and labor or to act as a bargaining agent for the workers. Article 10 would have given the council the right to petition the Moscow chief of police on behalf of workers, sanctioning what existed in practice.

Although these statutes were never officially approved, the council operated in the first few months of 1902 as if it had received such broad powers.[14] Thus encouraged, the workers began to act more militantly to gain their demands, not excluding the use of the strike weapon. The council, moreover, had ambitions to represent and lead the entire Moscow working class, not just the machine workers; in the beginning of March it rented headquarters and renamed itself the Council of Workers of the City of Moscow.[15]

The labor movement set in motion by Zubatov did not remain restricted to machine workers. As news spread of the economic benefits they had gained, Moscow workers in other professions —button makers, joiners, box makers, confectioners, tobacco workers, perfumers, and printers — petitioned for administrative

12. *Ibid.*; Shmeleva, Moscow *Uchenye zapiski*, p. 39.

13. Morskoi, pp. 73–74.

14. Slepov, writing in *Moskovskiia vedomosti*, July 9, 1903, held that the council never had official sanction. The statutes were printed in full in *Byloe*, no. 14, 1912, pp. 89–91, and Morskoi, pp. 71–75. According to the *Byloe* source these statutes were drawn up on the basis of article 16 of the council's Instructions that were approved by Trepov on October 11, 1901. That article states that the council could petition the Moscow chief of police for changes or additions to the Instructions. Ainzaft (*Zubatovshchina*, p. 39) maintained that these statutes, which were given to Trepov in 1902, are for a Society of Workers of Mechanical Factories of the City of Moscow and are different from those of the Society of Mutual Help. Morskoi (p. 76) maintained that these statutes were not acceptable to Trepov. Shmeleva (Moscow *Uchenye zapiski*, p. 39) refers to them as the council's statutes, which were worked out in March 1902. Most likely they were the "draft statutes" referred to by Burtsev in his letter to Zubatov on March 11, 1908, and which Zubatov, in reply, admitted were written by Tikhomirov (Koz'min, pp. 83, 85).

15. *Russkoe delo*, July 23, 1905.

approval to organize into mutual-aid societies. The most important of these were the textile workers, the largest single force in the city, among whom Zubatov's supporters had propagated the idea of self-organization toward the end of 1901. On January 3, 1902, Trepov authorized a district assembly for weavers; by the close of the year there were ten district assemblies for the Moscow textile workers in addition to others exclusively for workers at several of the largest textile mills. In February an autonomous Consultative Commission of Weavers was established, affiliated with the council and headed by F. Zhilkin, a protégé of Zubatov. Statutes for a mutual-help society among the textile workers were submitted in June and approved by the Ministry of Interior toward the end of the year.[16]

The textile workers, unskilled and among the poorest-paid factory workers, were viewed by the socialist intelligentsia as more backward and "unconscious" than the mechanical workers. Among the workers attracted to the Moscow Zubatovshchina, however, they proved to be the most militant. Following in the footsteps of the machine workers, they drew up petitions of complaint for presentation to the factory administration, displaying an unusual degree of solidarity in support of their demands. In February, for example, the workers at the Kondrashev silk-weaving mill declared their intention to leave work when the factory administration refused to accede to their demands; only when an officer of the council had obtained concessions from the management through means tantamount to collective bargaining did they agree to continue work.[17]

## Guzhon, Trepov, and the Moscow Council

The Guzhon affair was the *cause célèbre* which removed the council and the Moscow Zubatovshchina from their local context into the limelight and battlefield of national politics and policy. The case revolved around the demands of the weavers at the Guzhon and Mussi plant of the Association of Silk Mills. Its notoriety derived from the intervention of the council and a subsequent clash between the chief of police, who willfully interfered and attempted to extract

16. Ainzaft, *Zubatovshchina*, pp. 58–59; *Russkoe delo*, July 23, 1905; Shmeleva, Moscow *Uchenye zapiski*, p. 40; *Moskovskiia vedomosti*, Aug. 26, 1902.

17. Shmeleva, *ibid*. At the Kolosov weaving mill the council intervened and was able to prevent the discharge of workers, who were demanding a wage increase and a shorter workday.

concessions, and the factory administration, which stubbornly refused to compromise.

The dispute began on February 1, 1902, when two workers who had been given notice of discharge petitioned Trepov and the local factory inspector on behalf of the weavers.[18] Among the demands was an unusual claim for monetary compensation for time during which the weavers had been without work because of what they considered the factory administration's negligence, an amount computed to be 25 per cent of their wages since the previous Easter, or roughly 42,000 rubles. The factory administration refused to concede, and on February 7, 932 weavers gave notice of intent to leave work after passage of the fourteen days required by law.

On the evening of February 14, Zhilkin and Krasivskii, council members from the Consultative Commission of Weavers, appeared at the factory office requesting permission to speak to the workers, ostensibly to pacify them. The two reported back to the factory administration in less than an hour that the weavers had withdrawn their demands and were prepared to continue work under the prevailing factory rules and wage rates until Easter, provided the two discharged workers were rehired. The factory director, Iulii Guzhon, né Jules Goujon (he was French, as was the codirector, Moussy), refused, thereby continuing the dispute.

Unable to reach a satisfactory agreement, the weavers appeared at the factory office on February 21 to receive severance pay. Zhilkin and Krasivskii were to oversee the distribution of payments but were denied entrance on Guzhon's orders, even though Trepov had sent word to have them admitted.[19] Four days later the management gave two weeks' notice of dismissal to 660 other employees, whose labor was dependent on that of the weavers.

On February 26 the directors of the Association of Silk Mills sent a statement of their views on the dispute to both Trepov and the Ministry of Finance. Absolving themselves of all responsibility for strained labor relations at the mill, they warned of possible disorders provoked by the two discharged workers and the two council representatives. These four, in contravention of the law and the

18. The following description is based on the declaration made by the administration of the Association of Silk Mills in Moscow to the Industrial Section (of the Ministry of Finance), March 3, 1902 (Bukhbinder, "Zubatovshchina v Moskve," pp. 126–31); also see *Russkoe delo*, July 30, 1905.

19. Bukhbinder, *ibid.*, pp. 117, 127.

objections of the factory administration, were urging the weavers not to evacuate their living quarters in the factory barracks and to stand guard at the factory gates, forcibly impeding any of their number from defecting and preventing the hiring of new workmen. Under the influence of these irresponsible labor agitators, said the statement, the weavers had become "an extremely restless and dangerous element."[20]

The Moscow administration's close association with and support of the council made it sensitive to the rebuff administered by Guzhon. Trepov, moreover, was irked by the challenge to his personal authority. Responding to the statement the day it was received, Trepov expressed acute dissatisfaction with management's refusal to make concessions and intemperately threatened to order an official inquiry into the mill's compliance with sanitary regulations, violations of which, he warned, would lead to arrest of the factory administration "for a maximum length of time—up to three months."[21] Trepov, however, still appeared to believe the dispute could be resolved through the council's mediation; on the following day the local factory inspector informed the management that the weavers were ready to negotiate through Zhilkin and Krasivskii, both of whom were prepared to urge the weavers to return to work. Guzhon again refused to enter into talks with members of the council, whom he accused of fomenting labor strife, until a formal written request was received from the Moscow authorities. Trepov thereupon telephoned Guzhon and ordered that Zhilkin and Krasivskii be permitted to meet with the workers. Guzhon was compelled to give ground, and Zhilkin and Krasivskii entered the factory barracks to talk with the weavers.

Little was accomplished by these efforts, for the workers turned down the minor concessions offered by the factory administration. There was no basis for a compromise; the weavers renewed the demands that their two comrades be rehired and reimbursement be made in wages totaling 42,000 rubles, conditions clearly unacceptable to the management. That evening Krasivskii, under orders from the Okhrana, told the workers they must vacate the factory barracks within two days in compliance with a court order; lodging would be provided for those who did not wish to return to

20. *Ibid.*, p. 132.
21. *Ibid.*, p. 128.

their native villages. The majority decided to return home; 300 who remained in Moscow were housed in an empty factory rented by the council.[22]

On February 28, Trepov made good his threat and dispatched a commission to make an exhaustive study of sanitary facilities at the plant. As expected, the commission reported violations of sanitary regulations. That night the factory directors received a telegram to appear before the chief of police the following afternoon. The confrontation, however, failed to end the stalemate. Trepov attempted to intimidate the factory directors into negotiating and granting concessions to the workers, warning of harmful consequences for the association and its directors should they refuse, but Guzhon was unyielding.[23]

The Moscow administration, having devoted more than a year to cultivating the confidence of the working class, could not back down from its support of the weavers; in Zubatov's words "it was compelled to place itself on the side of the workers for the maintenance of its reputation."[24] From the beginning of the labor dispute until the workers received severance pay it sought through the council a compromise which would keep the mill running. When compromise proved impossible and the weavers left the mill, the Moscow administration became their benefactor. Zubatov advised the workers to hold out until the factory administration gave in to their demands. Through the council the Okhrana distributed 250 rubles a week to the weavers for sustenance, thus contributing to what in essence was a strike fund.[25] Financial support from the Okhrana enabled the weavers to continue their walkout for more than a month.

This benevolence no doubt accounted for rumors among the weavers that one of the plant's owners had been arrested and banished from Moscow on orders from the Grand Duke Sergei and that the state would shortly take over the silk mill.[26] There was some foundation to the first rumor. Irritated by the factory management's defiance, Trepov threatened Guzhon, a French national,

22. *Ibid.*, pp. 118, 129–30; Zubatov, "Zubatovshchina," p. 165; *Ocherki po istorii revoliutsionnogo dvizheniia i bol'shevistkoi organizatsii v Baumanskom raione* (Moscow-Leningrad, 1928), pp. 21–22.
23. Bukhbinder, "Zubatovshchina v Moskve," pp. 130–31.
24. Zubatov to Rataev, April 3, 1902 (*ibid.*, p. 117).
25. *Ibid.*; *Ocherki po istorii*, p. 21; *Russkoe delo*, July 30, 1905.
26. *Russkoe delo*, July 30, 1905; Bukhbinder, "Zubatovshchina v Moskve," p. 117.

with banishment from the empire as a dangerous alien; the threat might have been carried out had not Guzhon obtained the intercession of the French ambassador and Witte.[27]

The Moscow administration faced one of the most aggressive defenders of the interests of the capitalist class in Guzhon, a highly influential figure among industrial circles in Moscow and Petersburg. In 1883, Guzhon had founded the Moscow Metal-lurgical Plant, more commonly known after its owner; in the next two decades it grew into one of Russia's largest metallurgical plants.[28] Among the Moscow industrial community Guzhon was considered to be an enlightened industrialist, attentive to his workers' needs. Guzhon ruled his plant with a patriarchal hand; old-timers looked upon him as a father they could turn to in time of need. A workers' cooperative existed at the plant; Guzhon had even financed the construction of *dachas* for his employees. Nor were their spiritual needs overlooked. Church services were conducted regularly in the plant; each shop possessed its own ikon and celebrated its own religious holiday.[29]

Guzhon was also reputed to be a tough and outspoken defender of the interests of his class, unyielding to any demands made by his workers. An industrialist of the first rank, he was an active member of the Moscow Stock Exchange Committee, the Moscow branch of the Council of Trade and Manufacture, the Permanent Advisory Office of Ironmongers, and from its inception in 1905 until 1917 was chairman of the Society of Mill and Factory Owners of the Moscow District.[30]

27. Bukhbinder, *ibid.*, p. 106; Zubatov, "Zubatovshchina," p. 165. Trepov several years earlier was reported to have threatened Prokhorov with banishment from Moscow if he did not comply with the economic demands of his workers (*Osvo-bozhdenie*, no. 17 [Feb. 16, 1903]).

28. V. Meller, "Iz istorii zavoda 'Serp i molot,'" *Bor'ba klassov*, 1931, no. 6–7, p. 123; "Metallurgicheskii zavod 'serp i molot,'" *Bol'shaia sovetskaia entsiklopediia*, 2d ed., XXVIII (1954), 251; McKay, p. 53. *Rabochaia gazeta*, a Menshevik organ, on July 2, 1917, commented on the order of the Special Council on Defense of the Provisional Government to confiscate the Guzhon factory: "To appreciate this fact fully, it is necessary to take into consideration the following circumstances. First, Guzhon is not a nobody. He is a recognized leader of the Moscow metal industry. The Guzhon factory is of exceptional importance to the Moscow region, supplying 85 per cent of its metal" (Robert Paul Browder and Alexander F. Kerensky, eds., *The Russian Provisional Government, 1917* [Stanford, 1961], II, 765). The plant was nationalized in 1918, and its name changed in 1922 to "Serp i molot" (hammer and sickle).

29. *Rabochii zavod "Serp i molot,"* pp. 13–14; A. Koniaev, "Guzhon," *Istoriia zavodov*, no. 3 (1932), p. 68.

30. Olga Crisp, "Some Problems of French Investment in Russian Joint-Stock

The encounter with Zhilkin and Krasivskii at the silk mill was not Guzhon's first contact with the workers' council. The Society of Machine Workers had a large following at his metallurgical plant; in December 1901, the workers complained to Trepov about unsanitary facilities, the first of several declarations against the management.[31] Guzhon was determined not to recognize the council on grounds it was an illegal organ bearing the characteristics of a labor union. When the council intervened in the dispute at the silk mill, he used his considerable influence to thwart its efforts, forwarding detailed accounts of the dispute to Witte.[32] At the root of the prolonged labor conflict, Guzhon contended, lay the Moscow Okhrana:

If the Okhrana section did all in its power to explain the absurd rumors among the workers, if they explained to some that they have nothing to fear and confirmed to others that remuneration is only paid for work and not for truancy and that we do not live under the rule of socialism, in which one can confiscate the property of the factory owners for the benefit of the workers, if there followed an authoritative explanation of their misunderstanding, the strike would immediately end to the advantage of both parties.[33]

Guzhon also marshaled the Moscow industrial community in his support. Finally, he personally took his case to the Petersburg authorities. Traveling secretly to the northern capital, he successfully sought the help of the French ambassador, the Marquis de Montabello, whose intervention proved decisive.[34] After holding out for forty days the weavers returned to work with nothing to show for their sacrifice.[35]

The Moscow industrialists were already up in arms against the council when Guzhon appealed for their backing. Weavers at other mills had made monetary demands similar to those made at the

Companies," *Slavonic and East European Review,* 35 (1956), 232; *Rabochii vopros v komissii V. N. Kokovtsova,* pp. 37, 39; *Trudy vysochaishe uchrezhdennago vserossiiskago torgovo-promyshlennago s"ezda 1896 g. v Nizhnem Novgorode* (St. Petersburg, 1897), I, xviii; Buryshkin, pp. 255–56; *Sovetskaia istoricheskaia entsiklopediia,* IV (1963), 880.

31. Ainzaft, *Zubatovshchina,* p. 53; Meller, p. 124; Gaisinovich, p. 163.

32. Bukhbinder, "Zubatovshchina v Moskve," pp. 126–32; Vovchik, pp. 137–38.

33. Statement of the administration of the silk mill, March 21, 1902 (Ozerov, *Politika,* p. 254).

34. Report of C. Kinsky, attaché in the Austrian-Hungarian Embassy in St. Petersburg, to Count Goluchowski, May 2/15, 1902, in A. Ascher, "The Coming Storm," *Survey,* October 1964, p. 151. Witte also intervened on behalf of Guzhon (*Times* [London], May 17, 1902).

35. *Ocherki po istorii,* p. 22; *Torgovo-promyshlennaia gazeta,* Feb. 14, 1906.

Guzhon plant, whereupon the team of Krasivskii and Zhilkin had brusquely intruded, speaking high-handedly to the management on the workers' behalf.[36] Early March saw an outbreak of strikes in the city, including partial or total work stoppages at five of Moscow's most important plants.[37] Shortly before Easter, when hiring contracts were usually renewed, a general strike of Moscow weavers appeared imminent. On March 27, in an unusual display of solidarity, 1,500 weavers under the direction of the council pledged not to return to work after the Easter holiday until the factory owners recognized their representatives as bargaining agents, agreed to a closed shop, and accepted the terms of hiring the weavers put forward.[38]

The Moscow industrialists, perturbed over labor unrest in February and March, were perplexed over the proper course to take. The workers appeared to have the backing of the Moscow administration; surely, they surmised, the Petersburg authorities must have given their approval. Therefore it was best to accede to the workers' demands and meet the council halfway. So concluded many Moscow manufacturers. Others complied with the council's demands under pressure from Trepov's office. Some, like Guzhon, stubbornly stood their ground.[39] All, however, were confused and disconcerted and looked to the factory inspectors and the Ministry of Finance as bulwarks of support.[40]

Deterioration in labor relations throughout the city caused the Moscow industrialists to unite. Under Guzhon's prodding, they met in the first week of March at the headquarters of the Stock Exchange Committee and drafted a common declaration to be forwarded to Witte; a decision was also taken to lodge a complaint

36. *Iskra*, no. 22 (July 19, 1902), no. 23 (Aug. 1, 1902); Witte to Sipiagin, March 6, 1902 (Bukhbinder, "Zubatovshchina v Moskve," pp. 103, 120).

37. Veillet-Dufrêche to Delcassé, March 20, 1902, n.s.

38. Veillet-Dufrêche to Delcassé, April 25, 1902, n.s.; Ozerov, *Politika*, pp. 234–35; Shmeleva, Moscow *Uchenye zapiski*, p. 41; Laverychev, p. 155; *Perepiska V. I. Lenina i redaktsii*, I, 482.

39. *Russkoe delo*, March 19, 1905; Ozerov, *Politika*, p. 250; Vovchik, p. 137; "Novoe o zubatovshchine," p. 311.

40. Report of *okrug* factory inspector, March 17, 1902 (Ozerov, *Politika,* p. 234). Zubatov, in a communication to Rataev on April 2, 1902, divided the Moscow industrialists into three groups: those who supported the labor policy of the Moscow administration, those who were indifferent, and those who militantly opposed it and looked for support in the highest government circles. Zubatov did not assess the relative size and influence of each group ("Novoe o zubatovshchine," p. 311).

against the council with the Grand Duke Sergei. The declaration set forth their many grievances against the council and questioned its legal standing. The workers, it was alleged, had discussed questions of general state importance at their meetings, a charge sure to arouse Petersburg authorities. If it had been the intention of the government to stir up the workers against their employers, the government was playing with fire, they warned:

> If in granting them a certain degree of organization there is intention to attract them away from participation in political activity, then it appears no less dangerous to allow them anticapitalist activity, which undoubtedly has equally political significance, especially as coping with masses who have been attracted by any success in this regard can consequently appear extremely difficult, if not impossible.[41]

Of more immediate concern, the council was making extraordinary demands at many Moscow factories; substantial concessions might spread its influence throughout the central industrial region. In Moscow "the situation is extremely dangerous," the industrialists warned Witte.[42] On March 12 the Moscow section of the Council of Trade and Manufacture composed a similar declaration, accusing the workers' council of inciting the workers to make excessive demands under threat of strike.[43]

The imminence of a general textile strike welded the Moscow industrialists together in opposition to the workers' council. In the first part of April, they assembled and unanimously resolved not to recognize the council and to close down their factories rather than accede to the demands of the weavers. A delegation was sent to Petersburg to plead their cause before Witte, known as a strong champion of the interests of the business community.[44]

## Witte and the Moscow Zubatovshchina

The establishment of citywide labor associations for machine workers and weavers and the interference of the council in labor

---

41. Bukhbinder, "Zubatovshchina v Moskve," p. 120.
42. *Ibid.*
43. *Torgovo-promyshlennaia gazeta,* Feb. 14, 1906.
44. Veillet-Dufrêche to Delcassé, April 25, 1902, n.s. In 1905 the Moscow industrialists in reports to government authorities placed the blame for existing labor unrest squarely on the shoulders of the Zubatovshchina. L. B. Skarzhinskii, *Zabastovki i rabochiia sotovarishchestva* (St. Petersburg, 1905), pp. 260–61, 356–65; A. Kats and Iu. Milonov, eds., *1905: Professional'noe dvizhenie* (Moscow-Leningrad, 1926), pp. 147–52.

relations intensified the feud between the Ministry of Finance and the Moscow administration. To Witte the council was an illegal institution whose meddling in labor affairs eroded the authority and prestige of the factory inspector. Witte opposed the inspectors' having any dealings with the council whatsoever; he denied a request that the inspectors give lectures to the machine workers.[45] Throughout the course of the Moscow Zubatovshchina Witte used his ministerial position and considerable personal influence in the bureaucracy and at court toward stifling the council.

The Ministry of Finance was well informed by its agents of developments in Moscow. The factory inspectors, shunted aside by the Moscow authorities and the council, watched helplessly as labor relations in Moscow deteriorated and repeatedly warned the Ministry of the dangers implicit in the council's activities. Supported by the Moscow governor-general, who exerted his influence to wrest concessions from the factory owners, the Moscow workers, one inspector reported, were led to expect "a rapid and great improvement in their position at the expense of the factory owners," as well as backing from the government should they strike.[46]

Confidence that the government approved of their movement reportedly ran high among the Moscow workers. Cautioned by an inspector that the factory administration might well close down a plant if faced with a long and stubborn strike, a group of Moscow workers replied with assurance that in such event the factory owner would be compelled by the government to keep the plant running. Administrative intercession had replaced regular channels of procedure, an inspector complained, leaving the impression that "the council possesses the prestige of a government organ, created specifically for the defense of the workers' class interests."[47] Commenting on the Guzhon case the inspector predicted: "If the council will stand on this point of view, then the movement will embrace all the factories, the workers will demand a state salary of seventy-five kopeks a day and the transfer of the factories to the state."[48]

From many quarters information poured into the Ministry of Finance on the broadening influence the Moscow labor movement and the council exerted on the working class throughout the central

45. *Torgovo-promyshlennaia gazeta*, Feb. 7, 1906; Vovchik, p. 134.
46. Ozerov, *Politika*, p. 249.
47. *Ibid.*, pp. 249, 252.
48. *Ibid.*, p. 253.

industrial region. Factory inspectors in the provinces of Vladimir, Iaroslav, Riazan, and Perm reported that workers in their areas were discussing the Moscow Society of Machine Workers and had formed several labor organizations along similar lines. Through the reports ran the premonition of impending disorders after Easter, when, it was feared, news from Moscow might incite the workers in the provinces to labor disturbances.[49] Demands similar to those put forward by the council were made upon factory owners in the provinces. Strikes and collective workers' petitions, which in January and February were confined almost solely to the city of Moscow, noticeably increased the following month in nearby districts.[50]

Witte was in complete sympathy with the complaints against the council, which he believed was inflicting damage upon Russian industry.[51] In conversation with A. A. Polovtsev in early January he attacked the labor policies of the Grand Duke Sergei and those around him who, he maintained, believed they could bring industrial peace by giving the factory workers everything the socialists had promised them. Moreover, he feared that the Moscow program might be universally adopted, for the grand duke had succeeded in interesting the tsar in his labor program.[52]

Witte knew from bitter experience not to lock horns directly with the Grand Duke Sergei; discretion dictated a more cautious and indirect approach. Perhaps through pressure on the Ministry of Interior he could bring the august grand duke to task.

Sipiagin, it will be recalled, was well aware of Russian labor conditions, having conducted a personal investigation of factory life in 1901. His report, urging greater government intervention in factory affairs and a broad program of paternalistic measures to improve living standards, placed him closer in outlook to Zubatov than to Witte, who had opposed his proposals. Sipiagin, moreover, had good reason not to antagonize the Moscow governor-general. A special interministerial conference called for March 9, 1902, to consider Sipiagin's labor recommendations, was to be chaired by the Grand Duke Sergei. Witte, nevertheless, counted on Sipiagin's

49. *Ibid.*, p. 235.

50. *Ibid.*, p. 234; Shelymagin, p. 48.

51. E. J. Dillon, *The Eclipse of Russia* (New York, 1918), p. 158; Witte, *Vospominaniia*, II, 217.

52. "Dnevnik A. A. Polovtseva," *Krasnyi arkhiv*, 1923, no. 3, p. 108.

support, for he had promoted Sipiagin's candidacy to succeed Goremykin at the Ministry of Interior and continued, everyone said, to have considerable personal influence over his fellow minister.[53]

Witte set out to convince Sipiagin that the council had unlawfully encroached upon the authority of the factory inspector, interfered in relations between management and labor, and openly incited the workers to strike. He cited Sipiagin's own recommendations against permitting concessions to striking workers. He maintained that the special state conference of 1898 had, with the emperor's approval, delimited the sphere of activity of the factory inspector and the police with regard to factory surveillance. He was well aware that the council had thrived under the protection of the Moscow authorities, but he could not refrain from embarrassing Sipiagin by pretending ignorance, and confessed not to know "in what manner, with whose permission, and by what legislative decrees 'Unions of Workers' and their 'Councils' had been organized in Moscow."[54]

Witte also tried to restore the Ministry of Finance's initiative in labor affairs and undermine the Moscow Zubatovshchina and the influence of the Moscow administration by proposing the legalization of mutual-aid societies and the practice of electing factory *starosta* (elders), which would give the workers greater material security and spokesmen through which to express their needs; the Ministry of Finance felt the workers would thus realize the advantages of acting through legal channels.[55] On February 19 he requested Sipiagin to place this proposal before the inter-ministerial conference scheduled for March 9.

Witte followed up his correspondence with Sipiagin with a critical report to the tsar on the subject of the Moscow labor movement. Charging that Trepov had initiated a program which even the French socialist leaders Millerand and Jaurès had not dared to enact, Witte proposed a broadly representative state conference to discuss the matter. Meanwhile he kept in close touch with the factory inspectors. In a secret circular of March 26 he warned that labor unrest at the Moscow textile mills might worsen after the Easter holiday and reminded them of the duty to impress upon the workers that the government would not allow them to retain concessions

53. Von Laue, *Sergei Witte*, pp. 162, 167; Gurko, pp. 86–87.

54. Witte to Sipiagin, March 6, 1902 (Bukhbinder, "Zubatovshchina v Moskve," pp. 121–22).

55. *Materialy po rabochemu voprosu*, I, 20–27; Laverychev, pp. 146–48.

wrested illegally even if the factory administrations were willing to comply with their demands.[56]

Sipiagin took up the issue of the council in a letter to the Moscow governor-general on March 16. Referring to the Moscow industrialists' declaration and Witte's charges, Sipiagin declared his general agreement with administrative surveillance of the daily life of the workers as long as it remained within legal limits—a distinction, he asserted, the Moscow administration had not observed. Sipiagin, however, was not prepared to make demands on the Moscow authorities, for he meekly requested Trepov to respond to Witte and the industrialists.[57] Ten days later, no doubt on Witte's prodding, Sipiagin again wrote to the grand duke. He cited recent reports of the council's expanding activities and its recruitment of workers in industries other than textile and mechanical production, facts which had given the factory owners further cause for vexation. This time Sipiagin boldly suggested that, pending a final outcome of the issue, "it would be extremely desirable" to suspend the council's activity.[58]

Witte brought pressure to bear from another quarter to put a brake on the council's operations. Toward the end of March the Grand Duke Vladimir Aleksandrovich, on the initiative of Polovtsev, a confident of Witte and an outspoken critic of the labor policies of the Moscow administration, visited Moscow to make inquiries about the Moscow labor societies. Trepov, to whom the Grand Duke Sergei directed his brother, declared that the Moscow working class was more oppressed by the factory owners than were the serfs by the *pomeshchiki* in former times, a dangerous situation which bred discontent. Labor unions and clubs were efficacious means of arresting the causes of labor disorders. Apparently these arguments struck home, for to the chagrin of Polovtsev and Witte, the Grand Duke Vladimir returned to Petersburg a staunch supporter of his brother's policies.[59] Opposition to the Moscow experiment still remained strong, however, among influential circles in the capital; it

56. "Dnevnik A. A. Polovtseva," p. 128; *Revoliutsionnaia Rossiia*, no. 9 (July 1902); Ozerov, *Politika*, p. 28.

57. Bukhbinder, "Zubatovshchina v Moskve," pp. 124–25.

58. *Ibid.*, p. 133. Vovchik (p. 139) quotes the letter in part, dating it as March 22. On that date Witte had written to Sipiagin that "if energetic measures are not taken for the modification of the existing conduct of the police authorities then the most regrettable consequences can be expected."

59. "Dnevnik A. A. Polovtseva," pp. 128, 132.

was touch and go at the end of March whether the Moscow Zubatovshchina would continue operations or be officially terminated.

## Zubatov Counterattacks

As criticism of the council increased, Zubatov mounted a spirited
defense of his labor program. In a report to Sipiagin on March 4 he
stressed how his program had weakened the potential force of the
working class: "Having broken up the working masses into cells in
the form of various types of societies and having ruled the will of the
workers who head up these institutions, the government authorities
deprive such an organization of laboring masses of its elemental
force and make it capable of consistent and systematic activity which
is without any danger."[60]

In two long letters to L. A. Rataev, chief of the Special Section of
the Department of Police, written in the first days of April, Zubatov
rebutted point by point the Moscow industrialists' criticism of the
council. In particular he vigorously defended it and the Moscow
administration against allegations of anticapitalism: "the protective
attitude of the authorities to the labor organizations in Moscow is to
be explained not by enmity to the capitalists and partiality toward
the workers, but by official duty, which obliges the Orthodox-
autocratic state to treat equally, justly, and completely impartially
the workers and the owners, the poor and the rich."[61] The
assumption that trade unionism was anticapitalist by nature had no
basis in truth. In contradistinction to a socialist or revolutionary
labor movement, the Moscow council and its followers were
distinguished by their support of the government and the capitalist
system. Zubatov also took a verbal swipe at his critics within the
bureaucracy, especially provincial authorities who interpreted the
rising number of court suits filed by the workers as evidence of
growing political agitation.

This misunderstanding springs from the inability to differentiate a
*revolutionary* working class movement from a *peaceful* one, and of course can
in practice give rise not to the regularization of relations between the owners
and the workers, but the attainment of directly opposite results. In itself
such "discontent" is a completely healthy and desirable phenomenon,
which gradually heals the chronic sores of the factory-plant mode of life,
and which immunizes the latter from unexpected explosions and shocks. It

60. Korelin, "Krakh ideologii," p. 121.
61. Zubatov to Rataev, April 2, 1902 ("Novoe o zubatovshchine," p. 313).

is extremely burdensome and disturbing for persons in authority, but essentially it is very desirable for state interests and completely safe.[62]

The character of the Guzhon strike, Zubatov maintained, had validated his theories, directed as they were to sustaining the loyalty of the working class to the autocracy. Rumors that Zhilkin and Krasivskii were agents of the tsar sent to investigate factory conditions and that Krasivskii was an illegitimate son of Alexander II indicated that the workers, aware of receiving government support in their efforts to attain justice, put a monarchical interpretation on events at the Guzhon silk mill. These rumors, Zubatov boasted, "give graphic proof that I correctly caught and mastered the meaning of our national state ideal, and, on the other hand, figuratively depict those ends in which undoubtedly the legalization of the workers' movement will result, that is, precisely the strengthening and magnificent flowering of the monarchical idea, and not the liberal-democratic one."[63]

The utility of the council in maintaining peace among the factory masses was Zubatov's main tactical argument in persuading his superiors to sustain his experiment. The council had attained a prominent position among the working class; suspension of its activities would be "extremely undesirable, inopportune and dangerous," and would only benefit those inimical to the autocracy. If the council were to be abolished the masses would seek outlets for their grievances through factory terror and a struggle against the government; it would be a windfall for the revolutionaries, providing tangible proof of their oft-repeated propaganda that the monarchy was the servant of the ruling class and that a legal labor movement was an impossibility under the autocracy. The Moscow administration had formed the council to guide the labor movement; cut adrift from the Moscow authorities the working class would naturally seek shelter with the revolutionaries, turning from an upholder into an enemy of the autocracy, Zubatov warned.[64]

Zubatov firmly defended the role of the Moscow administration in the Guzhon affair. The dispute was attributed to the malpractices of the silk mill's administration; its protraction was due to

62. *Ibid.*, p. 314.
63. Zubatov to Rataev, April 3, 1902 (Bukhbinder, "Zubatovshchina v Moskve," p. 116). There was also a rumor among the workers to the effect that Slepov was a natural son of Alexander II (*Iskra*, no. 22 [July 1902]).
64. "Novoe o zubatovshchine," pp. 309–11.

management's determination to maintain the status quo in labor relations at all cost and to flaunt its power before the helpless workers. The Moscow administration realized that the eyes of all Moscow were on the Guzhon case; its decision to permit the Moscow workers to raise strike funds for the weavers was intended to prevent the authorities from being placed "in an extremely humiliating position in the opinion of the whole population of the capital."[65] This specific dispute, moreover, had great general significance: it revealed concretely the mutual need of the workers and owners for each other and the loss each would sustain should either take an uncompromising stand leading to a lengthy strike. The workers realized the financial impossibility of sustaining their striking comrades over a long period; the owners, in turn, were compelled to act more attentively toward the demands of their workers, who represented "a very considerable and at the same time a very dangerous force."[66]

These arguments were bound to be greeted scornfully by Zubatov's critics. Nor was his disclosure that the procurator's office had cleared the council of any imputation of criminal conduct likely to assuage the opposition. Strike funds were illegal whether their source was the factory workers or the Okhrana; the council and the society of weavers had no standing in law. The Moscow manufacturers continued to inveigh against the council and petition the Petersburg authorities for its closing. Witte remained determined to have that "sworn anarchist Zubatov" removed from power and bring an end to factory disorders in Moscow.[67]

## Zubatov Sets Out to Convert Moscow Society

Zubatov's correspondence with his superiors reached a limited but influential audience in the higher bureaucracy. To popularize and propagate his labor policies, he utilized the conservative press. Ambitious to have his program adopted throughout the empire, he sought nothing less than to re-educate Russian society on the labor question, to assure it that labor societies under administrative tutelage were compatible with the existing economic and political order. The "theoretical basis" of his movement, to use Zubatov's

65. Bukhbinder, "Zubatovshchina v Moskve," p. 118.
66. "Novoe o zubatovshchine," p. 314.
67. Veillet-Dufrêche to Delcassé, April 25, 1902, n.s.; "Dnevnik A. A. Polovtseva," p. 135.

words, was expounded in two series of articles appearing in March 1902.[68]

The most consistent public endorsement of Zubatov's program was to be found on the editorial pages of the reactionary daily, *Moskovskiia vedomosti*. Edited by V. A. Gringmut, later leader of the Russian Monarchist Party, the paper stood inflexibly for traditional Russian values, above all faith in tsar and Orthodox church. Editorials and articles in the paper were frequently concerned with the labor question. Here the usual denials of Russia's similarity with Western Europe were combined with realistic appraisals of developments in Russia leading to large-scale industry and a growing working class. The paper favored further government intervention in labor relations and government tutelage of the working class. It championed mutual-help societies and factory legislation, including state insurance and the election of factory elders. State intervention in labor relations was viewed as the best way to prevent exploitation of the working class and minimize the noxious influence of "political ideologies and liberal doctrines" among the factory population.[69] The paper favorably publicized the societies of machine workers and weavers and the council. Slepov was a regular contributor; its editorial writers, L. Voronov and Lev Tikhomirov, placed their pens at Zubatov's service.[70]

Voronov's contribution was a long series of scholarly articles under the title "Fallen Idol." Since the early nineteenth century, Voronov contended, Russian society had come under the spell of numerous foreign doctrines, each adopted after having been discarded in Western Europe. Marxism was the latest in the line of fallen idols to have become fashionable in Russia. Voronov summarized contemporary European criticism of Marxist theories and cited studies of contemporary labor conditions which tended to disapprove Marxist predictions. Bernstein's revisionism was discussed at length, as was the crisis it reflected in German social democracy. Russian propagators of Marxism such as Struve, Tugan-Baranovskii, and Il'in (one of several pseudonyms of

68. Zubatov to Rataev, April 2, 1902 ("Novoe o zubatovshchine," p. 314).
69. *Moskovskiia vedomosti*, Feb. 28, March 1, 24, 26, 1902; Jan. 10, Feb. 5, May 1, 19, 25, 1903.
70. Voronov's series of articles appeared daily in *Moskovskiia vedomosti* from March 3 through March 17, Tikhomirov's from March 20 through March 25. Both series were published shortly thereafter as brochures.

Vladimir Il'ich Ul'ianov, or Lenin) according to Voronov, ignored recent evidence disproving Marx's theories and confidently foresaw the rule of capitalism in Russia, to be followed inevitably by revolution. It was true, Voronov agreed, that large-scale production existed in Russia; it was untrue, however, that class struggle was a necessary concomitant of industrial growth. Indeed wages and other conditions of labor were considerably better in large plants than in small ones, where patriarchal relations between employer and worker existed only in theory. This, however, was not universally true: "Unfortunately, not all capitalists recognize the economics of high wages and the necessity of looking after the well-being of labor."[71] Factory legislation was thus a necessity.

Russian factory legislation had lagged behind the needs created by industrialization. The mere congregation daily of thousands of workers led to increasing communication among them and an awareness of common interests and the need to unite. The law, however, denied them the right to organize. Here lay the root of labor unrest, which the political agitator exploited. To remedy the situation, Voronov prescribed a charter of rights for the working class: "Giving the workers the possibility of independently looking after the improvement of their economic position through trade-union organizations would completely undermine the basis of political agitation."[72] Russia could destroy the Marxist idol and preclude a struggle between capital and labor by following Western Europe's example and legalizing labor organizations and collective bargaining. In any case, Voronov concluded, "the Government can save Russia from pernicious worship of the fallen idol only *if it consciously and firmly takes the peaceful regulation of relations between labor and capital into its own hands.*"[73] The words were Voronov's; the ideas and line of argument were Zubatov's.

Lev Tikhomirov's "The Labor Question and Russian Ideals" followed Voronov's articles. At one time a leading figure in the revolutionary Narodnaia Volia, Tikhomirov had made a full turnabout; from abroad he had made an abject confession of error, received amnesty, and returned to Russia to take up a career as a publicist, having become a true believer and faithful servant of autocracy and Orthodoxy. As an editor of *Moskovskiia vedomosti* he

71. *Moskovskiia vedomosti*, March 15, 1902.
72. *Ibid.*, March 16, 1902.
73. *Ibid.*, March 17, 1902; italics in original.

contributed numerous articles on the labor movement in support of Zubatov: he also wrote several brochures commissioned by Zubatov, whose ideological position was similar to his own. Tikhomirov was far and away Zubatov's most able and prolific propagandist.[74]

"The Labor Question and Russian Ideals" was directed at an audience of conservative monarchists; its object was to convince skeptics that the working class could be peaceably incorporated within the traditional order. Tikhomirov lauded the time-honored ideals of Holy Russia and lashed out at the modern intelligentsia; he stressed the conservative ideal of a union of tsar and people, including the newly emerging Russian working class in the latter category: "In reality the factory workers are the very same Russian people as any other, and are even more Russian in blood and spirit than our intelligentsia. In the factory population live the same beliefs and traditions of the Russian people that are in the peasantry."[75]

Yet Western European experience was not without lessons for Russian conservatives bent on denying social democracy a home, Tikhomirov held. In Europe social democracy was on the decline because trade unionism had satisfied the workers' materialistic appetite. The European factory workers longed for a better life without having to wait for the revolution. Through their trade unions they had made great gains and were beginning to live the life of the typical bourgeois. Trade unionism was thus anathema to the revolutionary, who thrives on bad times. So far this lesson had not been learned in Russia, where the working class had been ignored by all except the Marxists. To redress this situation Tikhomirov recommended that the Russian working class be recognized as a separate estate. When each class had an organizational basis for furthering its interests, which would be mediated and balanced by the state, the monarchist ideal would be realized in Russia: a truly Russian intelligentsia (in contrast to the Europeanized intelligentsia) would emerge, the unity of people and monarch would be

74. Spiridovich, "Pri tsarskom rezhime," p. 150. Zubatov discussed Tikhomirov and his writings in a letter to Burtsev on March 5, 1908 (Koz'min, p. 85). In addition to the pamphlets, Tikhomirov wrote editorials on the labor question and articles in defense of the Moscow societies of mutual help; see "Rabochiia obshchestva vzaimopomoshchi," *Moskovskiia vedomosti*, May 20 and 21, 1902. Unlike many conservatives, he found capitalism "necessary and useful" (*ibid.*, May 21, 1902).

75. Lev Tikhomirov, *Rabochii vopros i russkie idealy* (Moscow, 1902), p. 65.

cemented, and both class struggle and the social question would disappear.

While Voronov and Tikhomirov wrote to persuade conservatives, Professor Ozerov publicized Western European labor institutions in the pages of the liberal journal *Russkaia mysl'* (Russian Thought). Ozerov's scholarly articles detailed the history and workings of cooperatives, mutual-help funds, factory committees, and other organizational forms through which workers abroad had improved their material position. He contrasted with this the position of unorganized workers (that is, in Russia), urging them to establish strong organizational ties and disciplined unity as means of defending their common interests and raising their standard of living. Only when workers were organized would the owners take their demands seriously; organized and disciplined they could exert pressure for better wages by threatening to withhold their labor. Writing on factory committees and collective agreements abroad, Ozerov described the stages of labor organization, a process not dissimilar to the development of the Moscow Society of Machine Workers and its council: "Hitherto people sat like spiders in their corners; now the factory has united them and this horde of people under one roof contribute to the development of mutual-help funds, and subsequently these latter take upon themselves the further task of establishing the conditions of labor by means of a collective agreement."[76]

Ozerov took pains to assure his readers that measures taken abroad for the well-being of the workers were likewise of benefit to the government and the industrialists. Bismarck had justified labor legislation as a means of undermining revolutionary social democracy; the development of trade unions in the West had strengthened social peace in the industrial world; a Russian working class free to develop initiative and self-activity, as workers were in England, would greatly contribute to industrial growth.[77] Implied, of course, was that Russian industrialists had nothing to fear from the Moscow Society of Machine Workers; news of such societies should be greeted "as the dawn of a new [and] better future."[78]

76. Ozerov, *Iz zhizni truda*, p. 140.
77. *Ibid.*, pp. 150, 182, 198.
78. *Ibid.*, p. 198.

## Plehve and the Zubatovshchina

No amount of favorable publicity and pleading for the council and its labor societies appeared sufficiently convincing to make their continuation secure. The notoriety of the Guzhon affair, the united opposition of factory inspectors, Moscow industrialists, and the Minister of Finance, and the criticism from the Minister of Interior should have sufficed to end the Moscow labor experiment within a year of its inception. An order abolishing the council apparently was issued by the Minister of Interior and would have been executed were it not for the intercession of the Grand Duke Sergei.[79] Equally important was the assassination of Sipiagin on April 2, 1902, and the appointment of Viacheslav Plehve, who could be expected to be less pliable to Witte's prodding, as Sipiagin's successor.

Plehve came to the Ministry of Interior with an unsavory reputation among the Russian liberal intelligentsia; his two-year tenure as minister further intensified its hatred of him as a symbol of the reactionary and arbitrary despotism of the tsarist bureaucracy. Time, in the absence of an adequate biographical re-evaluation of Plehve, has done nothing to erase this judgment.[80] Plehve had entered government service in 1867 after graduating from Moscow University with a law degree. For the next thirty-five years he served in a variety of responsible official posts, first in the public prosecutor's office, then as director of the Department of Police, Assistant Minister of Interior, Imperial State Secretary, and finally as State Secretary of the Grand Duchy of Finland, before succeeding Sipiagin. Like Zubatov he had experience both in counter-revolutionary police work and in dealing with the labor problem. Named director of the Department of Police shortly after the assassination of Alexander II, Plehve gained prominence in the liquidation of the revolutionary *Narodnaia Volia*. A few years later as Assistant Minister of Interior he further distinguished himself as chairman of an interministerial commission drafting the factory legislation enacted in 1886, showing himself during the hearings more partial to the interests of the workers than the factory owners.[81]

79. Shmeleva, Moscow *Uchenye zapiski*, p. 41; *Russkoe delo*, July 30, 1905; *Rabochaia gazeta*, no. 40, 1906.
80. Paul Miliukov, *Russia and Its Crisis* (New York, 1962), pp. 15–16; Donald W. Treadgold, *Lenin and His Rivals* (New York, 1955), p. 22.
81. There are short accounts of Plehve's career in *Moskovskiia vedomosti*, April 6,

Plehve took up his ministerial post supremely confident in his own abilities and prepared to institute broad reforms in the areas of police activities, the central and local administrative apparatus, and peasant legislation.[82] He was the first to challenge seriously Witte's decade-long domination over his fellow ministers; for more than a year the two engaged in bureaucratic combat until Plehve emerged victorious and Witte was forced to step down.

Two decades had passed since Plehve had dealt with the labor question. He was conscious, however, that he had not kept informed on the question, which had become more serious and complicated since the mid-1880's.[83] An opportunity to discuss it arose shortly after his appointment. In early May 1902, Ianzhul, an old acquaintance of Plehve's, in an interview with the new minister elaborated his views on the labor problem in Russia and the steps necessary to ensure peaceful labor relations. Well acquainted with the labor movement at home and abroad, Ianzhul maintained that a proletariat similar to that in Western Europe now existed in Russia. The factory legislation of 1886 no longer sufficed. He therefore recommended a three-point program: legalizing the right to strike, legalizing labor unions, and transferring government labor policy from the Ministry of Finance, which was generally responsive to the demands of the industrial community, to the Ministry of Interior. Plehve responded favorably to the essence of Ianzhul's program, expressing his intention to seek immediate transfer of the factory inspectorate to his ministry, without which the other elements of Ianzhul's proposals stood little chance of being implemented.[84]

These were plans for the future; more immediate was the problem of large-scale peasant disorders in Poltava and Kharkov provinces. Before Plehve's departure for southern Russia to investigate the disorders, Witte hurried to meet the new minister and impress upon him the danger inherent in the recent labor unrest in Moscow, urging that Zubatov, without whom Trepov and the Grand Duke Sergei could not supervise the Moscow labor societies, be re-

---

1902; Gurko, pp. 589–90; *Otchet ... za sessiiu 1904–1905 g.g.*, p. 702. Plehve's chairmanship of the interministerial commission on labor legislation is described in Ianzhul, *Iz vospominanii*, pp. 65–68.

82. Gurko, p. 112.

83. Kokovtsov, p. 27; Pogozhev, "Iz vospominanii," p. 260.

84. Ianzhul, "Vospominaniia," *Russkaia starina*, no. 144 (Oct.–Dec. 1910), pp. 271–72, 491.

moved from office. Plehve, in reply, expressed opposition to the Zubatovshchina as a harmful and stupid experiment and declared he expected to resolve the issue during a conference with the grand duke in Moscow.[85] A delegation of Moscow factory owners visiting Petersburg to present their case against the council to Witte were warmly received by Plehve and encouraged to believe he was on their side.[86]

During his conference with the Moscow governor-general Plehve learned, as his predecessor had, that the Grand Duke Sergei was inflexible in support of Zubatov and that little could be done to end the Moscow experiment.[87] Plehve also took the opportunity to meet with the renowned chief of the Moscow Okhrana, of whose police methods and activities he disapproved. Three meetings were held, the major subject of conversation being the effective means of rooting out the forces of revolution.[88] There was no meeting of minds. Speaking from experience derived two decades earlier in combating Narodnaia Volia, Plehve held to the opinion that the security police should concentrate on destroying the revolutionary centers and little else. Zubatov criticized without effect Plehve's simplistic approach emphasizing "that reform activity is the most sure medicine against disorders and revolution" and stressing "the extreme desirability of granting a certain freedom of public self-activity."[89] Plehve thus left Moscow without having fulfilled his promise to Witte; indeed in the following months, as he became aware how far the labor movement and revolutionary activity had progressed since the 1880's, he even grew somewhat sympathetic to Zubatov's approach to state problems.[90]

From the start Plehve was acutely aware of criticism against the Zubatovshchina. The outcome of the Guzhon affair had failed to

85. Witte, *Vospominaniia*, II, 217–18; Laverychev, p. 156; Suvorin, p. 290; "Dnevnik A. A. Polovtseva," p. 135; *Rabochii vopros v komissii V. N. Kokovtsova*, p. 23.

86. Veillet-Dufrêche to Delcassé, April 25, 1902, n.s.

87. Witte, *Vospominaniia*, II, 217; *Rabochii vopros v komissii V. N. Kokovtsova*, p. 23; Ozerov, *Politika*, p. 237; Laverychev, p. 156.

88. "Pis'ma Mednikova Spiridovichu," *Krasnyi arkhiv*, 1926, no. 4(17), p. 193; Zubatov, "Iz nedavniago proshlago," p. 435. Plehve, during his visit to Moscow, told Trepov of his disappointment in the activities of Zubatov and the Moscow secret police (Gurko, p. 113).

89. Zubatov, *ibid*. In an interview at the end of May 1902, with a correspondent of the French newspaper *Matin*, Plehve stressed the efficacy of police methods in weakening the revolutionary parties (*Times* [London], June 2, 1902).

90. Gurko, p. 113.

satisfy the Moscow industrialists, and their conflict with the Moscow authorities continued. Protests too were heard from mill owners and provincial officials as the council sought to organize factory workers in areas surrounding Moscow. Reports that representatives of the council were responsible for a rash of strikes in Moscow province aroused opposition from A. G. Bulygin, the provincial governor, who issued a circular ordering the arrest of such factory agitators. In the same vein Bulygin, in a letter of March 20 to the Grand Duke Sergei, advised that the council's activities be limited to the city of Moscow.[91] Trepov, in reply, refused the request and came to the council's defense. Reports of impending strikes were to be attributed to animated discussions among the workers regarding the renewal of factory contracts and wage rates after Easter. The council's operations were in the government's best interests. Trepov went so far as to suggest that a council be organized for the province as a means of ascertaining the wishes of the factory masses.[92]

The factory owners and provincial authorities were further vexed by a flagrant case of labor agitation resulting from the intervention of the council in the town of Bogorodsk, just outside Moscow. In early June, Timofei Ianchenkov, Platon Vasiutin, and Andrei Chibrikov, recently employed weavers at the huge Bogorodsko-Glukhovskii cotton mill, were arrested on the charge of making threatening demands to the factory director. Interrogation revealed they were associated with the council and the Moscow society of textile workers; on instructions from the council they had planned to open a branch of the society in the cotton mill. Under detention they remained remarkably defiant. Claiming to speak on behalf of the entire work force of the mill, numbering more than 8,000, the three weavers demanded a nine-hour workday, abolition of night work, the allotment of free apartments and public baths from workers, establishment of a consumers' society, and improved sanitary conditions. Ianchenkov boldly asserted that the mill workers, when organized, would have Bulygin's protection, prophesying that "even slaves will live like masters."[93] The weavers' confidence in official protection was fully justified; after arrest they were

91. Vovchik, p. 139; Bukhbinder, "Zubatovshchina v Moskve," p. 106; Ainzaft, *Zubatovshchina, p. 58.*
92. Bukhbinder, *ibid.,* p. 107; Ainzaft, *ibid.,* p. 57.
93. *Russkoe delo,* Jan. 29, 1905; Bukhbinder, *ibid.,* p. 108.

transferred to Moscow on orders of the Moscow administration, which immediately had them set free. The astonishment of the management of the cotton mill at the extraordinary outcome of the affair did not end there; after release from prison the three promptly brought a court suit against the factory administration demanding compensation for their forcible removal from the mill.[94]

The militancy of the weavers, nevertheless, caused the Moscow administration to place a tighter rein on their activities. After the Easter holiday the Moscow weavers returned to work, having renounced their earlier demands and their hopes for a citywide textile strike.[95] It was now thought desirable to end the autonomy enjoyed within the council by the Consultative Commission of Weavers. In a report to a meeting on June 19, Afanas'ev recommended that the council be broadened beyond the machine workers to represent mutual-help societies recently formed among workers in other professions. The authorities were not prepared to accept a rejection of the proposal. Either the weavers would have to place their commission under the direct authority of the council, Afanas'ev warned, or official recognition of the commission would be withdrawn and it would have the status of an illegal organization. Soon thereafter the council was reorganized as Afanas'ev had recommended; so-called consultative commissions of twelve members were established to administer the individual mutual-help funds organized by professions. Three members of each commission served as delegates to the general council, which continued to retain control over the entire movement.[96]

## Zubatov and the Moscow Tycoons

The flowering of the Zubatovshchina in Moscow and the surrounding province just three months after complaints had been lodged against the council to the Ministry of Finance tended to confirm the worst fears of the Moscow industrialists. On July 8 a group of manufacturers went directly to Zubatov and warned him of the danger of his continuing to interfere in factory affairs.[97] This

94. *Russkoe delo,* Jan. 29, 1905; E. Popova, ed., *1905 v Moskovskoi gubernii* (Moscow-Leningrad, 1926), pp. 21–25.

95. Veillet-Dufrêche to Delcassé, April 30 and May 13, 1902, n.s.

96. Ainzaft, *Zubatovshchina,* p. 59; *Russkoe delo,* July 23, 1905; Sher, p. 129; Kats and Milonov, pp. 3–4.

97. *Russkoe delo,* Feb. 5, 1905; V. I. Shtein, "Neudachnyi opyt," *Istoricheskii vestnik,* no. 129 (July 1912), p. 235; Vovchik, p. 141.

meeting was a preliminary to Zubatov's well-known private talk with a small number of the city's most important industrial magnates behind closed doors at Testov's restaurant on July 26.[98] Zubatov's goal was to convince the industrialists of the wisdom of his policy, for their support was crucial to his program.

Pervading Zubatov's talk was an air of smug assurance that labor peace and stability could be maintained only through the intercession of the Moscow administration and the Okhrana in factory affairs. Administrative intervention was held to be of benefit not solely to the workers but to the existing order and even to the factory owners. The industrial estate, Zubatov alleged, was generally held in low esteem by all segments of public opinion, an assertion scarcely aimed to please his audience. The industrialists were beset by criticism from the intelligentsia, the clergy, and the press, which stigmatized them as "swindlers" for their exploitation of the working class. The trade-industrial estate could find true sympathy and defense of its legal rights only in the Moscow Okhrana, which would do all in its power to prevent and suppress criminal action by the working class and intelligentsia. The factory inspector had lost the workers' confidence and thus became ineffective in dealing with labor relations; this, along with considerations of state order, justified the encroachment of the Okhrana in that area. The Okhrana had already gained the confidence of the workers, who now believed that for each humiliation and insult they would receive from the Okhrana "fatherly attention, advice, support, [and] help by word and deed."[99] By nuturing the working-class movement the local authorities had enabled Moscow to avoid a wave of labor disorders similar to that in Petersburg during the summer, Zubatov contended.

The Okhrana, Zubatov further asserted, had concluded from its observations of factory life that labor strife could be prevented by expanding the rights of the factory workers through extralegal

98. The contents of the talk were first published in *Osvobozhdenie*, no. 8 (Oct. 2, 1902), with a note by the editor that the published version was based on a summary written immediately after the speech was delivered and then verified. The anonymous donor of a copy of the speech assured the editor that it was almost stenographically correct. The major points of the speech were also printed in *Russkoe delo*, Feb. 5, 1905, and in *Morskoi*, pp. 86–96. There are slight differences in the three versions. Zubatov ("Zubatovshchina," p. 163) challenged the accuracy of the printed versions. Vovchik (p. 141) lists the industrialists who attended.

99. *Osvobozhdenie*, no. 8 (Oct. 2, 1902).

measures rather than the normal legislative channels contemplated by the Ministry of Finance. The industrial estate could help to realize the Okhrana's aim by agreeing to negotiate with factory committees chosen by the workers. The committees would be under the surveillance of the Okhrana, which would select for their membership "special agents from the ranks of experienced and reliable workers, who have grown wise by long experience in the art of ruling great masses of people." The concurrence of the trade-industrial estate, added to existing support by the clergy, intelligentsia, and workers, would "to a significant degree facilitate the difficult task of putting into practice, not only in Moscow and Moscow *guberniia*, but also in all Russia—although outside the law— the only salutary means of regulating mutual relations between owners and workers."[100]

The Moscow industrialists had not come to Testov's to be lectured to; before the evening was over they had rebutted Zubatov's theses point by point. They vigorously denied the charges of labor exploitation and connivance with the factory inspectors, placing the blame for factory disturbances on agitators, malcontents, and drifters among the workers. They felt that Zubatov's plan to organize the workers into special unions directed by committees was borrowed from such countries as the United States and Australia; for Russia it "is not only completely inappropriate but even harmful, since it will give people with bad intentions a chance to subjugate the semieducated ignorant masses to their influence, and by such means make them an obedient weapon for reaching political goals." The industrialists also questioned the policy of giving preferential treatment to the working class, which they held to be a mere one per cent of the empire's population. If the police authorities intended to replace the factory inspectors with individuals like Krasivskii and Afanas'ev, the manufacturers warned, they would retaliate, and "close the factories and dismiss the workers, leaving it to the police to find them work."[101]

Shortly after the meeting at Testov's, Guzhon forwarded an account of the talks to Witte, who reportedly responded by vowing to bring police machinations in Moscow to an end. Zubatov, in defense, hastened to inform A. A. Lopukhin, the newly appointed

100. *Ibid.*
101. *Russkoe delo*, Feb. 12, 1905.

director of the Department of Police, that Guzhon had presented a distorted version of his talk with the industrialists.[102] Zubatov's relations with the Moscow factory owners soon came to an end; on August 17, 1902, four days after his letter to Lopukhin, Zubatov was transferred to St. Petersburg, where he served as chief of the Special Section of the Department of Police until his ignominious discharge a year later.

Zubatov's departure from Moscow was not universally hailed by the Moscow factory owners, for to his credit he had won over a part of the industrial community. After the talk at Testov's some of the industrialists concluded that labor societies were destined to spread throughout Russia, having evidently received the sanction of the Ministry of Interior. Plehve's failure formally to condemn the council lent weight to this belief and dashed expectations that the Moscow Zubatovshchina would be terminated once the Petersburg authorities were thoroughly aware of its unlawful activities. Since nothing had changed despite their protests, the industrialists reconsidered their position. The old guard among them held to the status quo, regarding the prevailing laws as sufficient for the existing state of Russian industrial development; reforms, they held, should be put off to the future in view of the industrial crisis Russia was undergoing, and at best should be initiated gradually. In contrast, a new party, small in number but nevertheless influential, had formed among the industrialists. Whether motivated by sympathy with the plight of the working class, by belief that all protest was futile in the face of governmental indifference, or simply by dint of threats, cajolery, and promises from the Moscow administration, as critics charged, several pillars of the Moscow industrial world were willing to meet Zubatov's program halfway.[103]

102. Zubatov to Lopukhin, Aug. 13, 1902 (Bukhbinder, "Zubatovshchina v Moskve," p. 115).

103. *Russkoe delo,* March 19, April 2, 1905; Zubatov, "Zubatovshchina," p. 178.

# CHAPTER 6

# The Zubatovshchina in Petersburg and Moscow, 1902–1905

Plehve's decision to bring Zubatov to Petersburg was part of his plan to overhaul the Department of Police and transfer all political cases to the courts, plans which were never realized. While touring the southern provinces Plehve had recruited Lopukhin, then public prosecutor in Kharkov, as director of the Department of Police with promises of these reforms. Zubatov, an old acquaintance of Lopukhin, was invited to Petersburg in August to take charge of the Special Section of the Department.[1]

The appointment was a definite promotion. Whether it was offered to Zubatov as a well-earned reward for his outstanding record in counterrevolutionary intelligence or as a tactful means of removing him from Moscow and appeasing the Moscow industrial community is not clear from the evidence. Most probably Plehve had both considerations in mind.

The Special Section had been established in 1898 as a separate inner bureau of the Department of Police to combat subversive activity. Assigned the crucial task of suppressing the revolutionary movement, it directed the Russian secret police at home and abroad from its secret headquarters along the Fontanka. Under Zubatov's direction, the "flying squadron," the pride of the Moscow Okhrana, was absorbed by the Department of Police, along with former colleagues trained by Zubatov. New branches of the Okhrana were opened in Kiev, Odessa, and Vilna, among other cities, staffed by young gendarme officers trained in modern methods of combatting

1. Testimony of Lopukhin and Zubatov (*Delo A. A. Lopukhina*, pp. 40, 113). On Zubatov's earlier contacts with Lopukhin see Boris Nikolajewsky, *Azeff the Spy* (Garden City, N. Y., 1934), p. 7.

conspiratorial operations and given authority to operate largely independent of provincial officials. The reorganization of the investigatory system was anathema to the older and more heavy-footed gendarme chiefs, who, taking umbrage at interference with their authority, became outspokenly bitter critics of Zubatov's methods of police investigation as well as his labor policies.[2]

From his desk at the Department of Police, Zubatov was able to continue his labor program; those who anticipated a speedy end to "police machinations" were disappointed, for during Zubatov's year in Petersburg the experiment spread to other cities, no doubt with the permission, if not enthusiastic support, of Plehve.

## The Petersburg Zubatovshchina

Shortly after Zubatov's arrival in Petersburg he initiated steps to found labor societies along the lines of those functioning in Moscow. The first move, as before, was to recruit leaders from the worker-intelligentsia; the next was to seek the support of the local administration, the Petersburg higher bureaucracy, and the clergy. V. I. Pikunov, a worker at the Lessner machine construction plant, a former resident of Moscow, and a one-time Social Democrat with a record of several arrests, was chosen to lead the Petersburg Zubatovshchina. Approached by Krasivskii, Afanas'ev, and Dolin, Pikunov was promised financial aid, the support of unnamed but highly placed persons, and the assistance of the academic community if he agreed to organize the Petersburg workers. As a first step he was advised to form an inner circle of organizers composed of workers sympathetic to the project from the major Petersburg mechanical plants.

Further advice came from Zubatov himself. Promising secret assistance, he emphasized the need for the support of society and the higher authorities. Thus approval for the workers to assemble should be sought from General N. V. Kleigels, the city governor of St. Petersburg; a delegation of workers should call upon Metropolitan Antonii and the archpriest F. N. Ornatskii, chairman of

2. Fredric Scott Zuckerman, "The Russian Political Police at Home and Abroad (1880–1917)" (Ph.D. dissertation, Department of History, New York University, 1973), pp. 16–17, 25–26, 56, 65–66; *Bol'shaia sovetskaia entsiklopediia*, XLIII (1939), 706; A. P., "Departament politsii v 1892–1908 gg.," *Byloe*, Nov.–Dec. 1917, pp. 19–20; Lopukhin, *Nastoiashchee*, p. 34; Spiridovich, *Pri tsarskom rezhime*, pp. 27–28; Men'shchikov, II, no. 2, pp. 122–23.

the Society of Religious and Moral Enlightenment, which might furnish a meeting place free of charge. The venture also needed to gain the backing of the press, for which Zubatov promised to introduce Pikunov to the editors of several Petersburg dailies.[3]

With the wheels oiled by Zubatov and the leaders of the Moscow council, the machinery was set in motion. A preliminary meeting was held by those interested in the plan, at which Pikunov was chosen chairman and S. A. Gorshkov secretary. On the following Sunday, November 10, 1902, a group of workers gathered at the Vyborg Inn on Finskii Avenue in the Vyborg district of the city to discuss plans for a new labor society, to select its leadership, and to hear a report from I. S. Sokolov of the Moscow council.

The leaders of the society took Zubatov's advice and, led by Sokolov, next sought the approval of the higher authorities. On November 13 they met with the deputy governor of the city, V. E. Frish who agreed to allow the workers to assemble on condition that the police receive prior notification. When they visited the Department of Police, Lopukhin expressed his sympathy with their aims and plans. Meanwhile Zubatov had persuaded Plehve to receive a delegation of Petersburg workers who allegedly shared his "wish to fight against sedition."[4] On November 21 the minister urged the workers to unite and organize to obtain benefits for the working class. Of greater significance, he pledged his support and expressed the desirability of leading the working class, through experienced leaders like those before him, away from precipitous action and toward social· peace. Lastly the delegation obtained general assurances of assistance for their project from the archpriest Ornatskii and Metropolitan Antonii.[5]

Zubatov's plans had moved unhindered with such rapidity that it was decided to reveal them before representatives of Petersburg high society. On December 10 six of Zubatov's followers addressed a session of the council of Russkoe Sobranie (The Russian Assembly), an ultraconservative and patriotic society newly founded under the chairmanship of Prince Dmitrii Golitsyn. The meeting was one of the

3. *Rabochaia gazeta,* Oct. 2, 9, 16, 1906. This newspaper, which appeared irregularly in 1906 and 1908, contains a series of anonymous articles on the Petersburg Zubatovshchina.

4. *Rabochaia gazeta,* Oct. 30, 1906.

5. *Ibid.;* "K istorii Zubatovshchiny," p. 87; Vovchik, p. 132; "Peterburgskoe dukhovenstvo i 9 ianvaria," *Krasnyi arkhiv,* 1929, no. 5 (36), p. 196.

few times in Russia's history when representatives of upper society and court circles had occasion to meet formally with members of the working class.[6] Among the dignitaries present were the Minister of Interior, high military and court functionaries, prelates of the church, officials of the local city administration, and several newspaper editors.

Each of the six workers discussed the current state and needs of the working class and the activities of the Moscow council, and appealed for the support of Russian society and government. The Moscow labor societies were described as instruments for undermining the appeal of radical agitators and forestalling labor strife. Dwelling on the Moscow factory owners' lack of sympathy for their mutual-aid societies, the speakers beseeched members of the audience to use their influence to further the education of the workers and to obtain government subsidies and credits. Any success attained by socialist propaganda was attributed to unsatisfactory working conditions; the best means to refute socialist propaganda and discredit the agitators was to improve the living standards of the workers.[7]

The members of the Russian Assembly were sympathetic to the workers' disavowal of Western European labor practices and loyalty to indigenous Russian principles of autocracy and Orthodoxy. They reacted negatively, on the other hand, to the idea of labor councils. Pikunov had lauded such institutions as enabling working-class representatives to restrain the workers from making unwarranted demands while at the same time expressing their true needs and wishes. He made a major blunder, however, in recommending to his ultraconservative audience that such councils be united into a central labor council, which could represent working-class interests before the government.

The most severe criticism came from two publicists Zubatov had

6. On the Russian Assembly see Gurko, p. 27; Hans Rogger, "Was there a Russian Fascism? The Union of Russian People," *Journal of Modern History*, 36 (1964), 401; Walter Laqueur, *Russia and Germany* (Boston and Toronto, 1965), p. 84.

7. *Moskovskiia vedomosti*, Dec. 15, 1902; Feb. 4, 1903. Slepov's account of the meeting was published in the form of a letter to the editor. Lenin's biting attack on Slepov's letter was published in *Iskra*, no. 31 (Jan. 1, 1903), under the title of "Moskovskie zubatovtsy v Peterburge." A second report of the meeting, less favorable to the workers than Slepov's account, is found in the journal of the Russian Assembly: "Zasedanie Soveta 'Russkago Sobraniia,'" *Izvestiia russkago sobraniia*, 1, no. 1 (1903), pp. 46–60.

felt would be sympathetic to his plans. V. V. Komarov, the editor of *Svet* (The Light), assured the Russian Assembly that a central labor council was unnecessary in Russia, where no sharp struggle between labor and capital as yet existed. V. L. Velichkov, the editor of *Russkii vestnik* (The Russian Herald), accused the invited workers of having adopted political issues, and retorted: "The state must protect property, and the workers must know that the interests of the factory owners are as dear to the state as are the interests of the workers."[8]

Prince V. P. Meshcherskii, the influential editor of *Grazhdanin* (Citizen), expressed second thoughts about the meeting in his column. He criticized the speakers for having dared to leave the ranks of the working class to appear before an alien audience. While not opposed to secret support for the labor organizations, he was against having the support publicized, for he held it was a dangerous precedent likely to encourage further demands. The meeting indicated that the labor question had become fashionable in some quarters; since it involved hundreds of thousands of workers, great caution was needed, Meshcherskii concluded, lest one's fingers get burned.[9] The conservative press, which Zubatov had so counted upon in the past, thus proved hostile in Petersburg and unwilling to popularize his movement.

Despite rapid progress among the workers, Zubatov and his followers were unable to establish firm foundations in St. Petersburg. The Petersburg Zubatovshchina inherited from the Moscow movement a legacy of rumors and suspicions about the covert role of the police that had a divisive effect on its leaders and members. Moreover, the local social-democratic intelligentsia had anticipated that the organizers of the Moscow Zubatovshchina would eventually try their luck in Petersburg; consequently Zubatov's Petersburg followers were openly harassed as police agents to a degree unknown in Moscow. The December 12 meeting of machine workers, for example, was dramatically disrupted by the delivery and reading of an anonymous letter addressed to the workers that charged Sokolov with being Zubatov's agent,

8. "Zasedanie Soveta," p. 57. The journalist S. N. Syromiatnikov, a contributor to the reactionary *Novoe vremia*, also subjected the workers' presentation to scathing, all-round criticism.

9. *Grazhdanin*, Dec. 15, 1902; *Moskovskiia vedomosti*, Feb. 8, 1903. Editorial criticism also appeared in *Rodnaia rech'*, Dec. 29, 1902.

employed to entrap the activists among them. The letter had its intended effect, for the workers refused to allow Sokolov to speak in his own defense.[10] At the following meeting, opposition speakers daringly arose from the audience to challence the authenticity of a letter from a worker who had written favorably about the organizers of the Petersburg Zubatovshchina. From the audience came demands that the Petersburg workers organize their society along the lines of labor unions in the West, and that each speaker at the meeting be guaranteed personal immunity. A proposal by the chairman to establish a workers' library to be stocked with books of interest to the membership brought a rhetorical question from the floor: "And what about Marx and Engels?" When the chairman announced that General Kleigels had approved the meetings, the crowd responded with the chant: "Zubatov, Zubatov, Zubatov." The Petersburg workers appeared to have a broad knowledge of Western European trade unionism: time and again the chairman was challenged on a variety of issues.[11]

It is doubtful if the religious and monarchist orientation of the new society did anything but further alienate potential members. On Sunday, February 2, 1903, the first formal gathering of the Petersburg Workers of Mechanical Factories was held in the hall of the Society of Religious and Moral Enlightenment in the Troitskii church. The meeting was opened by the Reverend Sergei, rector of the St. Petersburg Ecclesiastical Academy, who spoke on the force of mutual help in Christianity. A long letter addressed to the archpriest Ornatskii from the archconservative General E. V. Bogdanovich was read to the gathering. Bogdanovich stressed the time-worn theme that Russia differed from other countries where the working-class question was a burning issue because in Russia one powerful master, the tsar, through loving care as father of his people would secure justice and well-being for all. *Moskovskiia vedomosti,* in reporting the meeting, could truthfully state that "as in Moscow the workers place their affairs under the canopy of the Holy Orthodox Church . . . in distinction form any analogous labor movement in the West."[12]

10. *Rabochaia gazeta,* 1908, no. 1; I. I. Egorov, "V riadakh petersburgskikh sotsial-demokratov nakanune vtorogo s"ezda," *Krasnaia letopis',* 1928, no. 2 (26), pp. 42–43. The Petersburg Social Democratic Committee issued a number of leaflets attacking the Zubatovshchina, among them *Listovki peterburgskikh bol'shevikov 1902–1917* (Leningrad, 1939), pp. 26–30, 42–46, 53–57, 76–78.

11. *Revoliutsionnaia Rossiia,* no. 16 (Jan. 15, 1903).

12. *Moskovskiia vedomosti,* Feb. 5, 1903.

Opposition within the government, at both the local and ministerial levels, also inhibited the growth of the Petersburg Zubatovshchina. News of the new labor society soon reached the factory inspectors and the industrialists. Factory inspector V. P. Litvinov-Falinskii, for one, learned of the development when workers questioned him about labor unions and asked him whether they might receive substantial benefits from joining a mutual-aid society. The first stirrings of the Zubatovshchina in the capital coincided with a noticeable increase in labor demands at the Petersburg factories; although they had no direct evidence, the Petersburg authorities were not slow in linking the two. Thus when the factory inspector A. P. Iakimov received demands for a wage increase from workers at the Nevskii textile mill and learned that similar demands were going to be made elsewhere, he surmised they had been prompted by the new labor organizations.

To clarify the standing of the new society, General Kleigels hastily called a meeting with a senior factory inspector and Captain Sazonov, chief of the Petersburg Okhrana. Kleigels was a critic of Zubatov's approach to the labor problem; he had earlier urged Plehve to take the organization of labor out of the hands of the Department of Police, "the activity of which, in view of special conditions inherent in it, can frequently call forth in the public completely unmerited insinuations."[13] He had first learned of the labor meetings among the Petersburg workers through newspaper accounts while on vacation; he was particularly incensed that both he and the factory inspectors, the officials with primary responsibility for investigating labor problems in the capital, were kept uninformed. At the meeting, Sazonov explained the purpose and history of the Petersburg Zubatovshchina; a report of the meeting was forwarded to Witte on January 11, 1903.[14]

Witte played a major part in stifling the development of the Zubatovshchina in Petersburg. To his advantage, a schism had occurred among proponents of mutual help among the Petersburg workers. One group, terming itself "Independents," opposed involvement of the police or intelligentsia and favored labor organizations initiated and led by rank-and-file workers. The

13. *Osvobozhdenie*, no. 20/21 (April 18, 1903).

14. Three days later Witte forwarded the report to Plehve with a letter requesting, with sly innocence, further information on the matter, in order that proper instructions could be given to the factory inspectors (N. A. Bukhbinder, ed., "K istorii 'Sobraniia russkikh fabrichno-zavodskikh rabochikh g. S. Peterburga,'" *Krasnaia letopis'*, 1922, no. 1, p. 292).

"Independents" had composed the letter that had disrupted the December 12 meeting of machine workers. On February 2 their delegates met with Witte and attacked the Petersburg society as an instrument in the hands of Zubatov and the police to snare the more militant workers. Witte expressed agreement with their allegations and advised them to boycott the Zubatov societies as harmful to the development of the labor movement and of industry.[15]

On the same day Witte took another step to thwart Zubatov's plans. Writing to Plehve that he had learned the Ministry of Interior was preparing to approve the statutes of a mutual-help society for the Petersburg machine workers, he strongly recommended that action be delayed until a commission under the chairmanship of the Assistant Minister of Finance, Prince A. D. Obolenskii, could study the general question of labor societies and mutual-help funds. Plehve, for reasons that are not clear, readily agreed, and directed Lopukhin to communicate this to the commission.[16]

A series of lectures on religious and educational themes, similar to those begun in Moscow in the summer of 1902, were also planned for the Petersburg workers. However, the open baiting of the speakers at the labor meetings by political agitators caused members of the academic community, who had promised to take part, to withdraw for fear of public censure, and the lecture series was stillborn. Moreover, the cooperation of the clergy and the use of the facilities of the Society of Religious and Moral Enlightenment were ended on orders of Metropolitan Antonii after Witte informed Father Ornatskii that the police were implicated in the movement to organize the Petersburg machine workers.[17] By the spring of 1903 dissension among the leaders had reached the members and strengthened their suspicion that the meetings were a police trap. The Petersburg Zubatovshchina ground to a halt, with scheduled meetings frequently cancelled for lack of popular interest.[18]

15. *Rabochaia gazeta*, nos. 1 and 2, 1908; *Grazhdanin*, Feb. 6, 1903; *Russkiia vedomosti*, Feb. 15, 1903.

16. Bukhbinder, "K istorii 'Sobraniia,'" pp. 296–97; "K istorii Zubatovshchiny," p. 88; Vovchik, p. 133. The commission was established to examine the late D. S. Sipiagin's recommendations. On February 6, Plehve testified in favor of mutual-aid funds at individual plants; he opposed common funds for workers at several plants (Shelymagin, p. 49).

17. *Zapiski Georgiia Gapona* (Moscow, 1918), pp. 41–42; *Rabochaia gazeta*, 1908, no. 2; Skarzhinskii, p. 262; "Peterburgskoe dukhovenstvo i 9 ianvaria," p. 196.

18. *Zapiski Georgiia Gapona*, p. 41; Varnashev, p. 185.

The Petersburg labor movement initiated by Zubatov was revived by the priest Georgii Gapon in the summer of 1903 after the dismissal of Zubatov and Witte. In November 1903 statutes drawn up under Gapon's direction for an Assembly of Russian Factory and Mill Workers of the City of St. Petersburg were forwarded to the city governor. Plehve approved the statutes in February 1904, after which the assembly, under Gapon's leadership, quickly spread its influence among the Petersburg workers and was the center of events leading to Bloody Sunday in January 1905. In March 1904 Plehve also approved the statutes of the St. Petersburg Society of Mutual Help of Workers in Mechanical Factories, led by M. A. Ushakov, a worker in the state printing office, a former labor organizer for Zubatov and later a protégé of Witte.[19] The further history of these labor organizations, however, lies outside the scope of this work.

## The Moscow Zubatovshchina without Zubatov

Zubatov's departure for Petersburg probably aroused ambivalent feelings among Muscovites hostile to his views. His removal from Moscow might, as Witte among others believed, deprive his supporters of guidance and bring the Moscow Zubatovshchina shortly to a halt. But others felt that at the Ministry of Interior Zubatov would be in a better position to propagate his ideas among influential court circles and to promote the adoption of his program throughout the empire.

The Guzhon affair and the interministerial discussion of the Moscow Zubatovshchina that ensued did put a temporary brake on the Moscow Society of Mutual Help of Workers in Mechanical Factories. Although its statutes had been approved on February 14, 1902, the first general meeting of the society did not take place until September 14. Registration in the society, which had been opened as of March 1, produced by September a disappointing membership of 197 and a treasury of but 900 rubles, of which one hundred had been donated by Bishop Parfenii and ten by Lev Tikhomirov. Afanas'ev

19. Bukhbinder, "K istorii 'Sobraniia,'" pp. 289–90, 298; *Zapiski Georgiia Gapona,* p. 43; "K istorii Zubatovshchiny," p. 88; *S.-Peterburgskiia vedomosti,* April 14, 1904; *Rus',* Oct. 4 and 11, 1904. Relations between Zubatov and Gapon are discussed in Walter Sablinsky, "The Road to Bloody Sunday" (Ph.D. dissertation, Department of History, University of California, Berkeley, 1968), pp. 161–74, 179–81; Zubatov, "Zubatovshchina," pp. 169–72.

and Slepov addressed the first assembly, dwelling on the society's significance for the workers and predicting that the factory owners would in time cooperate with it. In the future the society planned to hold a lottery, present concerts, and establish a network of stores. The new, more conservative approach of the Moscow administration was expressed in the society's honorary membership, among which were Bishop Parfenii, the priest I. Fudel', Lev Tikhomirov, V. F. Dzhunkovskii, chairman of the Capital Guardianship of Popular Sobriety, and General Trepov.[20]

The Zubatovshchina made considerable progress among the Moscow textile workers, particularly late in 1902, after the statutes of the Moscow Society of Mutual Assistance of Workers in Textile Production were approved by the Ministry of Interior. The statutes of the new society, which was open to weavers, spinners, and laborers in the print and dye works of Moscow and its suburbs, allowed for police surveillance and supervision, as well as intervention by the Moscow administration; they reveal how far the latter had moved toward patent conservatism. Candidate-membership in the society was open to factory inspectors, administrative personnel of the factories, clergymen, and even policemen. The group's administrative board was selected by the Moscow chief of police; they could do little without his authorization or that of the Moscow governor-general.[21]

The textile workers, nevertheless, exhibited an avid interest in mutual help. At their first general meeting, held on January 9, 1903, registered membership of 800 was announced; two months later the number exceeded 1,300. Honorary members included the same group of prelates and bureaucrats as in the Society of Machine Workers, with the addition of V. A. Gringmut, the editor of *Moskovskiia vedomosti.*[22]

At Easter the directors of the Moscow textile mills had protested against the council and were prepared to shut down their plants and rebuff the demands of their workers; now they accepted honorary

20. *Russkoe slovo,* Sept. 15, 1902; *Moskovskiia vedomosti,* Sept. 16, 1902. Ozerov was likewise elected to honorary membership but publicly renounced the honor in protest against the manner in which the original statutes of the society had been altered (*Russkoe slovo, ibid.*).

21. Kats and Milonov, pp. 87–88; *Rabochii soiuz,* no. 1 (Oct. 3, 1906).

22. *Moskovskiia vedomosti,* Aug. 26, Sept. 12, 1902; Jan. 22, March 18, 1903; 1,216 members were registered as of the beginning of 1904 (Shmeleva, Shuia *Uchenye zapiski,* 1960, p. 71).

membership in the new society and even generously contributed to its treasury, once they had been assured that its goals were conservative. Krasivskii, who was elected president, told those gathered at the first general meeting that the society had the support of the government, the local authorities, and the factory owners.[23]

*Moskovskiia vedomosti*, which supported mutual-aid societies "as the best institutions which secure the correct distribution of the uneven income of the working man," hailed the change of heart among the Moscow industrialists.[24] "Knowing from the example of the West what kind of role workers play in preparation of social revolution, the Moscow factory owners had been firmly convinced that in Russia any labor movement could have solely a socialistic, revolutionary character"; the appearance of socialist agitators at the factories reinforced the owners' view that mutual-aid societies were "a harmful, criminal matter," to be opposed by "all means open and secret." Recently, however, the Moscow factory owners had begun "to examine more closely the living conditions of the Moscow workers and are convinced of their mistake; they see now that the Moscow workers unite not in order to submit to the socialist movement, but, on the contrary, to oppose it more successfully; consequently they see that the workers and the factory owners have one and the same goal and that the factory owners must not push the Moscow workers away but give them a helping hand in their good patriotic undertaking."[25] Thus, following Zubatov's departure from Moscow, there was the making of a rapprochement between the Moscow industrial community and the labor organizations Zubatov had nurtured.

23. *Moskovskiia vedomosti*, Jan. 22, Feb. 27, June 28, 1903; Laverychev, p. 161; *Rabochie Trekhgornoi manufaktury*, p. 32. The latter work includes memoirs of workers at the Prokhorov plant and valuable material on the Zubatovshchina among the Moscow textile workers.

24. *Moskovskiia vedomosti*, Jan. 11 and 24, 1903. Most likely the editorials were written by Lev Tikhomirov. As recognition of the new conservative course of the Moscow Zubatov societies, the Ministry of Finance on August 19, 1903, granted Trepov's request for financial assistance; 20,000 rubles were transferred to the Department of Police which, in turn, lent the money on an interest-free, long-term basis to the Society of Machine Workers (8,000 rubles) and the Society of Mutual Help of Workers in Textile Production (12,000 rubles) (Laverychev, p. 160). Other evidence indicates that the loan was not forthcoming until the following year (Shmeleva, Moscow *Uchenye zapiski*, p. 69; Bukhbinder, "Zubatovshchina v Moskve," pp. 102, 108; Tikhomirov, "25 let nazad," p. 23).

25. *Moskovskiia vedomosti*, Jan. 24, 1903.

During the course of 1902 and 1903 groups of Moscow button makers, tobacco workers, perfumers, woodworkers, confectioners, and box makers petitioned the government for permission to establish mutual-help societies, which in most cases began functioning without the sanction of the Petersburg authorities, who seemed in no hurry to give approval.[26] At Easter in 1903, Tsar Nicholas visited Moscow and warmly received a delegation of button makers, confectioners, perfumers, and tobacco workers in the Kremlin, but the results did nothing to advance the cause of their mutual-help societies.[27] In June of that year V. V. Ratko, the new chief of the Moscow Okhrana, complained that the delay in approving the statutes was destroying interest in the societies.[28] Not until January 1904, well over a year after the earliest had been submitted to the Petersburg authorities, were these statutes approved.

The Moscow Zubatovshchina gave the confectioners, perfumers, and tobacco and cigarette workers (about which relatively little is known) the rudiments of organizational unity and experience in economic agitation.[29] Among the woodworkers—joiners, button makers and box makers—the Zubatovshchina was popular from its outset, many joiners having previously been members of the Society of Machine Workers. In the first months of 1902, the woodworkers, encouraged by the council's efficacy in gaining benefits for the Moscow workers, began to hold meetings of their own under capable working-class leaders who were agents of Zubatov. Although the council in the summer of that year ceased to function in the capacity of an agent representing working-class demands, the woodworkers were not discouraged and continued to gather at their assemblies and discuss common interests. The leaders of the

26. Ainzaft (*Zubatovshchina*, pp. 58–59) states that in February 1902 the button makers received permission to hold meetings, the confectioners and perfumers in May of that year, the tobacco workers in October, and the box makers in May 1903.

27. *Moskovskiia vedomosti*, April 8 and 9, 1903; *Iskra*, no. 41 (June 1, 1903); Shmeleva, Moscow *Uchenye zapiski*, p. 57. Slepov tried to use the Moscow council leaders' visit to the tsar on April 7, 1903, to encourage workers to join the Zubatovshchina. On April 21 he called upon the workers to join because "the tsar knows about our organization," and said that they could obtain his favor "if we ourselves take the peaceful road" (Shmeleva, *ibid.*).

28. Ainzaft, *Zubatovshchina*, p. 68.

29. *Moskovskiia vedomosti*, Aug. 5, 1902; *Russkiia vedomosti*, Aug. 5 and 26, 1902; Ev. Evsenin, *Ot fabrikanta k Krasnomu Oktiabriu* (Moscow, 1927), pp. 19–20; *Sputnik Pishchevika*, 1922, as cited in S. Ainzaft, *Pervyi etap professional'nogo dvizheniia v Rossii* (Moscow-Gomel', 1924), I, 40; Kats and Milonov, p. 4; Ainzaft, *Zubatovshchina*, p. 58.

Zubatovshchina, now charged by Trepov with maintaining social peace, often found themselves helpless to prevent economic strikes caused by labor grievances the council previously would have taken up. For the woodworkers the Zubatovshchina brought a consciousness of self-interests beyond the individual workshop, exhibited at times in the collection and distribution of common strike funds.[30]

With the approval of the statutes of the new mutual-help societies in early 1904, the original plan to have workers in each major sector of industry organized in close association with the local administration had been realized. The achievement was superficial, however, for the eager interest shown by the Moscow workers in the first months of 1902 had waned. Moreover, without Zubatov's presence at the helm the movement lacked coordination and direction, drifting on its own inertia until the revolution of 1905. Further weakening the movement after Zubatov's departure was a leadership struggle among the ambitious officers of the council, who now came under more frequent and open attack for being police agents.[31] After the summer of 1902 the Moscow Zubatovshchina lacked any real continuity.

The Moscow administration continued to give its blessing to the council. No longer was it a focus of working-class grievances, however; it had become a convenient instrument for prevention of strikes and other factory disturbances. Beginning in the summer of 1902, the council no longer willingly received collective complaints or petitions or acted as a bargaining agent. Events at the Levisson furniture plant in the spring of 1903 illustrate the new course.[32] On May 31, on the initiative of a certain Kurochkin, Zubatov's leading supporter at the factory, a petition demanding a ten-hour workday was transmitted to the factory owner with the signature of 200 joiners. When the owner refused to concede, the workers decided to strike. When Kurochkin failed to discourage them, he threw in his lot with the strikers. Slepov was then dispatched to the plant but also failed to talk the joiners out of striking. Consequently, as a

30. *Russkiia vedomosti*, Aug. 5, 1902; S. Chernomordik [P. Larionov], "Dvadtsat' let tomu nazad," *Put' k Oktiabriu*, no. 3 (1923), p. 47; *Ocherki po istorii revoliutsionnogo dvizheniia*, p. 20; Ainzaft, *Istoria*, pp. 83–89; Milonov and Rakovskii, pp. 35–36, 41–43, 46–50, 52–55, 59–63, 69, 72–74.

31. *Russkoe delo*, July 30 and Aug. 13, 1905.

32. Archival material indicates that beginning in May 1902, the number of petitions received by the council sharply decreased (Ainzaft, *Zubatovshchina*, p. 64).

warning Trepov demanded that Afanas'ev and Slepov sign a statement that they understood that should any similar grievance, complaint, or petition be drawn up on behalf of workers for transmittal to a factory owner, they would be prohibited from all further activity "with regard to the leadership of the Moscow workers."[33]

The termination of the council's adversary role on behalf of the working-class demands is reflected in the reports of the factory inspectors for 1903. A sizable decrease from the previous year in the number of grievances filed by workers is noted, along with a corresponding increase in the percentage of those found upon investigation to be well-grounded. The change was attributed to the decline of the Moscow Zubatovshchina: "Apparently those temporary conditions that stimulated the workers, which took place chiefly in Moscow *okrug*, about which there was mention in the report for 1902, lost their validity in the current year."[34]

The Moscow administration's *volte-face* since the days of the Guzhon affair was well illustrated during the strike at the Bromlei machine plant in 1903. On June 29, 250 turners at the plant left work rather than submit to further abuse by the foremen who levied fines. Two days later they resolved to remain away from work until the factory administration made concessions in the workday and ended the rigid application of fines for tardiness. The turners, however, declined to choose representatives to negotiate with the factory administration, since those chosen under similar circumstances the previous year had been discharged. The local police officer, as well as Afanas'ev and Slepov, who were assigned by Trepov to report on the strike, emphasized the unusually orderly manner in which the strikers conducted themselves.[35] Nevertheless, on July 2, Trepov ordered the local police officer to post a notice that all those refusing to return to work would be permanently discharged and banished from Moscow. The factory inspector also urged the strikers to return to work, since he had found their complaints to be unjustified and the management had rejected their demands. On July 5, Trepov

---

33. *Ibid.*, p. 65; Piontkovskii, p. 99; Milonov and Rakovskii, p. 55.
34. *Svod otchetov fabrichnykh inspektorov za 1903 god*, p. vii.
35. "Stachka rabochikh zavoda br. Bromlei v 1903 g.," *Krasnyi arkhiv*, 1933, no. 1 (56), p. 141. It has been charged that Slepov exhorted the strikers to return to work (Piontkovsii, p. 99).

ordered that workers who had refused to resume work receive terminal wages and their passports. The entire work force of 945 was discharged, several being placed under arrest. Lacking financial sustenance for a long strike, more than a third of the employees reregistered for work on the day they had been discharged. Because of the presence of socialist agitators, troops were sent to surround the plant on July 7, after which the remaining strikers returned to work.[36] The Moscow administration had turned from an influential advocate of the workmen's cause into a rigid and harsh enforcer of the laws.

After Zubatov's forced retirement in August 1903, the Moscow administration acted against the workers' economic demands and agitation with even less restraint. Trepov increasingly resorted to force, the instinctive response of a police official. The strike of the Moscow printers in September 1903 well illustrates this. The printers were among the highest paid Moscow workers, their yearly wage nearly double that of the average worker. Since 1869 they had had their own mutual-help association, the Printers' Auxiliary Fund, in which representatives of the local administration and the higher bureaucracy served as honorary members; in 1903 the association had a membership of 460.[37]

Plans to unify the Moscow printers around common economic demands were begun in April 1903. On July 16 the printers, bypassing the existing fund, petitioned Trepov for permission to gather and discuss common interests; they also sought his support for their demands. The printers were not in agreement on a further course of action; some opposed a strike under any condition.

Trepov's response, however, forced unity and triggered a strike. He would neither permit the printers to hold a meeting to work out their demands nor allow their representatives to negotiate with their employers. Consequently they gathered secretly outside the city. When Trepov, in turn, precipitously arrested several of their

36. "Stachka rabochikh zavoda br. Bromlei," pp. 141–44; A. V. Ushakov, "Rabochee dvizhenie v Moskve nakanune pervoi russkoi revoliutsii," Karelo-finskii pedagogicheskii institut, Petrozavodsk, *Uchenye zapiski,* 2, pt. 1 (1955), Seriia obshchestvennykh nauk, p. 75; *Revoliutsionnaia Rossiia,* no. 30 (Aug. 20, 1903); *Iskra,* no. 45 (Aug. 1, 1903). During a strike at the Rontaller button factory in the fall of 1903, Trepov sent a representative of the council to warn the workers either to end the strike or face punishment (Shmeleva, Moscow *Uchenye zapiski,* pp. 66–67).

37. Sher, pp. 33, 74–75, 77.

leaders, they decided to strike. On September 9, 5,255 printers at some fifty-six Moscow plants went on strike; within a short time their number reached 15,000. Trepov responded with strict measures. Groups of strikers were dispersed by police patrols; policemen were posted at the print shops; Cossack detachments were placed at key points throughout the city to prevent the general public and the university students from joining the strikers in a mass demonstration. On September 10, Trepov ordered that printers who did not return to work be immediately discharged and banished from Moscow; mass arrests among the printers followed.

The actions of the strikers did not warrant repressive measures. The strike was notable for the absence of unreasonable demands and the peaceful, orderly conduct of the strikers. At no time did they organize a street demonstration or express hostility to their employers; mostly they just idled away their time. Moreover, their demands were either purely economic in terms of wages and hours, or primarily concerned with improvements in sanitary conditions. The professional solidarity of the printers made the strike unique for its time. The strikers refused to negotiate with individual owners, declaring they would bargain only on an industrywide basis with the Society of the Promoters of Printing to which their employers belonged.[38]

The employers, many of whom were sympathetic to the strike demands, readily agreed to institute uniform working conditions throughout the industry. Most of the printers' demands were met. Thus the strike resulted in a victory for the workers not because of support from the Moscow administration, as in the early days of the Zubatovshchina, but because the owners found the demands compatible with their own interests. Had Trepov not acted so hastily and forcefully, had he permitted representatives of the printers to bargain collectively, the strike could have been avoided. Zubatov would not have allowed the Moscow administration, as representatives of the autocracy, to oppose the just demands of the printers or deny them the right to assemble. Least of all would he

38. Sher, pp. 123–24; Piontkovskii, p. 100; *Iskra*, no. 49 (Oct. 1, 1903); no. 50 (Oct. 15, 1903); "Grève des ouvriers typographes à Moscou," Vautier, Consul General of France in Moscow, to Delcassé, Sept. 28, 1903, n.s.; "K istorii vseobshchei stachki na iuge Rossii v 1903 g.," *Krasnyi arkhiv*, 1938, no. 3(88), pp. 110–11. The history of the strike is in Sher's book, pp. 108–27; he describes the Society of the Promoters of Printing at pp. 98–107.

have forcibly dispersed their peaceful gatherings, leaving the impression that the state opposed their interests.

The Moscow administration soon tried to make amends for its harsh policy, and after the strike was over let it be known through the council that it would countenance a legal organization of printers, but it was rebuffed. The officers of the council took matters in their own hands and undertook to organize the printers. At Krasivskii's urging a group of printers petitioned to establish a new organization to be affiliated with the council. Permission was granted, and toward the end of 1903 the Society of Typography Workers began functioning with a program similar to other labor organizations associated with the Zubatovshchina. Despite attempts on the part of the socialist Union of Printers to boycott the society and charges that the society's leaders had ties with the Okhrana—ties which its officers proudly acknowledged—many printers were attracted to it; from fifty to three hundred attended each meeting. Many joined the society convinced by the September events of the need for more permanent unity. V. V. Sher, who interviewed its members, found that the average printer was not alienated by the society's association with the Okhrana and genuinely believed the society could best serve his professional interests.[39] The impulse to organize, which had imbued the Russian working class since the mid-1890's, swept many printers into the fold of the council.

Nevertheless, by 1904 the Moscow Zubatovshchina was in decline. By December 1903 membership in the Moscow Society of Mutual Help of Workers in Mechanical Factories had dropped to 190. An inspection commission established by Trepov reported in early 1904 that out of a nominal membership of 316 only 35 regularly paid dues. Equally discouraging was the finding that most workers who joined the society soon left it, convinced it was incapable of producing tangible benefits for its members. Moreover, many were reluctant to join, the commission reported, because of their comparatively secure material position—the machine workers being among the highest paid factory workers. The commission had an equally pessimistic report about the Zubatovshchina among the

39. Sher, pp. 132–36; Piontkovskii, pp. 99–100; Shmeleva, Moscow *Uchenye zapiski*, p. 65; Ushakov, p. 75. Krasivskii earlier had tried to dissuade the printers from striking (Pletnev, p. 21).

textile workers. Of the 1,200 members of their society less than a quarter attended its meetings, and the vast majority had ceased to pay dues. The society could hardly exist for another year, a member of the commission regretfully concluded.[40] The officers of the council gave other reasons for the poor progress of the Moscow Zubatovshchina: opposition by factory owners, the failure of the workers to understand the significance of mutual-aid funds, and the relatively small amount in the funds due to the insignificant amount contributed by each member.[41]

Thus by 1904 Zubatov's bold plans for controlling the labor movement had failed. In Petersburg his labor program met with hostility from influential circles in society and the bureaucracy; he could do little without strong support from his superiors. In Moscow, Trepov and the Grand Duke Sergei, Zubatov's champions and protectors, lacked his tact and patience; without a sensitive understanding of the worker's outlook and grievances they could little hope to retain a mass following.

### The Moscow Zubatovshchina in 1905 and After

The Moscow working class entered the revolutionary year of 1905 without having committed itself to the leadership of either the socialist intelligentsia or the Zubatovshchina. By the end of 1904, Moscow Social Democrats had succeeded in establishing an illegal union among the printers; the only organizations existing among the machine and textile workers, the largest work force in the city, were those associated with the Zubatovshchina.

The great strike wave that followed Bloody Sunday brought the struggle for the allegiance of the working class more out in the open. For the next few months the workers once again flocked to the mass meetings held by the Zubatov organizations, whose legal standing apparently guaranteed freedom of discussion not easily available elsewhere in those stormy days. Zubatov's followers, as in the past, tried to keep the workers' demands within an economic framework. They were also prepared to aid in the formulation of the economic demands of the workers.

The high point in the council's success during 1905, and the last

40. Ainzaft, *Zubatovshchina*, p. 67; Shmeleva, Moscow *Uchenye zapiski*, pp. 57, 68–69.
41. "Zasedanie Soveta 'Russkago Sobraniia,'" p. 49.

time it was able to gain a measure of collective support from the Moscow workers, occurred on March 30, when Krasivskii and Afanas'ev led a delegation to the Ministry of Finance to deliver a petition signed by 2,575 Moscow workers. The petition had been discussed at a number of meetings of the labor societies and had been opposed by socialist speakers who appeared at the meetings. The petition's eleven-point program called for legalization of trade unions, an end to criminal prosecution of strikers, state insurance for industrial accidents, a shorter workday, revision of factory legislation to equalize labor's rights with those of the factory owners, and additional working-class representation in consultative bodies drafting labor legislation.[42]

Trepov's appointment to the post of Petersburg governor-general in late January and the assassination of the Grand Duke Sergei the following month removed the shield of authority that had surrounded the Moscow Workers' Council and its labor societies. Socialist agitators took advantage of the council's weakness and addressed large gatherings of the Zubatov societies, attacking the Zubatovshchina and calling for greater labor militancy and an emphasis on political demands.[43] In July, the officers of the council suffered a personal blow when the Okhrana announced that individual monetary subsidies totaling four hundred rubles a month would no longer be paid after August.[44] The Zubatovites, nevertheless, still took to the field against their socialist opponents. At times they tried to recruit new members, hoping to take advantage of the inclination for organization among the factory workers. The Zubatovshchina was not unaffected by the strike movement in 1905; in October strike funds were distributed to workers from the treasury of the Society of Textile Workers.[45]

The Moscow Zubatovshchina gave the trade-union movement a

42. *Novoe vremia*, April 1, 1905; Ovsiannikov, p. 46; Sher, p. 135; Kats and Milonov, pp. 167–68; Skarzhinskii, pp. 5, 167–71.

43. *Iskra*, no. 89 (Feb. 24, 1905), no. 94 (March 25, 1905); *Rabochie Trekhgornoi manufaktury*, p. 55; N. Morozov-Vorontsov, ed., *Zamoskvorech'e v 1905 g.* (Moscow, 1925), p. 9.

44. Men'shchikov, *Okhrana i revoliutsiia*, III, 71–72; Ainzaft, *Zubatovshchina*, pp. 48–49.

45. P. Kolokol'nikov [K. Dmitriev], "Otryvki iz vospominanii (Glava III)," *Materialy po istorii professional'nogo dvizheniia v Rossii*, 3 (1925), 225–26; *Biulleteni Muzeia sodeistviia trudu*, no. 2 (Nov. 26, 1905); V. V. Simonenko and G. D. Kostomarov, eds., *Iz istorii revoliutsii 1905 goda v Moskve i Moskovskoi gubernii* (Moscow, 1931), pp. 147–48; Pletnev, p. 18.

rich legacy of trained labor leaders, among them the organizers of the Union of Tobacco Workers and two of the founders of the Moscow Union of Metal Workers.[46] It also left a temporary legacy of mistrust among the Moscow workers toward labor unions. The leaders of the new trade unions established in 1905 among the textile, confectionery, and tobacco workers had to defend their organizations and goals from charges of similarity to Zubatov societies.[47]

In general the Zubatov labor societies suffered further depletion in their ranks during 1905, and several came to an end. The Society of Machine Workers, the oldest of the Moscow organizations associated with the council, continued to exist for some time alongside the Moscow Union of Metal Workers, formed in 1906. Some metal workers joined both organizations; a few individuals held official posts in the rival societies. In 1910 the Society of Machine Workers was finally liquidated; the Society of Textile Workers ended its existence shortly thereafter. Some labor societies originally associated with the Zubatovshchina were known to be functioning as late as 1914.[48]

46. "O dvizhenii," pp. 145–46; Z. Shchap, *Moskovskie metallisty v professional'nom dvizhenii* (Moscow, 1927), pp. 59, 64–65; Sher, p. 128; Kolokol'nikov and Rapoport, p. 223.
47. Kolokol'nikov and Rapoport, p. 222; Grinevich, p. 44.
48. Sviatlovskii, pp. 73–74; Ainzaft, *Zubatovshchina*, p. 69; Bukhbinder, "Zubatovshchina v Moskve," p. 103.

# CHAPTER 7

# The Struggle against Social Democracy

Zubatov's aim had been to persuade the workers that they could fulfill their needs within the existing order, and thus to destroy any modicum of faith they might have in the radical intelligentsia. His chief enemy was Russian social democracy. The Social Democrats on their part could be expected to launch an all-out attack on the Zubatovshchina, sworn as it was to isolate them from those they counted upon to become the shock troops of a socialist revolution.

From the first days of the Zubatovshchina the Moscow authorities took precautionary measures to safeguard their infant labor movement from penetration by subversives bent on disrupting it. The societies were encouraged to police their own meetings through a screening committee assigned to make note of suspicious persons in attendance and to prevent outsiders from gaining entrance. In some instances members gave officers of the council the names of fellow workers who had called on them to oppose the Zubatovshchina, although the practice was not common. Only infrequently did opposition speakers dare to come out openly and attack Zubatov and the leadership of the council, for fear of arrest.[1]

Zubatov had faith that the workers, having been granted a degree of independence, would ensure that the labor organizations remained under their own control. He was confident that his hand-picked supporters on the council could more than hold their own in open debate with the opposition before the masses. When, for example, the Petersburg Social Democrats dispatched

1. Ainzaft, *Zubatovshchina*, p. 48; Shmeleva, Moscow *Uchenye zapiski*, p. 44; Bukhbinder, "K istorii 'Sobraniia,'" p. 323; *Russkoe delo*, July 9, 1905. Slepov maintained that the Okhrana made very few arrests among those who attended the meetings (*Russkoe delo*, July 11, 1905).

representatives to investigate the Moscow Zubatovshchina, he ordered that they be permitted to attend its meetings and speak freely. The officers of the council were able to best their socialist visitors in public confrontation, thus heightening their prestige among the workers.[2]

Zubatov felt that the clandestine attacks and allegations by the opposition could best be countered by meeting the charges head on. Handbills of the Moscow Social Democratic Committee and copies of *Iskra* containing articles critical of the Zubatovshchina were distributed by the council at labor meetings and read aloud. Matters which otherwise might have been left to guarded, secretive discussions among the workers were brought to the surface by the council leaders, who used the occasions to sow distrust of the revolutionary intelligentsia and defend themselves as loyal to the workers' cause.[3]

The ideology propagated by the Zubatovites aimed to widen the breach between the workers and the radical intelligentsia. The intelligentsia, it was maintained, was to be differentiated into the higher intelligentsia, such as the learned academic lecturers who devoted their time freely to the workers and wholeheartedly wished to further the cause of labor, and the petty, or revolutionary, intelligentsia who wished only to utilize the factory masses in a temporary alliance for the attainment of political power. The revolutionary intelligentsia enticed the workers into activities which could only bring them harm and eventual arrest while at the same time opposing organizations such as mutual-aid societies which benefited the working class. The revolutionaries, therefore, were enemies of the workers and as such deserved arrest, Afanas'ev and Slepov declared to their followers.[4]

2. Spiridovich, "Pri tsarskom rezhime," p. 151. Zubatov, writing to P. N. Lemtiuzhnikov on July 2, 1901, boasted that the Society of Machine Workers had concluded that the Social Democrats who attended their meetings were the worst and most stupid orators. Socialist agitators were hissed and whistled into silence; many of them stopped attending the meetings altogether (Ainzaft, *Zubatovshchina*, p. 48).

3. Shmeleva, Moscow *Uchenye zapiski*, p. 48; Piontkovskii, pp. 68–72; *Revoliutsionnaia Rossiia*, no. 6 (May 1902). Zubatov allegedly distributed 150 copies of such an issue of *Iskra*, advising the workers to determine for themselves how the alleged friends of the people, the Social Democrats, acted toward institutions that the Moscow workers found beneficial (*Iskra*, no. 16, Feb. 1, 1902).

4. Shmeleva, Shuia *Uchenye zapiski*, 1959, p. 146; *Revoliutsionnaia Rossiia*, no. 3 (Jan. 1902), no. 6 (May 1902); *Iskra*, no. 14 (Jan. 1, 1902), no. 19 (April 1, 1902); Piontkovskii, p. 71.

The council's officers, true to Zubatov's program, urged their followers to avoid the pitfalls of political action, and preached loyalty to the throne and the economic benefits of peaceful organizational activity. Through mutual help the workers could lessen their material insecurity and unify and strengthen themselves into a collective force. The workers likewise were told they were in need of education and to this end were informed about the labor movement abroad and the desirability of adapting Western European labor organizations to the Russian environment without changing the existing political order. There was allegedly no need for a constitution in Russia, nor for the workers to follow the illusory path marked out by the enemies of the working class, for within the tsarist autocracy the workers could find just fulfillment of their needs. Restraint and the avoidance of excessive demands in the immediate future were all that was required from the working class if it wished to gain sympathy and recognition from society and government.[5]

A brochure which was to serve as a guide for the worker-intelligentsia who led the Zubatovshchina omitted the principles of Orthodoxy and autocracy then being stressed in the lectures for the Moscow workers and concentrated on working-class interests. The brochure, said to be composed in late 1902 or early 1903 and attributed to Zubatov but anonymously signed by "A Group of Aware Workers," presented a sober analysis of the working-class question and an appraisal of tactics by which the Marxist appeal to the working class could be undermined. It posited the thesis that struggle was a necessary means of progress embedded in life itself and equally inherent in individuals, classes, and nations. The struggle of the working class for its interests was therefore "inevitable and irrepressible."[6] The working class desired equal rights with other classes. Strike funds and labor unions would support the struggle of the working class once it achieved unity. Only if the workers were led into violent action and disturbed the peace would the Russian government, like any other, take repressive measures. Strikes, save for the interference of the revolutionaries, most likely would end peacefully with concessions,

5. Varnashev, pp. 182–84, 187; Piontkovskii, p. 98; Bukhbinder, "K istorii zubatovshchiny," pp. 195–96.

6. *Rabochaia gazeta,* Oct. 2, 1906. The brochure was published in *ibid.,* Oct. 2, 9, 16 and 23, 1906.

for the factory owners would gladly sacrifice part of their income in return for order and tranquility in the factory. The revolutionaries counted on the owners to reject strike demands, thus helping the dispute to escalate into violent disorders, police intervention, and arrests, all of which could be blamed on the government.[7] The brochure, when viewed through the experience of Western European labor history, presented a realistic appraisal; the Moscow industrialists, however, could only label it anticapitalistic, although not as inflammatory as the views expressed by the officers of the council.

Afanas'ev, Slepov, and Krasivskii, as we have seen, often threw caution to the wind in the heat of discussion and attacked the capitalist class before the workers. In contrast to Zubatov's vision of a beneficient monarchy dispensing justice impartially to all classes, they promised that the government would take the workers' side in their struggle against capital.

The more conservative Moscow workers most likely were receptive to Slepov's views, which were unique among the council's leaders. Slepov's thoughts reflected the xenophobic and anti-Semitic sentiments of Sergei Sharapov, the editor of *Russkoe delo* (The Russian Cause), and are further evidence of the Moscow Zubatovshchina's bent in its latter phases toward the ideology of Official Nationality. Slepov was a frequent contributor to *Moskovskiia vedomosti* of articles on the labor question, for which he received personal praise from the tsar and Plehve.

In his writings Slepov denied that the establishment of mutual-aid societies in Moscow implied that the labor question existed in Russia or intent to organize trade unions in the Western European fashion; there was no labor question in Russia and "thank God, never will be, in the sense that it exists in the Western European states." All truly Russian people, regardless of class and station, must join in one family under the banners of Orthodoxy and autocracy to combat the alien philosophy of socialism, which was "born on the putrid soil of the West, under the flag of Judaism, Marx, Lassalle, Engels and company."[8] In addressing the Moscow

7. Ainzaft, "Zubatovshchina v Moskve," p. 73; *Rabochaia gazeta*, Oct. 9 and 23, 1906.

8. *Moskovskiia vedomosti*, Jan. 5, April 9, 1903; Korelin, "Russkii 'politseiskii sotsializm,'" p. 55. On the views of Sharapov, see Von Laue, *Sergei Witte and the*

workers, Slepov often invoked the words of Alexander III, "Russia for the Russians"; he attacked the Jews and foreign capitalists for allegedly draining the Russian economy at the expense of the Russian workers, and urged their banishment.[9] Slepov's simple, unquestioning faith in the autocracy and his hatred of foreign capitalists may explain his extreme promises to the workers in the name of the monarchy.

## Social Democracy, Lenin, and the Moscow Zubatovshchina

The Moscow Zubatovshchina began at a time when Russian social democracy was in a weak state, wracked by internecine theoretical and fractional disputes and badly in need of a firm organizational base. Lenin and Martov, to remedy these problems, began publications of *Iskra* abroad in December 1900, for the purpose of preserving ideological orthodoxy. Party structure and the relationship between the émigré centers and Social Democrats inside Russia were central issues during the historic second congress of the party in the summer of 1903. During the intervening years Moscow social democracy was helpless against the Zubatovshchina, impotent to prevent loyal servants of the autocracy from taking the leadership in organizing the working class. As a consequence the editors of *Iskra* had to take the struggle into their own hands. Try as they might, however, neither the émigré intelligentsia nor the Moscow Social Democrats could bring down the Moscow Zubatovshchina; the causes for its failure are primarily to be found elsewhere.

Police infiltration and the frequent arrest of its leadership left their marks on Moscow social democracy. Experienced party activists often refused to work in Moscow, while others out of fear and suspicion limited their contacts with the Moscow working class and with other socialists. Workers similarly feared contact with socialists; in social-democratic literature this became known pejoratively as the period of *kustarnichestvo* ("amateurish work"), a far cry from the early 1890's, when the Moscow Social Democrats had great expectations of leading the city's working class.[10] The Moscow

*Industrialization of Russia*, pp. 287–88. Slepov's memoirs were published in Sharapov's newspaper, *Russkoe delo*, in 1905.

9. *Rabochaia gazeta*, 1908, no. 1; Piontkovskii, pp. 68–72. Slepov's open anti-Semitism often led him into polemics (*Rabochaia gazeta*, ibid.; *Russkoe delo*, Aug. 13, 1905).

10. "Doklad moskovskogo delegata Veismana (Tseitlina) na II s'ezde RSDRP,"

Committee was also weakened through the schism created by the trend known as "Economism," as well as resentment against its subservience to the representatives of the *Iskra* émigré organization.

Despite these difficulties, Moscow Social Democrats labored to divert the workers away from the societies affiliated with the council. Without a printing press, they managed only to have handbills of rather poor quality infrequently hectographed. Other proclamations were smuggled abroad in handwritten form and published by the *Iskra* organization.[11] The message that they tried to drum into the workers' minds was a simple one devoid of abstract Marxist dogma. The central theme was suspicion of the motives of the police and the government in permitting labor organizations in the light of what they saw as the autocracy's history of repression against the working class and refusal to confer civil rights. Police repression was the richest source of resentment the proclamations endeavored to exploit; stressing the unsavory reputation of the police, the handbills charged Zubatov and officials of the council with organizing labor societies for no other purpose than to root out the most outspoken and militant labor leaders and stunt the burgeoning labor movement. The government was still the implacable enemy of the workers and the friend of the capitalists:

Comrades, they are deceiving us, corrupting us; they want to turn all of us into spies; they [try to] persuade us that the government, that very government which deprives us of freedom, which helps the capitalists, which hurls at us armed troops, Cossacks with whips, policemen with bludgeons, [and] which starves us, this very government is not an enemy of ours—say these henchmen of Trepov and Zubatov. Comrades, the assemblies which they granted us have a single goal—to bring into our midst treachery and to make it easier for spies to identify the really good and honest ones among us.[12]

The proclamation dismissed as illusory any advantages arising from the limited right of association allowed by the Moscow administration and stressed the importance of political and civil liberties, which could be attained only through a militant struggle

---

*Iskrovskii period v Moskve*, pp. 54–55; Allan K. Wildman, "Lenin's Battle with Kustarnichestvo," *Slavic Review*, 23 (1964), 479–503; Tseitlin, pp. 113, 119.

11. Bauman, p. 82; Angarskii, p. 55; Vovchik, p. 151; *Pochemu russkim rabochim nuzhna politicheskaia svoboda?* (Geneva, 1902); L. O. Kantsel' to the editors of *Iskra*, March 21 (April 3), 1902, in *Perepiska V. I. Lenina i redaktsii*, I, 461.

12. Quoted in Piontkovskii, p. 75.

similar to that of the Western European working class not as the result of abject petitions. To repair any breach between the working class and the radical intelligentsia which the ideology of the Zubatovshchina may have caused, socialist propaganda counter-attacked with the charge that the government had concealed its true aims, which were inimical to the workers' interests, in contrast to the openly enunciated aims of the social democratic intelligentsia, the real defenders of the working class.[13]

The Moscow Committee's handbills, produced in amounts of five and ten thousand, reached only a small proportion of that number of workers. Arrests, confiscation, and paucity of personnel for distribution limited their impact. Rumors branding the labor assemblies a police trap reached a broader audience and were effective in persuading some workers to cease attending the meetings and not register as members.[14] At times the Social Democrats took more direct action, attending district meetings and general assemblies to criticize the inactivity of the council, accuse its leaders of provocation, and direct the attention of the audience to the urgency of political struggle. Sometimes the audience turned on socialist speakers and fisticuffs ensued. The arrest of their speakers led the Social Democrats to conclude that the Okhrana welcomed such outbursts in order to pluck critics of the mutual-help societies from the audience, and after a time greater hesitation was shown.[15] The success of the Moscow Committee in advancing the socialist cause and countering the appeal of the Zubatovshchina was therefore limited and sporadic.

13. Iu. Polevoi, *Iz istorii moskovskoi organizatsii* (Moscow, 1947), p. 86; Piontkovskii, pp. 73–81; *Iskrovskii period v Moskve*, pp. 117–31; *Legal'nye soiuzy i russkoe rabochee dvizhenie* (Munich, 1902); *Iskra*, no. 31 (Jan. 1, 1903).

14. Pletnev, p. 17; Bukhbinder, "K istorii zubatovshchiny," pp. 192, 195–96. The Moscow workers often burned social-democratic handbills for fear they would be caught with them (Tseitlin, p. 94).

15. Shmeleva, Shuia *Uchenye zapiski*, 1960, pp. 65–72; *Rabochii zavod "Serp i molot,"* p. 64; Lenin, XXXIX, 100; XLI, 35. There is some question as to the degree of socialist opposition openly expressed at the meetings of the Moscow Zubatovshchina. It has been charged that the Social Democrats boycotted the meetings and thus facilitated Zubatov's success (Grinevich, pp. 25–26). Some workers who participated in the Zubatovshchina maintained that they did not remember having heard social-democratic speakers at the meetings (Pletnev, pp. 15, 25). Some testified that Social Democrats did speak (*ibid.*, pp. 21–22; "O dvizhenii sredi moskovskikh metallistov," p. 133). The difficulties Social Democrats encountered at meetings in the autumn and winter of 1904 are mentioned in N. A. Rozhkov and A. Sokolov, *O 1905 gode* (Moscow, 1925), pp. 30–31.

The *Iskra* organization aided the committee for reasons of its own. Agents supervising *Iskra's* distribution in Moscow were instructed to establish ties with the Moscow Committee and enter its leadership and, most important, to secure its commitment to the *Iskra* organization. *Iskra* agents faced formidable difficulties in Moscow. Nikolai Bauman, who arrived there in early 1901, found the committee loosely organized and its members resentful of interference by outsiders.[16] Furthermore, committee members were divided in loyalty to the rival émigré organizations of *Iskra* and the Union of Russian Social Democrats Abroad. Bauman's work was also complicated by the existence of a deep hostility toward the *Iskra* organization for allegedly trying to dominate the local committeemen. In early 1902, moreover, after the arrest of its leaders, the Moscow Committee came under control of the Union's followers. When Lydia Dan arrived in Moscow as an *Iskra* agent in January 1902, she found party work at a low ebb. Social Democrats still at large lacked contacts with bourgeois society, while ties with the factory workers had been cut short by arrests. Little money was available to finance the party's work despite secret contributions from the noted writer Maxim Gorky and the publisher S. Skirmunt.[17] Arrests, reconstitution of the Moscow Committee, and renewed arrests were, in short, the cyclical history of Moscow social democracy for the next two years.

Bauman's report to the second party congress on behalf of the Moscow party organization did little to hide the bleak record of the Moscow Committee in its struggle against the Zubatovshchina: "We keenly know that the history of the social-democratic movement in Moscow gives too little satisfaction to the congress. But nevertheless we consider it our duty now to tell the naked truth, however lamentable it is. In Moscow, revolutionary social democracy was powerless to deal with police socialism."[18]

Bauman, who supported Lenin's plans for party reorganization, offered no other curative for the weakness of Moscow social democracy than its complete control by the émigré party center: "We do not propose any specifically new means for the rebirth of the

16. *Perepiska V. I. Lenina i redaktsii,* I, 313, 321, 331; III, 288, 321.
17. N. E. Bauman to the editors of *Iskra,* written shortly before November 16, 1901 (*ibid.,* I, 313); Polevoi, pp. 90–93; statement by Lydia Osipovna Dan, personal interview, Aug. 30, 1962; *Martov i ego blizkie* (New York, 1959), p. 44.
18. Bauman, pp. 82–83; *Vtoroi s"ezd RSDRP,* p. 635.

social-democratic labor movement in Moscow. There are no such means. It is only necessary that organizational work pass into experienced hands."[19]

A report to the congress by a Moscow delegate, L. S. Tseitlin, was limited to the history of Moscow social democracy during 1902 and the first half of 1903. This report, which was not published in official protocols of the congress or in Soviet republications of the protocols, was even more depressing than Bauman's. Frequent arrests had left the Moscow Committee with too few experienced organizers and propagandists, factory committees, and workers' circles. Ties with factory workers were minimal; the few individuals who led workers' circles shunned association with the committee for fear of arrest. Consequently even those who were most sympathetic to the socialist cause drifted away:

Of the workers already affected by propaganda, the most gifted and covetous for knowledge, owing to the absence of a sound s[ocial]-d[emocratic] education [and] illegal literature which might satisfy their needs, turned to legal literature and the Sunday schools. The consequence of this was a certain rise in intellectual development and the complete absence of a revolutionary frame of mind, disillusionment and skepticism. These are worker-academicians, if one can put it that way. The less far-sighted of them fall under the influence of Ozerov and Co[mpany]; the more intelligent and sincere ones, understanding the political deception hidden in the lectures of the Zubatov professors, all the same give no evidence of revolutionary activity. The workers in mechanical factories for the most part produce such types.[20]

The reports of Bauman and Tseitlin, partly based on personal experience, are evidence enough of the sorry state of Moscow social democracy in the years before the revolution of 1905 and contradict the contention of some overenthusiastic Soviet writers that Moscow social democracy should be credited with destroying the Moscow Zubatovshchina. If it is true that in 1904 the Zubatovshchina showed symptoms of stagnation, so did socialist democracy. At the huge Prokhorov plant, moreover, the socialist revolutionaries, not their rivals, the Social Democrats, did battle with the Zubatovshchina; at the large Guzhon metal plant Social Democrats were few in number and did not form a party organization until 1905.[21]

19. Bauman, p. 87; *Vtoroi s"ezd RSDRP,* p. 639.
20. *Iskrovskii period v Moskve,* p. 56; Tseitlin's report appears on pp. 50–59.
21. *Rabochii zavod "Serp i molot,"* p. 13; *Rabochie Trekhgornoi manufaktury,* pp. 31, 33.

The editors of *Iskra* used their newspaper to heighten the militancy and loyalty of their followers inside Russia. Far from the center of battle *Iskra* chronicled the working-class struggle throughout Russia and provided an orthodox Marxist interpretation of contemporary Russian political and economic life, in addition to attacking its ideological rival for control of Russian social democracy. The Zubatovshchina, which held the center of the labor stage inside Russia, was drawn naturally into the vortex of internecine disputes plaguing Russian social democracy at the turn of the century.

The Moscow Zubatovshchina presented a tactical problem to the *Iskra* organization. Martov's biting attacks in *Iskra* on the mutual-help societies and the public lectures delivered by the Moscow academicians did not go unquestioned by some workers who were sympathetic to the cause of social democracy but attracted to the possibility of self-activity. This dilemma was revealed in a letter to the editors of *Iskra* signed by "A Well-Wisher." While acknowledging that Zubatov had fostered labor societies and mutual-aid funds for the purpose of undermining the appeal of the revolutionaries, the writer argued that Social Democrats would be placed in an unenviable position should they take a completely negative stand toward these labor organizations. "Would not such an attitude," he asked, "enable Zubatov to convince the ignorant mass of workers that the revolutionaries are against any real expansion of the workers' rights [and] are against any real improvement of their material position!" Better tactics for the socialists would be to explain to the workers that the authorities allowed them to form such institutions as the Zubatov societies only because they feared revolutionary agitation: "An unconditionally negative attitude toward [mutual-help] funds and cooperative stores is advantageous to Zubatov, and therefore it should not be taken. A wise and militant tactic requires economy of forces and therefore demands making use of any institution of the adversary, as if the very revolutionaries called them into being, and turning this new weapon of the enemy against him."[22]

The editors of *Iskra*, in an unsigned reply, were at pains to deny unconditional and general opposition to mutual-help funds and cooperatives. Their opposition was to the use of mutual-help societies for the political perversion of the working class; they would

22. *Iskra*, no. 15 (Jan. 15, 1902).

gladly support labor societies if they were completely unfettered by administrative shackles, for the masses in that case would mature and inevitably clash with the government.[23]

Lenin discussed social-democratic tactics toward labor reforms and reformers in a *Letter to the Northern League of the R. S. D. R. P.* in April 1902. For Lenin political considerations were vastly more important than support for reforms to improve the workers' lot. Social democracy had to strive to raise the political consciousness of the workers: "We neither can nor will further 'in every possible way' improvement in the conditions of the workers under existing circumstances. For example, we cannot assist in the Zubatov way... We fight only for such improvement of the workers' position as will *raise* their ability to conduct class struggle."[24] The sham reforms sponsored by the autocracy were a means of warding off revolution; Social Democrats had to draw "a clear line of distinction" between themselves and "all sorts of reformers." Here as elsewhere in his writings Lenin expressed fear of association with "reformers" lest revolutionary social democracy become corrupted.

The Zubatovshchina was frequently cited by Martov and Lenin in the dispute with their opponents in Russian social democracy. In the spring of 1900, Plekhanov and some of his followers left the Union of Russian Social Democrats Abroad, which at the founding congress of the party in 1898 had been designated as the representative of the party outside Russia, and created a new organization, the Revolutionary Group of Social Democrats. The focal point of the schismatics' attack on the parent organization was the union's alleged adoption of the so-called heresy of Economism, that is, emphasis on the economic struggle of the workers at the expense of revolutionary, political agitation.[25] The Zubatovshchina was tailor-made to fit this criticism. In an article in the November 1901 issue of *Iskra*, Martov linked the "Economists" with Zubatov in

23. *Ibid.* In 1906 Lenin wrote: "We also went to the Zubatov assemblies but were never members of them" (XII, 195).

24. Lenin, VI, 368.

25. Recent studies tend to reject the charges of Lenin and Plekhanov as a politically motivated device to remove their rivals as alleged falsifiers of Marxism: Jonathan Frankel, "Economism: A Heresy Exploited," *Slavic Review*, 22 (1963), 263–84; Schapiro, *The Communist Party of the Soviet Union*, pp. 31–35. Wildman maintains: "By 1901, when *Iskra* launched its attack on Economism, there was not a trace of this dangerous heresy in the Social Democratic movement" (*Making of a Workers' Revolution*, p. 144).

their support of mutual-help societies and funds. The Economists allegedly favored these institutions in the belief they would give the workers experience in self-activity and create a sense of solidarity, inevitably leading in the distant future to political consciousness and political struggle; Zubatov favored them as a means of crushing the revolution. Of the two, Martov asserted, Zubatov's assessment of mutual-help societies was closer to the truth.[26]

An anonymous group of "Comrades" counterattacked in "A Letter to the Russian Social-Democratic Press." *Iskra* was sharply censured for dogmatic sectarian intolerance and for exaggerating the influence ideologists exert on the socialist movement inside Russia—criticism to which the journal was vulnerable. *Iskra* was charged with ignoring the harsh environment in which the Russian labor movement had developed and with giving too little credit to the Economists for preparing the ground for labor militancy, as exemplified in the street demonstrations of February and March 1901. "*Iskra* is entirely wrong and unhistorical in its appraisal of that period and the direction of the activity of Russian social democrats," and in "failing to differentiate between 'the struggle for minor demands,' which broadens and deepens the labor movement, and minor concessions,' whose purpose is to paralyze every struggle and every movement."[27] The attribution of Zubatov's success among part of the working class to the influence of the journal *Rabochaia mysl'* was but typical of the intolerance of *Iskra*, which placed Social Democrats who differed with its point of view in the enemy camp.

Lenin responded for the *Iskra* editorial board in an article in that organ on December 6, 1901, "A Talk with Defenders of Economism," the title itself designed to damn *Iskra's* critics. Here Lenin expounded on the necessary role of the politically "conscious" ideologist in directing the otherwise vacillating or "spontaneous" movement of the masses, a thesis he was to elaborate upon at greater length in his now famous tract *Chto delat'? (What Is to Be Done?)* Rejecting the charge that *Iskra* had intended to identify the tactics of the Economists with those of Zubatov, Lenin opened new wounds in questioning whether *Rabochaia mysl'* could deny that the

---

26. *Iskra*, no. 10 (Nov. 1901).
27. *Iskra*, no. 12 (Dec. 6, 1901); Lenin, V, 361. Ushakov (p. 56) maintains that the anonymous letter-writers were Moscow Social Democrats.

spread of Economism had aided and abetted Zubatov's program.[28]

Lenin viewed the Zubatovshchina within the context of general state policy toward the maturing working-class movement. Since the Petersburg strikes of the late 1870's and the growth of socialist agitation the autocracy, as protector of the capitalists' interests, has had to employ a new tact toward the workers, namely a policy of "guardianship."

In our time guns, bayonets, and whips are not a sufficiently reliable guardian; it is necessary to convince the exploited that the government stands above classes, that it does not serve the interests of the nobility and the bourgeoisie, but the interests of justice, that it is concerned with protecting the weak and the poor against the rich and the powerful, etc. Napoleon III in France and Bismarck and William II in Germany exerted no little effort to play up to the workers in this way.[29]

In Lenin's judgment the Zubatovshchina was to be understood as part of a policy of intrigue against the revolutionary movement. "Promises of more or less extensive reforms, an actual readiness to carry out the tiniest fraction of what had been promised, and the demand to refrain from political struggle [in return ] for this—such is the essence of the Zubatovshchina," Lenin wrote in *Iskra*.[30] In *Chto delat'?*, published in March 1902 but written several months earlier, Lenin discussed at length the Zubatovshchina and the legacy he expected it would leave to the Russian working-class movement. The discussion, which was tangential to the major theses of the work, occurred in a chapter devoted to the relationship between social democracy and working-class organization.[31] The party, Lenin argued, should gain a paramount influence over working-class organizations without giving up its separate, independent existence. Even in Russia, where trade unions were previously unknown, legalization of labor organizations was progressing,

28. *Iskra*, no. 12. Soviet writers have also associated the Zubatovshchina with Economism: Piontkovskii, p. 67; M. Lebedev, "Politseiskii sotsializm v Rossii," *Propaganda i agitatsiia*, Dec. 1938, p. 42.

29. Lenin, V, 74. The quotation is from an article published in *Iskra* in July 1901, which concerns the government's general labor policy, not specifically the Zubatovshchina.

30. *Iskra*, no. 26 (Oct. 15, 1902). The article was reprinted in Lenin's collected works under the title "Politicheskaia bor'ba i politikanstvo" (VII, 37).

31. For a discussion of Lenin and the trade union movement see: Solomon Schwarz, *Lénine et le mouvement syndical* (Paris, 1935); Thomas T. Hammond, "Lenin on Russian Trade Unions under Capitalism, 1894–1904," *ASEER*, 8 (1949), 275–88; Thomas Taylor Hammond, *Lenin on Trade Unions and Revolution* (New York, 1957).

encouraged in part by supporters of the existing political order, in part by the working class and the liberal intelligentsia. The Zubatovshchina was part of this process, supporting legalization to counter the rapid spread of social democracy among the working class.

Lenin had little new to suggest in the way of tactical opposition; Social Democrats were urged to expose the hidden role of the police, attack the mutual-help societies as a police trap, and ridicule Zubatov's dogma of class harmony. Although the Zubatovshchina had perverted part of the working class, "in the long run the legalization of the working-class movement will be to our advantage, and not to that of the Zubatovs," an optimistic view echoed in other of Lenin's writings.[32] Social Democrats must expose the Zubatovshchina,

attract the attention of increasing numbers of the more backward sections of the workers to social and political questions, and free ourselves, the revolutionaries, from functions which are essentially legal (the distribution of legal books, mutual aid, etc.), the development of which will inevitably provide us with an increasing quantity of material for agitation. Looked at from this point of view, we may and should say to the Zubatovs and the Ozerovs: Keep at it, gentlemen, do your best! So long as you place a trap in the path of the workers (either by the way of direct provocation, or by the "honest" corruption of the workers with the aid of "Struvism"), we will see to it that you are exposed. To whatever real step you take forward, even if it is a "timid zigzag," we shall say: Please continue! Only a real, if small, extension of the workers' field of action can be a real step forward. And every such extension will be to our advantage and help to hasten the advent of legal societies, not of the kind in which agent-provocateurs hunt for socialists, but of the kind in which socialists would hunt for adherents.[33]

Bloody Sunday and the revolution it touched off seemed to Lenin irrefutable proof of his accurate prediction about the downfall of the Zubatovshchina, as his writings during 1905 frequently stressed.[34]

### The Moscow Zubatovshchina: Summary

The Moscow Zubatovshchina arose naturally from the policy, begun by Zubatov and Trepov in the mid-1890's, of using administrative pressure to extract economic concessions from the

32. Lenin, VI, 115; VII, 319.
33. *Ibid.*, VI, 115–16.
34. *Ibid.*, IX, 174–75, 210–11, 218, 220–21, 262, 300; Schwarz, *The Russian Revolution of 1905*, pp. 70–71.

Moscow factory owners. Its purpose was to thwart a union of the socialist and working-class movements through economic betterment for the working class and the removal of poor working conditions, upon which socialist propaganda thrived. It owed its early and rapid success to the attunement of its working-class leadership to the mood and aspirations of the Moscow proletariat. It provided the Moscow workers with education, mutual aid, a sense of unity, and an effective outlet for their grievances; it also permitted them self-organization and a limited right of assembly, privileges unique for the time in Russia.

The Kremlin procession of February 19, 1902, was the high point of the Moscow Zubatovshchina and essentially justified Zubatov's contention that the autocracy still maintained an emotional hold on the working class. The Kremlin celebration and the Guzhon affair brought an end to the successful period of the Moscow Zubatovshchina and inaugurated its second and more conservative phase. Both incidents dramatically brought the movement out of its limited, local context and onto the level of national policy, where its powerful critics could wield greater influence to terminate an experiment they considered dangerous both for industrial capitalism and the autocracy. This forced Zubatov to alter his original program of gaining cooperation with the liberal intelligentsia and labor concessions from the factory owners.

The substitution of lectures on moral and religious themes, infused with the ideology of Official Nationality, for talks on economic themes, the council's intervention in labor disputes with a view to bringing about their termination rather than obtaining concessions, and the honorary membership of the Moscow industrialists in the mutual-help societies were marks of the Zubatovshchina's new conservatism. It failed, however, to win over critics in the Moscow industrial community and the Ministry of Finance. Zubatov's departure from Moscow, moreover, fatally weakened the Zubatovshchina. Neither Trepov nor the Grand Duke Sergei had the sensitive understanding to deal with the labor movement alone; without Zubatov's presence their commitment to his program faltered and their recourse to repression increased.

In the final analysis the working class joined and participated in the mutual-aid societies as long as they continued to provide tangible benefits; when these stopped after the spring of 1902, thanks to the concerted opposition of Witte and the Moscow industrialists, the workers by and large became indifferent to the societies. Cut adrift from the Zubatovshchina, the Moscow proletariat remained loyal to the autocracy and unprepared as yet to follow the lead of social democracy. Moscow social democracy could not boast of victory over the Zubatovshchina; it barely survived the continual police raids and provocation.

The Moscow Zubatovshchina outlived its progenitor's tenure of office. It lingered on out of inertia, cut off from the mainstream of the Moscow labor movement long after similar experiments by Zubatov in Minsk and Odessa had dramatically been terminated. The three experiments had much in common but, as we shall see, they were separated by national and religious differences.

CHAPTER **8**

# Zubatov and the Bund

The story of the Zubatovshchina among the Jews of White Russia and the Ukraine forms a small chapter in the history of the Jewish community in Russia and its efforts to better its economic position and attain civil equality. The Zubatovshchina acquired among the youthful Jewish intelligentsia a militant and devoted leadership thoroughly convinced that Zubatov's program would work to the economic benefit of the Jewish masses. The Zubatov movement had, in fact, been called into being at the turn of the century in reaction to the rise of a Jewish socialist movement closely tied with the older labor movement among the Jewish artisans; its purpose was to break the link between the Jewish socialists and the artisans.

The modern problem of incorporating a sizable Jewish population into Russian state and society had begun with the partitions of Poland in the last quarter of the eighteenth century. The large areas of White Russia, the Ukraine, Lithuania, and of Poland proper incorporated into Russia at that time had a Jewish population of a million; a century later the figure had reached five million.

Tsarist policy toward Jewish subjects lacked consistency; the Jewish community, on its part, was always deeply divided over how to respond to the government's Jewish policies. The one measure of continuity throughout the period was the legal establishment of a specified area of the empire to which the Jews, with rare exceptions, were confined. The Pale of Settlement, as it was known, was demarcated in a statute enacted in 1835. In this vast ghetto, consisting of a belt of provinces in the western part of European Russia that ran from the Baltic to the Black Sea, resided 94 per cent of the Jews in the Russian Empire in 1897.

The tsarist government discriminated against its Jewish subjects in civil and property rights, taxation, and education, the severity of the measures dependent upon whether reform or reaction was in the ascendancy in Petersburg. Until the end of the reign of Alexander II, government policy was hesitant and vacillating; during the reign of Alexander III the Jews suffered harsh treatment as the government codified and increased Jewish disabilities. Laws were enacted to restrict Jewish residency to urban areas of the Pale; consequently, in 1897, 82 per cent of the Jews in the Pale were concentrated in cities and market towns. Jews who had settled with permission outside the Pale were herded back into its confines. The most notorious government action was the brutal and abrupt deportation in the spring of 1891 of 30,000 Jews from Moscow by police and Cossacks under special orders from the Grand Duke Sergei Aleksandrovich.[1]

The pogrom against Jewish persons and property following the assassination of Alexander II frightened the Jewish community, already disturbed by the government's harsh measures. Pogroms were not unknown in Russia before then. Those that occurred in 1881, however, were more widespread and destructive than before, inaugurating a period in which pogroms became more common.

From the first, Jewish leaders sensed that the court, led by the sovereign, gave tacit or even direct encouragement to mob violence against Jewish property and persons. The leniency of local officials toward the rampaging mobs and their apparent refusal to give immediate protection to the Jewish populace at each outbreak supported the conclusion that the pogroms were not sponta-neous outbursts by the ignorant masses. Both Alexander III and Nicholas II, moreover, were known to harbor strong anti-Semitic sentiments.[2]

The pogroms and the stringent government measures of the 1880's proved to most Jews that the dream of emancipation through assimilation was illusory. New solutions were offered to resolve the plight of the Jews, none fully acceptable to the entire Jewish community. Jewish intellectuals bitterly differed on issues of

1. Louis Greenberg, *The Jews in Russia* (New Haven, 1944), II, 30–32; S. M. Dubnow, *History of the Jews in Russia and Poland* (Philadelphia, 1918), II, 399–413; Mitskevich, *Revoliutsionnaia Moskva*, p. 272; G. B. Sliozberg, *Dela minuvshikh dnei* (Paris, 1933), II, 42; Aizenberg, pp. 80–81, 94.
2. Greenberg, II, 19–23, 39–40, 48, 103–4.

nationalism, assimilation, and socialism. For the Jewish masses the most obvious outlet was flight abroad; encouraged by government officials, who were glad to rid Russia of its Jews, emigration to the United States reached mass proportions for the first time during the 1880's.

Some Jewish thinkers questioned whether their people would ever cease to suffer as an alien minority until they acquired a land of their own; long before the first Zionist Congress was held, Jewish intellectuals in Russia pointed to the need for a Jewish homeland. Zionist clubs which existed in many parts of the Pale in the early 1880's raised funds for the settlement of Russian Jews in pioneer colonies in Palestine.[3]

Flagging interest in a Palestinian homeland was revived by the first worldwide Zionist Congress, which met in Basel in August 1897. Theodore Herzl, the leading spirit of the congress, led Zionism in a political direction, seeking an agreement from the Turkish government to allow colonization of Palestine at a faster rate. For most Russian Jews, however, the Palestine venture remained at best an unrealizable dream. Some still believed that assimilation would bring an end to discrimination; they feared that the spread of Zionism would add fuel to the arguments of Russian nationalists who questioned the loyalty of the Jewish population. Zionism was greeted still more hostilely by the Jewish socialists of the Pale, who founded an illegal party a few weeks after the meeting of the Zionist Congress.

## The Jewish Working Class and the Rise of Socialism

Socialist roots among the Jews of the Pale first developed in the administrative area known as the Northwest *krai*. In this area, composed of the Lithuanian and White Russian provinces, Jews formed more than a quarter of the population. Here, as elsewhere in the Pale, Jews were compelled by legislation to become urban dwellers; seven out of eight Jews in the Northwest region lived in the cities and market towns, comprising 57 per cent of its urban inhabitants.[4] The region was little industrialized for most of the nineteenth century. In White Russia the factory work force at the turn

3. *Ibid.*, pp. 66–67, 169–74; Ben-Adir, "Modern Currents in Jewish Social and National Life," in *The Jewish People Past and Present*, II (New York, 1948), 304.
4. Solomon M. Schwarz, *The Jews in the Soviet Union* (Syracuse, 1951), pp. 11–12.

of the century came to 50,000; those employed in artisan handicraft totaled 200,000.[5] Domestic handicrafts predominated, with the artisan supplying local needs rather than a broad market. At the end of the century handicraft production became infused with a new capitalist spirit. The master artisan began to lose his independence by working on orders for large stores that supplied him with raw materials and tools. The finished product was then either sold through local stores or shipped to distant markets. In some professions, such as bristle making and tanning, a number of artisans were gathered under one roof in a manufactory where they worked manually, their status approaching that of hired laborers.[6] Under the new conditions, the position of the journeyman-artisan also greatly deteriorated. Pitted in competition against his fellow workers, he became more dependent on his employer and subject to long working hours at meager wages. Laboring chiefly in workshops with few employees the artisans were deprived of the legal protection of the factory inspector, whose surveillance of factory legislation was limited to larger establishments. Discontent with oppressive working conditions thus spurred the formation of an organized labor movement in the Pale.

The Jewish working class in the White Russian and Lithuanian provinces was overwhelmingly composed of artisans; in enterprises with mechanized production Jews represented an insignificant percentage of the proletariat. The largest number of Jewish artisans in these provinces, about a third of the total, were engaged in production of clothing; combined with those employed in leather, wood, and metal handicrafts, they formed 65 per cent of Jewish artisans in Lithuania and 74 per cent in White Russia.[7]

The beginning of revolutionary activity among the Jews of the Pale can be traced to the early 1870's and associated with the Narodnik movement. These pioneer Jewish socialists felt a strong bond with the Russian revolutionary movement, and like their Russian comrades looked to a peasant *jacquerie* to overturn the monarchy and transform Russia into a land of agrarian socialism. Drawn to socialism by its supranational goals and

5. S. Agurskii, *Ocherki po istorii revoliutsionnogo dvizheniia v Belorussii* (Minsk, 1928), p. 10.

6. M. Rafes, *Ocherki po istorii "Bunda"* (Moscow, 1923), pp. 3–4.

7. I. Cherniavskii, "Promyshlennyi kapitalizm v Belorussii i Litve i obrazovanie evreiskogo proletariata," *Istoriia proletariata SSSR*, 7 (1931), 101–111.

cosmopolitanism, they were little concerned with, if not outrightly scornful of, those who emphasized the distress of the Jewish people and distinctively Jewish problems. No thought was given to founding an independent socialist movement among the Jews; most young Jewish radicals left the Pale, dissociated themselves from the Jewish religion and culture, and became Russified.[8]

The pogroms which followed the assassination of Alexander II shook the conviction of the small radical Jewish intelligentsia that the Narodnik movement would bring about a universal solution to the national problem. Further disillusionment resulted when some leaders of Narodnaia Volia voiced approval of the pogroms, holding that these popular acts of violence revealed the innate revolutionary stirrings of the peasantry. Disenchantment with the Russian revolutionary movement and renewed repression of the Jewish population caused those returning to the Pale to feel a heightened sense of Jewish nationalism and a new awareness of distinctively Jewish problems; they also came to a greater awareness of solidarity with the Jewish masses. Some now saw the solution in Zionism. Others, unwilling to forsake their socialist faith, turned to the Jewish working class.

Wide cultural and intellectual differences, however, separated the Jewish intelligentsia from the Jewish masses, posing a problem analogous to the one the Narodnik intelligentsia had faced in working among the Russian peasantry. The Jewish masses spoke Yiddish and were bound to religious and cultural traditions centered around the synagogue; the radical intelligentsia, on the other hand, were mainly from the middle class and were secular in outlook, having assimilated Russian culture and having adopted the Russian language, the lingua franca of the revolutionary movement.[9]

The first Jewish workmen's circles with a Marxist orientation were established in Minsk and Vilna in the mid-1880's. The Vilna circles were led by a new generation of young Jewish intellectuals who around 1890 organized the Jewish Social Democratic Group, or

8. N. Nedasek, *Bol'shevizm v revoliutsionnom dvizhenii Belorussii* (Munich, 1956), pp. 28–32; N. A. Bukhbinder, "Iz istorii revoliutsionnoi propagandy sredi evreev v Rossii v 70-kh gg.," *Istoriko-revoliutsionnyi sbornik,* 1 (1924), 37–66; Sliozberg, I, 90; Ezra Mendelsohn, *Class Struggle in the Pale* (Cambridge, 1970), p. 29.

9. A. I. Patkin, *The Origins of the Russian-Jewish Labour Movement* (Melbourne and London, 1947), pp. 83–90; Sliozberg, I, 93; Abraham Menes, "The Jewish Socialist Movement in Russia and Poland," in *The Jewish People Past and Present,* II, 365; Rafes, p. 12.

Vilna Group. In the circles small groups of workmen were taught the rudiments of reading and writing, and then given a lengthy course of study ending with indoctrination in socialism and graduation as worker-intelligentsia. The leaders of the circles had no intention of developing an exclusively Jewish revolutionary movement; emancipation of the Jewish masses was expected to come from the victory of the broader all-Russian revolutionary movement.

In the early 1890's the Jewish socialist intelligentsia changed tactics and forged a close alliance with the working class of the Pale, something which eluded Russian social democracy for another decade. The tactical changes were accelerated by the spontaneous emergence in the late 1880's of a Jewish working-class movement with a stable organizational structure capable of sustaining a successful wave of strikes. The new organizational form was the labor fund, a form of mutual-aid society. The funds, or *kases*, which were organized by professions, were distinguished from the older mutual-aid funds, the *khevrat*, by their exclusively working-class membership and their increasing utilization in support of strikes. Temporary strike funds were known to exist in the early 1880's; more permanently organized strike funds existed in many professions by the end of the decade. [10]

The growing dependence of the Jewish journeyman-artisan on his employer and the deterioration in his working conditions severed the once patriarchal relations existing in the workshops of the Pale. As late as 1900 a workday of fifteen or more hours was not unheard of among the bookbinders, hatters, weavers, and confectionery workers. [11] Long before the Jewish artisans came into contact with socialist propaganda they protested against working conditions through strikes. Until 1892–1893, when mass strikes among bristle makers and tailors in Vilna spread throughout the Pale, strikes were sporadic, localized, and usually limited to artisans in a single profession. The strike movement of 1893 was fought for the enforcement of a long-neglected law enacted in the time of Catherine the Great limiting the workday in handicraft workshops to twelve hours. In some cases the workers petitioned the local

10. Henry J. Tobias, *The Jewish Bund in Russia from Its Origins to 1905* (Stanford, 1972), p. 21; Mendelsohn, pp. 28, 41–44, 54.
11. N. A. Bukhbinder, *Istoriia evreiskogo rabochego dvizheniia v Rossii* (Leningrad, 1925), p. 12; Agurskii, p. 13; Mendelsohn, pp. 11–12.

authorities, including the police, for enforcement of the law and gained their support. Pressure from local administrative authorities compelled employers to abide by the law, although they continued to ignore it at every opportunity. [12]

The emergence of a militant strike movement caught the socialist intelligentsia unawares. New tactics were deemed necessary. Workmen's circles had been an exceedingly slow means of politicizing the masses. The educational process was lengthy; small numbers of workmen, some selfishly interested in their own advancement, had received instruction, while the broad mass of workers had been ignored by socialist propagandists. Agitation among the working masses was now considered the immediate task. The new tactic, however, was not warmly accepted by the workmen's circles; the worker-intelligentsia, the main beneficiary of the circles, put up stiff resistance and sharply criticized the intelligentsia for abandoning them. [13]

The new goal was to unite the Jewish labor movement solidly behind social democracy. Central to the new tactics were to be agitation on the basis of the workers' immediate needs and the formation of close ties between the socialist intelligentsia and the organized strike funds. Agitation among the masses was conducted with the supposition that in the process of economic struggle the workers would inevitably clash with the police power of the state and become politicized; political consciousness would naturally involve a demand for political change and social and economic revolution. *Ob agitatsii,* by Kremer and Martov, was the text setting forth the new tactics of social democracy.

## The Jewish Labor Bund

Agitation among the Jewish artisans gave the cosmopolitan Jewish socialists, believers in revolution through a countrywide alliance of the working class and social democracy, a greater

12. Nedasek, p. 37; Tobias, p. 27; Bukhbinder, p. 54; Mendelsohn, pp. 50–51; *Materialy k istorii evreiskago rabochago dvizheniia* (St. Petersburg, 1906), p. 36; Kol'tsov, p. 200. The law called for a twelve-hour day with two breaks for meals, a half hour for breakfast and an hour and a half for dinner (*Revoliutsionnoe dvizhenie sredi evreev* [Moscow, 1930], p. 86).

13. *Materialy,* pp. 28–30; Bukhbinder, pp. 58–62; Mendelsohn, pp. 45–49; Ezra Mendelsohn, "Worker Opposition in the Russian Jewish Socialist Movement, from the 1890's to 1903," *International Review of Social History,* 10 (1965), 271–72.

awareness of the needs and problems of the Jewish masses both as workers and as Jews. Increasingly, despite their Marxist ideology, they found themselves concerned with distinctively Jewish problems. Yet only cautiously and hesitantly did they decide to found a social democratic party representing solely the Jewish working class.

The need for such a movement was the theme of a speech delivered by Martov before a gathering of socialist activists in Vilna in May 1895. The speech came to be regarded as "a turning point in the history of the Jewish labor movement," the phrase under which it was published abroad in 1900. Martov began by condemning the Jewish socialists for looking to the Russian workers as the revolutionary hope of the future while ignoring the Jewish masses in their midst. The Russian labor movement was still in its youth; it could not be expected to bring about the liberation of the Jewish proletariat. In its struggle for political and economic rights the Russian working class faced such strong opposition that it would probably have to sacrifice certain of its demands, most likely "demands which solely concern Jews, as for example, freedom of religion or equality of rights for Jews." The Jewish intelligentsia had a revolutionary force of great potential in its own backyard: "The Jewish working class represents a sufficiently compact mass; being organized, it will represent a very impressive force." In conclusion, Martov exhorted Jewish socialists to found "a special Jewish labor organization, which would be the leader and educator of the Jewish proletariat in the struggle for economic, civil and political liberation."[14]

Vilna became the center of the effort to create a unified Jewish labor movement. Socialists there had developed close contacts with leading Russian revolutionaries abroad and social-democratic committees within Russia. These contacts facilitated the spread of socialism throughout the White Russian and Lithuanian provinces; from Vilna, Jewish socialists set out to organize the Jewish artisans for socialism in the towns of the Pale. The tactical change to agitation among the masses prompted the adoption of Yiddish, the mother tongue of the Jewish workers, as the language of the movement.[15]

14. *Materialy,* p. 154.
15. In the census of 1897, 99.3 per cent of the Jews in the Northwest region listed Yiddish as their mother tongue (Schwarz, *The Jews,* p. 13).

In the 1890's the number of organized workers and strike funds significantly increased. In 1894 strike funds were organized in twelve professions in Vilna and four in Minsk; by 1897, their number had reached twenty in both cities, with membership totaling fifteen hundred in Vilna and a thousand in Minsk.[16] There was no letup in the strike movement for better working conditions. In Vilna in 1895 fifty-six strikes occurred among workers in twenty-seven different professions, with the strikers claiming victory in more than 80 per cent of the cases.[17] By the mid-1890's a mass labor movement, highly organized and stressing the efficacy of economic struggle, could be said to exist in White Russia and Lithuania.

Encouraged by the success of the new tactics, thirteen delegates representing socialist groups in five cities met secretly in Vilna in September 1897 and established the General Jewish Labor Union in Russia and Poland, popularly known as the Bund.[18] A central committee was established to direct the party's organization and maintain contacts with local committees; to ensure the central committee's immunity from arrest, its members were to avoid contact with the masses. The Bund henceforward was to be subjected to frequent police raids; its emphasis on conspiratorial techniques, however, permitted the organization to continue functioning even when its central forces were almost totally depleted. The Bund congress also reaffirmed the recent commitment to Yiddish. A party newspaper and a periodical were to be published in Yiddish; agitational literature in Yiddish was to be greatly increased.

The founders of the Bund regarded it as an integral part of the larger social-democratic movement then in its formative stage in European Russia. For this reason they readily accepted the call to form a nationwide Marxist party; three Bundists were among the nine delegates who secretly gathered in Minsk for the first congress of the all-Russian Social Democratic Labor Party in March 1898. Kremer, a leader of the Bund, was chosen by the congress to the new party's central committee.

During the first three years of its existence the Bund suffered temporary setbacks through police raids, but its ties with the Jewish labor movement remained unbroken. In a report to the International

16. Tobias, p. 37; *Materialy,* pp. 44, 50–51.
17. *Materialy,* p. 53.
18. Tobias, pp. 60–69; *Materialy,* p. 65.

Socialist Congress in Paris in 1900, the Bund declared the base of its organization to be the strike funds organized in each profession; each organized profession in a city or town had a structure resembling a trade union, that is, a statute of its own, a treasury, and elected bodies, including a commission. One member of each commission served as a delegate to a central commission or assembly *(skhodka)* which administered those funds set aside for strikes. Funds were also appropriated for a library commission which handled the acquisition and distribution of legal and illegal literature.

The local Bund committee organized a network of circles in each profession and directed the movement throughout the city.[19] Figures from the aforementioned Bund report and police estimates placed the total membership of the funds, exclusive of several large cities such as Lodz and Warsaw, at approximately 5,600, making the Bund the most broadly based social-democratic organization in Russia for its time.[20] The strike movement for improvements in wages and hours continued successfully in these years. Information available to the Bund on strikes among artisans and factory workers of the Pale from the end of 1897 to the summer of 1900 indicated that more than 90 per cent concluded in the workmen's favor. The high degree of success was attributed to the strong discipline and common front shown by the workers, who usually went on strike *en masse*.[21]

## Zubatov, the Bund and the Jewish Labor Movement: The Early Stages

The rise of a mass Jewish labor movement and the spread of social democracy in the Pale went unheeded for some time by the authorities. As strikes increased, however, local officials ceased to be tolerant, and arrests of strikers became more common. Officials, however, knew little, if anything, of the Bund or of its role in energizing the labor movement in White Russia and Lithuania. G. K. Semiakin, a high official of the Department of Police, during a discussion with Sergei Zubatov in 1897 confessed that the department lacked reliable information on the Bund. "Despite my

19. M. G. Rafes, *Ocherki istorii evreiskogo rabochego dvizheniia* (Moscow-Leningrad, 1929), p. 55; *Materialy,* pp. 68–69.
20. *Materialy,* p. 68; Tobias, p. 98.
21. *Materialy,* pp. 82–83; Nedasek, p. 76.

poverty, I would give twenty-five rubles to the one who would tell what kind of a thing this 'Bund' is," Semiakin added, half in jest.[22]

The St. Petersburg authorities, who already highly valued Zubatov's ability to ferret out the revolutionary nests, now entrusted him with the direction of counterintelligence investigation of revolutionary activities in Lithuania and White Russia. Within a short time the area was flooded with agents of the Okhrana's "flying squadron." Zubatov called on his agents to follow the Bund leaders from city to city, biding his time until he had sufficient information to raid the Bund branches in one fell swoop. On the night of July 26, 1898, police raids were carried out in several cities; a large number of Bundists were arrested, including the entire central committee.[23]

With a view to recruiting *sotrudniki* (collaborators) who would keep the Okhrana abreast of developments inside the Jewish revolutionary movement, Zubatov ordered the prisoners transferred to Moscow, where they were placed in solitary confinement prior to lengthy interrogation. Their cases were processed slowly in the hope of wearing them down and eliciting information of use to the police; not until April 1901 were the prisoners sentenced. The delay was occasioned by the adamant self-discipline of the Bundists; the large majority denied they belonged to the Bund and provided little information of value to the police. Nor did the prisoners succumb to Zubatov's powers of persuasion or ideological appeal.[24] Writing of his first contacts with the Bundists, Zubatov described the prisoners as "malicious, impudent, wily, united and disciplined in regard to their leaders."[25] On another occasion he acknowledged that their obstinacy disheartened their interrogators, upon whom "the Jewish movement produced something of a grandiose impression, almost of an inaccessible influence."[26] The threat of new repressive measures against the Jewish people failed to move the prisoners to give testimony; Zubatov's invitation to individual

22. Men'shchikov, *Okhrana i revoliutsiia*, II, no. 1, pp. 12–13.
23. *Ibid.*, pp. 112, 164; Tobias, pp. 81–83; Bukhbinder, *Istoriia*, p. 75; Nedasek, p. 65; N. A. Bukhbinder, "Razgrom evreiskogo rabochego dvizheniia v 1898 g.," *Krasnaia letopis'*, 1922, no. 4, p. 149; B. M. Frumkin, "Zubatovshchina i evreiskoe rabochee dvizhenie," *Perezhitoe*, 3 (1911), 198–201.
24. Bukhbinder, *Istoriia*, pp. 78, 81; Frumkin, p. 202.
25. "K istorii Zubatovshchiny," p. 94.
26. "Novoe o zubatovshchine," p. 292.

leaders of the Bund to hold private talks was no more successful.[27]

Zubatov next attempted to acquire a direct influence over the Jewish labor movement; the bristle makers might well have served his purposes. They were among the most exploited workers in the Pale: low wages, a sixteen-hour workday, unsanitary working conditions, and cruel treatment at the hands of their employers led them to band together in 1898 into the Jewish Bristle-Workers' Union of Poland and Lithuania, whose central committee unified the movement and established contacts with other labor organizations. Almost all the bristle makers in the Northwest region joined the union, which possessed an underground organ, *Der Veker* (The Awakener).[28]

The bristle makers in the early 1890's had limited their activities to economic strikes and other means of furthering their professional interests. Under the influence of socialist agitators, however, they became more politically motivated and in 1898, the year of its founding, their union declared its allegiance to the Bund. The union's political orientation and its involvement in the transport of illegal literature brought it to the attention of the police. Zubatov, for one, however, believed that the bristle makers were not so politically committed as to reject an offer of legalization from the government and recommended that policy to his superiors. In so doing he exaggerated the union's strength: "The contemporary Jewish movement which has embraced the entire Northwest area has as its basis a very firm, strong, and stable organization in the form of the so-called 'Union of Bristle-makers.'" Its strength derived from the fact that "all its members are Jews, who speak one language, and most important of all, that this organization gave great material benefit to the bristle makers." To render the union harmless to the government Zubatov recommended that politically inclined elements be removed. Once that was accomplished new statutes could be prepared to legalize the union and end its need for conspiratorial activity; Zubatov predicted: "with subordination to the statutes the activity of the 'union' most likely would again be engaged in the economic sphere."[29]

Zubatov followed up these ideas in talks with prisoners closely

27. Frumkin, p. 202; Tobias, p. 121.
28. Rafes, *Ocherki istorii*, p. 56; Mendelsohn, *Class Struggle*, pp. 72–73; Rafes, *Ocherki po istorii "Bunda,"* pp. 331–34.
29. Rafes, *Ocherki po istorii "Bunda,"* p. 334.

associated with the union, promising them his support if they would use their influence to have the bristle makers return to their former economic orientation. One prisoner who supported legalization of the union was allegedly promised 20,000 rubles to publish a legal organ for the bristle makers. Although several prisoners, including some leaders of the bristle makers' movement, apparently agreed to agitate on behalf of Zubatov's ideas, nothing came of the project, for reasons that are not evident.[30] The attempt to work through existing Jewish working-class organizations having failed, Zubatov would encourage the establishment of a labor organization to rival the Bund and weaken its hold over the artisans of the Pale.

Zubatov's interrogation of the Bundists aroused his interest in the Jewish question. A second wave of mass arrests in Minsk in 1900 gave him the opportunity to study the Bund closely once more. Previous experience helped him to ascertain the psychological makeup of the prisoners and to adjust his line of argument skillfully to persuade them of fallacies in socialist ideology.[31] As a result of long dialogues with young Bundists, he was able to acquire a small group of converts who promised to propagate his ideas upon their return to Minsk; these recruits were to become the founders of the Jewish Independent Labor Party a year later. To comprehend Zubatov's success in recruiting followers among the Bund intelligentsia and the rapidity with which the Independents gathered a mass following among the Jewish artisans of the Pale, we must examine the critical evolution the Bund was undergoing as well as the complex political scene in the city of Minsk.

Crises in the Bund

The founding congress of the Bund had established the party's organizational structure but left unresolved serious programmatic and tactical questions. No clear-cut decisions were reached for some time on such important issues as the role and dimension of political struggle, the relative emphasis to be given to economic strikes, the nationality question, and the nature of relations with other socialist organizations. During the next few years, the Bund re-evaluated its

30. Frumkin, pp. 207, 209; *Listok "Rabochago dela,"* no. 5 (Jan. 1901); Tobias, pp. 126–27.
31. "K istorii Zubatovshchiny," p. 94; "Novoe o zubatovshchine," p. 292.

tactics. The outcome, a decision to emphasize political agitation and downgrade economic struggle, stirred strong opposition within its ranks and threatened it with loss of support by the Jewish masses. Thus at the time Zubatov's plans for a rival Jewish labor organization were taking shape, the Bund was undergoing a profound internal crisis.[32]

Toward the turn of the century, the conviction had begun to grow among the Bund's leadership that the old methods of economic struggle based on illegal funds and strikes had reached the point of diminishing returns and that greater weight should be given to political action. At the Second Congress, in September 1898, local committees reported that strike funds were ceasing to be the sole medium for uniting workers and making them conscious of their political and economic interests. Economic struggle was still deemed significant, but the stiffening resistance of employers to their workers' demands and increasing cases of police intervention and arrests appeared to lessen the efficacy of strikes as a labor weapon. The Second Congress thus advised local committees to use greater discretion in calling on the workers to strike.[33]

The economic recession that began in the fall of 1899 harshly affected the working class of the Pale; among the artisans, unemployment became widespread, competition for jobs intensified, and working conditions deteriorated. Strikes under these conditions were chiefly defensive in purpose — that is, designed to preserve the existing terms of hire.

The Fourth Congress of the Bund, in May 1901, almost completely ignored the issue of strike funds. A resolution recommended that local committees show caution in calling for strikes. Only defensive strikes were justified in professions in which the strike movement had made all the economic gains that could be expected; strikes were to be restricted chiefly to industries where working conditions were particularly bad and the workers had not yet participated in economic struggle.

The Fourth Congress also endorsed broad political action. Not a single voice protested against the new emphasis on intensive political agitation, the Bund proudly reported:[34] "Political struggle

32. Frumkin, pp. 205, 211–13; Zaslavskii, "Zubatov i Mania Vil'bushevich," pp. 100–101.
33. Tobias, pp. 87–88.
34. *Materialy,* p. 107.

must be waged as an independent action and must occupy a prominent place in the activities of the organization. It should not be considered as a mere outgrowth of economic struggle and must be waged by means of purely political agitation, political demonstrations, and May Day strikes with political demands."[35]

The primacy of political agitation was upheld in the resolutions of the Fifth Congress, in September 1902, although resistance to the new course at the lower levels was noted. Some local committees still hindered the execution of the party's program by "dependence on and adaptation of the organization to the trade-union movement, which remains a survival of the past." The congress resolved to combat this tendency by demanding that local committees be independent of trade-union organizations. The foremost duty of the committees was revolutionary agitation. The committees, in the words of a congress resolution, without "renouncing the leadership of the economic struggle, must in their activity conform to the general interests of the revolutionary proletarian movement, and consequently look upon themselves not as representatives of trade-union organizations, but as revolutionary organizations, which put into practice the principles of international revolutionary social democracy."[36]

The new party line was not acceptable to a large part of the Bund's working-class following. Some workers had earlier abandoned the Jewish socialist intelligentsia in protest against the shift from workmen's circles to mass agitation. Others had complained that the leadership of the local Bund committees was not elective and thus not sufficiently representative. Now the de-emphasis on economic struggle alienated many more workmen, and rifts developed between the local committee intelligentsia and their working-class following.

The Jewish workers, moreover, did not share the socialist intelligentsia's antipathy toward the police and the local authorities and preferred to remain within a legal framework.[37] The strike movement had taught them that tangible gains were to be made through economic struggle, and they were not ready to abandon the

---

35. Raphael R. Abramovich, "The Jewish Socialist Movement in Russia and Poland (1897–1919)," in *The Jewish People Past and Present*, II, 372.

36. *Posledniia izvestiia*, no. 88 (Oct. 4, 1902).

37. Mendelsohn, "Worker Opposition," p. 276; Mendelsohn, *Class Struggle*, pp. 97, 127, 139; memoirs of M. Frumkina (Ester), in "Novoe o zubatovshchine," p. 327.

tactic. Many artisans, and some elements within the party, felt that "the Bund, in the name of purely s[ocial]-d[emocratic] principles, is sacrificing the vital interests of the workers."[38] Moreover, the workers could argue that the success of the strike movement was not a thing of the past, for the great majority of strikes still terminated in their favor.[39]

The Bund had not abandoned economic struggle altogether, but its disinclination to encourage further development of the strike movement led many workers to forsake it and seek out other organizations where the old ways prevailed.[40] They found shelter in the new groups that amalgamated socialism and Zionism and in the Jewish Independent Labor Party, which made its first inroads in the Bund stronghold of Minsk.

## The Socialist and Labor Movements in Minsk

Minsk at the turn of the century had a population of 90,000, half of it Jewish. As in other centers of the Northwest region, large mechanized industry was insignificant, the number of factory workers few. A mass labor movement began in Minsk in the early 1890's; by 1896, artisans in most Minsk handicraft trades possessed their own strike funds and had engaged in strikes. The Minsk Committee of the Bund did not direct the strike movement, which was in the hands of the workers.[41]

The city's diversified population, which included large numbers of White Russians, Ukrainians, Great Russians, Poles, and Jews, explains the cross-currents of nationalism and socialism and the wide political spectrum which characterized Minsk at the end of the nineteenth century. Minsk, as Zubatov often remarked, was a revolutionary city par excellence.[42] Since 1897 Minsk had been a

38. "Novoe o zubatovshchine," p. 327.

39. Tobias, pp. 98–99.

40. "Jewish craftsmen were concerned, first and foremost, with the improvement of their economic conditions, and were therefore prepared to follow whomever would promise them such improvements. They allied themselves with the Marxist intelligentsia not because it was Marxist so much as because it held out to them, through the implementation of the 'agitation' program, the hope for a better future" (Ezra Mendelsohn, "The Russian Jewish Labor Movement and Others," *Yivo Annual of Jewish Social Science*, 14 [1969], 96).

41. Tobias, p. 101. This situation was also found in other cities; Mendelsohn, *Class Struggle*, p. 70.

42. Frumkin, p. 203; Mendelsohn, *Class Struggle*, pp. 4–5; N. A. Bukhbinder, "Evreiskoe rabochee dvizhenie v Minske," *Krasnaia letopis'*, 1923, no. 5, pp. 122–23;

center of the revived Narodnichestvo (Populist) movement that eventually culminated in the formation of the Socialist Revolutionary Party. The Minsk group was led by Ekaterina Breshko-Breshkovskaia and Grigorii Gershuni, both of whom were later prominent in the party.[43] Breshkovskaia had a large following among the youth from the Minsk gymnasia; Gershuni led another group which debated tactical questions with local Social Democrats in much the same way that the Narodniki and Marxists had done several years earlier at student gatherings in Moscow and Petersburg. The evening lectures of the Society of Refined Arts were turned into a forum for these debates; in the words of a participant, "this whole ideological life flowed almost openly," members of the rival political groups being well acquainted with one another.[44]

The Bund was strongly entrenched in Minsk. After its First Congress, the central committee and the party's press were moved to Minsk, where police surveillance was considered to be weak. The Bund had harnessed the labor movement among the Minsk artisans for its own ends. By 1900 it also had supporters among the young radical intelligentsia and was the only political group in Minsk with a following among the working masses; a stable social-democratic group independent of the Bund did not rise in Minsk until 1903.[45]

The tension between the intelligentsia and the working class, which characterized the socialist movement throughout Russia in the 1890's, was evident in Minsk in the opposition of the worker-intelligentsia to the tactical change from educational workmen's circles to mass agitation. The issue precipitated a crisis in the spring of 1899, when Albert Zalkind, representing the Bund's central committee, scolded the Minsk Committee for its continuing devotion to workmen's circles. After a lively debate, which brought the Minsk group to the verge of a schism, it acquiesced to Zalkind, fearful that the central committee would otherwise withhold agitational literature in Yiddish upon which the Minsk Committee

---

Mark Wischnitzler, "Minsk," *Universal Jewish Encyclopedia* (New York, 1942?), VII, 577; "Minsk," *Bol'shaia sovetskaia entsiklopediia*, 2d ed., XXVII (1954), 545.

43. Spiridovich, *Zapiski zhandarma*, pp. 43–44.

44. Frumkin, p. 205.

45. Ef. Belen'kii (Sergei), "Vospominaniia o bol'shevistskoi organizatsii v g. Minske v 1903 g.," *Proletarskaia revoliutsiia*, Nov. 1924, p. 196. A recent Soviet source maintains that an *Iskra* circle was founded in Minsk in 1901 and later became the nucleus of the Minsk group of the R.S.D.R.P. formed in the fall of 1903; "Minsk," *Sovetskaia istoricheskaia entsiklopediia*, IX (1966), 471.

depended. Zalkind did not have his way for long. At Easter the rank-and-file workers making up the support of the Minsk Committee declared they would depose it if it refused to return to the tactic of workmen's circles. Within the committee, debate over the issue raged all summer; in August it yielded to the workers and was reorganized under the leadership of Girsh Iakelev Shakhnovich and Mania Vladimirovna Vil'bushevich, both of whom were to become prominent in the Jewish Independent Labor Party.[46] The rift within the Minsk Committee, however, continued unhealed.

The committee had other internal difficulties. Party agitators objected because committee members were not elected; workers complained they were not sufficiently represented on the committee, which they alleged was dominated by intellectuals. In July, the Minsk joiners announced they would no longer attend committee meetings because of its neglect of economic struggle and failure to include a representative from their profession in its composition.[47] Thus the Minsk workers, like many other artisans of the Pale, were prepared to welcome a movement supporting the tactic of economic struggle, a tactic that had been acceptable to the Bund in its prepolitical stage.

46. Bukhbinder, "Evreiskoe rabochee dvizhenie v Minske," pp. 126, 128, 131–32; Mendelsohn, "Worker Opposition," p. 272; Mendelsohn, *Class Struggle,* pp. 58–59.

47. Bukhbinder, "Evreiskoe rabochee dvizhenie v Minske," p. 137; Tobias, pp. 36, 100–101; Mendelsohn, *Class Struggle,* p. 62.

# CHAPTER 9

# The Jewish Independent Labor Party

Zubatov's plans to break the link between the Bund and the Jewish working class took shape with the arrest of a large part of the Minsk Committee on the night of March 6, 1900. The new prisoners upon interrogation turned out to be less fanatical than those arrested in 1898. The Bund now contained, Zubatov reported, a large number of "green youths" with a tendency "to renounce their views just as soon as one managed to convince them of the opposite."[1] Through interrogation Zubatov learned that these "green youths" had been drawn into the revolutionary movement out of sympathy with the plight of the masses rather than through indoctrination in political theory, with which they had little acquaintance. Here was raw material that the Okhrana's master in brainwashing could fashion into a product serviceable for his future plans. The prisoners, including the more hardened revolutionaries among them, were subjected to re-education in Zubatov's course on the spirit of enlightened autocracy.

Aleksandr Chemeriskii, who was arrested on May Day in Minsk, has described Zubatov's training program for political prisoners in his memoirs. Prior to his interrogation Chemeriskii was escorted to a nearby restaurant, where he was allowed to eat freely at government expense. Upon return to prison he was brought, to his surprise, before an officer in civilian clothes: "Instead of asking questions . . . he simply began to speak about the labor movement, about strikes," Chemeriskii recalled. The talks with Zubatov made a great impression on Chemeriskii, and the books he was given to

---

1. "K istorii Zubatovshchiny," p. 94.

read from the Okhrana's library on the labor movement in Western Europe proved to be "a complete revelation."[2]

Zubatov summarized his approach to the prisoners in a report to the Department of Police on November 28, 1901:

Talks about the radiant idea of Christian monarchy; about the difference between supreme and government authority, between central organs and provincial representatives of the administration; about the difference between the idea of a peaceful labor movement and a revolutionary one; about the antithesis between the interests of the members of the first and the interests of agitators, which, owing to the difference in aims, amounts to the latter's exploitation of the laboring masses; about the inability of extremist elements, in the interests of the masses, even to make use of the direct requirements of the law, such as the establishment of the twelve-hour workday for handicraft enterprises; and finally, acquaintance, through original documents, with the practice of the Moscow police with respect to the workers, in the spirit of the principles stated in the 1898 Report of the Moscow chief of police addressed to His Imperial Highness, the Moscow governor-general, had a stunning impact on those arrested as facts and considerations which completely contradicted their ideas and conceptions, and among them appeared persons who firmly decided to enter on a new road of activity.[3]

The prisoners at first were neither asked to betray their comrades nor enticed to enter the Okhrana's service. Instead, Zubatov endeavored to recruit ideological followers, picturing himself to the prisoners not as a police officer but as a bearer of an idea of consequence. Long uninterrupted dialogues, sometimes lasting six hours or more, on the most varied intellectual subjects, from contemporary literature to the Jewish question, left a strong impression on hardened revolutionaries as well as novices. Zubatov's soothing persuasiveness, moreover, contrasted favorably with the rough physical treatment the prisoners suffered at the hands of a Minsk gendarme colonel noted for his hatred of Jews and revolutionaries.

When Zubatov had ascertained that a prisoner was won over, he requested a written confession, promising that no harm would come to anyone as a result, and in this respect Zubatov kept his word. Among the prisoners converted to Zubatov's ideological views were the Minsk Bundists Shakhnovich and Vil'bushevich, future leaders of his labor program among the Jews. Unlike the leaders of the

2. "Novoe o zubatovshchine," p. 316.
3. *Ibid.*, pp. 292–93.

Moscow Zubatovshchina, who came from the working class, Zubatov's Jewish followers were of the intelligentsia.

The most energetic and capable organizer in the group was Mania (Maria) Vladimirovna Vil'bushevich (Wilbushewitch), the daughter of a Grodno merchant. Vil'bushevich had earlier been involved in the circle led by Evgeniia Gurevich, a long-time socialist propagandist in Minsk; by the time of her arrest at the age of twenty she had become a leading member of the Minsk Committee of the Bund. Mania Vil'bushevich was destined to lead a full and dramatic life dedicated to fighting the Bund in Russia and the United States before becoming a prominent pioneer in Zionist colonies in Palestine.[4] Of all the partisans Zubatov recruited from among the Jewish youth of the Pale, she became his most fervent disciple. Her correspondence with him, portions of which have been published, reveals her troubled soul and the great tribulations facing Zubatov's recruits who returned to Minsk in the summer of 1900. Strong-willed and given to complete but changing emotional commitments, Mania Vil'bushevich before leaving prison had become captivated by Zubatov's views on the monarchy and of a peaceful, evolutionary labor movement. Moreover, she freely told him what she knew of the Bund committees in Minsk, Grodno, and elsewhere in the Pale, suggesting the arrest of her former party comrades in order that they might likewise go through Zubatov's course of indoctrination.[5]

Zubatov kept Sipiagin informed of his conversations with the prisoners; in June and July 1900 they were released and allowed to return to Minsk.[6] Their early return caused a great stir in Minsk and led to wide-ranging disputes over Zubatov's reliability and his proposals to legalize the labor movement. A few of the prisoners returned home emotionally depressed for having made a confession in prison and soon left the labor movement altogether; others upon release felt that "those dreams about legal work, which earlier

4. Frumkin, p. 204; Zaslavskii, p. 101; "Vil'bushevich, Mariia," *Bol'shaia sovetskaia entsiklopediia*, X (1928), 786; Bukhbinder, "Nezavisimaia," p. 223; Manya Shochat (Vil'bushevich's married name), "The Collective," in *The Plough Woman*, ed. Rachel Katzenelson-Rubashow (New York, 1932), pp. 19–26; *Encyclopedia of Zionism and Israel*, ed. Raphael Patai (New York, 1971), II, 1218; *Encyclopaedia Judaica*, XIV (1971), 1441–42.

5. Bukhbinder, "Evreiskoe rabochee dvizhenie v Minske," p. 135; Zaslavskii, pp. 106, 123–25.

6. Bukhbinder, *ibid.*; Frumkin, p. 209.

inspired them, remained dreams";[7] some, like Gershuni, who also had made a written confession to Zubatov, returned from the Moscow prison adamant in their old ways and determined to fight against Zubatov's machinations and his "new course." The latter group maligned Zubatov, accusing him of being a wily bureaucratic careerist totally insincere about the program he espoused. Sufficiently intelligent to realize that the theory of tsarism he propagated was divorced from reality, Zubatov would at most grant the workers minor concessions "in the form of fictitious trade unions and the right to strike," concessions which would be withdrawn as soon as the workers demanded more basic rights. An utterly unprincipled careerist, Zubatov cared neither "about the tsar nor the labor movement nor the Russian people." Gershuni, in particular, propagated in Minsk this view of Zubatov, which Vil'bushevich felt "penetrated the consciousness of all with the speed of lightening."[8]

Disturbed by the interest aroused by Zubatov's supporters, the Bund felt it necessary to warn Bundists against cooperating with the plans of the Okhrana chief. In August 1900 its central committee issued a proclamation accusing Zubatov of directing counter-revolutionary activities against the Bund and using his spies to repress the Jewish labor movement. "How could one enter into a conversation with such an enemy of the workers?" the Bund rhetorically questioned.[9] Individuals entering into relations with Zubatov or his followers were neither revolutionaries nor friends of the working class: they would be openly branded as traitors and provocateurs, the Bund warned.

The central committee's proclamation was a rebuff to Zubatov, who had convinced himself, after converting some minor Bundists, that the leadership could be similarly won over. "Animated by success, I wanted to dislodge Kremer's faith and through him the whole group of '98," Zubatov informed his superiors; "I sent him a telegram, he answered me, I again sent a telegram, but this time did not receive an answer, for their escape abroad was accomplished and a proclamation appeared."[10]

7. Vil'bushevich to Zubatov, Aug. 2, 1900 (Zaslavskii, p. 104); Frumkin, p. 209.
8. Vil'bushevich to Zubatov, Aug. 2, 1900 (Zaslavskii, pp. 105–6); see also Frumkin, p. 209.
9. *Rabochee delo*, no. 7 (Aug. 1900).
10. Zubatov's report of Sept. 6, 1900 (Zaslavskii, p. 103); see also Tobias, p. 121; *Revoliutsionnaia Rossiia*, no. 4 (Feb. 1902).

The sustained attack upon Zubatov in Minsk intellectual circles and the Bund's stern warning to its members shook the confidence of even the most enthusiastic supporters of the "new tactic." Not for the last time did Zubatov's Jewish followers find themselves laboring as a small minority in a hostile atmosphere. Material compensation in no way accounted for their loyalty to the cause of the Zubatovshchina; there is no evidence they received individual stipends from the Okhrana, as did the officers of the Moscow Workers' Council. [11] Determination to struggle against the majority coupled with strong conviction in the righteousness of their cause accounts for their willingness to face material sacrifice, public discomfort and humiliation, and even physical attacks. Shakhnovich, for example, upon returning to Vilna was greeted with such a hail of criticism, including denunciation as a provocateur, that he became embittered and resolved to emigrate abroad. Had not Mania Vil'bushevich hurried to Vilna and exhorted him to continue the struggle, he doubtless would have left the movement. [12]

Mania Vil'bushevich, too, knew moments of desolation and despair. Depressed by malicious rumors that she was a mere pawn in Zubatov's game of espionage, she could not for some time bring herself to write to Zubatov as she had promised. Cut off from Zubatov and adrift in a hostile environment, she slowly began to give way to the barest suspicions that Zubatov's talks with her "about tsar, God, the soul" was but a clever means of recruiting "an ecstactic young girl as an assistant."[13] These suspicions were causing her to hate him, she confessed in a letter to Zubatov; she implored him to convince her otherwise. Difficulties mounted for Mania Vil'bushevich; the Bund's proclamation attacking the Zubatovshchina caused many Minsk workers, whom she had begun to organize, to turn against her.

During these months of travail, Mania Vil'bushevich underwent another intellectual and emotional awakening. She remained an

11. Zubatov held that he did not have to pay his Jewish followers: "But the work of Jewish agents in the legal labor movement (Minsk and Odessa) really did not cost me a cent, because here the whole matter was organized exclusively for intellectual ends" (Zubatov, "Zubatovshchina," p. 166). He did admit that some money from the funds of the Department of Police was sent to the Odessa Independent leader Khunia Shaevich ("K istorii Zubatovshchiny," p. 96). For a discussion of the Independents' financial support see Schwarz, *The Russian Revolution of 1905*, pp. 279–80.

12. Zaslavskii, pp. 106, 116, 122.

13. *Ibid.*, p. 107.

advocate of a nonrevolutionary labor movement, although on grounds other than those held by Zubatov, her letters reveal. Zubatov's tactics had practical weakness in their applicability, she wrote to him on October 14, 1900. For one thing, the socialist intelligentsia could not be persuaded to lead a working-class movement dedicated to economic struggle, for they had already gone through that stage and become disillusioned with it. Nothing but a full-scale revolution would satisfy them. Moreover, Zubatov's ideology centering upon "that wonderful, powerful theory of tsarism" might be understood by the intelligentsia but not by the working class, which could have little interest in such a "fascinating dream." Nevertheless she was of the opinion that "the Jewish movement . . . very soon will take a purely economic direction, clearly rejecting any sort of revolution whatsoever."[14] The cause for the renewed dedication of both Vil'bushevich and Shakhnovich to Zubatov's plans for a legal, evolutionary Jewish labor movement was their passionate conversion to Zionism, which had made inroads among the Minsk intelligentsia.[15]

### Zubatov and the Jewish Question

The Zionists were the first group seriously to challenge the Bund's leadership over the Jewish masses of the Pale. Their program, in contrast to the Bund's was directed at all classes and elements within Jewry. The Bundists, as Social Democrats, believed that the emancipation of the Jews and other peoples in Russia was dependent on the success of the general revolutionary movement; the interests of the Jewish workers therefore were considered bound up with those of the working class throughout the empire. The Bund, moreover, challenged the Zionist contention that Russian Jews could end their desperate plight only through exodus to a homeland. From the Bund's point of view, Zionism was a utopian, middle-class dream, diverting the Jewish working class from the struggle for political rights. Above all the Bund detested Zionist

14. *Ibid.,* p. 120.
15. *Ibid.,* pp. 120, 122. In an autobiographical sketch published in the 1930's, Mania Shochat (her married name) states that until she was fifteen she received religious training in the Bible and the Talmud as well as in Hebrew. Both her brothers were Zionists prior to her conversion to the cause. She maintains, however, that when she arrived in Palestine in January 1904 she was not a Zionist (Katzenelson-Rubashow, pp. 19, 21).

opposition to political activity and struggle.[16] The Third Congress of the Bund in April 1901 branded Zionism "a reaction of the bourgeois classes against anti-Semitism and the abnormal legal position of the Jewish people" and the Zionist goal of a territory for the Jewish people "utopian and not feasible."[17] Zionists were prohibited by the Bund from entering its economic and political organizations. Nevertheless, Zionism acquired a large following. More than 700 delegates from various parts of Russia and from Palestine met in a Zionist conference in Minsk in August 1902.[18]

The antipathy between Zionism and socialism was not so absolute as to preclude a synthesis of the two on national and social questions. Poale Zion (Workers of Zion), which arose simultaneously in Minsk and Ekaterinoslav in 1900, was the first organization that endeavored to bridge the gap. The Minsk group in the next two years developed followers in other towns of White Russia and Lithuania. In contrast to the Ekaterinoslav faction, which had a social-democratic orientation, the Minsk Poale Zionists opposed political activity, maintaining that an effective class struggle could be carried on only when the Jews had obtained a homeland. Abstention from politics, however, did not preclude advocacy of cultural activity and economic struggle to better the lot of the Jewish working class. The Minsk Poale Zionists' position on the labor question bore similarities to that of Mania Vil'bushevich and her cohorts, making them natural allies against the Bund.[19]

The Zionist-Socialists also tried to fuse socialist and nationalist tendencies among Russian Jews. Nachman Syrkin, their ideological leader, believed Russian Jewry would be emancipated only when it possessed a socialist state of its own. Mania Vil'bushevich became an enthusiastic convert. The government had nothing to fear from Zionism, she wrote Zubatov, for, as Syrkin postulated, "the Jewish workers, as workers, must acknowledge a purely *economic movement, they must not be interested in the politics of that country in which they live; Zionism must become their politics.*"[20] Mania

16. Greenberg, II, 173; Abramovich, p. 387; Ben-Adir, pp. 300–302.
17. *Materialy,* pp. 126–27.
18. Greenberg, II, 180; Wischnitzer, p. 576.
19. On the Minsk Poale Zionists see Ben-Adir, pp. 306–7; Abramovich, p. 388; Patkin, p. 218; Greenberg, II, 157; Frumkin, p. 213; Bukhbinder, *Istoriia,* p. 342; Nachman Syrkin, "Beginnings of Socialist Zionism," in Marie Syrkin, *Nachman Syrkin, Socialist Zionist* (New York, 1961), pp. 240–41.
20. Italics in original; Vil'bushevich to Zubatov, Oct. 14, 1900 (Zaslavskii, p. 120).

Vil'bushevich may have misread or misquoted Syrkin, but her commitment to Zionism was never in doubt.

Strengthened by their new-found attachment to Zionism, Shakhnovich and Vil'bushevich began the task of organizing the Jewish artisans and recruiting additional leaders for their movement from among socialist activists. Working under the most trying conditions, which at times meant "one going against all," they suffered frequent setbacks but continued "with a thirst for struggle."[21] Their propaganda stressed the benefits to be reaped by the workers if they would but follow the purely economic and legal road. Artisans in each profession were encouraged to prepare statutes of organization for approval by the authorities.

In some cases Mania Vil'bushevich was unable to dispel the workers' fears, based on past experience, that the signatories of workmen's petitions would be arrested. In Grodno, however, she was able to persuade the local printers, most of whom supported social democracy, to call off an imminent strike and act "by the legal method" by sending the statutes of their society to Petersburg for confirmation. Fearful that the local gendarmes would intervene and undo her work—she had promised the printers immunity from arrest if they agreed to follow her program—Vil'bushevich pleaded with Zubatov to restrain the local authorities: "For the sake of all that is dear to us, use influence so that they are not arrested here for a strike," for the printers needed proof that the police and the government were not the enemies of the working class.[22]

In the final analysis the success of Zubatov's plans depended on whether the government was prepared to sanction the program his followers expounded among the artisans. Although, as Mania Vil'bushevich reported, the workers were not interested in politics, they had little faith in the government, which for the most part they hated as the defender of the bourgeoisie. If their common plans were to attain success, she wrote to Zubatov, the local gendarmes must be curbed and literature promoting the legalization of the labor movement widely circulated.[23]

---

Zaslavskii unfortunately did not publish the entire letter. Presumably Vil'bushevich was referring to Syrkin's "The Jewish Problem and the Socialist-Jewish State," written in 1898. The essay is to be found in Arthur Hertzberg, ed., *The Zionist Idea* (New York, 1970), pp. 333–50. A reading of the essay does not support Mania Vil'bushevich's interpretation of Syrkin's views.

21. Zaslavskii, p. 122.
22. *Ibid.*, pp. 114–15.
23. *Ibid.*, pp. 109, 118.

The support of General Trepov and the Grand Duke Sergei had been sufficient to permit the inauguration of the Moscow Zubatovshchina; approval by the Ministry of Interior, however, would be necessary to get Zubatov's program under way in Minsk, for it involved state policy on the Jewish question which could only be resolved on the highest levels. From the government's point of view, the Jewish working-class movement was particularly dangerous, having been linked closely for several years with the revolutionary intelligentsia, unlike the labor movement among the Russian workers. Many high officials feared that encouraging the Jewish working class to organize was a dangerous game that would eventually backfire against the monarchy.

While his disciples were out in the field laboring to enlist the Jewish artisans under the banner of legalization and economic struggle, Zubatov sought government approval of his plans. During the summer and fall of 1900, he wrote constantly to Petersburg officials setting forth his views on the contemporary labor movement and the Jewish problem, explaining the benefits the autocracy would derive from implementing his program.

Zubatov's acquaintance with the Jewish question had begun in his student days, when he had friends among the Jewish radical youth; later, during his years with the Okhrana, he devoted much study to the problem. Slepov, who knew Zubatov well, maintained that he sympathized with the plight of the Jews.[24] According to a colleague in the Okhrana, Zubatov considered the Jewish question a "temporary phenomenon, which must be resolved by following the example of Western European governments, that is, all restrictive laws against the Jews must pass into history."[25] Discriminatory legislation against the Jews was irrational, he told his Jewish prisoners, and would be rescinded.[26]

---

24. Slepov, in *Russkoe delo,* no. 33 (Aug. 13, 1905); Zubatov to Burtsev, Nov. 22, 1906 (Koz'min, p. 54).

25. Zavarzin, *Zhandarmy,* pp. 58–59. It is maintained that in these years, P. I. Rachkovskii, chief of the Russian secret police abroad, instigated the forgery later known throughout the world as "The Protocols of the Elders of Zion" (Norman Cohn, *Warrant for Genocide* [New York and Evanston, 1966], pp. 78, 83, 106–7). However, General Spiridovich, who knew Zubatov and other officials of the Department of Police quite well, asserts that he never once heard of the Protocols at that time (General A. I. Spiridovich, "Evreiskii vopros v Rossii v poslednee tsarstvovanie: Petr Ivanovich Rachkovskii" [manuscript, Aleksandr Ivanovich Spiridovich Papers, Yale University Library], p. 3).

26. Moshe Mishkinsky, "Ha-sotsializm ha-mishtari u-megamot ba-mediniut ha-shilton ha-tsari legabay ha-yehudim," *Zion* (Jerusalem), 25 (1960), 240–41.

In his reports to the Department of Police, which were forwarded to Sipiagin for consideration, Zubatov emphasized the possibilities of using the deep cleavages among the Jewish people and within the Bund itself to draw the Jewish masses away from the Bund. His conversations with Jewish revolutionaries, despite complications of "national, religious, and other peculiarities," had yielded positive results, he wrote Leonid Rataev, chief of the Special Section of the Department of Police:

Summarizing all this, I'll say one thing: it's necessary to encourage the Jews. After that one can twist them around one's finger. Thanks to their solidarity, the slightest attention to them is instantly transmitted to all corners, and everyone learns about it. Bring the crowd to heat by your attention and the masses will follow you, and thanks to their unity, they themselves will betray the revolutionaries.[27]

For the government the lesson was clear; "give simple measures to their advantage and you are master of the situation."[28] These measures were spelled out in Zubatov's communications to Sipiagin.[29]

The spread of Zionism among the Jews of the Pale strengthened these sentiments in Zubatov. "Inside Jewry such a great internal fermentation is taking place, a reformation (for us not only harmless but, owing to the circumstances of the time, also advantageous) whose process we can only hinder by unwarranted interference," he wrote to his superiors in commenting on Mania Vil'bushevich's conversion to Zionism. The government should take advantage of all forces which could be used to further its end; with regard to the Jews this meant "it is necessary to support Zionism and in general to play upon nationalistic aspirations."[30]

In a report to the Department of Police in November 1901 on the Minsk labor movement, Zubatov further elaborated on the theme that autocracy was compatible with the fundamental outlook of the Jewish people. Interrogation of Jewish prisoners had taught him that "the autocratic ideal appeared understandable to them; since the Jewish religion teaches belief in the coming of the Messiah and

27. Bukhbinder, "Nezavisimaia," p. 209.
28. *Ibid.*
29. Mishkinsky, pp. 239–41; Zaslavskii, p. 110; *Listok "Rabochago dela,"* no. 5 (Jan. 1901), p. 5. The measures Zubatov recommended are not certain, for those sections of his communications pertaining to the Jewish question have not been published.
30. Zaslavskii, p. 121.

the re-establishment of a Jewish state with the accession to the throne of a type of David, the democratic political idea is completely foreign to the national political thought of Jewry."[31]

Zubatov urged the government to ease censorship regulations in the Pale and permit publication of works in Yiddish, which would further his plans for a legal movement, as a letter to the Department of Police in September 1900 reveals:

Documents would convince you that, even burning with a desire to work legally, it is impossible for the Jews to do so: the Jewish masses do not understand Russian, and there is no legal literature in jargon [Yiddish]. There is a mass of illegal ones, and they circulate freely as do popular books among us. If one completely accepts that the interest of culture and revolution are contradictory, then creation of a daily and periodic legal jargon literature will establish a cornerstone in the struggle against the mass revolutionary movement.[32]

A year later Zubatov was still pleading with the Department of Police for "a legal newspaper in jargon, without which the masses can only learn of news from the illegal Bund press."[33] Apparently the authorities were reluctant to approve a newspaper by a group of former Bundists; as late as January 1902, Zubatov complained that his plans were being thwarted by censorship and the lack of a paper in Yiddish.[34]

Although Zubatov planned to undermine the Bund chiefly through enticing away its mass following, he still had recourse to police methods. Thus, for example, he recommended the arrest of the leaders of a social-democratic center that had brought about a series of strikes in Minsk and other cities of the Pale.[35] In his view it would be best if the "most harmful and disturbing elements" were banished from the Pale.[36] The removal of the most active socialist agitators from the Pale would smooth the path for his followers. The rest was up to the higher authorities. "Thus I did everything. Now it is the turn of S. E. [Zvolianskii], who promised to support my public with corresponding ministerial measures for the well-being of Jewry

31. "Novoe o zubatovshchine," p. 293.
32. Zaslavskii, p. 112. The following month Zubatov wrote that the most immediate need of the moment was "permission for literature in jargon" (*ibid.*, pp. 121, 123).
33. "Novoe o zubatovshchine," p. 294.
34. Bukhbinder, "Nezavisimaia," pp. 259–61.
35. Men'shchikov, II, no. 1, p. 119.
36. *Ibid.*, p. 184.

and the workers," Zubatov wrote to the Department of Police in the late summer of 1900.[37] Apparently Sipiagin did allow Zubatov to proceed on an experimental basis but was unwilling to give official sanction to his full program.[38] As in Moscow, so in the Northwest region, the Zubatovshchina began without formal legal authorization.

## The Beginnings of the Minsk Zubatovshchina

During the first year after their conversion — that is, until the summer of 1901—Vil'bushevich, Shakhnovich, and their associates concentrated on attracting labor agitators to their cause and organizing the Jewish artisans. The government was at first hesitant to encourage the new tactic as the case of the Kreslavl' bristle makers exemplifies. In the summer of 1900, Shakhnovich wrote to Zubatov on behalf of the 250 Kreslavl' bristle makers, who had been on strike for almost four months. Attributing the strike to the employer's arbitrary lowering of wages, Shakhnovich pleaded with Zubatov to "compel the manufacturer to cease his illegal actions" and thereby convince the union to change tactics and seek legalization. Zubatov forwarded the petition to the Department of Police with a favorable comment: "In the given moment this case can have deep political significance in the sense of raising the workers' faith in the importance of the central government." His superiors, however, disagreed and replied that the dispatch of an investigator to the scene of the strike was "inconvenient."[39]

Fortunately for the plans of Mania Vil'bushevich and her Minsk associates, Zubatov found an able supporter of his program in the person of the chief of the Minsk *guberniia* gendarme administration, Colonel Nikita Vasil'evich Vasil'ev, whose role in the Minsk Zubatovshchina was analogous to Trepov's in Moscow.[40] Vasil'ev's aggressive intervention in labor disputes in support of the workers, which began toward the end of 1900, served to give the lie to Bund propaganda, which branded the government as defender of the interests of the capitalists. Vasil'ev's activities provided tangible evidence that the government would sanction a purely economic movement and, in part, explains the willingness of a large part of the Minsk working class to forsake the Bund.

37. Zaslavskii, p. 110.
38. Spiridovich, "Pri tsarskom rezhime," p. 151.
39. Bukhbinder, "Nezavisimaia," p. 211.
40. *Ibid.*, p. 213.

The disregard of the legal twelve-hour workday norm for handicraft workers by the employers of the Minsk metal craftsmen led to a strike in May 1901, offering Vasil'ev grounds to intervene. Calling representatives of the strikers and their employers to his office, Vasil'ev acted as a stern mediator, scolding both parties for breaking the law: the strikers, for leaving work without proper notice, the employers for insisting on an unlawful workday. On Vasil'ev's recommendation, work was resumed, with the legal workday enforced, a special declaration to that effect, signed by the governor, Prince Trubetskoi, having been posted in all workshops. For the metal craftsmen Vasil'ev's intervention meant a twelve-hour day rather than the previous fourteen.

Vasil'ev's stand in the metal workers' strike had an electrifying effect on the city's working class. Artisans in other professions began to seek his intercession on their behalf. The new tactic placed those politically conscious workers who supported the Bund in a difficult position, as the case of the Minsk joiners illustrates. The Bundists, of course, opposed the joiners' cooperation with Vasil'ev, but to denounce those who sought his support would jeopardize their own hold over the masses, for many joiners were attracted by the material gains to be made through Vasil'ev's influence. In the end they compromised, toned down their attacks on Vasil'ev, and even sanctioned tentative cooperation with him.[41]

Mania Vil'bushevich fully supported Vasil'ev's initiative among the joiners. She debated against Bundists for the support of the leading activists among the joiners; when the joiners decided to strike, she addressed a huge gathering of their profession on the need to avoid political issues and conduct a purely economic strike for a twelve-hour day. When the strike took place it was conducted as Vil'bushevich advised. The gendarme authorities chose to look the other way, and after a single day off the job the joiners obtained their employers' agreement to the new workday.[42]

Colonel Vasil'ev's intervention in labor relations went beyond the mere enforcement of the law. On occasion he acted on behalf of the workers, presenting their demands to their employers, and extracting concessions under duress. He also encouraged the workers to organize, as in the case of the Minsk housepainters, who went on strike in the spring of 1901. Inquiry had revealed to Vasil'ev

41. *Ibid.*, pp. 214, 217–18.
42. Ainzaft, *Istoriia,* pp. 90–91.

that the housepainters had no common demands, each worker bargaining on his own. Offering his residence as a meeting place, Vasil'ev urged the painters to gather, work out common demands, and then send a delegation to meet with him. In seeking to better their working conditions, the painters could be assured of his support, for "the gendarmes must take the part of the working people."[43] The painters complied in full with Vasil'ev's recommendations; Vasil'ev, on his part, studied the painters' demands, pronounced them just, and had the employers called to his office to discuss the strike. Without mincing words, he accused the owners of exploiting their workers and arousing them to strike, thus engendering conditions dangerous for order. In short, he demanded that they capitulate and accept the strikers' terms. The employers, cowed by the show of administrative authority, meekly submitted. The scene was repeated by Vasil'ev with employers in other professions, although not always with the same positive results.[44]

The new tactic was also applied to the shop assistants, who had established a *ferein* (union) and strike fund in May 1900. Shortly thereafter the *ferein* began a campaign of strikes accompanied by publication of agitational literature condemning their exploitation by the store owners. The union, which had branches throughout the Pale, was autonomous but had ties with the Bund.

The energetic activity of the union caused uneasiness among the police and prompted Zubatov to order the arrest of its central committee in the last days of June 1901. Iulii (Iudel) Samoilovich Volin and Aleksandr I. Chemeriskii, two of those arrested, within a short time were to join Vil'bushevich and Shakhnovich as the mainstay of the Minsk Zubatovshchina.[45]

The 9,000 Minsk shop assistants were undoubtedly the largest work force in the city. In earlier times they had formed a fairly privileged group among Jewish workers; most had expected to remain shop assistants only until they saved sufficient capital to

43. *Revoliutsionnaia Rossiia,* no. 4 (Feb. 1902).
44. *Ibid.*
45. Men'shchikov, II, no. 1, 143–45. In 1901–1902, Volin wrote articles on the Minsk labor movement for *Budushchnost'* (The Future), a Petersburg weekly, I. F. Masanov lists Volin as a writer, dramatist, and journalist, in his *Slovar' psevdonimov russkikh pisatelei, uchenykh i obshchestvennykh deiatelei* (Moscow, 1960), IV, 110. Volin and Chemeriskii were Bundists who joined the Independent cause shortly before the founding of the party ("Novoe o zubatovshchine," p. 317; Bukhbinder, "Nezavisimaia," p. 218; Bukhbinder, "Evreiskoe rabochee dvizhenie v Minske," p. 137).

open their own shops. But times had changed, and the salesmen were more frequently employed in large stores; no longer was he an employee of high status. By 1901, when Zubatov's supporters tried to organize the Minsk salesmen, their working conditions had deteriorated below that of the artisans. The average workday in Minsk shops was fourteen to fifteen hours; while the artisans finished work at 8:00 P. M. the salesmen labored beyond midnight.[46]

In the late spring of 1901 Colonel Vasil'ev seized the opportunity to win the shop assistants' confidence. Learning of an impending strike, he proposed that they meet openly to discuss their professional needs. A special invitational ticket was sent by the Minsk gendarme administration to each shop assistant; on Vasil'ev's orders proclamations were posted throughout the city inviting the shop assistants to the meeting and offering the use of a printing press, if the shop assistants would act within legal bounds.

On June 11, 400 shop assistants gathered in the Paris hall, the highlight of the meeting being an impassioned speech by Colonel Vasil'ev. Preaching the need for collective action if the salesmen wanted their employers to take their demands seriously, Vasil'ev promised to act on the salesmen's behalf if they would forswear revolutionary activity: "I am ready to help you. I am a representative of the tsarist authorities and therefore nothing is so dear to me as the happiness of the working class. You can always depend on my help. But woe to you if you take it into your head to go against the state order. Then do not expect mercy—I will be implacable."[47]

The speech became the subject of heated discussions throughout the city's shops, many salesmen arguing in favor of Vasil'ev's offer of support. Representatives of the salesmen met a few days later and agreed on common demands for a wage increase and an earlier closing hour in the shops. The store owners, summoned by Vasil'ev to answer the salesmen's demands, reluctantly appeared on June 21, but they could not agree on the terms they would offer. On Vasil'ev's insistence they met again at the city hall the following week. This time Vasil'ev exerted sufficient pressure to extract a

46. *Budushchnost'*, no. 10 (March 9, 1901), no. 7 (Feb. 15, 1902); Mendelsohn, *Class Struggle*, pp. 79–80.
47. *Revoliutsionnaia Rossiia*, no. 4 (Feb. 1902); see also *Iskra*, no. 6 (July 1901); Bukhbinder, "Nezavisimaia," p. 215. Gershuni, who wrote the article (anonymously) in *Revoliutsionnaia Rossiia*, maintained that Vasil'ev previously acted in a contrary manner, arresting many salesmen during a peaceful strike in 1900.

promise of compliance with part of the salesmen's demands, the store owners, however, still stubbornly resisting any change in the closing hour of the shops.[48]

The Jewish Independent Labor Party

Zubatov kept the Department of Police abreast of events in Minsk, summarizing in his reports the activities of Colonel Vasil'ev and quoting verbatim from letters he received from his Jewish followers. In a letter on June 27, 1901, Zubatov defended the "new course" among the Jewish workers. The mass of unorganized workers, incapable as yet of either conducting their own affairs in an intelligent and systematic manner or formulating their own needs, was the key to the labor question in Minsk. To prevent the ignorant masses from falling prey to the radical intelligentsia, the gendarme authorities, as representatives of the government, had to be attentive to the workmen's needs and well-being. This was a time-consuming and difficult task.

It can be facilitated by the appearance of a new group of persons, alien to radicalism, who, after becoming assistants to the government authorities, would become competitors of the revolutionaries in the matter of leading the unorganized masses. The organization of such a force is the urgent task of the moment. It will facilitate the activity of the government authorities, paralyze the revolutionaries, and render assistance to the masses in their material position.[49]

The force Zubatov had in mind was his own Jewish supporters, who were now ready to give their movement formal organization as a party to counteract the Bund.

On July 27, 1901, some twenty to twenty-five persons gathered for the founding meeting of the Jewish Independent Labor Party, the most prominent being Mania Vil'bushevich, Aleksandr Chemeriskii, Iosif Gol'dberg, and Iulii Volin.[50] The party's program, Chemeriskii tells us in his memoirs, had been drafted by Gol'dberg, a Poale Zionist, and edited by the other leaders.[51] The meeting of July 27, besides adopting the party program, drafted a manifesto announcing the formation of the new party.

48. Bukhbinder, "Nezavisimaia," pp. 215, 217; *Revoliutsionnaia Rossiia*, no. 4 (Feb. 1902); *Posledniia izvestiia*, no. 27 (July 23, 1901); *Vestnik russkoi revoliutsii*, no. 2 (Feb. 1902); *S.-Peterburgskiia vedomosti*, Oct. 23, 1901.

49. Bukhbinder, "Nezavisimaia," p. 218.

50. *Ibid.*, p. 255; N. A. Bukhbinder, "O zubatovshchine," *Krasnaia letopis'*, 1922, no. 4, p. 312.

51. "Novoe o zubatovshchine," p. 317.

The manifesto was at once a statement of party views on the character and needs of the working class and an attack upon recent trends in the Bund. Closely following Zubatov's line of reasoning, it was clearly designed to appeal to the self-interest of the working class. In the view of the Independents the Jewish working class, in need of "bread and knowledge," should not sacrifice its material concerns to political goals alien to its interests. Economic and cultural organizations free of manipulation by political groups and solely dedicated to workmen's interests were a necessity for the Jewish workers. At this point the manifesto went far beyond what the autocracy acknowledged until the revolution of 1905, for it maintained that "the worker, just as every person, has a right to be a partisan of any political party be chooses."[52]

The second half of the manifesto emphasized the incompatibility between the workers' economic aims and interests and the Bund's political goals. The Bund's past contributions to the working-class movement were not denied, but its new tactics were held to be inimical to the workers' interests: "The Bund fulfilled a great historical mission, having developed in the working class a spirit of dissatisfaction with its economic position, but when this is achieved and the entire mass of workers seeks organization, it becomes impossible to keep economic and cultural activity in the political clutches of the 'Bund.'" For the Bund, economic struggle was primarily a means of revolutionizing the masses rather than a method of improving the worker's economic status. Even the Bund's mass economic organizations served as a vehicle to "thrust upon the worker its own political views and aspirations, disregarding his psyche, affections, and aspirations." The Bund's intolerance was illustrated in its unwillingness to permit workers not fully sharing its views to enter its economic organizations; it was also seen in demands on its members to terminate contacts with intelligentsia in disagreement with the Bund's official policies.

The program of the Independent Party was designed to attract a broad membership from the working class. Limited to four points, it set as the party's major goal an improvement of the material and cultural level of the Jewish proletariat. The party was prepared to act illegally to reach this goal; cultural-educational organizations both

52. Frumkin, pp. 214–15. The program and manifesto are given verbatim in Bukhbinder, "Nezavisimaia," pp. 242–43.

"illegal and legal as far as possible," were deemed necessary.[53] In practice this meant the founding of "broad economic organizations (trade unions, funds, clubs, associations)" and the spread of scientific and professional knowledge among the working class as well as "its education for collective life." Ignoring the fact that their intent to found illegal organizations made the party political in the eyes of the government, the Independents went on to vow they had no political goals and would "touch upon political questions only so far as they affect the daily interests of the workers." The government would hardly have been pleased by the program's invitation to workers of "any political views" to become party members. Aware of the workers' resentment of alleged undemocratic control of the Bund committees by the intelligentsia, the program pledged that the Independent Party would be organized "democratically, that is, directed from below, and not from above."

The Independents needed a press to popularize the idea of legalization among the artisans and to respond effectively to vitriolic attacks from the Bund. The strict censorship laws were patently defied, as the Independents, following in the steps of the clandestine revolutionary parties, acquired an illegal printing press and published their own literature. On Chemeriskii's suggestion, a periodical, *Arbayts-mark* (The Labor Market), was printed in Yiddish to chronicle news of strikes and the labor movement in general. The Minsk gendarme administration knew of the press but looked aside and permitted the Independents to operate without interference.[54] Apparently the Department of Police acquiesced in the strange situation in which the Independent Party found itself, that is, "compelled to remain illegal for lack of other, legal forms."[55] During the next two years the party was to live in a twilight zone of legal-

53. Frumkin, p. 215. The party program exists in three versions, which contain several differences. Frumkin's version appears to be the most complete; it is the only version to include a section in part 1 on illegal activity. A report to the Department of Police of January 22, 1902 (Bukhbinder, "Nezavisimaia," p. 255), attributed to Zubatov, differs in some regards from both the version in Frumkin and a report found among Shaevich's papers (Bukhbinder, "O zubatovshchine," p. 312).

54. "Novoe o zubatovshchine," p. 317. Some Independent Party proclamations were countersigned by a representative of the Minsk *guberniia* gendarme administration (Bukhbinder, "Nezavisimaia," p. 253).

55. Bukhbinder, *ibid.*, p. 258. Writing from a first-hand knowledge of the history of the Independent Party in Minsk, Frumkin (p. 215) came to the same conclusion: "Circumstances compelled them to spread the idea of legalization and economism not by the negation of everything illegal, conspiratorial, of everything political and revolutionary, but by means of the acknowledgment of all this."

ity, permitted to exist by the Petersburg authorities with many misgivings, but given no formal status in law.[56]

The publication of the manifesto and program was followed by a series of proclamations to the working class further delineating the party's aims. Except for the absence of political slogans, the artisans must have found the contents of the Independent broadsides little different from Bund leaflets. With rampant unemployment and intolerable working conditions in the Pale many workers likely agreed with an Independent leaflet that attributed their suffering to exploitation by their employers, the insecurity of work, and their own ignorance.[57]

Speaking a language clearly understood by the workers, the Independents in a second leaflet pledged to use all available means to promote working-class interests:

Comrades! we are not for destruction but for creation; we wish to create a powerful and broad movement, which would protect the worker from exploitation by the capitalists and from all accidents in his life. We set ourselves the goal—the most sacred goal, which can only be namely: to raise the material and cultural position of the working class, to show it by what way to attain bread and knowledge.... We will use every means both legal and illegal—if only they be of benefit to the working class in its present terrible position.[58]

Political parties, bent on revolutionizing the working class, hindered its full development by disregarding legal means such as mutual-aid funds and artels, which provided workers abroad material security during illness or unemployment. "But the laboring masses do not wish, and must not wish, that their material interests be sacrificed to some political goal," the Independent leaflet argued.[59] The road to improved working conditions would be opened if the workers shunned the political parties and founded legally approved institutions of self-help to supplement their strike funds.

Another Independent leaflet cited such socialist luminaries as Bernstein, Bebel, and even Lenin in support of legalization. If the workers would bring into being a peaceful, nonpolitical trade-union movement, the government would ultimately conclude it had

56. Vovchik, pp. 128–29; *Mladorosskaia iskra,* April 22, 1935.
57. Frumkin, p. 216; *Iskra,* no. 17 (Feb. 15, 1902).
58. *Letuchii listok,* no. 1, quoted in *Iskra,* no. 17.
59. *Ibid.*

nothing to fear and would take the necessary steps for legalization.[60] The Independents thus assured the workers, on the basis of Zubatov's vague commitment given in the depths of a Moscow prison, that the government would sanction working-class unity and economic struggle.

While the Independents vigorously opposed the Bund and other revolutionary parties, they never were staunch defenders of the autocracy and the existing political order. "Let the workers know that their well-being depends not on a monarchy or a republic or a constitutional government in our country, but on the degree of strength of labor organizations," the party's committee wrote in response to an attack by the Socialist Revolutionaries. The party's tasks were capable of realization "independent of one or another form of government (be it an autocracy, a constitutional one, or a republic)."[61]

### The Minsk Zubatovshchina in Action

Aided by Colonel Vasil'ev, who granted them freedom to assemble, the Independents began to gain a mass following among the Minsk artisans. In July 1901, Zubatov was informed that a large number of Minsk metal craftsmen, joiners, bookbinders, and bristle makers were ready to forsake the Bund and join the Independents.[62] Three months later one of his Minsk correspondents joyfully reported further success: "The bricklayers are almost all ours, the bookbinders also. The metal craftsmen with all their heart and soul. Half the joiners, half the salesmen, almost all the tinsmiths."[63]

The ad hoc arrangement by which Colonel Vasil'ev had permitted striking workers to assemble and elect representatives to draw up common professional demands now became regular practice. General meetings for the Minsk working-class followers of the Independents were held in a large hall on Saturdays. Artisans in each profession also met separately; each group elected a committee to conduct its meetings and other activities and determine demands to be made on their employers. The committees were also

60. Frumkin, pp. 217–18.
61. Bukhbinder, "Nezavisimaia," pp. 269–70.
62. *Ibid.*, p. 218.
63. "Novoe o zubatovshchine," p. 294; *Iskra*, no. 9 (Oct. 1901). The Independents also organized the Minsk tailors and purveyors (*S.-Peterburgskiia vedomosti*, Feb. 28, 1902).

responsible for keeping discussions free of political issues and for keeping Vasil'ev informed of their proceedings. When the artisans had determined their demands Vasil'ev would convene their employers and seek to convince them of the justice of their workers' case.[64]

The Minsk joiners and turners, 800 to 900 strong, received permission to meet in the Paris hall on August 26. Almost half that number attended the meeting, which resolved to organize a Jewish Woodworkers' Club. Draft statutes were adopted at the next meeting on September 15 and forwarded to the Ministry of Interior for approval ten days later. The statutes provided for a library and reading rooms as well as lectures and discussions in Yiddish. Without waiting for approval from Petersburg, the joiners began meeting regularly on Saturdays under the leadership of Volin and Gol'dberg of the Independent Party intelligentsia and with the presence of Colonel Vasil'ev. A special commission established by the joiners observed the enforcement of the legal twelve-hour day for artisans and sought intervention in cases where the employers proved recalcitrant.[65] Similar commissions were to be found in the other unions organized by the Independents.

The Independents likewise attempted to win over the shop clerks, hoping to capitalize on Vasil'ev's earlier efforts. They addressed a proclamation to the Minsk salesmen on the subject of pilfering, a practice the Independents deplored but for which they blamed the store owners, who, by their exploitation of labor, forced their employees to steal. Other methods could give the salesmen more certain rewards and prevent their exploitation:

If it is desirable for us to better our lives, then we have many other radical means than stealing. There is a single means to help ourselves. It is the way by which the workers and salesmen of the whole world reduced their work and increased their pay and attained human conditions. The main thing is unity, brothers and sisters; enter our *ferein* so that we might help ourselves through our own efforts.[66]

64. Bukhbinder, "Nezavisimaia," pp. 212–13, 257; "Novoe o zubatovshchine," p. 294.

65. *Budushchnost'*, no. 39 (Sept. 28, 1901), no. 40 (Oct. 5, 1901), no. 42 (Oct. 19, 1901); *Posledniia izvestiia*, no. 33 (Sept. 23, 1901), no. 37 (Oct. 17, 1901); Bukhbinder, "Nezavisimaia," p. 256; *S.-Peterburgskiia vedomosti*, Oct. 23, 1901; Jan. 1, 1902; Aug. 20, 1903.

66. Bukhbinder, *ibid.*, p. 253.

The salesmen accepted the invitation and with the permission of the Minsk chief of police began to meet on a regular basis in November 1901. Three hundred salesmen attended the first meeting; according to the Bund press, 700 to 800 attended subsequent meetings in the Passazh hall to discuss their professional needs and the benefits of self-help.[67] On January 21, 1902, they approved statutes for a proposed mutual-help society and forwarded them to Petersburg for approval. The meeting also heard demands for an earlier closing time and shorter working hours in general. Reports that salesmen in neighboring cities had benefited from the local governor's order that stores be closed by 9:00 P. M. led to a decision to petition Prince Trubetskoi, governor of the province, to issue a similar order for Minsk.[68] The salesmen, however, did not reckon with the store owners' stubborn opposition or with Prince Trubetskoi's support of the owners. Without obtaining Trubetskoi's approval, Vasil'ev had peremptorily ordered that Minsk shops be closed at 9:00 P. M. The merchants curtly refused to obey the order even after Vasil'ev had personally tried to bully them into compliance. Prince Trubetskoi rejected the salesmen's petition and, angered by Vasil'ev's usurpation of authority, ordered notices posted throughout the city that stores need not close before 11:00 P. M. Vasil'ev having failed them, the salesmen would turn to more militant methods to improve working conditions.[69]

The general meetings and literary evenings organized for the working-class following of the Independents proved popular. Reportedly, as many as 1,500 workers crowded the hall to hear speeches on legalization of the labor movement and the need for the workers to raise their cultural level. Here too plans for an organization uniting all Minsk artisans were discussed. At one of these gatherings the statutes of the proposed Society of Mutual Help of Jewish Artisan Workers of the City of Minsk were approved and, like those prepared by the salesmen and woodworkers, sent to Petersburg.[70]

67. *Posledniia izvestiia*, no. 56 (Feb. 14, 1902); *Budushchnost'*, no. 7 (Feb. 15, 1902).

68. *Budushchnost'*, no. 7; *S.-Peterburgskiia vedomosti*, Oct. 23, 1901.

69. *Revoliutsionnaia Rossiia*, no. 4 (Feb. 1902); Frumkin, p. 222. The Independents and Vasil'ev allegedly discussed using terror against recalcitrant owners but rejected it as a weapon. The Independents in June 1902 urged the salesmen to strike to attain their ends.

70. "Novoe o zubatovshchine," p. 295; *Budushchnost'*, no. 5 (Feb. 1, 1902); Bukhbinder, "Nezavisimaia," p. 257; *S.-Peterburgskiia vedomosti*, Feb. 28, 1902.

The Independent Party resembled the Bund in its relations with the artisans in each profession it organized, the Party Committee having replaced the Minsk Committee of the Bund. The Independent Party Committee represented both the intelligentsia and the workers. Each profession had a *ferein* and an elected council of eight to ten members, which settled disputes, administered the *ferein's* strike fund and library, and organized readings, study courses, and evening parties for members.[71] Each council selected a representative to sit on the committee with the intellectual leaders and organizers of the party. Limited to an advisory role in the professional matters of each *ferein*, which was autonomous in matters of concern solely to its members, the committee could make decisions for the entire working-class membership on issues of significance to all workers; it organized lecture courses and general meetings, at which decisions were made by majority vote, administered the party's library, and published party literature, duties usually performed in the social-democratic structure by the local party committee. Ten per cent of each worker's contribution to his *ferein* was forwarded to the committee to finance its activities.

The Independents were concerned with the worker's desire for knowledge as well as bread and hoped to provide their followers with services available to the Moscow machine workers. The proposed mutual-help society planned a school for workers' children, a workshop for the unemployed, a Yiddish newspaper, distribution of books, and legal advice for the workers by a group of eminent local jurists. These plans were only partially fulfilled because the Petersburg authorities refused to approve the society's statutes. A credit union was formed; permission was locally obtained for a series of lectures in Yiddish by teachers from state schools, provided that political questions were avoided. With the local liberal intelligentsia in large part hostile to the Independents, the lectures fell to the few members of the intelligentsia who were willing to brave public opinion. The lectures, as in Moscow, were on topics of general education and on the labor movement and were followed by discussions. "Without doubt, these lectures on the labor question, the trade union movement, on history, etc., were a great magnetic force for the workers," a contemporary witness testified.[72]

---

71. Bukhbinder, "Nezavisimaia," pp. 258–59.
72. Frumkin, pp. 223, 233; see also Bukhbinder, "Nezavisimaia," pp. 212, 256; "Novoe o zubatovshchine," p. 293; *Posledniia izvestiia*, no. 43 (Nov. 8, 1901); *S.-Peterburgskiia vedomosti*, Feb. 28, 1902.

The lectures soon came to an abrupt end, however, for their leading organizer was persuaded to abandon the Independents.[73]

The cultural and educational aspects of the Independent program were subordinate to the party's campaign for a revival of economic struggle. After Vasil'ev's intervention failed to extract substantial concessions ("the workers turned to the 'Independents' in complete confidence that the external pressure which the 'Independents' could bring on the owners would force the latter to yield and free the workers of the necessity to risk the carrying on of a steady and sustained struggle"), the Minsk artisans, led by the Independents, resorted to their familiar militant tactics: "There began a strike wave which by its extent and virulence was not inferior to the movement of the 90's."[74] When, for example, Vasil'ev failed to obtain an earlier closing hour in the Minsk shops, the Independents recommended that the salesmen go on strike until they got their way.[75]

At the center of the Minsk strike movement was the *ferein*. The workers in each profession had come to view the *ferein* and its council as representative organs to which they could bring their professional grievances. The council formulated the professional demands of the workers, made the decision as to whether to strike, and conducted negotiations as sole bargaining agents for the workers. When a strike was contemplated the council would invite the employers to settle differences through either direct negotiations or arbitration. Should the employers refuse, the workers would be called to strike and Vasil'ev's intervention might be sought to bring recalcitrant employers to reason.[76] In some cases the council drew up a code for a profession regulating relations between the master employer and his workers and apprentices. One such set of norms, worked out by a joint commission representing the *ferein* and the owners of the local photographic studios, contained detailed rules governing relations between the owner and

73. "Novoe o zubatovshchine," pp. 294–96; *S.-Petersburgskiia vedomosti*, Feb. 28, 1902; Mendelsohn, "Worker Opposition," p. 281.

74. Frumkin, p. 220; see also *Materialy*, p. 42. Discussing the strike movement of the 1890's in the Pale, Mendelsohn concludes: "The origins of the Jewish mass strike movement are thus intimately linked to the idea of legalism, the same type of legalism that was later to haunt the socialists in the guise of police socialism" (*Class Struggle*, p. 51).

75. Frumkin, p. 222.

76. *Ibid.*, p. 221; Bukhbinder, "O zubatovshchine," p. 328.

his apprentice photographers, prescribed the length of the workday and minimum monthly wages, and restricted the period during which an employee could be discharged to the three months of spring. The rules were not unfavorable to the employer, for they made the *ferein* financially liable for a breach of contract by any of its members. If the general aim of the Jewish labor movement at the turn of the century was to formalize labor relations on a contractual basis, as Ezra Mendelsohn holds in his study *Class Struggle in the Pale,* the Minsk photographers could consider themselves well off.[77]

In 1900, the Bund had reported that a thousand Minsk artisans were organized under its leadership; two years later the Independents could boast of a larger working-class following in the city. The Independents, for the moment at least, had broken the back of the revolutionary movement in Minsk.[78] Gershuni, in a "Letter from Minsk," which appeared anonymously in an émigré organ in September 1902, reported with chagrin that the revolutionary movement among the Jewish workers in Minsk had reached a low point. The demoralization of the Minsk working class was attributed to the Independents, as evidenced by their ability to attract from 600 to 800 followers to a recent celebration.[79]

It is not hard to account for the success of the Independents among the Minsk working class. Conditions in Minsk were conducive to the development of the type of labor organization which the Independents offered. When the Independents arrived on the scene the city's artisans were facing hard times, with unemployment and hunger common. In March 1901 a Minsk correspondent reported to *Budushchnost'* (The Future), that the idea of mutual-aid societies and artels had recently caught on among the Minsk workers, owing primarily to stagnating working conditions.[80] Two years later the Minsk correspondent of the Bund in a similar vein described the general meetings of the Independent Party: "It is painful to see the masses, who attentively listen to the words of the orator, avidly searching for a way out of their terrible position."[81] Undoubtedly the Bund's de-emphasizing of economic

77. Bukhbinder, "Nezavisimaia," pp. 253–54; *S.-Peterburgskiia vedomosti,* Aug. 20, 1903; Mendelsohn, *Class Struggle,* p. 88.

78. *Materialy,* p. 68; Nedasek, p. 77.

79. *Revoliutsionnaia Rossiia,* no. 11 (Sept. 1902).

80. *Budushchnost',* no. 10 (March 9, 1901).

81. *Posledniia izvestiia,* no. 113 (March 7, 1903).

struggle and the lack of organization on the part of the great mass of Minsk workers facilitated the work of the Independents. The workers found the Independents' call to economic struggle and legalization of more immediate concern than the Bund's agitation on behalf of the uncertain and distant goal of revolution. The Minsk workers, moreover, did reap material benefits from the strike movement in which the Independents were involved and supported. The Independents' close association with Vasil'ev did not weaken their standing among the artisans, for the workers did not see in the police an enemy and often turned to the police for support of their demands.[82]

No evaluation of the causes for the Independent Party's success should overlook the contribution of its leaders. Few in number, they were energetic, able organizers, persuasive in spreading the party's message among the Jewish working class. Their understanding of the revolutionary milieu and prior contacts with the Minsk artisans and the Minsk Committee of the Bund were invaluable to them. They were of the intelligentsia. Yet such was their political acumen that the Independent Party never was subjected to the tension between workers and intelligentsia or the charges of elitism and undemocratic practices that rent the Bund and social democracy in general. Undoubtedly the police smoothed their path by widespread arrests of Bund activists and by permitting their followers freedom of assembly. However, without the perseverance and great organizational capacities of Mania Vil'bushevich and her colleagues the party's success would have been unthinkable; the economic and cultural benefits the party brought the Jewish masses surely gave them inner satisfaction and reward.

## The Independents, Poale Zion, and the Bund

The Bund's attack on Zionism was beneficial to the Independents. The anti-Zionist campaign led at times to fisticuffs between members of Zionist circles and their Bundist adversaries. Since the Bund's campaign was aimed at the Jewish working class, the Zionists redirected their propaganda and recruitment toward the workers.[83] A report entitled "The Participation of Zionists in the

82. Mendelsohn, *Class Struggle,* pp. 96–97; Mendelsohn, "Worker Opposition," p. 277.

83. Bernard K. Johnpoll, *The Politics of Futility* (Ithaca, 1967), p. 29; undated communication of the central Zionist group in Grodno, as cited in a report on the

Improvement of the Position of Jews," delivered at the Congress of Russian Zionists in Minsk in August 1902, recommended Zionist support for "the establishment of artels, savings banks, artels for migrants—mutual-help societies, etc."[84] Before the congress opened Zionist intelligentsia and Minsk workers met together to discuss Zionist agitation among the working class and the Zionist cultural and economic programs for workers. "The reason for [Zionist] agitation among the workers," Colonel Vasil'ev informed his superiors, "is the necessity to give the workers something more substantial than Zionism has given them to now, in order by that means to win them over to its side and divert them from the social-democratic and revolutionary organizations, [and] to give them the best spiritual nourishment and a peaceful means of attaining improvement in their economic life."[85] These goals were analogous to those of the Independents, thus making possible an alliance between the Independents and the Zionists, particularly the Minsk Poale Zionists.

The Independent cause gained immeasurably from the acquisition of the Minsk Poale Zionists as allies. The Zionists supplied additional intellectual leaders and activists, of which the party was in need. The Minsk liberal intelligentsia, to whom the Independents had first turned to fill the gap, had publicly spurned the Independents, thirty-six of them publishing a declaration of boycott against the party.[86]

Zubatov had long realized the strength the Zionists could bring to the Independent cause and encouraged Zionist efforts to organize the Jewish workers. The Minsk Poale Zionists thus were given

history of Zionism prepared in 1903 by the Department of Police and signed by Lopukhin, its director (Departament Politsii, *Sionizm* [St. Petersburg, 1903], pp. 65–66). The Grodno report concluded: "It is necessary to establish between the Russian and the émigré circles a more frequent exchange of thoughts on the question of fighting against social democracy with a view to attracting the working class to our movement." The Department of Police's report described a new phenomenon in Zionism in 1902: the Zionists, and especially the "democratic faction among them, begin to pay great attention to the Jewish workers, aiming at diverting them from a union with the social democrats and placing them under the influence of Zionism" (*ibid.*, p. 127).

84. *Budushchnost'*, no. 35 (Aug. 20, 1902). A Soviet writer recently claimed that support for the Zubatovshchina was expressed at the Minsk Zionist Congress in 1902 (L. Vostokov, "Antinarodnaia deiatel'nost' sionistov v Rossii," *Voprosy istorii*, March 1973, p. 25).

85. Department Politsii *Sionizm*, p. 130.

86. Frumkin, p. 227; *Revoliutsionnaia Rossiia*, no. 11 (Sept. 1902).

the same freedom to organize the local artisans and hold meetings as the Independents had. Apparently the Independents and the Minsk Poale Zionists, both of whom had considerable success in forming workers' circles, came to a programmatic and working agreement.[87] Of the Minsk Poale Zionists, Iosif Gol'dberg became one of the leaders of the Independents, and I. A. Berger frequently lectured to the Independents' *fereins.*[88]

Further Zionist support of the Independent Party came at a Minsk conference of Zionist labor leaders from a number of Lithuanian cities held in November 1901. As reported to Zubatov, the conference agreed on friendly relations with the Independent Party: "Recognizing the great significance of the J[ewish] I[ndependent] L[abor] P[arty] for making the Jewish masses into Zionists and the necessity of independent labor unions for the Jewish workers, the conference decreed to assist every undertaking of the J[ewish] I[ndependent] L[abor] P[arty]."[89] The conference further agreed to encourage Poale Zionists to enter the Independent Party wherever the party had branches and to assist in the foundation of new branches where none existed.[90]

The Independents also searched for recruits in the ranks of the Minsk Bund. Several Independent Party leaders had been members of the Minsk Committee of the Bund. They retained friendship with former Bund colleagues for some time; it is even alleged that until the founding of the Independent Party they remained in the Bund in order to weaken the Minsk Committee from within.[91] Despite the scathing attack on Zubatov and his supporters by the Bund's central committee in August 1900, the Minsk Bundists and the Independents maintained contacts and attended each other's meetings: "In life itself, in the workshops, at labor exchanges, even at meetings and assemblies and, in particular, in the intelligentsia

---

87. Zaslavskii, p. 123; Agurskii, p. 67; *Posledniia izvestiia,* no. 113 (March 7, 1903); *Vozrozhdenie,* no. 1-2 (Jan.–Feb. 1904); Frumkin, p. 213.

88. Bukhbinder, *Istoriia,* p. 342; *Budushchnost',* no. 42 (Oct. 1901); "Novoe o zubatovshchine," p. 327. The Independent Party has been recently called a "'socialist' faction in Zionism," and its leaders Vil'bushevich, Volin, Gol'dberg, and Chemeriskii, labeled Zionists. E. S. Evseev, "Iz istorii sionizma v tsarskoi Rossii," *Voprosy istorii,* May 1973, p. 72). Evidence does not indicate, however, that Chemeriskii was a Zionist.

89. Bukhbinder, "O zubatovshchine," p. 315.

90. "Novoe o zubatovshchine," pp. 296–97.

91. For the evidence see, Ia. Sh. Gerts and S. M. Shvarts, *Zubatovshchina v Minske* (New York, 1962), pp. 5–9.

circle, the demarcation line was not at once put into practice. The Minsk organization of the Bund was bound to all the representatives of the new trend by personal ties."[92]

In July 1901, just as the Zubatovites were on the point of formally establishing the Independent Party, Aleksandr Chemeriskii, a member of the Minsk Committee of the Bund, was converted to the Independent cause. The committee, unnerved by the defection in its ranks as well as from among its working-class following, was said to be willing to enter into discussions with the Independents with a view to working out an agreement. After a full night of negotiation, according to Zubatov's informant, the Minsk Committee capitulated and recognized the need to legalize the labor movement, agreeing to send a representative to inform the Bund central committee of its decision.[93] The published materials give no indication whether the central committee responded; yet a year later reports persisted that the Bund leadership was ready to make peace with the Independents.

Charges that the Bund took an equivocal stand toward the Zubatovshchina and that its central committee contemplated cooperation with the Independent Party have been the subject of controversy to the present day. The debate centers around the reliability of information Zubatov received from Minsk in August 1902 describing an alleged Bund conference at which the Bund's central committee decided to send one if its representatives to open talks with the Independents. In the name of the central committee the representative proposed making peace with the Independent Party on the following terms: the Independent Party would become solely a labor organization, cease attacking the Bund, adopt a neutral position toward the revolutionary movement, and totally break its ties with the police. In turn, the Bund would end its boycott of the Independents and cease further economic activity, leaving it completely in the hands of the Independents. Lastly, Bund members would enter the Independent *fereins*.[94]

The Bund has steadfastly held the report to be a fabrication on the grounds that no Bund conference took place at the time and place indicated in the report to Zubatov.[95] On the other hand,

92. Frumkin, p. 224; see also Bukhbinder, "Nezavisimaia," p. 255.
93. Bukhbinder, *ibid.*, p. 218.
94. "Novoe o zubatovshchine," pp. 305–6.
95. Testimony of former Bundists M. Rafes and M. Frumkina (Ester), *ibid.*, pp. 325, 327; Gerts and Shvarts, pp. 6–8.

Solomon Schwarz, who recently subjected the charges to thorough investigation, holds there is sufficient circumstantial evidence to suggest there is a kernel of truth to the report. In his view the reference to Bundists' meeting in Minsk most likely refers to influential elements in the Bund's leadership, who favored the formation of an organized and broadly based labor movement separate from the politically oriented Bund. This explains, according to Schwarz, the offer to let the Independents become the exclusive leaders of a Jewish labor movement.[96] The evidence still remains too inconclusive to say with certainty that the Bund made a peace proposal to the Independents; we do know, however, that no deal was consummated and that the Bund press never let up in its criticism of the Independents.[97]

Increasingly irked by the close association between the Independent Party and the police, the Minsk Committee of the Bund eventually felt it necessary to come out forcefully in opposition to the Independents. Since further attendance at Independent gatherings might lead to arrests, the committee channeled its attack through word of mouth and proclamations.[98] The increasing number of workers and intelligentsia who left the Bund for the Independents alarmed the Minsk Committee and caused it to concentrate on isolating its remaining followers from the Independents. In March 1902, a year and a half after the Bund's central committee had first cautioned members against contact with Zubatov and his partisans, the Minsk Committee felt compelled to repeat the warning. All "decent persons" were urged to break off relations with members of the Independent Party, shun its meetings, and reject its literature. These demands were "unconditionally obligatory" for all Bundists; disobedience would bring expulsion from the party.[99]

Bundist appeals to misguided former comrades who had joined the Independents stressed the allegedly traditional role of the

96. Gerts and Shvarts (Schwarz), pp. 13–18.

97. Zubatov stated in a report of August 12, 1902, that no agreement with the Bund's central committee was possible because the Independents refused to end their contacts with the police and become the economic wing of a revolutionary party ("Novoe o zubatovshchine," p. 306).

98. Frumkin, p. 224. Bund agitators did try to attend Independent Party meetings and speak out against the Independents; *Deiatel'nost' Bunda za poslednie 2 goda* (London, 1903), p. 8; *Vtoroi s"ezd RSDRP,* p. 504.

99. Frumkin, pp. 226–27; *Posledniia izvestiia,* no. 64 (April 10, 1902).

police as persecutors of the working class. The activities of the Independent Party and Vasil'ev's support of the artisans were deemed nothing more than government tactics to destroy both the Bund and the unity of the working class. In the long run those who followed the Independents would be deceived, for the government would not fulfill the Independents' promise to legalize the labor movement.[100] Bund propaganda also indicted the Independents and Zionists for cooperating with the tsarist government, the oppressor of the Jewish people: "We Jewish workers in our struggle against the autocracy do not have for the time being allies in our society. Our saviours—Zionists, legalizers, Zubatovites, and others —strain all their efforts in order to lead the Jewish proletariat away from the revolutionary path and educate it in the spirit of slavish worship of the autocracy."[101] In reality, then, the Independent Party was not, as it claimed to be, a trade union organized for defense of working-class interests, but purely a political organization serving the monarchy.[102] Political struggle, not cooperation, was the order of the day toward a government which oppressed the working class and the Jewish nation, the Bund insisted.

The line taken by Bund propaganda against the Minsk Independents had little chance of persuading the Jewish masses. The arguments were too general; while readily understood by fellow socialists they were not likely to convince the average worker, who was more receptive to the down-to-earth message of the Independents.[103] In desperation the Minsk Committee, its ranks decimated by arrests and defections, took a more extreme means to oppose the Independents and began to disrupt their meetings.[104]

Their efforts did not bear fruit. Writing in March 1903, four months before the disbanding of the Independent Party, the Minsk correspondent of the Bund sadly admitted that the local organization had put up a weak struggle against the Independents: "Unfortunately, thanks to the sad concurrence of circumstances, the local Bund organization during the last year was so weakened that it was not in a position to give a proper rebuff to the debauchers

100. Bukhbinder, "Nezavisimaia," pp. 243–45, 248.
101. *Posledniia izvestiia*, no. 71 (May 29, 1902).
102. Bukhbinder, "Nezavisimaia," p. 249.
103. Tobias, p. 142; Frumkin, pp. 225–26.
104. *Posledniia izvestiia*, no. 75 (June 26, 1902). The Independents tried to keep Bundists from attending their meetings, *ibid.*, no. 56 (Feb. 14, 1902).

of the working masses."[105] A survey of the state of the Jewish labor movement during the summer of 1903 appearing in a Bund organ came to a similar conclusion.[106] We therefore have to look beyond the Bund for the main causes of the Independent Party's dissolution.

105. *Posledniia izvestiia,* no. 113 (March 7, 1903).
106. *Di Arbeiter Stimme,* no. 35 (Oct. 1903), cited in Rafes, *Ocherki po istorii "Bunda,"* p. 366.

1. Grand Duke Sergei Aleksandrovich

2. Dmitrii F. Trepov

3. Ivan L. Goremykin

4. Dmitrii S. Sipiagin

5. Viacheslav K. von Plehve

6. Lieutenant General Aleksandr I. Panteleev

7. Major General Nikolai V. Kleigels

8. Vladimir N. Kokovtsov

9. Sergei Iu. Witte

10. Major General Dmitrii G. Arsen'ev

11. Mania Vil'bushevich (Wilbushewitch) in 1903 (courtesy of the Bund Archives, New York)

12. Mania Vil'bushevich Shochat (courtesy of the Zionist Archives and Library, New York)

13. Aleksandr Chemeriskii (courtesy of the Bund Archives, New York)

# CHAPTER 10

# The Vilna Episode
# and the End of the
# Minsk Zubatovshchina

The applicability of the Independent program to the Jewish working-class movement made feasible the party's expansion to other centers of the Pale. Furthermore, if the Independents were to eradicate the Bund's influence, they would have to emulate the Bund's network of local branches. Heartened by the Minsk success, the Independents in early 1902 planned to do just that. With permission of the gendarme authorities party organizers were dispatched to other towns and cities of the Pale, among them Grodno, Bobruisk, Ekaterinoslav, Odessa, and Vilna.[1]

The most determined of these efforts in the Northwest region was made in Vilna. Vilna had a reputation as an early home of the Russian Jewish labor movement and a center of Jewish socialism. Beginning in the early 1890's, Vilna artisans in most professions had organized strike funds and participated in economic strikes. Vilna Social Democrats had been the pioneer organizers of the Bund and colonized the major centers of the Pale with their activists. The Bund had its largest following in Vilna; at the Paris International Socialist Congress in 1900, it reported 1,400 adherents in Vilna organized around strike funds.[2] The Independents thus could expect strong opposition from the local Bundists and their working-class followers in Vilna.

In May 1902, Mania Vil'bushevich journeyed to Petersburg to

1. Bukhbinder, "Nezavisimaia," p. 259. In one case, on Vasil'ev's initiative Independent Party agitators were dispatched to a town where the Bund's influence was strong (Bukhbinder, "O zubatovshchine," p. 319).

2. *Materialy*, pp. 27–28, 68. Of Vilna's population of 154,000 in 1901, 76,000 were Jews ( *Budushchnost'*, no. 9 [March 2, 1901]).

discuss the future of the Independent Party with government officials. She apparently made a favorable impression, for Plehve sanctioned the extension of the Independent Party outside of Minsk, agreeing to permit a party representative to be sent to Vilna "for the establishment of a corresponding labor movement."[3] The assignment went to Aleksandr Chemeriskii.

The Vilna project started inauspiciously. Before Chemeriskii departed for Vilna several threats were made against his life, and Zionist acquaintances warned him that his presence in Vilna would lead to certain death. Undaunted, Chemeriskii in early June went ahead with his plans. At the Minsk railway station he was given a rousing send-off by a crowd of Independent enthusiasts. The ebullience of the demonstrators, however, frightened the local police, who placed them under arrest; Chemeriskii, in turn, was dragged off the train en route to Vilna and returned to Minsk. Through the intervention of the gendarme office, the Independents were shortly released and Chemeriskii began his journey to Vilna once again.

Chemeriskii arrived in Vilna at a most critical moment. Mass unemployment, hunger, and police repression had bred violence and unrest in the city. The new governor, General Viktor von Wahl, responded with stern measures, further alienating the Vilna workers. Warning the population against giving way to "senseless dreams," he declared a state of emergency and ordered an early evening curfew to discourage labor meetings. Von Wahl, like a true representative of the Ministry of Interior, had alternated repression with measures to improve the working conditions of the artisans;[4] in general, however, his policy was repressive.

The anticipated clash between the workers and the Vilna governor was not long in coming. On May Day a crowd of workers was dispersed by Cossacks with whips, who flogged those arrested. Four days later Gersh Lekert, a Bundist, attempted to assassinate von Wahl in revenge, but failed and was arrested. Lekert's execution by hanging made him a martyr among the radical youth, who felt that the repressive measures taken against the workers justified the attack on von Wahl.[5] Thus the Independents could expect that the Vilna workers would greet with hostility the suggestion that they

3. Bukhbinder, "O zubatovshchine," p. 289.
4. *Posledniia izvestiia*, no. 58 (Feb. 27, 1902), no. 65 (April 17, 1902).
5. Bukhbinder, "O zubatovshchine," p. 290; Men'shchikov, II, no. 1, 147; "Girsh Lekert i ego pokushenie," *Krasnyi arkhiv*, 1926, no. 2 (15), pp. 95, 102.

cooperate with the local authorities or take the path of legalization.

Chemeriskii, nevertheless, took up the challenge. He arrived in Vilna in the first part of June with a letter of introduction to local Zionists, who were in the process of organizing the artisans into artels. Through the assistance of Kunin, the leader of the Vilna Poale Zionists, Chemeriskii was able to make contact with the Vilna factory workers and artisans. As the sole Independent organizer in the Bund's stronghold, Chemeriskii showed great fortitude. His first letter to party comrades in Minsk acknowledged his difficulties: "The Bund here is very powerful. It is the ruler of men's minds. It is strong not so much in numbers, as by representing the prevailing mood."[6] For one thing, he ignored local Zionists' warnings that the Bund was prepared to resort to violence to prevent the Independents from taking root in Vilna and met Vilna Bundists at their invitation. During these days Chemeriskii suffered material privation, living for some time on a kopek a day and often going hungry. Despite these hardships, he was at first optimistic about chances for success thanks to the favorable response from the Vilna workers whom he addressed.[7]

Chemeriskii alone could not get the Independent Party message to the city's large working class. In his first letter to Minsk he requested the Independent Party committee to produce a brochure setting forth in popular style the party's program and inviting workers to become members. The brochure, which was published a week later, was designed to destroy the barrier the Bund had erected between the working class and the Independents and in turn erect a barrier between the workers and the Bund. The Vilna Bundists, the brochure charged, had declared a boycott against the Independents as part of a program to enslave the working class for their own ends:

Yes, a boycott is a precious thing for the Bund, but for you, men and women Vilna workers, it is an insult. It is terrible that you are so spiritually enslaved, that one can order, simply command, you exactly as soldiers in a regiment, not to speak, not to make the acquaintance of people, not to discuss, but to obey; it is shameful because your Bund generals and colonels consider you so stupid, that they are certain that they can present you with any falsehood they please, and you will accept it with satisfaction and believe it... This is done by people who, in their own words, are fighting for freedom of thought, freedom of speech, freedom of opinion.[8]

6. Bukhbinder, "O zubatovshchine," p. 290; see also Chemeriskii's memoirs, "Novoe o zubatovshchine," p. 319; Posledniia izvestiia, no. 63 (April 3, 1902).

7. Chemeriskii's memoirs, "Novoe o zubatovshchine," p. 318.

8. Bukhbinder, "O zubatovshchine," p. 295.

The brochure declared that workers and the Bund had sharply differentiated aims: "We say that to be a striker—that is, a person who understands the necessity to unite with one's workshop comrades in order to defend oneself against the owner's exploitation—and to be a social democrat—that is, a person who deliberately aims at a new order—are entirely different things." The Independents believed that "economic organizations must be independent of any political party whatsoever; they must neither be socialist nor Zionist, etc., but simply economic and moreover must contain the broad working masses." If the labor *fereins* do not come under socialist control the government will be less likely to repress them and "we can even hope that it will legalize, that is, authorize them." Legalization already had begun in Moscow and Minsk, the Independents told the Vilna workers, "and you will probably see it soon in Vilna."[9]

The Independent Party's appeal to the Vilna workers was cleverly framed to make the Bund respond to its charges. Openly accused of dictatorial control over the masses and of preparing physical attacks on Independent Party organizers to prevent the Vilna workmen from learning of the Independent program, the Bund was forced to refrain from actions which would substantiate the charges and embarrass it. The Vilna Committee of the Bund sternly warned party comrades not to use force lest the Independents become "sufferers for an idea."[10] Any member who defied the ban on violence would be excluded from Bund organizations.

The Vilna Committee sought to explain to the workers its extreme hostility toward the Independents.

Why don't we act toward them as toward ordinary ideological opponents, as for example Zionists, liberals, etc. Each person has the right to spread his views [and] ideas if he is truly convinced of them: however, if people do not disdain to use any means, stop at nothing, do not reject with scorn the "enlightened" cooperation of the gendarmery, when these "friends of the workers," yesterday's revolutionaries, without any shame maintain relations with such hangmen as Zubatov, Vasil'ev, and company, who have tortured hundreds, even thousands of lives—then we cannot act toward

9. *Ibid.*, p. 296.
10. *Posledniia izvestiia*, no. 81 (Aug. 14, 1902). M. Rafes, who was politically active in Vilna at the time the Independents were there, recalled that Chemeriskii was attacked with a knife by a Bundist; the incident evoked sympathy from the workers for Chemeriskii and caused the Vilna Bund Committee to demand that local Bundists limit criticism of the Independents to matters of ideology ("Novoe o zubatovshchine," pp. 323–24).

such persons as ordinary ideological opponents; they cannot call forth in us anything but hatred and contempt, for it does not matter to us if some of them even truly believe in their legalizing mission.[11]

The Bund appealed "to all honorable persons without distinction" to refuse to cooperate with the Independents: "You, Vilna workers, must not only have no relations with the legalizers, not only make no use of the services they offer you, not only carry on no debates with them and not visit their meetings, but besides that [you must] try to unmask before the broad masses the entire depth of depravity and falsities which their shameful activity carries with itself."[12]

The Bund enforced its boycott of the Independents by terrorizing the Vilna masses, Chemeriskii reported; those who ignored its warnings and attended Independent Party meetings were physically attacked.[13] The Vilna Committee, on the other hand, did send some of its partisans to Independent Party meetings in order to disrupt the proceedings with accusations of provocation.[14]

The Vilna Bundists' boycott of the Independents made Chemeriskii's task immeasurably more difficult, for the Independents had counted on enlisting Bund activists in Vilna. Having failed in this effort the Minsk party center decided to dispatch Volin, Vil'bushevich, Gol'dberg, and Shmul' Muliar a stonemason, who was an experienced labor organizer and capable orator, to assist Chemeriskii. Each encountered great practical difficulties in conducting agitational work, although they did not share fully the gloomy pessimism to which Chemeriskii was giving way.[15]

By late July, Chemeriskii had laid the bare foundation upon which the Vilna Independents might build a mass following. A small band of disciples had been gathered through a slow process of recruitment; an executive council of six persons and a discussion group of seven were in operation. Members of the discussion group were to graduate into the ranks of the council when they were deemed sufficiently loyal to the cause. Each of Chemeriskii's recruits had wide contacts with the Vilna workers and the local Bund committee and were counted on to win supporters for the Independent Party.

11. *Posledniia izvestiia*, no. 81.
12. *Ibid*.
13. *Ibid*., no. 76 (July 3, 1902); Bukhbinder, "O zubatovshchine," p. 293.
14. Bukhbinder, *ibid*., pp. 297, 300.
15. *Ibid*., pp. 293, 296–301; "Novoe o zubatovshchine," pp. 299–307, 319.

The police smoothed the path for the Vilna Independents. Chemeriskii's petition to hold labor meetings was forwarded by Zubatov to his superiors with the recommendation that "in case General Cherkassov turns to the Department of Police for permission to allow such assemblies, it would be extremely desirable to decide this question in a positive sense."[16] Lopukhin, in reply to an enquiry from the Vilna provincial gendarme office, advised that the Independents be given permission to conduct meetings and be rendered whatever assistance might be necessary.[17]

Police support in reality was circumscribed by the power of the local governor. In July 1902 the Bund press reported that the Vilna chief of police, in an effort to relieve unemployment, had ordered the posting of a declaration urging homeowners to give work to the local house painters. The declaration never saw the light of day, for the acting governor countermanded the order and castigated the chief of police as a dreamer.[18] The Vilna chief of police, nevertheless, assisted the Independents. Chemeriskii assured the Singer sewing machine salesmen that the police would not interfere if they went on strike. True to Chemeriskii's promise, the chief of police summoned the salesmen to his office, roundly cursed their employers for exploitation, and vowed that the salesmen had nothing to fear from him if they went on strike.[19]

The Independents had little to show for their nine months of activity in Vilna. At most they gained some allies among those opposed to the Bund; no following of any significance was acquired among the Vilna working class. The allies included Poale Zionists, some elderly workers, and a goodly number of shoemakers. The Poale Zionists, as we have seen, assisted the Independents in making their first contacts with the Vilna workers; they also allowed

16. "Novoe o zubatovshchine," p. 299.

17. Bukhbinder, "O zubatovshchine," p. 294. A Department of Police report on the history of the Zubatovshchina dated its communication to the Vilna gendarmery in support of the Independents as August 12, 1902 ("K istorii Zubatovshchiny," p. 89). Through the help of the local gendarmery Chemeriskii was able to secure the release of Independent Party members who had been arrested at a party meeting ("Novoe o zubatovshchine," p. 319).

18. *Posledniia izvestiia*, no. 77 (July 10, 1902).

19. The salesmen, nevertheless, refused to follow the lead of the Independents, declaring themselves unwilling to adopt tactics which appeared hypocritical and at variance with those traditionally employed by the local Bund committee in directing strikes (*Posledniia izvestiia*, no. 81 [Aug. 14, 1902]).

their followers to attend Independent Party meetings and, in turn, looked to the Independents to publish their proclamations against the Bund. Eventually they came to resent the Independent campaign to recruit party organizers from their ranks. As for the older workers, who predominated at Independent rallies in Vilna, they became "passive members," offering their apartments for labor meetings. Dissatisfaction with the Bund's program of class warfare had caused them to gravitate to the Independents, whom they hoped would stand for social peace in labor relations, a policy the Independents never favored.[20]

The Vilna shoemakers, around 200 in number were the only group of Vilna workers among whom the Independents might have acquired a mass following. The shoemakers had a reputation for militancy, having abandoned economic struggle for political organization several years earlier. Not all the shoemakers had approved the change; a recession at the turn of the century caused many to long for a return to former tactics. A *ferein* and strike fund were founded, with membership restricted to shoemakers who disavowed politics and had no contacts with the Vilna Bundists. One of the leaders of the *ferein* was an Independent supporter, and it was believed that the rank and file would follow his lead.[21]

It was all in vain. In February 1903 the Independent Party formally withdrew from Vilna, signaling its first major setback. An Independent proclamation announcing the withdrawal put on a brave face, calling it only a temporary retreat from the city. The Bund had not caused the cessation of party activities in Vilna, the proclamation asserted, for the Independents had anticipated attack from that quarter. At fault rather were the "unconsciousness" and "conservatism" of the masses, as exhibited in their unquestioning acceptance of the Bund's charge of provocation against the Independents. When the Independents had organized the workers in other cities and the benefit of these organizations had become apparent to the Jewish working class, the Independent Party would triumphantly return to Vilna. The Bund, of course, greeted the Independent announcement skeptically; the Independents' withdrawal from Vilna was viewed as a victory caused by the "sys-

20. *Ibid.;* Bukhbinder, "O zubatovshchine," pp. 299–301.
21. Bukhbinder, *ibid.,* pp. 298–99; *Posledniia izvestiia,* no. 135 (July 9, 1903); "Novoe o zubatovshchine," pp. 304, 319.

tematic unmasking of the Independents by Bund committees in articles, proclamations, at meetings, and in circles."[22]

## The Independent Party and the Tsarist Government

The expansion of the Independent Party beyond the confines of Minsk had necessitated its reorganization. Previously it had been directed by an executive bureau, established in Minsk before the founding of the party, which assigned party agitators wherever needed, published and supervised the distribution of party literature, maintained contact with party branches in other towns, and organized meetings for discussion of party issues. In 1902, ten representatives from the Minsk, Odessa, and (for a time) Vilna labor committees formed the Party Committee.

The large increase in the number of Independent *fereins* in Minsk probably accounted for the creation of the Minsk labor committee. Composed of representatives from each union, the labor committee was the only body connecting the otherwise autonomous labor unions. The committee conducted business of common interest to the Minsk artisans and administered a cultural commission as well as an agitational commission through which the idea of working-class unity was promoted in professions still unorganized. The committee's approval was necessary before a general strike could be called; it was also chiefly responsible for drafting the statutes of the labor clubs and published its own proclamations. Three members of the Minsk labor committee served on the Party Committee, where they acted as a link between the working class and the party hierarchy.[23]

More than ever in its structure the Jewish Independent Labor Party resembled the illegal parties with whom it was in open warfare.[24] By its encouragement and leadership of strikes, it parted with legality; no more legal were its collective bargaining efforts on behalf of striking workers or the strike funds established by its unions. The Independents possessed their own party organs which

22. *Posledniia izvestiia,* no. 140 (Aug. 4, 1903); see also Bukhbinder, "O zuba-tovshchine," p. 302.

23. Bukhbinder, *ibid.,* pp. 326–28.

24. Even Independent Party followers were confused as to whether their movement was political or solely economic; see the minutes of the Minsk Independent union of woodworkers found in the "Protokol-bukh fun ferayn fun di stoliares, Minsk, Dets. 1902–Yuli 1903," Bund Archives.

ignored censorship rules and freely discussed labor relations, local working conditions, and strikes; like the socialist parties the Independents published agitational literature to attract the working class. However, in contrast to the political parties, which had to lead a shadowy and precarious illegal existence, the Independents confidently expected the government to sanction their party. They encouraged the workers to unite, not to overthrow the political order, but to the extent necessary to extract legal recognition from the government.

At the end of 1902 labor unions in fifteen of the twenty most important professions in Minsk were in the Independent camp, a strong indication of the party's popularity among the artisans.[25] With the Minsk working class organized behind their party, the Independents awaited approval from Petersburg of the labor societies they had founded. In the final analysis legalization as an idea could have only a temporary hold over the Minsk workers and the Independent leaders themselves; unless the government was prepared to give recognition and support to the Independent Party and its unions, the party intelligentsia might well lose confidence in Zubatov's promises, and, under continual attack from the Bund, give up the fray.

Zubatov recognized that his standing with the Independent leaders depended on the degree to which the autocracy acted in the direction he had promised. In endless communications to Petersburg, Zubatov advised that the government satisfy more fully the material aspirations of the workers and give a tangible sign of endorsing the Independent Party. Typical was Zubatov's comment in a letter to Rataev in July 1902 that "some essential proof on the part of the government is desirable extremely soon to strengthen the Independents' hopes."[26]

In Moscow, where social democracy was not a vigorous enemy and lacked mass support, Zubatov was satisfied to establish semilegal labor societies under the protective authority of the Grand Duke Sergei and General Trepov. In the Pale, social democracy as represented by the Bund was stronger and had deeper roots among the masses; therefore legalization of the Independent Party and its unions, a more radical measure, was necessary, Zubatov advised the

Department of Police: "The whole practice of the social democratic movement in Minsk and the present situation shows that neither force nor arrests are capable of fighting against it. The sole force capable of eradicating revolutionary activity is legalization of the economic movement."[27]

Another report on the Minsk labor movement written on the same day, January 22, 1902, and attributed to Zubatov, similarly concluded that the Independents could carry on their struggle against the Bund successfully only when "trade unions and all other economic labor organizations" were legalized.[28]

After Zubatov was transferred to Petersburg, he had the leaders of the Independent Party visit the capital to acquaint officials with the party's program and activities. Mania Vil'bushevich had an audience with Prince Aleksei Obolenskii, Assistant Minister of Finance, to discuss government subsidies for the Independent Party. Obolenskii was impressed and expressed willingness to grant the subsidies, as did Plehve, but Witte's opposition was decisive, and the funds were not forthcoming. In late 1902 and early 1903, when Zubatov was planning the moves that brought the Petersburg Zubatovshchina into existence and contemplating extension of his labor program to other areas of the country, he held frequent strategy sessions with leaders of the Independent Party. Attending were Vil'bushevich; Khunia Shaevich, leader of the Odessa Independents; Dr. Shapiro (or Sapir), a Zionist; the archpriests N. A. Skvertsov and Ornatskii; Father Georgii Gapon; and General Aleksandr Skandrakov, chief of personal security in the Ministry of Interior[29]—a motley group to plan the labor policies of the tsarist government!

Zubatov did well to marshal all available support for his labor program, for there was formidable opposition both in Minsk and within the higher bureaucracy to his ideas on the labor question and the Jewish problem. No doubt he was embarrassed by the rash of strikes that occurred in Minsk at a time when criticism by the Petersburg authorities of the Guzhon strike and the activities of the Moscow Council brought an end to the militant phase of the Moscow Zubatovshchina. In a letter to Iosif Gol'dberg in August

27. Bukhbinder, "Nezavisimaia," p. 262.
28. *Ibid.*, p. 259.
29. *Rabochaia gazeta*, no. 41 (Sept. 25, 1906); 1908, no. 2; 1908, no. 3; Spiridovich, "Pri tsarskom rezhime," p. 152; *Zapiski Georgiia Gapona*, pp. 38, 42.

1902, Zubatov lectured the Independent leader on the negative impression strikes left on the general public and the difficulty of preventing violence during strikes even when they had been begun for peaceful purposes.[30]

The Minsk employers had reluctantly yielded to the demands of the Independent unions largely in response to pressure from the local police. Since appeal to local officials was of no avail, they directed their grievances to the Petersburg authorities, making the most of the point that the Independent Party had no legal standing. By initiating and supporting strikes the party had clearly violated criminal law. This was the gist of a petition submitted by the Minsk tailor-shop owners to Plehve in May 1903. The Independent *fereins* were accused of acting as a civil court, fining employers for conduct of which they disapproved or for breach of contract. The *fereins* acted as bargaining agent for the workers, demanding a new contract from employers under threat of a general strike:

Thereupon the *fereins* assume legislative power, publishing decrees which regulate relations between the owners and the workers, define the length of the workday and so forth, such questions in all European states being resolved only by legislative authority. In order to compel the owners to submit to their demands, the *fereins* continually have recourse to a very serious means, namely, labor strikes, with which they continually threaten the owners.[31]

The petitioners attributed the union's activities and the general deterioration of labor relations in Minsk to administrative protection of the Independents. Plehve was entreated to use his authority to have the unions abolished and the rights of the employers respected.

The Ministry of Interior, disturbed by the labor unrest associated with the Independent Party, had taken steps to end the militancy of the Independents even before it received the petition. In April 1903 the party leaders were summoned to Petersburg and warned by Lopukhin that further breach of the law would bring government prosecution.[32] This was but the first of several setbacks the Independents faced in the spring of 1903 that led to the dissolution of the party.

30. "Novoe o zubatovshchine," pp. 308–9.
31. Bukhbinder, "O zubatovshchine," p. 332.
32. "Zapiska direktora depart. pol. Lopukhina o stachkakh v iiule 1903 g. v Odesse, Kieve, Nikolaeve," *Krasnaia letopis'*, 1922, no. 4, p. 389.

The Government and the Jewish Question

The fate of the Independent Party was as dependent on the government's Jewish policies as it was on its labor policy; both the Jewish intelligentsia, which directed the party, and the Jewish workers were keenly sensitive to each move of the autocracy in dealing with the Jewish problem. In the winter of 1902–1903, the Jewish question was affected by the interministerial rivalry between Witte and Plehve.

In his memoirs Witte discussed at length his divergence with Plehve on the Jewish question. Witte maintains that while he was Minister of Finance he did all in his power to hinder the enactment of further Jewish disabilities and in general favored the removal of restrictive laws against the Jews.[33] As for Plehve, Witte charges that he played an influential role in shaping the government's anti-Semitic policies, a judgment that history has generally accepted. Plehve's severe critics have accused him of having a hand in the pogroms that followed the assassination of Alexander II, as well as the notorious Kishinev pogrom in 1903; indeed, Witte has named Plehve as the true author of the anti-Jewish measures of 1882 that were officially attributed to Count N. P. Ignat'ev. Later, as chairman of a commission charged with preparing legislation to strengthen the Temporary Rules of May 3, 1882, Plehve proposed still harsher Jewish residency restrictions. On this occasion Plehve, according to Witte, was not motivated by hatred for the Jews—for he allegedly understood the error of his anti-Jewish policies—but was led by the bureaucrat's natural bent to carry out the wishes of his superior, in this case those of the Grand Duke Sergei Aleksandrovich, a notorious anti-Semite.[34]

The Jewish question was debated by Witte and Plehve at a meeting of the Committee of Ministers on January 7, 1903.[35] The immediate issue before the committee was of minor significance: the petition of a Vilna Jewish society to open a workhouse for Jews. Ranged in opposition to the petition were von Wahl and Witte; in favor were Plehve and his assistant, P. N. Durnovo. Both parties

33. Witte, *Vospominaniia*, II, 210.

34. *Ibid.*, pp. 214–15; Sliozberg, *Dela minuvshikh dnei*, II, 165–66, 172–76; III, 51–55; G. B. Sliozberg, "Baron G. O. Gintsburg i pravovoe polozhenie evreev," *Perezhitoe*, 2 (1910), 107–8.

35. Witte discussed in his memoirs (II, 211) why aspects of the Jewish question were dealt with by the Committee of Ministers.

defended their position within the context of general state policy on the Jewish problem. A. F. Koni, an eminent jurist, attended the meeting, and on the suggestion of Baron P. L. Korf drew up an account of the proceedings the same day.

Koni's account reveals the discussion to have been replete with contradictions. Plehve, reputedly a supporter of restrictive measures against the Jews, on this occasion appeared as an advocate of mutual help to improve the economic position of the Jewish masses; Witte, a self-professed opponent of Jewish disabilities, took the lead in opposing the workhouse for Vilna Jews.

In his opening remarks Plehve declared he wanted it clearly understood that his support of the petition was no indication that he considered the presence of the Jews on Russian soil as anything but deleterious:

I consider Jewry a phenomenon hostile to the national and state well-being of Russia. The characteristics of the Jews and the manifestations of their activities, which are hostilely directed against the government and the existing order, are of such seriousness that the government not only has the right but even the obligation to impose binding irksome measures on them and not give them an equal position with the Christian population. From this point of view I am in complete solidarity with the views of my predecessor, and I consider any weakening of the measures taken against Jewry as not in conformity with the views and tasks of the government.[36]

Plehve, nevertheless, was not indifferent to the plight of the Jews. In his view, their hostility to their environment was conditioned by material hardship; tightly congested in urban areas, they faced unemployment, poverty, and unhygienic working conditions. Adding to the restlessness of Jewish youth was the breakdown of religious and familial authority. "Therefore, despite everything said by me," Plehve continued, "all steps toward relief for the Jews by mutual help — [from] their burdensome economic position must be supported, and I on my part consider the establishment of a workhouse completely feasible." Without referring to the Independent Party by name, Plehve tried to enlist official support for its activities. "If the committee is in agreement with me," he concluded, "then I will report about the cancellation of the order prohibiting unions of mutual help in the Western *krai* that was

36. A. F. Koni, *Na zhiznennom puti* (Leningrad, 1929), V, 284; the following account of the meeting comes from pp. 283–86. For a further discussion of Plehve's view on Jewish youth and the breakdown of the Jewish family, see the *Times* (London), July 23, 1903.

promulgated in accordance with the former tendencies of the Ministry of Interior."

When Witte's turn came, he likewise subordinated his remarks on the Vilna workhouse to the general issue of the Jewish problem. The Ministry of Finance, he maintained, always considered the Jews "useful intermediaries for trade and industry" and the restrictive measures against them unnecessary and unjust. The Vilna workhouse would have a good influence. But larger issues were involved here, for if permission were granted, the government would be inundated by petitions from Jews in other towns; having granted the Vilna Jews the right to a workhouse it could not logically deny Jews elsewhere the right to open mutual-aid societies. If that occurred, it would appear to all that the Jews enjoyed special privileges from the government, Witte added, addressing himself to the empress, who was present: "But then the opinion would be formed that Jewry, hitherto limited in its rights, enjoys the patronage of the committee, and your imperial highness and the committee will have to concern itself chiefly with matters of Jewish mutual aid. One cannot but see a certain danger in such a state of affairs, and I consider it necessary to turn the committee's attention to this."[37]

Plehve in rebuttal again stressed the pitiful living conditions among the Jews and denied there would be any danger to the government if it granted the right of mutual help to Russian Jewry. In Plehve's view "the government must not disregard the possibility of exerting a conciliatory influence; this is demanded by the interests of the state and a sensible policy." Witte's stubborn opposition and his admonition to the empress that the establishment of the workhouse would make her "the protectress of the Jews" were sufficient to have a decision on the petition postponed and presumably shelved.

Witte's stand on the issue of the Vilna workhouse becomes clearer when one considers that it indirectly touched the sensitive labor question, which the Ministry of Finance held to be in its domain. Behind the debate and Plehve's unexpected support of the Vilna project lay the question of legalization of the Minsk mutual-help societies and labor clubs, as well as the status of the Independent Party itself.

37. Koni, p. 285.

The statutes for the proposed artisan and salesmen's clubs were eventually rejected by the Petersburg authorities on grounds that are uncertain. In August 1903, the month Witte was dismissed as minister, the Ministry of Interior did approve statutes for a mutual-aid society in Minsk for workers in handicraft production, having made "certain significant changes which concern the participation of police surveillance of the affairs of the society."[38]

Approval came too late for Mania Vil'bushevich and her colleagues. In April the notorious Kishinev pogrom took place; three months later the Independent Party was disbanded. The Kishinev atrocities drew worldwide attention by its violence and charges of government complicity from liberal opinion at home and abroad. Although Plehve may not have had a direct hand in instigating the pogrom—even Witte and Prince Sergei Urusov, sharp critics of Plehve's Jewish policies, hesitated to go that far—he apparently was not disturbed by its violent nature and later approved of the Kishinev pogrom as a positive example of retaliation against the activity of Jewish revolutionaries. It was also alleged that Plehve had given orders to the local governor prior to the Kishinev events not to use arms in case of anti-Semitic disorders, thus explaining why the bloody excesses continued unabated as the Kishinev police temporarily stood idly by.[39]

When Plehve's secret circular of June 24, 1903, banning Zionist activity in Russia came to light, it reinforced the view that Plehve was the mastermind of the government's anti-Semitic policies. Restrictive measures against Zionism were necessitated, the circular maintained, by the recent tendency of the Zionists to delay indefinitely the goal of assisting Jewish emigration to Palestine.

Russian Zionists are directing their activities to the development and strengthening of the national Jewish idea, preaching solidarity in exclusively Jewish organizations in places [where Jews] presently reside. This tendency, being hostile to the assimilation of the Jews with other nationalities, aggravates the blood difference between the former and the latter, runs counter to the principles of the Russian state idea, and therefore cannot be endured.[40]

38. *S.-Peterburgskiia vedomosti*, Aug. 20, 1903.

39. Witte, II, 215; Prince Serge Dmitriyevich Urussov, *Memoirs of a Russian Governor* (London and New York, 1908), pp. 15, 77–82; Greenberg, II, 51; Zavarzin, *Zhandarmy*, p. 64; *Times*, May 27, 1903. For a discussion of Plehve, the Ministry of Interior, and the Kishinev pogrom, see Sliozberg, *Dela minuvshikh dnei*, III, 59–67.

40. *Osvobozhdenie*, no. 7(31) (Sept. 18, 1903).

Congresses and other meetings of Zionists were prohibited, as was the collection of money for the Zionist cause. Local officials were to maintain strict surveillance of educational institutions that taught "the ancient Jewish language, and other institutions for the development of the national isolation of Russian Jewry."[41]

In an interview with Theodore Herzl, the Zionist leader, the following month, Plehve expressed himself in terms consistent with the circular. He was in sympathy with the Zionist aim of Jewish emigration for purposes of founding a Jewish state; interdiction of Zionist activity in Russia had resulted from the decision of Russian Zionists at their recent Minsk conference to emphasize Jewish nationalism rather than emigration. The Russian government aimed at a homogeneous population and expected patriotism and loyalty from all its peoples; Russian Jews had not proven sufficiently compliant in either respect. Jewish assimilation had proceeded slowly; on the other hand, many Russian Jews had become enemies of the Russian government. The Jewish problem was unique to Russia because of the vast numbers of indigent Jews, said to be two to three million. The emigration of the less capable Jewish masses and the assimilation of the most intelligent and well-to-do would be a solution acceptable to the Russian government, Plehve confided to Herzl.[42]

The Kishinev pogrom and the ban on Zionist activity heightened the self-awareness and nationalism of Russia's Jewish population; together the pogrom and ban revealed that the position of the Jewish masses was dependent on the government's attitude toward the Jews and that the socioeconomic emphasis of the Independents could not appreciably benefit the Jewish masses. No doubt the Independent Party leaders now felt a greater sense of Jewishness, accompanied by hostility toward the government. The Zionist ban hit them particularly hard; many had either embraced Zionism or were sympathetic to its goals. The Independents had allied with

41. *Ibid.; Posledniia izvestiia,* no. 141 (Aug. 14, 1903); see also S. Ginzburg, "Poezdka Teodora Gertslia v Peterburg," *Evreiskii mir,* 2 (1944), 199; Ministerstvo Vnutrennikh Del, Departament Politsii, *Sbornik sekretnykh tsirkuliarov* [New York, 1929], pp. 34–36.

42. Ginzburg, pp. 202–3. During a conversation with representatives of the Jewish community in July 1903, Plehve warned that the most extreme measures would be taken if the antigovernment movement among the Jews did not cease. "We shall then be obliged to get rid of you. For that purpose we shall, on the one hand, facilitate your migration. On the other hand, we will exclude the Jews from all our schools and render their lives in Russia impossible" (*Times,* July 23, 1903).

the Minsk Poale Zionists, believing that their programs were compatible. The anti-Zionist measures indicated a rejection of Zubatov's recommendation for peaceful coexistence and cooperation between the Zionists and the autocracy; Plehve had delivered a deathblow to the Independent Party.[43]

## The Independents Disband the Party

Under the impact of the Kishinev pogrom and the Zionist ban and with Lopukhin's warning against further strikes still fresh in mind the Independents convoked a party conference in Minsk on July 3, 1903. Little is known of the proceedings except for the unanimous decision to dissolve the Independent Party.[44] The last act of the party committee was the publication of a proclamation explaining the considerations that led it to terminate the party and setting forth its views on the future of Jewry and the Jewish labor movement.

The committee saw no reason for the party to continue on its semilegal basis in light of contemporary conditions. It believed the government was prepared to enact further factory legislation and, after long vacillation, would permit the existence of a Jewish labor movement along the lines of the Moscow Zubatovshchina. It would not, however, sanction a movement which bore a class character; any labor organization which failed to identify the interests of the worker with that of his employer would meet with government opposition.

The Ministry of Interior's circular outlawing Zionism had broad implications for all Russian Jews. "This circular signifies a turn in government policy," the committee warned, "in the sense of the persecution of all Jewish social movements which are not revolutionary, [that is], the repression of all Jewish nationalism." In

43. Chemeriskii's memoirs, "Novoe o zubatovshchine," p. 318; Frumkin, p. 227; Greenberg, II, 180. On July 14, 1903, Shaevich, the leader of the Odessa Independents, wrote: "I arrived from Petersburg terribly depressed by . . . the official prohibition of Zionism and Zionist activity in Russia. This development . . . prompts me and my comrades in the movement to abandon that work in the labor movement which until now completely absorbed us" (Vovchik, p. 127). The enmity against Plehve reached such extremes that Mania Vil'bushevich allegedly left Russia at the end of 1903 "as the emissary of a Socialist Terrorist group which had been organized for the purpose of assassinating the Czarist minister von Plehve" (Katzenelson-Rubashow, p. 19).

44. "Novoe o zubatovshchine," p. 321; *Posledniia izvestiia*, no. 140 (Aug. 4, 1903).

view of the effect repression must have on all elements of the Jewish population, a legalized labor movement in any form could only seem "a sharp, meaningless, insolent dissonance." The existence of a Jewish labor movement demanding class legislation without support from a similar movement among the Russian workers would buttress the arguments of those who hold that "the root of all free-thinking evils lies in the Jews."[45]

Thus was sounded the death knell of the Independent Party. Many of its founders, including Mania Vil'bushevich, entered the ranks of Poale Zionism or other Zionist organizations. Chemeriskii was the exception; he drifted back to the Bund and eventually became a member of its central committee. After the formation of Soviet power he became secretary of the central bureau of Evsektskii, the Jewish Sections of the Communist Party.[46]

## Summary

The Minsk Zubatovshchina thus came to an end owing to the government's repressive nationality policies and its unwillingness to give full sanction to the Independent Party. The Bund's opposition did not lead to a defection of the Independent Party's working-class following in Minsk, where during its lifetime the party basically fulfilled Zubatov's goals. The Jewish Independent Labor Party led a shadowy existence for two years before its leaders realized the futility of economic struggle by the Jewish masses without concomitant civil rights and an end to Jewish disabilities.

For a time, then, Mania Vil'bushevich and her cohorts led the only party functioning in Russia with government acquiescence, since the Department of Police and the government authorities knew of its activities at all times. Indeed it was the only open political party in Russia, for despite its renunciation of political activity the Jewish Independent Labor Party had all the attributes of a political party. It made use of a limited freedom of assembly, possessed its own press, published party literature, and had a mass following. It even committed itself, if necessary, to illegal activity. In pre-1905 Russia, no other group—conservative, liberal, or revolutionary—could

45. *Poslledniia izvestiia*, no. 140.
46. "K istorii Zubatovshchiny," p. 93; memoirs of Chemeriskii, Frumkina, and Rafes, "Novoe o zubatovshchine," pp. 322–28. On the Evsektsii see Schwarz, *Jews in the Soviet Union*, pp. 100–101; Zvi Y. Gitelman, *Jewish Nationality and Soviet Politics* (Princeton, 1972).

have so acted without immediate suppression and arrest of its leaders. Until Lopukhin's warning, the government allowed the Independents to violate with impunity the prevailing laws on strikes and labor relations, doing little to uphold the rights of the employers. It was a measure of the degree to which the government feared and respected the Bund that it temporarily permitted a militant Jewish labor movement to thrive in the Pale as a counterforce.

Neither the tool of the government nor of Zubatov, the Independents took advantage of local administrative protection to preach the benefits of economic struggle against capitalist exploitation, a view of labor relations anathema to the higher bureaucracy. That the Independents were determined to improve the economic position of the Jewish workers and that they did so seems of little doubt.[47] They encouraged the Jewish artisans to organize for self-protection; their legacy was a more highly conscious Jewish working class, of which the Bund was in all probability the beneficiary.

The declaration of dissolution was not the final act in the short history of the Jewish Independent Labor Party. While the party was holding its final session in Minsk, far away to the south the most dramatic events in the history of the party and the Zubatovshchina were being played out. The Odessa general strike provided a major test of Zubatov's ideas. It also challenged the government's self-restraint and willingness to sanction a militant, nonpolitical, and loyal working class movement and embark upon a dynamic approach to the labor question.

47. Mendelsohn (*Class Struggle*, pp. 151–52), on the other hand, maintains that the Zubatov *fereins* "could not effect permanent changes for the Jewish artisan class." To Mendelsohn, "the failure of even legalism to improve the condition of the Jewish artisans was a major reason for the decline of Jewish Zubatovism."

CHAPTER 11

# The Odessa Independents

Odessa in 1900 could look back on a century of phenomenal growth which made it the third largest city in the Russian Empire and a port of world renown. Its modern history dates from Russia's conquest of portions of the Black Sea littoral from the Turks in the last decades of the eighteenth century. On Catherine the Great's orders, this southern "window on the west" was transformed into a naval stronghold and port for merchant shipping. Railroad construction after the 1860's connected Odessa with the rich farming hinterland, enabling the food products and raw materials of the Ukraine to reach the port for shipment around the world. Odessa's commercial fame largely rested on its export of grain, which, along with its other trade, made it second only to St. Petersburg as Russia's most important commercial port at the beginning of the twentieth century.

Odessa's population rose apace with its growth as a port. In 1808 a mere twelve thousand inhabited Odessa; by 1914 the population had reached a half-million. The presence of foreign ships, merchants, and sailors gave the city the cosmopolitan flavor of an eastern Marseilles that it still retains. The city's melting pot reflected the empire's multinational character. In the port labored a motley population from the Caucasus—Georgians, Ossetians, Armenians —alongside Turks, Greeks, Persians, Moldavians, Bulgars, and Poles. The greater part of Odessa's population, however, was made up of Russians and Ukrainians (together totaling 49 per cent) and Jews (31 per cent); the surrounding countryside was predominantly Ukrainian. Among Russian cities Odessa had a population with a high cultural and educational level; in 1904 almost half the population was literate, well above the national average.[1]

1. "Odessa," *Bol'shaia sovetskaia entsiklopediia,* 2d ed., XXX (1954), 520; D. R.,

Odessa's industrial growth became noteworthy only in the 1880's. In 1878, Odessa's 142 industrial enterprises employed fewer than 4,000 workers; by 1903 the number of private enterprises had tripled and the industrial work force had reached 21,000. Flour mills, sugar refineries, and other food processing plants, whose products were chiefly exported, formed a third of these enterprises, their production accounting for two-thirds of Odessa's industrial output. Eighty-two metal processing plants produced 10 per cent of Odessa's gross output. Other plants processed animal products, chemical products, and wood; cork, jute, and leather plants processed materials brought to Odessa. In addition to privately owned enterprises there were state controlled industries including distilleries, the railway shops of the Southwest Railroad and the large plant of the Russian Steamship and Trade Society; more than 3,000 laborers were employed in these state works. Large-scale enterprises employing upwards of 500 workers, common in Moscow and Petersburg, were a rarity in Odessa.[2]

## The Working Class

Industrialization did not fundamentally alter the basic economic character of the city, which was still dominated by its port. Odessa's factory workers were an insignificant share of the total population. They comprised only one-quarter of the entire force of hired laborers in 1903; salesmen and others involved in trade formed 40 per cent, 10 per cent worked for the railways or shipping industries. There were 20,000 artisans in the city, almost equal to the number of factory workers. Altogether the work force came to 80,000.[3]

The Odessa working class tended to be specialized along lines of nationality: peoples from the Caucasus, Moldavians, and foreigners worked in the port, Ukrainians and Russians in the larger plants and

"Odessa," *Novyi entsiklopedicheskii slovar'*, XXIX (1916), 271, 273, 279; Portal, pp. 112–13; D. Shlosberg and B. Shul'man, "Vseobshchaia zabastovka v Odesse v 1903 gody i 'nezavisimtsy,'" *Litopis revoliutsii*, 1929, no. 1 (34), p. 102; Rashin, pp. 353, 579; "Zapiska Lopukhina," p. 386; Garvi, p. 126; [Iu. M. Steklov and N. Trotskii], *Iz rabochago dvizheniia v Odesse i Nikolaeve* (Geneva, 1900), p. 116.

2. *Bol'shaia sovetskaia entsiklopediia*; Garvi, p. 78; *Otchet odesskago komiteta torgovli i manufaktur za 1903–1905 gody* (Odessa, 1906), pp. 122, 124, 127; M. Dzhervis, "K istorii professional'nogo dvizheniia v Odesse," *Materialy po istorii professional'nogo dvizheniia v SSSR*, 5 (1927), 5–7; F. E. Los', *Formirovanie rabochego klassa na Ukraine* (Kiev, 1955), p. 38.

3. Dzhervis, p. 5; Shlosberg and Shul'man, pp. 103–4.

railway shops, while the Jews predominated in the small-scale plants and artisan workshops. The Russian and Ukrainian workers were largely recruited from the impoverished peasantry of the neighboring provinces who migrated seasonally to the city. Mutual suspicion and a wall of cultural and religious differences separated the Russian factory workers living in the industrial suburbs of Peresyp' and Dal'nitskii, where the large plants and factories were located, from the Jewish artisans occupying a large sector of the city's center.[4]

Odessa had then as now a substantial Jewish population. A large influx of Jews from the Northwest *krai* in the 1890's gave Odessa at the end of the century a Jewish population of 150,000. Count P. P. Shuvalov, the city governor, in 1901 and again in 1902 petitioned the Ministry of Interior and the Committee of Ministers to prohibit further Jewish emigration to Odessa, probably because he feared racial disturbances among the already great number of Jewish poor in the city.[5] Odessa for some time had been a major center of Jewish intellectual life. Secular and cosmopolitan in outlook and largely Russified, Odessa's Jewish intelligentsia differed from their fellow Jews of the Northwest region by their physical appearance, assimilation of Russian culture and adoption of the Russian tongue, and by their break with religious tradition. Part of the Jewish working class was also Russified, although to a lesser degree.

Relations between the Jewish community and the more numerous Russians and Ukrainians were embittered by sporadic outbursts of anti-Semitic violence. Odessa was the modern home of the pogrom; acts of physical violence against Jewish persons and property occurred in 1820, 1859, 1871, 1881, and 1905.[6] Racial tension was heightened by labor unrest at the end of the century due to economic stagnation in the city. Among the Jewish population a third was supported by charity; another 30,000 were considered at the poverty level.[7] Unemployment and poverty affected the Russian no

4. Garvi, pp. 38, 78, 127; Godlevskii, "Kishinev, Odessa, Nikolaev," *Letopis' revoliutsii*, 1924, no. 2(7), pp. 128–29.

5. *Svod vysochaishikh otmetok . . . za 1899 g.*, p. 30; *Svod vysochaishikh otmetok . . . za 1901 g.*, p. 28. Approximately 82 per cent of the 50,000 Odessan Jews on relief had emigrated from other provinces (*Budushchnost'*, no. 18 [May 3, 1902]).

6. Greenberg, II, 19, 21; Howard D. Mehlinger and John M. Thompson, *Count Witte and the Tsarist Government in the 1905 Revolution* (Bloomington and London, 1972), pp. 58–64.

7. *Budushchnost'*, no. 18; no. 19 (May 10, 1902).

less than the Jewish workers, often leading to acts of aimless destruction. On July 16, 1900, unemployed port workers, disgruntled by the use of soldiers to load freighters bound for China vented their anger in the destruction of Jewish shops and physical attacks on Jews. The following day a mob destroyed many Russian and foreign-owned stores as well before armed troops and Cossacks restored a semblance of order. More than a thousand arrests were made by the evening of July 17; the pogrom nevertheless continued for another two days in the city's central section.[8]

The economic stagnation that set in during 1900 led to a further deterioration in the bargaining power of the city's labor force. Working conditions, already incredibly poor in many professions, worsened. Employers exploited the economic crisis to rid themselves of workers who had been active in pressing for better wages and hours, replacing them with juveniles and women.[9] The émigré socialist press and responsible government officials similarly reported that distressingly bad working conditions prevailed in the port, factories, and workshops of Odessa and that the workers were unable to better their lot in the face of adamant opposition by their employers.

Lopukhin, the director of the Department of Police, who investigated labor conditions during a visit to the city in the summer of 1903, concluded that the Odessa labor movement had risen in militancy in direct proportion to the harsh conditions of work. The stevedores were particularly hard-pressed. Their work was backbreaking and very poorly paid; mechanization, moreover, decreased the number of jobs available. As unskilled workmen they were unable to find employment in other occupations. The steamship lines, which paid for work on the basis of the weight of the goods hauled, conspired to drive down wage rates, well knowing that the stevedores had no legal recourse. Driven to despair, the stevedores found an outlet in violence; the contractors who hired them on behalf of the steamship lines were often set upon and in some cases beaten to death.[10]

The sailors and stokers of the Odessa steamships also had no legal

8. *Iskra*, no. 1 (Dec. 1900); "Khronika vnutrennei zhizni," *Russkoe bogatstvo*, Aug. 1900, pp. 159–162.

9. *Iskra*, no. 25 (Sept. 15, 1902), no. 32 (Jan. 15, 1903).

10. "Zapiska Lopukhina," pp. 385–89; *Budushchnost'*, no. 18.

protection; like the stevedores, according to Lopukhin, they were "completely dependent on their employers."[11] The wages paid by the Russian Steamship and Trade Society had remained unchanged for over two decades while the cost of living had increased considerably, as had the work load assigned each sailor. Job security and working conditions were no better for the conductors and drivers of Odessa's horse-cars and tramways under the management of the Belgian Society. Here the administration of the lines customarily recruited employees without stipulating the terms of hire; worse still, employees were frequently discharged without warning and replaced by workers hired at still lower rates. The minimum workday was eleven hours; it sometimes reached eighteen hours or more, with overtime work on those occasions obligatory. At times the tram conductors were required to work on their feet uninterruptedly for twelve hours without a break for a meal.[12] The stevedores, sailors, stokers, and tram conductors shared a common discontent over working conditions and were drawn naturally into the vortex of the Odessa general strike out of desire for improved working conditions.

Among the factory workers and artisans working conditions were little better. Labor conditions at the factories and quarries, where low wages were accompanied by a workday of twelve to eighteen hours, further deteriorated during the industrial crisis at the turn of the century. Many factory workers were either unemployed or working at reduced wage rates and a drastically curtailed work week. The city's artisans suffered from long working hours, the general slowdown in economic activity, and a changing structure of production and distribution. As the stages of production became more simplified and larger in number the intermediary who supplied the raw materials and sold the finished product increasingly utilized women and children, who gratefully accepted

11. "Zapiska Lopukhina," p. 387; *Times* (London), Aug. 8, 1903.
12. "Zapiska Lopukhina," pp. 388, 390; Consul Sauvaire to Delcassé, July 30, 1903, n. s.; Thomas E. Heenan, American consul in Odessa, wrote of the Odessa tramway workers in a report to the State Department of Aug. 3, 1903 (n. s.): "These men were obliged to report for work at 6 A. M. and many of them during the summer months were kept at work until 3 A. M. of the following day. This seems incredible but I am informed that it is true. For this work the conductors received 60 cents a day on the average, and the drivers still less" (Consular Dispatches, National Archives). The Odessa Tramway Company, according to McKay (p. 86), earned almost 20 per cent on its capital in 1899; as a result other Belgian firms were attracted to Odessa.

wages well below the norm paid to skilled artisans.[13] The artisans in the smaller workshops were not protected by factory legislation; the factory inspector's jurisdiction did not include them. Like the remainder of the Odessa working class, the artisans at the outset of the century were receptive to any movement, legal or illegal, dedicated to active engagement in a struggle for better working and living conditions.

## The Revolutionary Movement

Odessa had played a leading role in the history of the Russian revolutionary movement since the 1870's. Social Democrats had been active in Odessa from the early 1890's. Marxist propaganda was disseminated among factory workers as well as laborers who were not distinctively proletarian, a characteristic Odessa social democracy was to retain throughout the years under study. The sailors of the merchant fleet, shoemakers, and construction workers were the groups most receptive to socialist agitators. Progress among the merchant seamen moved so rapidly that a strike of sailors, stokers and machinists of the Black Sea steamers was planned for the summer of 1894. The port strike was to be accompanied by agitation for a general strike among the city's working class. These grandiose plans were cut short by widespread arrests in January 1894.[14] During the next few years repeated unsuccessful attempts were made to establish a stable party organization. As in other industrial centers the working-class movement toward organizational unity and self-help continued unabated irrespective of the presence of the intelligentsia; in the last years of the decade circles and strike funds were organized by the workers without the assistance of the intelligentsia.[15]

In 1900 the Odessa Committee of the Russian Social Democratic Labor Party was established. Propagandists and agitators of Jewish extraction, trained by the Bund in the Northwest *krai* formed the committee's best and largest group of labor organizers; owing to their talents the committee had considerable success among the

13. Garvi, p. 80; *Iskra*, no. 9 (Oct. 1901), no. 42 (June 15, 1903); I. [V.] Bortnikov, *Iiul'skie dni 1903 goda na iuge Rossii* (Odessa, 1953), p. 28; Los', p. 28.

14. Steklov and Trotskii, p. 7; S. Mel'nik, *V. I. Lenin i odesskaia partiinaia organizatsiia* (Odessa, 1960), pp. 6–7.

15. Steklov and Trotskii, pp. 8–12; Garvi, pp. 20–21; *Rabochee dvizhenie*, IV, 2, pp. 635–37.

city's artisans, most of whom were Jewish. Although a few circles were formed in the Odessa factories and railway shops, the committee was unable to organize and assume the leadership of the labor movement among the factory proletariat. The lack of trained organizers of Russian extraction and the low level of culture and literacy among the Russian proletariat, which was largely recruited from the village poor, made systematic agitation among the Russian factory workers difficult. The committee feared to send Jewish agitators into the factories owing to the tension in the city between Jew and Gentile. As a consequence, the Odessa Committee was reproached by critics for focusing attention almost exclusively on the Jewish workers.[16]

The Odessa Committee found the taverns where the artisans customarily gathered to exchange news and gossip convenient for the distribution of their literature and the maintenance of close contacts with the workers during strikes. The workers were also accessible during holidays, which they celebrated by staging fist fights outside the city for entertainment.[17] As the committee gained a following among the artisans it organized them separately by professions, each with its own leadership, study circle, and strike fund.

The trend in social democracy known as Economism—that is, concentration on mass agitation and economic struggle based on the workers' concrete demands—was predominant in the Odessa Committee, which took a hostile stand toward *Iskra's* political line. In the committee's view economic struggle would simultaneously bring improvements in labor conditions and revolutionize the masses; direct political agitation among the masses was to be conducted only with "a certain caution and gradualness."[18]

This trend was continued under M. S. Zborovskii, the leader of the committee after August 1901. Zborovskii, who was popular among the Odessa workers, was known as an accomplished labor organizer rather than as a Marxist ideologist. He stressed the need to reach the workers through a simple approach, avoiding

16. Garvi, pp. 23–4, 31, 38, 45, 47, 78; testimony of Kostich [Zborovskii] at the Second Congress of the R.S.D.R.P., *Vtoroi s"ezd RSDRP*, p. 64; *Doklad o russkom sotsial'demokraticheskom dvizhenii*, p. 33.

17. Iosif Kristalovskii, "Iz istorii zarozhdeniia i razvitiia bol'shevizma v Odesse," *Letopis' revoliutsii*, 1924, no. 2 (7), p. 137.

18. Garvi, p. 116.

controversial doctrinal questions then raging among the party intelligentsia which were beyond the understanding of the masses and of little interest to them. Under his influence the committee gave priority to organizing the economic struggle of the workers;[19] for this reason it supported a wave of economic strikes that broke out toward the end of 1901.

In its regard for the workers the Odessa Committee was not above calling into play the existing labor laws. It sought to have the local administration enforce the eighteenth-century law on the maximum workday for artisans and even insisted that factory inspectors make the rounds of those workshops as yet uninspected. A pamphlet on trade unions commissioned by the committee used as its sources the same books Zubatov had given his prisoners to read, another sign of the pervasiveness of Economism among Odessa Social Democrats.[20]

The Odessa Committee was criticized for Economism both from within its ranks and by the editors of *Iskra*. The dispute turned on questions of party politics and tactics. The committee by outlook was at first closely associated with the views of *Rabochee delo*, the organ of the Union of Russian Social Democrats Abroad, which rivaled the *Iskra* organization for leadership of Russian Social Democracy. The *Iskra* émigré center, determined to capture the Odessa Committee and gain its formal adherence, dispatched a number of agents to Odessa for liaison purposes.[21]

At the end of October 1901 several prominent propagandists on the committee, critical of its disinclination for political agitation, withdrew and formed the Southern Revolutionary Group of Social Democrats. The Group concentrated more on organizing factory

19. *Ibid.*, pp. 18–20, 25, 27, 77; E. Levitskaia, "Iz zhizni odesskogo podpol'ia," *Proletarskaia revoliutsiia*, 1922, no. 6, p. 136. D. Novomirskii, a Social Democrat who worked with the Odessa Committee, was told in early 1901 by a member of the committee to avoid discussion of democracy and revolution in speaking to workers: "The masses are still in a monarchist frame of mind and we risk pushing them away from us. It is best entirely not to touch upon politics. Economic interests are closer to the workers. With the passage of time they will go over to politics" (D. Novomirskii, "Iz istorii odesskogo podpol'ia," *Proletarskaia revoliutsiia*, April 1927, p. 183). Another member of the Odessa Committee told Novomirskii that in addressing the workers he should "not touch upon politics, not curse the tsar" (*ibid.*, p. 184).

20. Garvi, *passim*; Shlosberg and Shul'man, pp. 108–9.

21. Garvi, pp. 106–7, 140; Novomirskii, pp. 189–90; *Pravda*, Aug. 4, 1938; *Vtoroi s"ezd RSDRP*, pp. 567, 571. Among the *Iskra* agents sent to Odessa were K. I. Zakharova, D. I. Ul'ianov, and R. S. Zemliachka.

and railway shop workers than had the Odessa Committee. They accused the committee of wrongfully maintaining that the working class could acquire political rights under the autocracy and for ignoring the factory workers. While the schism lasted each faction strove to win over the Odessa working class to its own program.[22] The *Iskra* center naturally sided with the Southern Revolutionary Group; it hoped that the committee would come to understand the need for political agitation, end the schism, and pledge a reunified committee to follow *Iskra*.[23] The schism in Odessa social democracy lasted until the summer of 1902, when the two factions united as the United Odessa Committee of the R. S. D. R. P. The establishment of the United Committee, however, did nothing more than paper over the breach caused by differences over tactics, and tedious debates continued.

Disgruntled by continuing signs of Economism within the new body, many former members of the Group broke away once more in September 1902 and founded the Southern Revolutionary Union of Social Democrats, which unconditionally supported the *Iskra* organization; the committee, on the other hand, was sympathetic to the Bor'ba (Struggle) group led by N. Riazanov (D. B. Gol'dendakh), which opposed *Iskra*. The Union lasted a half year before its members, at the urging of R. S. Zemliachka, *Iskra* agent in Odessa, re-entered the Odessa Committee.[24] As Zemliachka had hoped, the former members of the Union were successful in winning the committee to the *Iskra* program; in April 1903, *Iskra* published a committee statement of solidarity with its organization. "Odessa— until this year the most hostile of the large cities—has now gone over to us," Martov wrote with satisfaction to P. B. Aksel'rod.[25]

The Odessa Committee during these years was also beset with

22. Garvi, p. 144; Novomirskii, pp. 191, 198, 200; Godlevskii, pp. 128–129.
23. Garvi, pp. 20, 139–43; *Vtoroi s''ezd RSDRP*, p. 763; Wildman, *The Making*, pp. 215–16; Novomirskii, pp. 190–91; *Revoliutsionnaia Rossiia*, no. 13 (Nov. 1902); *Iskra*, no. 11 (Nov. 20, 1901), no. 17 (Feb. 15, 1902); *Iskrovskie organizatsii na Ukraine* (Kiev, 1950), pp. 36–38; *Perepiska V. I. Lenina i rukovodimykh im zagranichnykh partiinykh organov s sotsial-demokraticheskimi organizatsiiami Ukrainy* (Kiev, 1964), p. 93.
24. Novomirskii, pp. 201–2; *Iskra*, no. 30 (Dec. 15, 1902), no. 31 (Jan. 1, 1903); Bortnikov, p. 34; Keep, p. 85; *Listovki revoliutsionnykh sotsial-demokraticheskikh organizatsii Ukrainy 1896–1904* (Kiev, 1963), pp. 257–60; *Perepiska V. I. Lenina i redaktsii*, II, 311, 409, 531, 547–48; *Leninskii sbornik*, XI, 339.
25. *Pis'ma P. B. Aksel'roda i Iu. O. Martova*, eds. F. Dan, B. Nikolaevskii, and L. Tsederbaum-Dan (Berlin, 1924), p. 84; Novomirskii, p. 202; *Iskra*, no. 31 (Jan. 1, 1903); Levitskaia, pp. 136–37; *Vtoroi s''ezd RSDRP*, p. 774.

opposition from within the ranks of the working class. This phenomenon, which was common to most social democratic committees then active inside Russia, had existed at the time of the
committee's founding in 1900. Suspicious that the intelligentsia was
out to dominate the labor movement through the committee's
practice of co-opting its leadership, the workers sought to break the
control of the intelligentsia by instituting the principle of electivity to
the committee. In the spring of 1902 members of the opposition
ceased to support the committee and formed the Odessa
social-democratic union Rabochaia Volia (The Will of the Worker).
As a separate organization the union lasted until September
1903, when it issued a manifesto announcing its return to the fold
of the Odessa Committee and adherence to Lenin's views on party
organization.[26]

A second workers' opposition appeared in the form of Makhaevism. The Makhaevists were the followers of the Jan Waclaw
Machajski, a revolutionist critical of social democracy and the role of
the intelligentsia in the labor movement. In Odessa his ideas were
popular among the unemployed and those who resented
intelligentsia's domination of social democracy.[27]

The chaos and disunity in the ranks of Odessa social democracy
were furthered in the first months of 1903 by the establishment of an
Odessa branch of the Bund. Individual Bundists had for some time
been influential in the Odessa Committee; much of the socialist
literature distributed by the committee had been supplied through
the Bund. News of a separate Bund committee operating in Odessa
was greeted hostilely by the Odessa Committee and the *Iskra*
group.[28]

The Odessa Committee and the Russian social-democratic
splinter groups did not have the labor field to themselves. The
Polish Socialist Party (P.P.S.) had followers among the Odessa

26. *Listovki revoliutsionnykh*, pp. 573–75; Garvi, pp. 73, 107–12; *Vtoroi s"ezd RSDRP*,
pp. 11, 356–57, 757–58; *Revoliutsionnaia Rossiia*, no. 13 (Nov. 1902); *Iskra*, no. 50 (Oct.
15, 1903).

27. Marshall Shatz, "The Makhaevists and the Russian Revolutionary Move-
ment," *International Review of Social History*, 15 (1970), 253. On the ideology of
Makhaevism and its congruity with Zubatov's ideas see Marshall Shatz, "Jan Waclaw
Machajski: The 'Conspiracy' of the Intellectuals," *Survey*, Jan. 1967, pp. 45–57.

28. Garvi, p. 55; *Vestnik Bunda*, no. 3 (June 1904); *Vtoroi s"ezd RSDRP*, pp. 63–64,
66–67, 501, 510; L. Martov, *Istoriia rossiiskoi sotsial-demokratii* (Petrograd-Moscow,
1923), pp. 57–58.

working class, as did the anarchists and Socialist Revolutionaries. The Odessa Committee of the Socialist Revolutionary Party, founded in 1902, won over some of the organized workers from social democracy.[29] Ideological differences among the social democratic groups and between the Social Democrats and their rivals did not prevent them from acting in common on the more practical matter of organizing economic and political agitation. The Odessa revolutionary underground groups evinced none of that sectarian narrowness so characteristic of political life among the émigré socialist leaders.[30]

Throughout these years the police were extremely active. Frequent raids were made on socialist headquarters resulting in large numbers of arrests. Consequently, the Odessa Committee became extremely cautious in its activity, generally opposing street demonstrations and other forms of political agitation. The Southern Revolutionary Group, on the other hand, favored mass meetings and street demonstrations which, as the committee predicted, ended in police raids and arrests.

The Odessa Committee temporarily withdrew its opposition and agreed to participate in the celebration of the anniversary of peasant emancipation on February 19, 1902. The police were alerted beforehand and during the night of February 8–9 made more than 300 arrests, including many leaders of the Group and the Committee. Further arrests on February 12 caused postponement of the demonstration. On February 23 forty to sixty workers, accompanied by several students and sympathizers, took to the streets carrying red banners and chanting revolutionary songs in what has been called the first street demonstration of the Odessa workers. For the Southern Revolutionary Group the demonstration was intended to be a practical realization of its plans to involve the workers in

29. Garvi, pp. 104–6; *Revoliutsionnaia Rossiia*, no. 13 (Nov. 1902), no. 25 (June 1, 1903); G. G. Sushkin, *Pod krovavym znamenen* (Moscow, 1933), p. 8. The Odessa anarchists were influenced by Makhaevism. They fought Zubatov's followers for the leadership of the Odessa bakers ("Ocherk anarkhicheskago dvizheniia v Odesse," *Buntar'*, Dec. 1, 1906, p. 30).

30. The Odessa Committee agreed to supply literature to the anarchists, who were organizing the quarry workers (Garvi, pp. 105, 186, 192). When the Socialist Revolutionaries decided to establish a training school for agitators in Odessa, the local social democratic leaders accepted their invitation to meet and discuss the matter; among them was D. I. Ul'ianov, Lenin's brother (N. Osipovich, "Rasskazy o sekretnykh sotrudnikakh," *Kandal'nyi zvon*, 1 [1925], 118–19).

political agitation. The price it paid, however, was high for almost its entire membership was arrested. The lesson of February 23 reinforced the Odessa Committee's opposition to political demonstrations.[31]

## The Independents and the Working Class

It was at this point in the political life of Odessa, with the socialist movement disorganized, splintered into several camps, and weakened by numerous arrests, that the Independents appeared on the scene. Their initial labor organizer in Odessa was Meer Kogan, a native of the city. Kogan had experience as a social-democratic organizer and had the confidence of large numbers of Odessa workers, many of whom he knew personally. Beginning agitation on behalf of the Independents in early July 1902, he visited his old haunts, the pubs and inns where the workers gathered, defying a boycott the socialist groups had declared against him. Shortly thereafter he reported to the party center in Minsk that he had found a fertile soil for Independent propaganda among the house painters, the tobacco workers, and the tinsmiths; needed to further the Independent cause were additional labor organizers and literature in Russian setting forth the party's program and aims.[32]

In response the party commissioned Iulii Volin to join Kogan. Volin likewise was struck by the vast potential open to the Independents among the Odessa working class. Neither the Odessa Committee nor the rival Southern Revolutionary Group, it appeared, had organized the labor movement behind socialism; together they had an insignificant following of 1,500 workers. In general they both lagged behind the spontaneous strike movement that involved a vastly larger number of workers. Volin was thus convinced that the Odessa working class, largely unorganized and with little understanding of strike funds, eagerly sought to establish the type of labor organizations with purely economic goals that the Independents had to offer.[33]

Volin's evaluation proved correct. Working-class recruits were

31. Novomirskii, 194–200; Kristalovskii, p. 141; Garvi, pp. 131, 192–97; *Iskra*, no. 18 (March 10, 1902), no. 23 (Aug. 1, 1902).
32. Bukhbinder, "O zubatovshchina," p. 303. It was reported that Independent Party branches were also opened in nearby Elizavetgrad and Nikolaev (*Iskra*, no. 25 [Sept. 15, 1902]).
33. Bukhbinder, pp. 304–6; "Novoe o zubatovshchine," pp. 301–3.

attracted to the Independents so rapidly that the membership soon awaited practical realization of the party's program. Consequently, by the end of July 1902, two weeks after Volin's arrival in Odessa, the Independent Labor Group, the first name given the Odessa branch, had plans under way for workers' funds, public lectures by local professors, a library, and a newspaper. Volin reported that several leaders of the Odessa Jewish intellectual community, including the prominent Zionist Ahad Ha-Am (Asher Zvi Ginsberg) and the distinguished historian of Jewish life S. M. Dubnov, had declared themselves sympathetic to the Independent Party's aims.[34] On August 4, Volin wrote to Zubatov of his unexpected success and joy that "we have a party in Odessa and its future is already secured!"[35] Volin had recruited capable labor organizers from the Odessa intelligentsia, and thus felt free to agitate on behalf of the party either in Kiev or Kharkov. Ten days later Zubatov informed his superiors that the Independents had already organized a *ferein* for the Odessa house painters and were in the process of organizing the milliners and workers at the box factories.[36]

Kogan and Volin received organizational assistance from Mania Vil'bushevich, Chemeriskii, and Shaevich, all of whom arrived from Minsk. Khunia (Genrikh Isaevich) Shaevich deserves particular consideration, for from January 1903, when he began as an Independent Party organizer, he became the soul of the Odessa Independent movement, amassing a great personal following among all segments of the working class; by July 1903, Shaevich had become Russia's first great labor organizer.

Materials concerning Shaevich's life are fragmentary and contradictory. He boasted of a doctorate from Berlin University (there was much skepticism about the existence of the degree—one account holds that he passed himself off as a former student, removed from the university for radical ideas) and was known among the Odessa Jewish community for his activity as chairman of an Odessa Zionist circle, Oir Zion; he also had served on the library commission of an Odessa Zionist organization and had directed a

---

34. Bukhbinder, p. 306; "Novoe o zubatovshchine," p. 302. Dubnov has denied the truth of Volin's report, maintaining that he never sympathized with the ideas of the Independents and that his relations with Volin were short-lived (S. M. Dubnov, *Kniga zhizni* [Riga, 1934], I, 401–2).

35. Bukhbinder, "Nezavisimaia," p. 229.

36. "Novoe o zubatovshchine," p. 306.

project to publish and distribute Jewish nationalist literature among his coreligionists.

While attending the Minsk Congress of Russian Zionists in the summer of 1902 as a delegate of the Odessa Zionists, Shaevich met Mania Vil'bushevich and fell under her spell. From the moment of his return to Odessa he gave himself wholeheartedly to the Independent cause without, however, forsaking his allegiance to Zionism.[37] Despite his Zionist leanings Shaevich's influence went beyond the Jewish masses, who considered him one of their own, for "the Orthodox were persuaded that he was a convert, believing that he was a member of the Imperial Ministry of Interior and a teacher at the Odessa orphanage of her Imperial Majesty, the Empress Marie Feodorovna."[38]

The youthful leadership of the Odessa Independents—Shaevich and Chemeriskii were in their twenties—was determined to withstand the most trying circumstances in order to plant the party firmly in Odessa. Socialist opposition at once branded the Independents as police spies and condoned physical attacks upon Independent Party organizers.[39] Chemeriskii frequently went hungry for want of money and slept coverless on the hard benches at party headquarters. Two decades later, he recalled: "We worked until we dropped. At four to five o'clock in the morning we were already at the (labor) exchange taverns of the various workshops."[40] Ideological conviction appears to have primarily motivated Odessa party leaders; there is no evidence they received regular payments from the state treasury, although Zubatov did admit that funds were sent them from his own account and that of the Department of Police.[41]

Both Kogan and Volin emphasized that their hold over the intelligentsia and workers drawn to the Independent movement would soon end if practical fulfillment of the party's promises was

37. On Shaevich's biography, activities, and popularity, see Bukhbinder, "Nezavisimaia," pp. 230–31; Bukhbinder, "O zubatovshchine," p. 311; *Revoliutsionnaia Rossiia*, no. 28 (July 15, 1903); "Novoe o zubatovshchine," p. 319; Kristalovskii, p. 147; *Soiuz metallistov v Odesse* (Odessa, 1925), pp. 12–22; F. Achkanov, "Zamety pamiati," *Kommunist* (Odessa), March 1923, p. 64; Sauvaire to Delcassé, Aug. 12 and 17, 1903, n. s.
38. Sauvaire to Delcassé, Aug. 17, 1903, n.s.
39. *Iskra*, no. 25 (Sept. 15, 1902).
40. "Novoe o zubatovshchine," p. 321.
41. "K istorii Zubatovshchiny," p. 96.

not forthcoming. Official permission was an absolute necessity for the party to function, Volin told party comrades in Minsk in late July: "A broad movement is possible here only legally. Odessa is not at all similar to Minsk, and it is impossible to organize here professional *fereins* illegally. With authorized meetings on a semilegal basis it can be done."[42] A week later he similarly informed Zubatov that the Independents were in a position to hold large labor meetings but were being held back by lack of official approval.[43]

The Odessa administration had shown itself sympathetic to the plight of the workers and on several occasions had brought terrible conditions to the attention of management. Count Shuvalov, the city governor, was reputed to be liberal in labor matters; in a report on the labor movement made in 1899 and discussed in an earlier chapter, he recommended a shorter workday and better educational opportunities for the workers. He rigorously enforced the law on working hours in handicraft workshops and sponsored the establishment of artels in order that the artisans and factory workers could "improve their position and free themselves from exploitation."[44]

The Independents had to contend with a number of administrative authorities in Odessa—among them the city governor, the chief of police, factory inspectors, and chief of the local Okhrana—some favorable, some unfavorable. The Ministry of Interior cleared the way for the Independents, informing the local authorities that the party's activities had higher approval. Although never legally recognized, the Independent Party branch in Odessa received sufficient crucial support from the ministry and its Department of Police to proceed on that minimal semilegal basis that Volin had felt necessary.

On September 4, 1902, the Department of Police sent instructions to General Bessonov, chief of the Odessa gendarmes, to render Volin all possible assistance including permission to organize labor meetings and distribute party proclamations. To an enquiry from Lieutenant Colonel Kritskii of the gendarme administration for

42. "Novoe o zubatovshchine," p. 302; Bukhbinder, "O zubatovshchine," p. 305.
43. Bukhbinder, "Nezavisimaia," p. 229.
44. *Iskra*, no. 2 (Feb. 1901); see also no. 15 (Jan 15, 1902), no. 16 (Feb. 1, 1902); Garvi, p. 98; Steklov and Trotskii, p. 5; "Zapiska Lopukhina," pp. 387, 390; Ozerov, *Politika*, p. 133; I. Premysler, *Revoliutsiinii rukh na Ukraini na pochatku XX stolittia* (Kiev, 1958), pp. 38–39.

instructions regarding Mania Vil'bushevich, who was holding meetings with Odessa workers, Lopukhin replied: "Vil'bushevich is personally known to me and to Count Shuvalov. Render Vil'bushevich, in case of necessity, complete cooperation."[45] On November 20, Lopukhin informed Count Shuvalov that the ministry was not opposed to the requests he had received from the Independents to lease halls for their assemblies, for meetings of that type had received recognition from the Ministry of Interior and were taking place in St. Petersburg and Minsk: "On the part of the Ministry the satisfaction of the petition of the group of Independents in Odessa would meet with no obstacle, on the indispensable condition, however, that one of the petitioners be personally known to the city mayor and that responsibility for order at their meetings be accepted by one of the petitioners."[46]

The strongest statement of official support by the Petersburg authorities came in December. General V. D. Novitskii, the chief of the Kiev gendarmery and a vigorous foe of Zubatov, had ordered the arrest of Vil'bushevich and Volin, charging that there was little difference between the revolutionary parties and the Independents. On December 19, Lopukhin informed Novitskii, as he had told the Minsk and Odessa gendarme chiefs, that the Independents were acting with the knowledge and approval of the Department of Police. Describing the goals and activities of the Independents, Lopukhin concluded: "Vil'bushevich and Volin are representatives of the labor movement in the said direction, which completely answers to the views of the Government "; thus "they must not, of course, meet with impediments on the part of Government organs."[47]

Ministerial protection was also afforded to Shaevich. Captain A. V. Vasil'ev (not to be confused with his Minsk counterpart) was sent to Odessa to head the Okhrana office with instructions to look after

45. Bukhbinder, "Nezavisimaia," p. 230; see also Bukhbinder, "O zubatovshchine," p. 306; *Iskra* no. 23 (Aug. 1, 1903); "K istorii Zubatovshchiny," p. 89; "Zapiska gen. Novitskago, podannaia na vysochaishee imia cherez kn. Sviatopolka-Mirskago," *Sotsialist-revoliutsioner*, no. 2 (1910), p. 82. Lopukhin later maintained that the Independents had received "semirecognition" from the Odessa authorities ("Zapiska Lopukhina," p. 389).

46. Bukhbinder, "Nezavisimaia," p. 231; see also Vovchik, pp. 128–29; "K istorii Zubatovshchiny," p. 90.

47. "Zapiska gen. Novitskago," p. 83; see also *Revoliutsionnaia Rossiia*, no. 28 (July 15, 1903); "K istorii Zubatovshchiny," p. 90.

Shaevich; at the same time a letter was transmitted to Count Shuvalov in Plehve's name, instructing the city administration not to impede Shaevich's plans to organize the working class.[48] The Independents, however, were not without strong critics in the Odessa hierarchy. The public prosecutor and the senior factory inspector vociferously opposed the militancy of the Independent labor organizations and kept their superiors in the Ministries of Justice and Finance informed of events in Odessa; both ministries in turn brought the issue before Plehve.[49]

Administrative protection strengthened the position of the Independent Party, lending weight to the conviction, common among the Odessa masses, that the party operated with the sanction of the highest authorities and, indeed, the tsar himself. Shaevich for many of these simple souls was an emissary of the tsar, sent to Odessa to improve the lot of the common workmen. After the Independents had organized the Odessa working class and led a number of strikes without encountering administrative interference, many workers concluded that the tsar had approved the strikes and ordered the local administration to force concessions from the factory owners. During July as a general strike unfolded without a sign of repressive reaction from the authorities these notions were reinforced, leading many more workers to join the strike.[50]

To acquire mass support the Independent Labor Group issued a series of proclamations expounding its program and intentions. Similar in form to those clandestinely distributed by revolutionary groups, but differing in content, they aimed to convince the workers through simple logic of the economic and cultural benefits to be derived from labor unions organized under their own control. Against the objection that labor unions were illegal in Russia, the Independents argued that the government would recognize labor organizations formed by the workers. In the past the "red spectre" had caused the government to confuse the working-class movement

48. Spiridovich, "Pri tsarskom rezhime," pp. 152–53; *Revoliutsionnaia Rossiia,* no. 28. Shaevich in banishment was reported to have declared that Plehve had given the Independents the right of assembly (*Osvobozhdenie,* no. 55 [Sept. 2, 1904]).

49. "Novoe o zubatovshchine," p. 321; Bukhbinder, "Nezavisimaia," pp. 281–84; "Zapiska gen. Novitskago," p. 86.

50. Sauvaire to Delcassé, Aug. 12 and 17, 1903, n.s.; *Revoliutsionnaia Rossiia,* no. 29 (Aug. 5, 1903).

with the revolutionary socialist one, leading it to view each strike or labor fund as a sign of protest against the existing order. In recent years, however, both government and society had begun to accept the view that labor unions were necessary for the defense of working-class interests. It could be expected, therefore, that if the workers organized purely economic unions entirely divorced from the political parties, the government and indeed the factory owners would recognize their benefit to industry and the country at large and bring about their legalization. Organizational unity then would enable the workers to pressure the government to respond to their interests.[51]

The workers should not passively wait for the factory owners and the authorities to promote their interests as Prince Meshcherskii had suggested in his newspaper, an Odessa Independent Labor Committee proclamation counseled: "The true friends of the workers will never advise them to sit idly by and place all hopes in policemen and factory inspectors. The workers' well-being and deliverance can be obtained only through their own efforts by means of united and mutual support, and at that time we will say: Lord, deliver us from such 'friends' and we ourselves will deal with enemies."[52]

Shaevich's appeal to the masses was more personal and emotional. For the workers he harangued (he was popularly spoken of as the "orator"), Shaevich, with his long hair and short beard, lost the appearance of the typical intellectual of the time: "Before the masses he became unrecognizable: true inspiration seized him—with eyes lit up, nostrils distended, his whole figure, his whole forward movement embodied protest. The auditorium with bated breath, devouring eyes, listened to him. . . . Shaevich spoke graphically, absorbingly."[53] Tears came to the workers' eyes as Shaevich depicted their miserable lives, from the deprivations of childhood to the high illness rate, premature aging, and general defenselessness of maturity. He evoked the workers' deep sense of humiliation and unworthiness for having humbled themselves before their employers and for being incapable of providing their families with a decent living or preparing their children for a life better than

51. Bukhbinder, "O zubatovshchine," pp. 306–19; Bukhbinder, "Nezavisimaia," pp. 268–71.
52. Bukhbinder, "O zubatovshchine," p. 335.
53. *Soiuz metallistov v Odesse*, pp. 12–13.

their own. Exploitation would cease, working conditions would drastically improve, and their employers would treat them with respect when they ceased competing with one another and united into a union. "All for one and one for all," Shaevich's jeremiad ended, as he pleaded for the brethren to join the Independent unions.[54]

From the moment Shaevich became the acknowledged leader of the Odessa Independents the tempo of party recruitment picked up considerably. Apartments were rented for discussion groups and headquarters opened in the industrial environs of Peresyp' where meetings were held two or three times a week and occasionally daily. Attendance grew rapidly. Forty to fifty were present at first; ten times that number crowded in at later gatherings.[55]

The Independents struck roots among all elements of the Odessa working class—factory and railway workers, artisans, and port workers. More remarkable, they were able to unite Russian and Ukrainian factory workers and Jewish artisans largely through the oratorical and organizing abilities of Shaevich, a young Jew of Zionist persuasion, at a time when the embers of the anti-Semitic pogroms still smoldered. Surprisingly the Russian factory workers and the port workers, multinational in composition, were more receptive to the Independents and flocked to their standards in greater number that did the Jewish artisans.[56] Shaevich had a personal following in the largest factories and railway shops of Odessa, as well as among workers in the brickyards, creameries, and tanneries.[57] Woodworkers and coachmakers, Russian in nationality, also joined the Independent Party in large numbers, as did the house painters, sailors, bakers, and the tram and port workers.[58] By April 1903 the Odessa party membership reached two thousand. Official figures are unavailable on total party membership at its peak; estimates place it as high as six thousand (the party's following was several times larger), making the Odessa Independents the leaders of the largest organized labor movement in Russia for its time.[59]

54. *Ibid.*, pp. 13–14; Achkanov, p. 64; Sauvaire to Delcassé, Aug. 17, 1903, n. s.
55. Bukhbinder, "Nezavisimaia," p. 281; *Revoliutsionnaia Rossiia*, no. 28 (July 15, 1903); *Soiuz metallistov v Odesse*, p. 12; Vovchik, p. 129.
56. "Novoe o zubatovshchine," p. 319; Bukhbinder, "O zubatovshchine," p. 304.
57. Bukhbinder, "Nezavisimaia," p. 281.
58. "Novoe o zubatovshchine," pp. 319–20; Shlosberg and Shul'man, p. 115.
59. Bukhbinder, "Nezavisimaia," p. 281; "Dva dokumenta," *Materialy po istorii professional'nogo dvizheniia v Rossii*, 3 (1925), 249.

At the head of this labor movement, directing party affairs in Odessa, stood the Independent Labor Committee, which administered the mutual-aid funds, organized labor meetings, and published the party's literature. Assisted by a group of thirty to forty working-class representatives, it set general policy and drafted the statutes for the mass labor unions attached to the Independent Party.

The unions, organized by professions, were the basic units in the structure. Independent unions were formed among the machine workers, woodworkers, tinsmiths, boilermakers, coach makers, sailors and stokers, and bakers. Union meetings, limited to members, were held with the foreknowledge of the police at the pubs where the workers in each profession habitually gathered.[60]

The statutes of the Union of Metal Workers of the City of Odessa, the only statutes published to date, were similar to those that governed strike funds, reflecting the militancy of the Independent labor movement in Odessa. The union ostensibly was established, according to the statutes, for the usual trade-unionist goals of raising the material and intellectual levels of the membership. The statutes clearly indicated that the union's economic goals were to be attained largely through strikes; each member contributed a fifty-kopek entrance fee and ten kopeks weekly in dues to the union's treasury, which was essentially a strike fund. The metal workers, moreover, expected to supplement the union's treasury with contributions from other Independent unions during strikes.[61]

To foes of the Independents, such as I. I. Popov, senior factory inspector of Kherson *guberniia*, these statutes were but one illustration of the Independent unions' exclusive devotion to militant methods. Popov criticized the police and the local administration for shielding the Odessa Independents and charged that the Independent unions fostered violence, class hatred and disrespect for the law, providing, in sum, an education "in the revolutionary spirit."[62]

### The Independents and the Strike Movement

The Independents' militant spirit infused their unions and the

---

60. "Novoe o zubatovshchine," p. 319; Bukhbinder, "Nezavisimaia," pp. 281–82; "Dva dokumenta," p. 249.
61. "Dva dokumenta," p. 250; *Osvobozhdenie*, no. 4(28) (Aug. 2, 1903); *Soiuz metallistov v Odesse*, pp. 14–15.
62. "Dva dokumenta," p. 250.

strikes they led. Shaevich was a firm believer in strikes as an efficacious means of improving the position of the workers and thus retaining their loyalty to the Independent Party, a view not entirely shared by Zubatov.[63] At a time when official reprimand had precluded support of strikes by the Moscow Council, the unions organized by the Independents began a campaign of economic strikes. Their first strikes were on a small scale and involved few workers. In December 1902, the boxmakers went on strike, and early the next year a number of strikes occurred in artisan workshops.

In March 1903 the twelve workers at the Priv mechanical workshop went on strike demanding that one of their comrades, released for insolence, be rehired. Shaevich twice requested Priv to meet with him regarding the strike, but Priv, on the advice of the factory inspector, ignored the invitations and fired his workers. The Priv case was notable for the efforts of the strikers, in defiance of the law, to keep scabs from replacing them. Strikebreakers were physically assaulted and, in the case of one newly hired worker, beaten to death.[64]

The following month the tinsmiths at the Sokolovskii cannery, the bakers, and the workers at the Restel' plant went on strike. The Sokolovskii strike directly challenged the employer's hiring right; his ten employees left work after he refused to hire an additional tinsmith who was seeking employment. Responsibility for the strike rested with the union of tinsmiths; several of the strikers wished to return to work but stayed away out of fear of the union, which was prohibiting the tinsmiths from working in the cannery.[65]

The strike at the Restel' iron foundry and mechanical plant in April 1903 was the first conducted by the Odessa Independents at a comparatively large plant and assumed in the history of the Odessa Independent movement the same importance as the Guzhon affair in Moscow. The ostensible cause of the strike was the dismissal of a worker who had been employed at the plant for over twenty years. The factory inspector, however, concluded that the true cause lay elsewhere; labor relations at the plant had traditionally been good,

63. *Zapiski Georgiia Gapona,* p. 43; *Russkoe delo,* no. 33 (Aug. 13, 1905); Sauvaire to Delcassé, Aug. 12, 1903, n. s.
64. "Dva dokumenta," p. 251; *Revoliutsionnaia Rossiia,* no. 28 (July 15, 1903); Ainzaft, *Istoriia,* p. 92.
65. "Dva dokumenta," p. 251; *Revoliutsionnia Rossiia,* no. 28; "K istorii Zubatovshchiny," p. 91.

and the issue at hand appeared too insignificant to warrant a strike by almost the entire work force of a 175. Interrogation of the strikers and of workers at other plants convinced Popov that the strike was part of a carefully calculated plan by the Independent leaders to give the Odessa workers practical experience in conducting strikes and to demonstrate to factory owners and workers alike the power and influence of the Independent union.

The first sign of unrest occurred on Friday, April 18, when one of his workmen informed Restel' that he would receive a letter demanding he rehire Semen Dragomiretskii, the worker in question. If Restel' did not wish to respond immediately he would be invited to meet with his workers; should he still refuse to concede, a strike would be called. That afternoon a letter to that effect signed by the council of the Independent Union of Machine Workers was transmitted to Restel'. No other warning of a strike was given.

On Monday, April 21, only seven employees showed up for work at the plant. On that day Restel' received a second letter from the council, designating Shaevich as its bargaining agent and warning Restel' he would have to pay his employees for the time the plant lay idle. Restel' refused to budge: encouraged by Popov, who feared that concessions would engender unrest at other plants, Restel' ignored the council's demands and gave notice that those strikers who failed to appear at work at the end of three days would be fired.

The strike was not favored by all the workmen despite the council's contention that it represented the views of the Restel' workers. Many older workers and those with families to support were not members of the union, felt no reason to strike, and remained home out of fear. The union had forbidden the strikers to seek work and kept observers near the factory gates, threatening potential strikebreakers with physical harm. The Restel' workers were confident that the factory administration ultimately would submit to their demands, for they boasted of having accumulated sufficient reserves in the state bank to endure a prolonged strike.

The Restel' strike was therefore unusually long, lasting twelve weeks. During this time the strikers received sustenance from the union's treasury, which contained contributions from members at other plants and workshops. The union kept observers a short distance from the plant to intercept and divert newly hired workers to union headquarters where they would be given food, financial aid, and arguments against working at the Restel' plant. If they insisted on entering the plant, however, a signal would be given and a large crowd would gather ready to use force to thwart the strikebreakers. Popov reported that cases of violence against strikebreakers, evident from the first days of the strike, grew in frequency as the strike progressed and the management succeeded in hiring a considerable contingent of new workers.[66]

The strike at the Restel' plant would have ended in short order were it not for the benevolent neutrality of the local authorities. On April 21, the first day of the strike, Popov sought the assistance of V. N. Starkov, the acting city mayor. Starkov agreed that it was "impossible and dangerous" for Restel' to yield to the strikers' demands. Yet the following day, after speaking with Shaevich, Starkov changed his mind and recommended that the management rehire Dragomiretskii. Although Starkov received reports from Popov describing beatings of newly hired workers at the Restel' plant, he took no action.[67]

On May 16 the strike took its most violent turn. Some eighty strikebreakers were set upon by two to three hundred union members; some of those attacked required hospitalization. In this instance, too, the police sheltered the Independents; a request for protection by the new workers at the Restel' plant was rebuffed by police officers who drove them off from the police station and threatened them with imprisonment if they gathered again in a crowd.

Starkov, to Popov's dismay, dealt with the union as though it had legal standing, agreeing to cooperate with a deputation of Restel' workers who petitioned him to intervene on their behalf.[68] In the end official support mattered little, for the strike dragged on to an unsuccessful conclusion and was finally overtaken by the July

66. *Revoliutsionnaia Rossiia*, no. 28; no. 31 (Sept. 1, 1903); *Soiuz metallistov v Odesse*, pp. 17–18; A. Pankratova, *Fabzavkomy Rossii v bor'be za sotsialisticheskuiu fabriku* (Moscow, 1923), p. 72.

67. *Revoliutsionnaia Rossiia*, no. 28. Social-democratic sources maintain that the idea for a strike came from the Restel' workers and was at first opposed by Shaevich because of insufficient strike funds in the union's treasury (Kristalovskii, p. 147; Achkanov, p. 64; *Soiuz metallistov v Odesse*, pp. 16–17). Some accounts maintained that the police did give protection to the strikebreakers (*Iskra*, no. 46 [Aug. 15, 1903]; Suskin, p. 13).

68. *Revoliutsionnaia Rossiia*, no. 31 (Sept. 1, 1903); *Soiuz metallistov v Odesse*, pp. 18–19; "K istorii Zubatovshchiny," p. 91.

general strike. Shaevich, who had adamantly ordered the strikers to hold out until management agreed to take them back, reluctantly consented at the end of June to their seeking work elsewhere. Dragomiretskii thereupon left for his native village, as did many strikers.[69] The Odessa Independents had suffered their first setback.

While the Restel' strike was in progress the Independents struck the Odessa canneries. The plant owners met the issue head on, resolving at a special meeting on May 3 neither to negotiate with the union of tinsmiths nor grant its strike demands; if necessary, they were prepared to seek workers for their canneries from outside Odessa. Unable to obtain satisfaction from the local police and Okhrana, both of which appeared to ignore the union's flagrant violations of the law as well as the pleadings of the factory inspector, they decided to petition the governor and the Petersburg authorities. Their petition ascribed primary guilt for the rash of labor disturbances in Odessa to Shaevich, who was said to have convinced the workers that their illegal actions were sanctioned by the gendarmes.[70]

The protection the Independents had received from the local authorities was put in question with the replacement of Shuvalov by Lieutenant General D. G. Arsen'ev as city governor. Popov hastened to get the ear of the new governor and to persuade him to end the lawlessness of the Independents. Arsen'ev evidently was impressed with Popov's arguments, for he ordered a full investigation of the charges. Apparently Arsen'ev also gave an order to halt the activities of the Independent Party which was never executed owing to the opposition of Golovin, the acting chief of police, and Vasil'ev, chief of the Odessa Okhrana. On June 30, Arsen'ev informed Plehve that the Odessa strike movement was led by the Independents and warned that if the Independent unions continued unchecked they would become the cradle of revolutionary cadres.[71]

Similar reports reached Petersburg from the procurator's office,

69. *Revoliutsionnaia Rossiia,* no. 31. The French consul in Odessa reported on August 17, 1903, n.s. (August 4 o.s.) that the Restel' strike was still in progress.

70. *Revoliutsionnaia Rossiia,* no. 28, July 15, 1903; Bukhbinder, "Nezavisimaia," p. 231.

71. "K istorii Zubatovshchiny," p. 91; "Dva dokumenta," p. 251; *Osvobozhdenie,* no. 23 (May 19, 1903), no. 2 (26) (July 2, 1903); *Revoliutsionnaia Rossiia,* no. 31.

factory inspectors, and Odessa manufacturers. On May 9, Restel' telegraphed Witte, ascribing the strike at his plant to Shaevich's initiative and giving details of attacks upon his newly hired workers. "The factory inspector and I informed the [Odessa] administration about this," Restel' complained, "but the coercion does not cease. I ask your excellency for protection."[72]

The numerous complaints against the Independents were effective. Shaevich and leaders of the Minsk Independents were called to Petersburg by Lopukhin and "warned that each attempt of theirs in violation of law and order will entail prosecution similar to the prosecution of any illegal circle."[73] Shaevich thereupon expressed his intention to terminate the Independent branch in Odessa, although he took no positive steps in that direction before July. During most of June, in fact, the Independent unions continued to recruit additional members, particularly sailors and stokers of the merchant fleet, stevedores, day laborers in the shipyards, and horse-tram conductors.[74]

Other troubles plagued the Odessa Independents on the eve of the general strike. Earlier in the year it was revealed that Volin, the party treasurer, had absconded with union funds; rumor had it that he had made his way to America. In June union members among the railway-shop workers and the boilermakers of the Russian Steamship and Trade Society, whose financial contributions had made possible the protracted Restel' strike, demanded an audit of union funds, charging that monies earmarked for the Restel' strikers had been squandered without any account kept of their distribution. Some workers critical of the procedures by which the funds were administered ceased to pay dues to the unions.[75]

The Kishinev pogrom and the ban on Zionist activities, as we have seen, greatly distressed the Jewish leaders of the Independent Party; among the Jewish community in Odessa they caused fear and uneasiness for the future. Shaevich, on the other hand, thrived on action, and the Independents under his leadership joined Odessa Zionists and some liberal elements of society in establishing a

72. D. Shlosberg, "Vseobshchaia stachka 1903 g. na Ukraine," *Istoriia proletariata SSSR*, 7 (1931), 68; see also "Novoe o zubatovshchine," p. 321.

73. "Zapiska Lopukhina," p. 389.

74. *Ibid.*; "Dva dokumenta," p. 251.

75. *Revoliutsionnaia Rossiia*, no. 20 (March 15, 1903), no. 21 (April 1, 1903), no. 31 (Sept. 1, 1903); Sushkin, p. 13.

Committee of Self-Defense to protect Odessa Jews against anti-Semitic disturbances that were expected to occur shortly after the Kishinev pogrom. The Bund and the Odessa Committee of the R.S.D.R.P. also held talks with the Independents on the subject of self-defense, according to Chemeriskii, but without tangible results. The Committee of Self-Defense, using lodgings previously set aside by the police for the Independents, issued an appeal for calm and order. Fearful that any labor disorder might be transformed into an anti-Semitic pogrom, the committee called upon all Jews, including "members of the S.R., S.D., and Bund parties to restrain from organizing demonstrations."[76]

Fears of a pogrom proved unfounded. The July general strike, which engulfed workers of all professions and nationalities in Odessa, was notable for its racial harmony.

76. *Revoliutsionnaia Rossiia,* no. 23 (May 1, 1903); see also *Iskra,* no. 40 (May 15, 1903); *Posledniia izvestiia,* no. 129 (June 3, 1903); "Novoe o zubatovshchine," p. 320.

CHAPTER 12

# The Odessa General Strike

The grandiose wave of strikes that swept through the major industrial centers and port cities of the Ukraine and Caucasus in July and August 1903 was by far the largest that Russia had yet experienced. Strikes were reported in Odessa, Kiev, Nikolaev, Baku, Tiflis, Elizavetgrad, Batum, Ekaterinoslav, Kerch, and several smaller cities as Russia witnessed its greatest demonstration of working-class discontent prior to the revolution of 1905.[1]

During July in Odessa, Russia for the first time underwent a general strike as the working class, made powerful through unity, brought the life of the city and port to a dead halt. Although strikes simultaneously developed in other southern cities, evidence indicates that the Odessa general strike arose from indigenous causes. Neither the socialists nor the Independents should be credited with beginning the July strikes in Odessa. Once begun, however, both tried to seize the leadership of the movement, the one to transform it into a small political demonstration, the other to keep the demands of the strikers within economic bounds.

The July strikes arose and fed on working-class discontent with mass unemployment and harsh working conditions; better hours and wages and an end to specific abuses were the sole aims of the strikers. "These strikes sooner or later could not but arise," Lopukhin concluded after personal investigation in Odessa at the

1. *Svod otchetov fabrichnykh inspektorov za 1903 god*, pp. ix, 99. Factory inspector reports vastly underestimated the number of strikes and strikers in July 1903. They gave the combined total as 296 strikes and 32,000 strikers (V. E. Varzar, ed., *Statisticheskiia svedeniia o stachkakh rabochikh na fabrikakh i zavodakh za desiatiletie 1895–1904 goda* [St. Petersburg, 1905], Table II, p. 4 of supplement).

end of July.[2] "The whole movement bears an elemental rather than an organized character," an eyewitness to the Odessa events reported to *Iskra*, a view taken by most observers.[3]

The strike at the Southwest Railway workers on July 1 is generally regarded as the starting point of the movement which culminated in the general strike. The immediate cause of the work stoppage was the discharge of a worker for apparently unjust causes. The strike demands were at first limited to the rehiring of the aggrieved worker and the discharge of several foremen notorious for ill-treatment of the workers. A day later additional demands were made for a wage increase, a nine-hour day, and an end to the humiliating physical search of employees.

The strike, confined at first to 200 boiler shop workers, embraced on July 2 the entire work force of over 2,000. It was soon called off, however, through the influence of the Independents and prompt action taken by the management. K. S. Nemeshaev, the director of the railway, hastened to Odessa and reached an agreement with the strikers on July 3; they pledged to return to work after he conceded most of their demands. Since changes in wages and hours needed the higher approval of the Ministry of Communications, Nemeshaev promised to place their demands before the Petersburg authorities and return with an answer within two weeks.[4]

The railway shop strike was marked by a sharp clash between socialist and Independent agitators, the first of many such battles during the July days. Agitators from the Odessa Committee of the R.S.D.R.P., which had a strong party cell among the railway-shop workers, addressed crowds of strikers, trying to turn the workers' discontent into general opposition to the capitalist class. The

---

2. "Zapiska Lopukhina," p. 389; see also *Times* (London), Aug. 4, 1903.

3. *Iskra*, no. 45 (Aug. 1, 1903). Our primary source of information about the Odessa general strike comes from dispatches and letters smuggled out of Odessa and published in the émigré organs *Iskra, Osvobozhdenie, Posledniia izvestiia,* and *Revoliutsionnaia Rossiia;* the dispatches of the Odessa correspondent of the *Times* are also of value. Correspondence between the Odessa administration and Petersburg officials is found in Bukhbinder, "Nezavisimaia"; Shlosberg, pp. 52–85; *Vseobshchaia stachka na iuge Rossii v 1903 godu* (Moscow, 1938). Also see the report composed by the Department of Police for the Minister of Interior, "K istorii vseobshchei stachki," pp. 84–85. The reports of Sauvaire, the French consul in Odessa, on the course of the strike are informative and perceptive.

4. "Zapiska Lopukhina," p. 386; Sushkin, p. 16; *Iskra*, no. 46 (Aug. 15, 1903); *Osvobozhdenie*, no. 4 (28) and its supplement (Aug. 2, 1903); *Vseobshchaia stachka*, p. 79; *Iskrovskie organizatsii na Ukraine*, p. 317.

strikers, however, were unmoved; when an agitator began discussing political issues they stopped him from speaking. The determination of the workers to confine their demands within economic bounds found expression repeatedly during the July days.

The Independents were active in the strike at the railway shops, where they had a following of about 150 workers. Their supporters effectively opposed the Social Democrats, threatening to break the united strike front and return to work if socialist literature was distributed or propagandists from the Odessa Committee were permitted to address the workers. On occasion agitators from the committee were attacked by Independent sympathizers while addressing the strikers. Under pressure from the Independents the strikers refused to circulate the committee's leaflets, and with the agreement of the committee itself the leaflets were destroyed. The first round in the protracted battle during the July days was thus scored in favor of the Independents.[5]

The success of the strike in the railway shops encouraged workers in other professions to embark on the same path to better their position. On July 3 the stevedores employed by the Russian Steamship and Trade Society left work demanding better wages and hours. The following day the strike spread to stevedores working on the docks of the Black Sea–Danube Society and privately owned shipping lines. By the evening of July 5 the number of strikers exceeded 4,000. The strike revolved around long-standing grievances —backbreaking hours and pitifully low wages, demeaning hiring practices, rough treatment from the foremen, and occasional nonpayment of wages. Popov, the factory inspector, however, blamed the Independents for instigating the strike and accused Shaevich, who had a large personal following among the stevedores, of contriving pretexts to justify the walkout.[6]

During the strike the local administration was placed in a crossfire between the shipping lines, financially damaged by the work stoppage, and the stevedores. The first demanded the banishment of the strike instigators and the requisition of soldiers to load their ships; the stevedores, on their part, petitioned the city ad-

5. *Iskra,* no. 46 (Aug. 15, 1903); Shlosberg and Shul'man, p. 124; *Listovki revoliutsionnykh,* pp. 446–48; "K istorii vseobshchei stachki," p. 112.
6. "Zapiska Lopukhina," p. 386; "Dva dokumenta," p. 252; *Iskra,* no. 45 (Aug. 1, 1903); *Vseobshchaia stachka,* pp. 79, 81–2; *Iskrovskie organizatsii na Ukraine,* p. 317; Shlosberg and Shul'man, pp. 124–25; *Revoliutsionnaia Rossiia,* no. 30 (Aug. 20, 1903).

ministration to intercede on their behalf with the steamship companies.

Golovin, the acting chief of police, endeavored to end the strike. On July 6 representatives of the striking stevedores were called to his office and advised to return to work, but to no avail. On the following day the contingent of regular police in the port was augmented. Police officers made the rounds of the docks interrogating groups of strikers and administering a beating to those who stubbornly refused to end the strike. The sharp stick wielded by the police and the carrot in the form of partial economic concessions offered by several firms led a number of stevedores to resume work; a large number, however, still held out. Despite the efforts of socialist agitators, official reports maintained that the strike to this point was conducted peacefully.[7]

On July 8 the strike took a turn indicative of things to come. That morning a Greek steamship firm announced it intended to hire stevedores to load one of its ships. The 300 workmen who showed up at the pier ready to be hired at wage rates considerably below those demanded by the strikers were surrounded by an angry mob of stevedores bent on preventing them from being hired. A police officer who attempted to arrest the ringleaders was threatened with bodily harm and driven off. In the evening Captain Vasil'ev warned the Department of Police of imminent disorders: "At the present time the situation begins to grow worse, for the workers are again gathering in a crowd, insisting on the fulfillment of the declared demands, and sometimes expressing reluctance to submit to orders of the police to disperse."[8] During the following days the stevedores placed unrelenting pressure on the strikebreakers to rejoin the strike and present a united front. This tactic, repeated in other strikes in July, largely accounts for the monolithic strike of the entire Odessa working class.

The port authorities were forewarned as early as July 6 that the sailors and stokers of the merchant fleet were on the verge of striking. Observers had predicted for some time that onerous working conditions would ultimately produce an outburst of discontent among the crewmen of the merchant ships. On July 10 a

7. *Vseobshchaia stachka,* pp. 79–90; *Iskrovskie organizatsii na Ukraine,* pp. 317–18; *Revoliutsionnaia Rossiia,* no. 29 (Aug. 5, 1903); *Iskra,* no. 46 (Aug. 15, 1903); "Dva dokumenta," p. 252; "Zapiska Lopukhina," p. 387; Shlosberg and Shul'man, p. 125.
8. *Vseobshchaia stachka,* p. 87; see also "K istorii vseobshchei stachki," p. 84.

number of seamen called on their comrades to leave work; on the following day they were joined by 1,200 to 1,500 engineers, sailors, and stokers employed on the ships of the Russian Steamship and Trade Society, the Black Sea–Danube Society, the Eastern Chinese –Russian Society, and other steamship lines, bringing the movement of traffic in the port to a standstill.[9]

Although the seamen's strike was brought about by long-standing grievances and was affected by the mood in the city, it nonetheless was generally attributed to the Independents owing to their great success in unionizing the sailors and stokers. Shaevich was a legendary figure among the port workers, while Ivan Efimovich Zhimoedov, a former ship's lackey and an assistant to Shaevich, was the chief organizer of the Independents' union of sailors. When the sailors struck, therefore, they naturally headed for Independent headquarters. Upwards of several thousand sailors congregated there on July 11 and 12 to work out terms of their common demands, which they forwarded to the office of Major General V. P. Pereleshin, chief of the port. Pereleshin met personally with a deputation of sailors, assuring them that many of their demands were already under consideration by a special conference and promising to consult with the management of the shipping lines and have an answer within the week; he urged the seamen in the meantime to return to their ships.

True to his word, General Pereleshin convoked a conference of representatives of the major shipping lines on July 12. The shipping companies, already facing a financial crisis due to competition from the railroads, balked at instituting uniform working conditions and pay scales, holding that work loads for each crew varied from voyage to voyage. Agreement was reached to establish a high-level commission to investigate the intricacies of the problem, thus delaying a settlement with the impatient workers. In general the small shipping concerns and foreign lines readily agreed to grant wage increases, while representatives of the larger firms demurred on grounds they were not empowered to make changes until they consulted the managing directors of the lines.[10]

Shaevich's activity during these days is not fully clear. Apparently

9. *Revoliutsionnaia Rossiia*, nos. 29 and 30; *Vseobshchaia stachka*, pp. 81, 90; *Iskrovskie organizatsii na Ukraine*, pp. 318–19; "Zapiska Lopukhina," p. 387; Steklov and Trotskii, pp. 7, 13; Sauvaire to Delcassé, July 30, 1903, n. s.; *Times*, Aug. 8, 1903.

10. "Zapiska Lopukhina," pp. 388–89; Shlosberg, p. 63; Shlosberg and Shul'man, pp. 115, 128; Bukhbinder, "Nezavisimaia," p. 283; *Listovki revoliutsionnykh*, p. 462;

during the first week of July he was at the Minsk conference of Independent leaders that disbanded the party, for early in the morning of July 6, Captain Vasil'ev telegraphed the Minsk gendarme office with a request that Shaevich return to Odessa since a stevedores' strike was in progress.[11] No doubt Vasil'ev believed that the presence of Shaevich, the acknowledged leader of the Odessa workers, would bring the hitherto anarchic train of events to a focus and forestall disorders.

Shaevich returned to Odessa "terribly depressed," unfit for the role in which Vasil'ev and the strikers had cast him. The Independent Party had gone out of existence, while the official prohibition of Zionism and Zionist activity, he wrote in mid-July, "impelled me and my comrades in the movement to abandon that work in the labor movement in which up to now we have been completely absorbed."[12] Thus when Shaevich appeared before the striking sailors for the first time on the afternoon of July 11 he seemed gloomy and agitated and spoke with unwonted hesitancy. His criticism of the strike action for its probable inefficacy and his recommendation that the sailors return to their ships were greeted coolly, and Shaevich hurriedly departed.[13] The force which Shaevich had made powerful now took on an elemental life of its own, disinclined to be deflected by the "orator" from moving in the direction he had previously charted.

While the striking sailors and stokers were restlessly awaiting a decision on their demands from the commission established by the shipping lines, groups of merchantmen led by Zhimoedov actively sought to create a united strike front through coercion against strikebreakers. General Arsen'ev and other responsible Odessa officials informed Petersburg that the strikers had not "violated external order," but they feared that the presence of vast throngs of unemployed workers in the port might lead to disorders and destruction of property. Security in the port was therefore tightened; a Cossack squadron and additional police were assigned to patrol the dockside.[14]

---

*Revoliutsionnaia Rossiia*, no. 30; *Vseobshchaia stachka*, pp. 90–91; *Times*, March 10, 1903; "Dva dokumenta," p. 253; *Otchet odesskago komiteta*, p. 175; Sauvaire to Delcassé, July 30, 1903, n. s.

11. Shlosberg and Shul'man, p. 128.
12. Vovchik, p. 127.
13. *Revoliutsionnaia Rossiia*, no. 29.
14. Shlosberg and Shul'man, p. 128; *Vseobshchaia stachka*, pp. 90–91.

Fear for order, too, moved the government to intervene in the strike and reactivate the port. The Petersburg authorities had been kept informed of labor unrest in Odessa. General Arsen'ev reported regularly to both Plehve and the Grand Duke Aleksandr Mikhailovich, director of the Russian merchant marine. On July 12, the government took decisive action. The Minister of the Navy sent a telegram to Commanders of the Black Sea Fleet of the Imperial Navy: "In agreement with the desire of the Minister of Interior, I ask that there be sent to Odessa on the steamships of the Russian Society as many sailors and stokers as can be spared without a great loss to the navigation of the fleet in order that they replace for a short time those who went on strike, with a view to setting minds at rest and terminating the strike."[15] To avert the dangerous possibility that the naval seamen might join the striking sailors, Plehve gave a supplementary order to separate the "lower ranks" from the strikers.[16]

On July 15 and 16 steamships arrived from Sevastopol' bearing 400 to 600 machinists, stokers, and helmsmen of the Imperial navy to man the passenger ships and freighters in Odessa harbor.[17] On July 16 the port was active again as merchant ships, idle for several days, departed Odessa with new complements of seamen. The employment of naval personnel undermined the bargaining power of the strikers. Some returned to their ships; others remained on strike and tried to interfere with scheduled departures.

Meanwhile the commission representing the major steamship lines dragged on its deliberations. By July 20, the day the commission presented its report, the Odessa strike wave had begun to recede. Not surprisingly therefore, all the basic demands of the sailors and stokers were rejected.[18]

On July 15 the center of the strike movement returned to the heart of the city. On that day the drivers and conductors of the Odessa Tramway Company struck. The tramway strike, along with the renewal of the railway-shop workers' strike (the management had refused to raise wage rates), was the first in a rapid train of events

15. *Vseobshchaia stachka*, p. 91.
16. *Ibid.*
17. *Ibid.; Revoliutsionnaia Rossiia*, nos. 29 and 30; *Iskrovskie organizatsii na Ukraine*, pp. 319–20; "Dva dokumenta," p. 253; Heenan to Francis B. Loomis, Assistant Secretary of State, Aug. 3, 1903, n. s.
18. "Zapiska Lopukhina," p. 390; *Vseobshchaia stachka*, p. 91; *Revoliutsionnaia Rossiia*, no. 30; *Otchet odesskago komiteta*, p. 175; *Iskrovskie organizatsii na Ukraine*, p. 321.

which brought the life of the city to a standstill. The tramway workers were moved to strike by news that the management of the line was about to discharge their entire number.

The strike was not unexpected, for the tramway workmen were known to be among the most exploited of the Odessa working class; their demands, including the call for a ten-hour day, were of a purely economic nature. The tramwaymen were attracted to the Independent Party by the success of its unions and the unity and mutual aid they provided. On July 13 their representatives visited Independent headquarters in the Peresyp' district and implored Shaevich to take the leadership of the proposed strike. Shaevich surprisingly advised caution; only when it became apparent that the tramway workers could not be dissuaded from striking did Shaevich reverse his position.[19]

On July 15 all work ceased on the tram lines as the conductors and drivers, more than 600 strong, enforced a shutdown. Groups of strikers encamped at the stables and tram depot, determined to prevent the operation of the cars and the employment of scabs. When the police ordered them to clear the depot entrance and disperse, they refused and asserted defiantly that they had been sent by the Independent Labor Committee to secure the depot and would depart "only with the permission of the committee."[20]

The strikers had sympathizers in the local administration. Golovin, the acting chief of police, advised their representatives how best to impede the movement of the trams without breaking the law and giving the police a pretext to intervene. Captain Vasil'ev of the Okhrana went a step further. Duplicating Trepov's role in the Guzhon affair, he threatened to have the vice-director of the tram line banished and the assets of the company seized unless all the demands of the workmen were unconditionally met.[21] The general

19. "K istorii vseobshchei stachki," p. 84. The anonymous reporters for the émigré organs as well as Lopukhin emphasized the significance of the tram strike in engendering the general strike; see *Osvobozhdenie,* supplement to no. 4(28); *Posledniia izvestiia,* no. 139 (Aug. 10, 1903); "Zapiska Lopukhina," pp. 390–91. On the tram strike see also M. Dzhervis, "Stachka tramvaishchikov," *Professional'naia zhizn'* (Odessa), Dec. 1923, p. 49; Shlosberg, pp. 63–64, 67; *Revoliutsionnaia Rossiia,* no. 30; *Iskra,* no. 46; *Posledniia izvestiia,* no. 140 (Aug. 17, 1903); Bukhbinder, "Nezavisimaia," p. 283. The tramway workers' demands are given in *Listovki revoliutsionnykh,* p. 462.

20. Bukhbinder, *ibid.,* p. 283; see also *Iskrovskie organizatsii na Ukraine,* p. 320; *Times,* July 31, 1903.

21. *Revoliutsionnaia Rossiia,* no. 30; Shlosberg, p. 68; McKay, p. 281; Sauvaire to Delcassé, July 31, 1903, n. s.

public, the primary victim of the halt in service, was likewise sympathetic to the strikers, believing in the justness of their case; the public voluntarily contributed money to sustain the tramway workers until the strike was settled. The workers justified this faith, for the strike was conducted with "complete order and peace."[22]

During the tramway strike both management and the strikers petitioned the local administration to intervene, the former requesting administrative action to terminate the strike, the latter, after their demands were rejected by the company, seeking to have the authorities compel the management to capitulate. Captain Vasil'ev sided with the tram workers; Osetrov, director of the office of the city governor, and the mayor, P. A. Zelenyi, both of whom, it was rumored, had been bribed by the Odessa Tramway Company, upheld the views of the management. General Arsen'ev, under pressure from both sides, chose to convoke a special conference to adjudicate the case.

The conference, called for July 16, was chaired by General Arsen'ev and included Osetrov, Zelenyi, Popov, Golovin, several other administrative officials, and two members of the city duma. At its first session a decision was made to issue a declaration in the name of the city governor calling on the tramway workers to return to work under the old conditions with the assurance that their demands would receive just consideration by the commission. The strikers replied firmly they would settle for nothing less than a written guarantee that their demands would be fulfilled. They also rejected a personal appeal from Arsen'ev, who visited the strikers encamped at the tram depot on the evening of July 18. He coupled a promise of complete satisfaction of strike demands if they went back to work with a warning that Cossack troops would be called in if they continued to block the movement of the trams.

By this time the tramway strike had merged with the general strike and the city administration was under instructions to impose order in the city by force if necessary. True to Arsen'ev's word the dreaded Cossacks appeared; strikers who had lain on the tram tracks were removed bodily and beaten. Several strikers were hospitalized; two were said to have died. On July 19 the streetcars were again in full operation, operated by new complements of conductors and coachmen and with policemen aboard as escorts.[23]

22. *Revoliutsionnaia Rossiia*, no. 30; "Dva dokumenta," p. 254; Dzhervis, p. 50.
23. *Revoliutsionnaia Rossiia*, no. 30; *Iskra*, no. 46; *Posledniia izvestiia*, no. 140;

Accompanying the walkout of the port workers, tram line employees, and railway shop workers were strikes at individual workshops and plants. Garthering momentum and unchecked by force or the threat of force the strike wave swept through Odessa until the city's entire machinery of life ground to a halt. The workers' demands almost everywhere were solely economic in character and not excessive. In some cases factory owners found it expedient to implement without hesitation the improvements demanded by their workers.[24] Many manufacturers, however, were unwilling to accede and made no overt effort to prevent their employees from walking off the job. In the French-controlled shoe polish and tin plant of Jacquot (Zhako), for example, Popov explained to the workers that the management was financially incapable of meeting their wage demands. If they wished to quit work they should give the proper two weeks' notice; otherwise they would be legally subject to dismissal after three days' leave. The workers, however, were in no mood to compromise. When Popov finished speaking the cry went up, "We do not agree! Everyone leave work!" and all 360 left the plant to join the ever growing mass of strikers.[25]

On July 15 work was halted at the railway stations, the quarries, the French-controlled Waltouch (Val'tukh) tin plant (250 workers), the tannery of the Southern Russian Association (150 workers), and the cement plant of the Southern Russian Society (80 of its 130 workers). Popov and two district factory inspectors visited plant after plant in a futile attempt to prevent the strikes from spreading. In most cases Popov found the workers willing to listen to reason. Most were not inclined to leave work but eventually joined the strikers under pressure from organized gangs of agitators. At the Waltouch plant, without prior notice or presentation of demands, the workmen simply did not appear after dinner. By midday Popov realized "the utter impossibility of visiting all the plants and taking

*Osvobozhdenie,* supplement to no. 4(28); *Vseobshchaia stachka* p. 105; *Odesskii listok,* July 20, 1903; *Times,* Aug. 7, 1903; "Zapiska Lopukhina," p. 392; Dzhervis, p. 50; *Russkiia vedomosti,* July 21, 1903; Sauvaire to Delcassé, Aug. 14, 1903, n.s.

24. "Dva dokumenta," p. 253. Lopukhin reported that such was the panic among the factory owners and other employers that it took only two to three persons from the crowd to compel the workers to leave their posts, and the owners would submit to their employees' demands ("Zapiska Lopukhina," p. 391).

25. "Dva dokumenta," pp. 252–54; Kristalovskii, p. 148; *Listovki revoliutsionnykh,* p. 463.

any measures to terminate or forestall disorders, besides advice, instructions, and approval given by telephone."[26]

Emboldened by their effectiveness in persuading fellow workers to join the strike movement without incurring repressive measures from the responsible city officials, the strikers pressed onward with the goal of completely emptying every factory, workshop, and store of its work force. The goal was reached the next day; "during July 16 and 17 the whole city was at the mercy of the crowd."[27] A catalogue of plants closed by strikes on July 16 is not available. Popov's report, incomplete by his own admission, included the following establishments (with figures on the number of employees): a tannery (150), a cement plant (130), the Dubskii chemical plant (38), the Shestopal chemical plant (15), a jute factory (1,200), the Aris cork plant (800), the Kravovshchinskii mechanical plant (60), the Shel' agricultural machine plant (90), and the tea weighing plants of Kuznetsov (160) and K. and S. Popov (400). Social-democratic sources listed strikes beginning on that day at macaroni plants, a rope yard, a candy factory, and a tin plant. Joining the movement too were warehouse workers, employees of small privately owned workshops, and employees of state and municipal enterprises.[28]

In the course of the day the workers congregated at various meeting places in the industrial districts of the city to exchange news of the strikes, listen to speakers, and discuss strike demands. At the Kursaki grove in the Mikhailovskii district, where a group of strikers estimated at from 300 to 600 congregated, mounted police appeared in mid-afternoon and dispersed the crowd, one of the few occasions in the early stages of the general strike in which the authorities decisively intervened. The crowd quickly responded by marching to the district police headquarters to seek the release of comrades who had been arrested, but they were driven off by Cossacks.[29]

At the Rubov gardens in the Bugaevka suburb, the most popular gathering place at the height of the July days, strikers began congregating in mid-morning on July 16, their number swelling to 7,000 or 8,000 by early afternoon. Speakers from both the Independent Party and the Odessa Committee of the R.S.D.R.P.

26. "Dva dokumenta," p. 255; see also *Listovki revoliutsionnykh,* pp. 462–63.

27. "Zapiska Lopukhina," p. 391.

28. "Dva dokumenta," p. 255; *Vseobshchaia stachka,* p. 103; *Listovki revoliutsionnykh,* pp. 463–64.

29. Sushkin, p. 19; *Iskra,* no. 46; "Dva dokumenta," p. 255; Achkanov, p. 65; *Iskrovskie organizatsii na Ukraine,* pp. 320, 322.

harangued the crowd. Independent orators attacked the Social Democrats as enemies of the working class and the tsarist government. Socialist speakers, in an effort to raise the strikers' political consciousness, impressed upon them the need to draft common demands and emphasized the interrelationship between economic and political struggle. The Social Democrats departed from the gardens around four P. M. to join their comrades in the suburb of Peresyp'. An hour later the crowd left the gardens and began wandering from factory to factory in the neighborhood, forcing each to shut down.

Police in small numbers were present at the meeting in the Rubov gardens, passively observing the proceedings except for the arrest of one speaker. Cossack forces stationed near several factories remained passive as the crowd forced each enterprise in its path to shut down. Apparently the Cossacks were under orders merely to protect property, for they made no attempt to clear the streets, a duty for which they were generally employed and had a fearful reputation. More significant were reports that the Cossacks listened sympathetically to political agitators who urged them to join the striking masses.

Between 6 and 7 P. M. the crowd quietly began to disperse homeward after agreeing to reassemble the next morning in the Rubov gardens. Meanwhile the Odessa Committee began feverish preparations for a hugh political demonstration the following day. Messengers were dispatched throughout the working-class sections of the city to spread news of the meeting scheduled for the Rubov gardens; at committee headquarters work went on through the night; red banners were made ready, themes and sequence of speeches mapped out, leaflets and pamphlets taken out of hidden storage, all in preparation for the day's momentous events.[30]

## Independents versus Socialists

The strike movement crested on Thursday, July 17. A clear and full picture of the day's happenings cannot be discerned from available accounts. What appears unmistakable, however, is first, that the masses never came under the control of any single group or party, and, second, that much of what transpired followed no preconceived plan.

The mood of the crowd, as on the previous day, was peaceful. The

30. *Iskra,* no. 46; no. 47 (Sept. 1, 1903); no. 49 (Oct. 1, 1903); Sushkin, pp. 19–20; "Dva dokumenta," p. 256.

strikers' demands were based on economic grievances peculiar to individual enterprises and professions and couched in such a way that all could understand the tangible benefits their fulfillment would bring. Socialist speakers throughout the day appeared at mass meetings in an attempt to convey their political message, but without any significant success.

Early on July 17 throngs of workers began to gather in the Rubov and Diukov gardens on the outskirts of the city. Speakers from the Odessa Committee were first to address the crowds, which grew ever larger as the morning wore on. At the Rubov gardens, where the workers arrived in a festive mood, the crowd listened politely as social-democratic orators endeavored to persuade it that a revolution was necessary to reach the economic goals the strikers had set for themselves. Socialist agitators, however, were never able to rivet the attention of the multitude on any but economic goals: "among the masses at this time the desire to formulate their own particular demands was dominant," an Odessa correspondent wrote in explanation to *Iskra*. [31]

Action, not words, pleased the restless crowd, parts of which at the slightest call would wander off to shut down nearby plants still in operation. The Social Democrats, moreover, had to contend with aggressive opposition from the Independents. Spokesmen from the Independent Labor Committee addressed large groups of workers, stressing the need to keep the focus of the strike on purely economic goals. Now and then followers of the Independent Party and the Odessa Committee fought each other for the speaker's platform, disrupting the orderliness of the meeting and causing some workers to wander away in disgust.

The Independents' point of view fitted the mood and aspirations of the strikers more closely than did the political line taken by the socialists. Some workers, displeased with the political orientation of the gathering, crossed themselves and departed. One of them was heard to say: "Lord, how is it possible to get along without him [the tsar]; and what does it got to do with him? We have to fight against the capitalists but not the tsar." [32] Expressions of opposition arose from the crowd when followers of the Odessa Committee began

31. *Iskra*, no. 46.
32. *Iskra*, no. 49. In September 1903, Emel'ian [Iaroslavskii] wrote from Odessa to the editors of *Iskra* about publishing a brochure or leaflet for the Odessa workers on the connection between economic and political struggle. "In view of the vague notion

chanting revolutionary songs. The crowd's negative reaction to any mention of politics were described in *Iskra* by one of the social-democratic speakers at the meeting: "At this time the influence of the 'Independents' began to tell noticeably. Cries were heard: 'Why do they have to speak about politics?' 'We didn't come here to sing!' 'We don't need the [Social] Democrats.'"[33] The socialists had thus failed in their first opportunity to seize control of the striking masses. "The disorganizing work of the 'Independents' on the one hand, and inadequate knowledge of the mood of the masses on the part of the committee, on the other, are the two basic causes for the fact that the Social Democrats failed to control the meeting," another *Iskra* correspondent acknowledged.[34]

By mid-morning the crowd had swollen to such proportions that many were out of the range of the speakers' voices. Having spent three to four hours in the park, the crowd was restless; temporarily attentive to a socialist orator discussing the formulation of their economic demands, the crowd, some 8,000 to 10,000 strong, soon lost interest and began to leave the gardens.

Once more the workers began their peregrinations, first compelling all enterprises in Peresyp' to close before heading for the port area. Another crowd of several thousand, which had been meeting since early morning in the Diukov gardens, marched toward the inner city with the same intent. Ever increasing in number with the accretion of newly enlisted strikers and sympathetic members of the general public, the crowd reached 40,000 to 50,000 at its height. Throughout it remained bent on peaceful action. Although in some cases the call for cessation of work was met passively by the work force and with opposition by management, the strikers succeeded in emptying the plants of their workmen without recourse to force or destruction of property. A large police contingent as well as patrols of soldiers and Cossacks, which since early morning had benevolently stood in the back-

---

about the role of the tsar which exists in some strata of the ignorant masses—which became apparent, by the way, in rather typical cries of 'Down with the autocracy, but keep the tsar'—it is desirable to publish a brochure, in which would be explained, on the one hand, the principles of autocracy and, on the other, the role of the personality of the tsar" (*Perepiska V. I. Lenina i rukovodimykh*, p. 376).

33. *Iskra*, no. 46; Achkanov, p. 66.

34. *Iskra*, no. 46. Another participant admitted: "we social democrats lost the leadership of the masses" (*ibid.*).

ground near the park, convoyed the crowd along its line of march, and silently stood aside as agitators from the Odessa Committee harangued the strikers on political themes and distributed socialist literature.[35]

As the huge crowd reached the interior of the city it split into several large groups, each roaming the city and halting work wherever a retail shop, plant, or workshop was found open. Hotels, restaurants, pubs, coffee shops, barber shops, bakeries, and butcher shops were invaded and their employees persuaded to join those thronging the streets. By nightfall the strikers had reached their goal of a "complete stoppage in the city of all trade and industrial activity."[36] The city was bereft of bread, meat, and other essential foodstuffs—patrols of workmen stood guard day and night at the bakeries to keep them closed—electric light, rail and ship transportation, and newspapers. In the words of an eyewitness: "on this day the city, one could say, was found in the hands of the workers."[37]

While the crowd went its way unrestrained in its control of the city, the Independents were gathering at committee headquarters in Peresyp'. Shaevich, who sometime earlier had reported being ill, did not appear at the meeting, which was presided over by his assistant. The Independents had earlier sent emissaries to all sections of the city to urge the workers in every factory and workshop to choose representatives to confer with the committee. When these delegates assembled they formulated common demands for the strikers; resolutions were passed calling for a 20 percent wage increase and an eight-hour work day. The latter resolution was passed only under strong pressure from socialist speakers who had penetrated the meeting hall. The Independents were firmly resolved to give battle to their enemy, for once the Social Democrats had left the hall the delegates unanimously pledged themselves to clear the parks of any socialist speakers who attempted to address the masses the following day.[38]

35. *Osvobozhdenie*, supplement to no. 4 (28); *Iskra*, nos. 45 and 46; *Revoliutsionnaia Rossiia*, no. 29; *Times*, Aug. 4, 1903; Sauvaire to Delcassé, July 30, 1903, n. s.

36. "Dva dokumenta," p. 256; see also Bukhbinder, "Nezavisimaia," p. 283; Achkanov, p. 65; Sauvaire to Delcassé, July 31, 1903, n.s.; Heenan to Loomis, Aug. 3, 1903, n.s.

37. *Osvobozhdenie*, no. 4 (28); see also Sauvaire to Delcassé, July 30, 1903, n.s.; *Times*, Aug. 18, 1903.

38. *Iskra*, nos. 46 and 49; *Posledniia izvestiia*, Aug. 17, 1903.

Meanwhile, bands of strikers began to head back to the Diukov and Rubov gardens where from about 5 to 8 P. M. they listened to speeches. The day's activities again ended with a decision to reassemble the following morning; "only late at night did the mass of workers, who had spent the whole day on their feet and without food, disperse to their homes in complete exhaustion but in a delightful...utopian mood."[39] Journalists caught up in the day's events unanimously reported on the buoyancy of the masses: "All were joyful, shared everything they had, rolls and water; all were comrades and believed, it seemed, they would achieve better times."[40]

Despite anarchy in the streets the day had passed without violence.[41] Credit for this state of affairs must above all go to the Odessa workers. They maintained strict self-discipline, avoiding acts of destruction and looting while firmly in command of the city. Rarely have the Russian masses exhibited such self-restraint when freed from strong bonds of authority. Fortunately, too, the Odessa authorities in their confusion had not resorted to force. "One can say without exaggeration, and it is admitted even by the Odessa city governor himself, that during the course of July 16 and 17 the whole city was at the mercy of the crowd, which did not behave violently only because there was no need for violent behavior," Lopukhin concluded after personal investigation in Odessa at the end of July.[42] The passivity of the Odessa authorities may well have convinced many strikers that the local administration sympathized with their interests and consequently would not interfere in peacefully conducted economic strikes, as the Independents had asserted. The strikers also met with no hostility from the Odessa middle class, part of which made no effort to hide its strong sympathy with the grievances of the workers.[43] Finally, the vital role of the Independents in the maintenance of order cannot be discounted. Not only was their presence felt in restraining the workers and keeping the socialists from turning the general

39. *Osvobozhdenie,* supplement to no. 4 (28).
40. *Iskra,* no. 49.
41. *Times,* Aug. 4, 1903.
42. "Zapiska Lopukhina," p. 391; see also the *Times, ibid.*
43. *Revoliutsionnaia Rossiia,* no. 29; I. V. Bortnikov, "Vseobshchaia stachka 1903 goda rabochikh g. Odessy," Odes'kii derzhavnii pedagogichnii institut im. K. D. Ushins'kogo, *Naukovi zapiski,* 8 (1947), 68; *Posledniia izvestiia,* no. 141 (Aug. 14, 1903).

strike into a mass political demonstration, but their movement, designed to discipline the working class to seek a peaceful, nonpolitical outlet for its grievances, was vindicated in the July days. In the words of an eyewitness: "On July 17, when along the streets moved a numberless crowd of workers, in the camps there were eight hundred soldiers in all; the arms and powder warehouses were extremely poorly guarded. If at that time the crowd was not so "economically" inclined, [if] at that time the "Independents" had not set the tone—the workers might have taken advantage of the confusion of the authorities and taken possession of the whole city."[44]

Yet the situation remained highly alarming to the authorities. Early on the morning of July 18 the French consul in Odessa telegraphed the Quai d'Orsay: "General strike since yesterday. Maritime service and railroads halted. No more bread. Situation grave. Conflict between strikers and troops feared." At mid-morning he telegraphed again: "Situation more and more serious. French establishments menaced. Authorities declared themselves powerless. All is feared."[45]

The Odessa Committee of the R.S.D.R.P. was determined to utilize the mass meetings on that day for political agitation with the goal of "direct control of the strike."[46] It planned to take the initiative in formulating the common demands of the strikers, presuming that as a consequence, recognition would be accorded its leadership. The committee intended to gain an advantage over the Independents and its other rivals by scheduling a meeting of its supporters at 7 A. M. in the Rubov gardens to map strategy for the mass rally expected later that morning.

The turning point in the general strike came on Friday, July 18. The morning began with a repetition of the previous day's events. In the Diukov gardens a huge crowd variously estimated at from 15,000 to 50,000 at its height began gathering at 7 A. M.; at the same hour a crowd of similar proportions began to gather at the Rubov gardens.[47] The Independents and the socialists again took to the

44. *Revoliutsionnaia Rossiia*, no. 29.
45. Sauvaire to Delcassé, July 31, 1903, n. s.
46. *Iskra*, no. 46.
47. Descriptions of the meetings in the Diukov gardens are found in *Posledniia izvestiia*, no. 140; *Osvobozhdenie*, supplement to no. 4 (28). The day's events at the Rubov gardens are described in *Iskra*, nos. 45 and 46; *Revoliutsionnaia Rossiia*, no. 29; Sushkin, p. 7.

battlefield; at times they descended to fisticuffs, the Independents displaying greater aggressiveness than previously. At the Diukov gardens the Independents arrived early and held the field against their opponents until the Social Democrats reached sufficient numbers to defy the Independents' threat of force. Speakers representing various political factions thereupon addressed the crowd despite interruptions by the Independents who occasionally attempted to seize and maul political agitators. The Independents implored the masses to keep strike demands within economic limits without committing themselves to "any definite program" and to pursue only "the instinctive motive to improve their material position."[48]

At the Rubov gardens the Independents stole a march on their rivals by appearing before the time scheduled for the meeting of social-democratic organizers. They stood alertly on guard around the outer perimeter of the gardens prepared to use force, if necessary, to prevent their enemies from penetrating the barrier. Socialist orators who had made their way inside were forcibly removed and threatened with deliverance to the police should they dare return. "This broke up the ranks of the Soc[ial] Dem[ocrats]," and the meeting planned by the Odessa Committee never did transpire.[49] Only after a considerable force of sympathetic workers had been gathered did socialist speakers, still with great difficulty, dare to mount the rostrum and address the crowd. Agitators from the Odessa Committee who harangued the workers from the branches of a tree were greeted from the audience below with cries of "Down with the socialists!" and "We don't need politics!"[50] One socialist speaker was dragged from the tree by Independent partisans; only after a long scuffle were his party comrades able to rescue him. Undaunted, socialist orators continued their efforts to win over the masses but with even poorer results than on the previous day.

Harassment by the Independents, the unwieldly size of the throng, and the separation of the strikers into groups all militated against any speaker's capturing the minds of the assembled masses. The mood of the crowd, moreover, was alien to political agitation; the distribution of leaflets by the Rabochaia Volia social-democratic

48. *Osvobozhdenie*, supplement to no. 4 (28).
49. *Iskra*, no. 46; see also Sushkin, pp. 30–32.
50. *Iskra*, no. 46; see also Achkanov, p. 66.

faction "gave rise to strong animosity in the crowd," reported an *Iskra* correspondent.[51] The socialists did not have the field to themselves; the Independents also obtained a hearing for their views, once again calling upon the strikers to shun politics and focus their attention on economic grievances.[52]

### The Dissolution of the General Strike

Up to this point the Odessa authorities had shown extraordinary restraint. On July 18, however, the military was unleashed. That morning 10,000 copies of a declaration bearing the signature of General Arsen'ev were posted throughout the city, warning that any further infringement of order would be immediately suppressed by force. The declaration was also printed the same day in the official organ of the Odessa administration, *Vedomosti Odesskogo Gradonachal'stva*, the sole newspaper functioning during the general strike.[53]

The first move by soldiers and Cossacks was triggered by the distribution of social-democratic leaflets at the Diukov gardens; the attack was thus directed against socialist agitators and not the workers, many of whom either remained in the gardens to continue their discussions or departed for the inner city. Since the crowd put up little or no resistance the Cossacks resorted to force only sporadically; consequently there were few casualties. The socialists, assuming that the workers were enraged by the Cossack assault, felt that the golden opportunity for a mass political demonstration was at hand; marching with the workers along the road to the city they unfurled red banners with party slogans and chanted revolutionary songs.[54]

The course of events was much the same at the Rubov gardens. There the Cossacks and soldiers, present throughout the mass meeting, tightly surrounded the gardens. A group of 2,000 or 3,000 workers bent on marching to the inner city charged at the soldiers and was able to break the cordon. After a preliminary warning to disperse was given by Golovin, the Cossacks and soldiers swooped

51. *Iskra,* no. 46; see also no. 45 and Sushkin, p. 33.
52. "K istorii vseobshchei stachki," p. 113.
53. "Dva dokumenta," pp. 258–59; *Vseobshchaia stachka,* pp. 99, 103, 105; *Iskra,* no. 45; *Odesskii listok,* July 20, 1903; *Russkiia vedomosti,* July 21, 1903; *Times,* Aug. 6, 1903; Sauvaire to Delcassé, July 31, 1903, n.s.
54. *Posledniia izvestiia,* no. 140; *Osvobozhdenie,* supplement to no. 4 (28).

down on the crowd, driving it off from the gardens. "Disorder and vacillation gave a relative handful of Cossacks and soldiers the opportunity to drive off 50,000 workers," an observer commented.[55] The attack lacked the ferocity for which the Cossacks were dreaded. Had the workers defiantly resisted the Cossack force the outcome might have been tragic. Had the crowd tried to win over the Cossacks, whom observers believed were sympathetic to the strikers, it might have peacefully disarmed them and created a revolutionary situation. But the strike movement remained focused on economic goals.[56]

Driven off from the gardens large numbers of workers gathered in columns and headed by different routes for the heart of the city, followed by the Cossacks. Along the route socialists staged political demonstrations, distributing leaflets, unfurling red flags, and chanting the *Marseillaise*. As on the previous day, the masses were self-disciplined and determined not to give way to looting and disorder. Proud of having transcended national devisiveness in forging a united labor front the marchers assured tradesmen on the route they need not bolt their doors: "Do not fear, do not fear, it is not a Kishinev [pogrom] for you; we want quite a different thing; among us there are neither Jews nor Russians; we are all workers; it is equally burdensome for all of us."[57]

The Cossacks eventually broke up the political demonstrations, but again without their wonted ferocity. No effort was made to pursue the demonstrators, the soldiers frequently looking aside as they fled. A few soldiers were reportedly persuaded to hand over their rifles to the crowd. The Cossacks and soldiers, who for several days had observed the strike from close quarters, "undoubtedly underwent the influence of the strike agitation which gripped the entire lower class of the Odessa population."[58] Arrests were made, although their number was small considering the magnitude of the strike.

By eventide the streets had been cleared; detachments of Cossacks and soldiers patrolled the city and the industrial suburbs. Work in the port was renewed that evening, a clear sign that the back of the general strike had been broken. The declaration of the city

55. *Iskra*, no. 46; see also Achkanov, p. 66; *Soiuz metallistov v Odesse*, pp. 21–22.
56. *Revoliutsionnaia Rossiia*, no. 29.
57. *Iskra*, no. 45.
58. *Revoliutsionnaia Rossiia*, no. 29; *Iskra*, no. 45.

governor, bolstered by the omnipresence of soldiers and Cossacks ready to enforce its terms, had the intended effect.

On the following day, July 19, the economic life of the city was slowly resumed with a minimum of overt force. Only in the aforementioned case of the tramway coachmen and conductors were brutal measures taken by the Cossacks to restore order. A group of workers bent on shutting the few remaining bakeries and butcher shops still open for business were surrounded by troops and arrested. A good part of the city, however, still lay idle; Odessa remained without newspapers, railway communications, and sufficient bread and meat; Socialist agitators continued to meet in the public parks for the next few days to discuss further strategy, a futile gesture in view of the strikers' return to work.[59]

By July 23 nearly the entire labor force was back at work as Odessa took on its normal appearance.[60] Through the streets where a throng of 50,000 workers had roamed traffic now went its usual way; shops and factories made idle by the strike were back in full production. For the better part of two days Odessa had witnessed anarchy in its streets. The strikers had submitted to the order of the city governor and dispersed without defiance and without having received promises of major economic concessions.

59. "K istorii vseobshchei stachki," p. 85; "Dva dokumenta," p. 259; *Iskra*, no. 49; *Revoliutsionnaia Rossiia*, no. 29.
60. *Vseobshchaia stachka*, p. 105; "Dva dokumenta," pp. 259, 263.

# CHAPTER 13

# The Authorities,
# the Socialists, and
# the General Strike

The Odessa authorities followed no logically thought-out plan of action during the July days. Indeed, several puzzling questions remain to be answered about their performance. Why had they delayed so long in suppressing the strike when it was manifestly clear to all that the strikers had broken the law? Why did they finally resort to force after the strikers had demonstrated remarkable self-restraint, neither assaulting the police nor destroying private or public property?

General Arsen'ev, upon whose shoulders rested primary responsibility for the maintenance of law and order in the city, was unduly slow in dispatching troops to clear the streets of strikers. Whether, as Lopukhin charged, he panicked and became ineffective in the midst of the confusion or whether he exercised prudence in view of the peaceful mood of the crowd and the inadequate number of troops directly at hand, as he stated in his defense, Arsen'ev did fail to deal promptly with the street demonstrations in the repressive manner prescribed for state officials.[1] Street disorders were not unheard of in Odessa. A secret military order of April 7, 1903, had anticipated just such an eventuality as the July days by providing that a special detail of the Odessa garrison be constantly in readiness for immediate summons by the city governor; the order included specific plans for the occupation of the city.[2]

While the July general strike was in its early stages Arsen'ev had at his command 750 men: one company of foot soldiers, a Cossack squadron, the regular police, and the guards that patrolled the port

1. "Zapiska Lopukhina," pp. 391–92. Arsen'ev's defense of his actions is found in his report to Plehve, July 28, 1903 (*Vseobshchaia stachka,* p. 102).
2. *Iskra,* no. 41 (June 1, 1903); *Times,* July 16, 1903.

area. The largest part of the Odessa garrison, including most of its Cossack troops, was stationed some distance from the city at summer quarters. On July 15 Arsen'ev requested the immediate dispatch of the Eighth Don Cossack regiment from Tiraspol' but was at first refused because of an infectious illness in the camp and the imminent visit of the inspector-general of the cavalry. The following evening, on Arsen'ev's orders, four companies of infantrymen were transferred from their summer quarters to Odessa with the assistance of General A. V. Kaul'bars. Another eleven companies opportunely arrived toward the evening of July 17, when the general strike was at its height.[3]

Lopukhin charged Arsen'ev with irresponsibility during the July days; he had failed to protect workers who wanted to continue on their jobs from coercion by the strikers and had not taken prompt measures to ring the industrial suburbs with troops to thwart the occupation of the city. Arsen'ev and Popov, in turn, laid the blame for the general strike at the feet of police officials. Golovin, they alleged, failed to take resolute action against the crowd as it roamed through the city streets. Instead, the police abetted the strikers' goal of a general work stoppage, advising factory owners to avoid violence by releasing their employees from work. Golovin, it was charged, failed to execute an order he received from the city governor's office to prevent the mass meeting scheduled for July 17 in the suburb of Bugaevka. If the orders had proved unenforceable, the gathering was to have been surrounded and the strikers seized and transported to places of detention. The police, however, pleaded there were insufficient forces to carry out the order, and instead dispersed the crowd, thus allegedly allowing the strike movement to gather force. Similarly the police were charged with failing to fulfill Arsen'ev's command to "take the most drastic measures" to preserve order in the city and the port; at the height of the strike, groups of strikers were able to board the merchant ships and remove their crews.[4]

The Odessa authorities were strongly divided in their opinion of

3. *Vseobshchaia stachka,* pp. 99, 102–3; "Zapiska Lopukhina," pp. 391–92; "Dva dokumenta," pp. 254–55; *Revoliutsionnaia Rossiia,* no. 31 (Sept. 1, 1903); *Odesskii listok,* Aug. 5, 1903; Sauvaire to Delcassé, July 30, 1903, n.s.; Heenan to Loomis, Aug. 3, 1903, n.s.

4. *Vseobshchaia stachka,* pp. 103–4; "Dva dokumenta," pp. 255–59; "Zapiska Lopukhina," p. 392; *Revoliutsionnaia Rossiia,* no. 31.

the Independents' conduct during the general strike. Captain Vasil'ev in general supported the Independents and tended to believe Shaevich's avowal that they participated in strikes only to keep the revolutionary parties from gaining control of the masses. Popov, long an opponent of Shaevich, and Osetrov, director of the office of the city governor, upon whom Arsen'ev depended for advice during the days of crisis, were the Independents' chief critics. In Popov's view, the militant labor movement Shaevich had nurtured broke adrift during the July days, giving the antigovernment parties the opportunity they had awaited to revolutionize the masses. The workers had been blindly led by the Independents' teachings into believing the righteousness and higher sanction of strike action. Many by their own admission, "were led astray by false assurances of their leaders, who promised them complete impunity and suggested that both the army and the civilian authorities would be on their side since they had supposedly received an order from above to assist in the improvement of their economic position."[5]

On July 12, Arsen'ev telegraphed Plehve to report the outbreak of a strike among the sailors and stokers of the merchant fleet; his information indicated the Independents had instigated the strike. An Odessa police inspector also cited Zhimoedov, Shaevich's assistant, as recognized leader of the striking sailors and stokers.[6] Captain Vasil'ev at this point was also skeptical toward Shaevich's claim that the Independents "only took part in the strike to restrain others" and felt that the Independent Party was directly implicated in the strike. Hundreds of strikers milled around Independent headquarters where they received instructions. "Shaevich leads the strike," Vasil'ev complained, "but does not speak to me about it."[7]

When this information reached the Ministry of Interior, which had shielded the Independent Party, Lopukhin telegraphed the Odessa mayor that Plehve demanded the arrest and banishment of the Independents if factual information existed that the Odessa strikes were the result of their agitation. By this time (July 14) Vasil'ev had altered his position and supported the Independents. "The sole restraining element among the strikers are the Independents," Vasil'ev telegraphed the Department of Police the following day,

5. "Dva dokumenta," p. 259.
6. *Vseobshchaia stachka*, p. 90; Shlosberg, p. 66.
7. Vasil'ev to Lopukhin, July 13, 1903 (Shlosberg, p. 67); see also Bukhbinder, "Nezavisimaia," p. 233; Vovchik, p. 131.

adding that Arsen'ev therefore had concluded "it is not now desirable to arrest them."[8] Thus for the time no action was taken on Plehve's order, and the Independents' involvement in the July days continued.

Further dispatches from Odessa indicating that a general strike was developing caused Plehve to demand immediate and firm measures by the local authorities to restore order. On July 17, the day the strikers were in command of the city, Plehve telegraphed the mayor and city governor "to take the most energetic measures against persons who incite to strike, including equally the Independents, and establish order on the streets even if by the use of arms."[9] Official opinion in Odessa was divided as to whether the Independents should be arrested and banished. Arsen'ev, on the basis of Plehve's telegram, was prepared to order Shaevich's arrest and banishment. Vasil'ev, in a telegram to Lopukhin the same day, vigorously championed the Independents. In his view the Odessa authorities were mistaken in thinking that the Independents had brought about the general strike. On the contrary, the Independents and "especially Shaevich, hold the strikers in check, otherwise there would have long since been a violent upheaval." The arrest of the Independent leaders at that crucial moment would gravely undermine efforts to keep the strike within orderly bounds: "In view of the agitated mood of the working masses over which the revolutionary organizations are now trying to spread their influence, the activity of the Independents as a moderating influence, restraining the workers, is recognized as desirable by me; their arrest and deportation can only decrease the chances for the maintenance of order and tranquility in the city by the authorities."[10]

The question of administrative action against the Independents was examined by a special commission established by the city governor to frame measures for restoring order in the city. The commission, chaired by Arsen'ev, included Popov, Zelenyi, Osetrov, the local procurators, and the chief of the Odessa gendarmery,

8. Vasil'ev to the Department of Police, July 15, 1903 (*Vseobshchaia stachka*, p. 92; Shlosberg and Shul'man, p. 130). In a message to Zubatov on the same day, Vasil'ev maintained he had taken control of the Independents and was directing them (Bukhbinder, "Nezavisimaia," p. 234).

9. Bukhbinder, *ibid.*, p. 233; "Dva dokumenta," p. 259.

10. Bukhbinder, *ibid.*, pp. 234–35; Los', pp. 252–53; "Dva dokumenta," p. 255. Zhimoedov was arrested on July 17, but released the same day on orders of the gendarme chief (Bortnikov, p. 77).

Bessonov. Golovin and Vasil'ev were also members but did not attend all the meetings and generally held views contrary to the majority.

At a meeting on the morning of July 18, from which Osetrov was absent, the commission recognized that the Independents at the moment were a moderating influence and proposed that Shaevich be invited to meet with Vasil'ev and urged to exert his utmost to restrain the masses. Apparently the decision of the commission was reversed through Osetrov's influence the same day and the activity of the Independents officially ordered suspended, for late that evening, after conferring with Vasil'ev, Shaevich addressed a large Independent rally, announcing the temporary suspension of the party.[11] The Odessa Independent center was thus suppressed at the moment when its members were joined in combat with the revolutionaries. The next day, July 19, it was reported that Independent followers had physically assaulted socialist agitators; no large gathering took place in the city on that day due to the counteragitation of the leaders of the Independent unions.[12]

Arsen'ev, determined to end Shaevich's influence, requested Plehve's permission to deport the Independent leader from Odessa. Plehve immediately ordered Shaevich arrested and sent to the Vologda governor for detention in Ust'sysol'sk *uezd* (district). On Saturday, July 19, Arsen'ev told Golovin to have Shaevich arrested and banished.[13] Members of the Independent unions visiting the headquarters of the Independent Labor Committee that day found a note posted on the door stating that "meetings will not take

11. "Dva dokumenta," pp. 256, 260; Shlosberg, p. 68; Bukhbinder, "Nezavisimaia," p. 233.

12. *Vseobshchaia stachka*, p. 99; Shlosberg and Shul'man, p. 139.

13. Bukhbinder, "Nezavisimaia," p. 235; "Dva dokumenta," p. 256; *Iskra*, no. 47 (Sept. 1, 1903); *Vseobshchaia stachka*, pp. 101–2; Shlosberg and Shul'man, p. 140; "K istorii Zubatovshchiny," p. 93. Shaevich's case was examined by a special conference, which sentenced him to banishment in Siberia under police surveillance for five years. In accordance with the Imperial Manifesto of August 11, 1904, he was released with the proviso that he was not to reside in Odessa or the capital for the duration of his sentence. This limitation was lifted after Shaevich petitioned the Department of Police for permission to rejoin his family in Odessa and agreed to the department's demand that he foreswear agitation toward legalization of the labor movement. Information on Shaevich and his outlook while he was in prison is found in Bukhbinder, pp. 224–28, 235–41; *Osvobozhdenie*, no. 55 (Sept. 2, 1904); "K istorii Zubatovshchiny," p. 93; G. Lelevich, "D-r. Shaevich v tiur'me," *Krasnaia letopis'*, 1922, no. 5, pp. 392–93; An. Gol'dman, "Dve popravki," *Krasnaia letopis'*, 1923, no. 8, pp. 250–51.

place henceforward until there is an order from the local administration."[14] On the same day the Department of Police, on Plehve's order, clarified the position of the higher authorities toward the Independent Party in a communication to Arsen'ev:

The "Independents" originally were opposed to any political tendency and had as goal the attainment of an improvement in the position of the working class on the basis of informing the authorities about the pressing needs of the workers, but strikes and coercion, to which the "Independents" subsequently proceeded, being prohibited and prosecuted by law, do not lose their illegal character because they were carried out by organizations which had originally set for themselves a goal desirable from the government's point of view. Therefore, the above-mentioned activities of the "Independents" are subject to prosecution just as are similar actions by other organizations. However, their activity aimed at spreading among the ranks of the workers ideas about the necessity of eliminating political tendencies in the labor movement, the establishment of mutual-aid funds, and the organization of talks on general education and professional matters, is not subject to prosecution.[15]

The suspension of the Independent unions was not accepted as final by either Shaevich or his followers. The port workers and sailors on July 28 sought permission of the city governor to hold further meetings and to keep their union functioning but were refused. In early August, Popov received information that workers in the Independent movement hoped for Shaevich's return to Odessa and the re-establishment of their unions. The Independent Party, however, had come to an end; the Odessa authorities, believing the Independents guilty of fomenting the general strike, feared the party's revival. "Such a union with an exclusively militant activity is inadmissible. The return of Shaevich is unthinkable."[16] So reported Popov to Petersburg, adding that Arsen'ev was in full accord.

## Petersburg Officialdom and the General Strike

The broad divergence of opinion among responsible Odessa officials during the July days was also found within the Ministry of Interior. During the strike Plehve stood for the application of force,

14. Bukhbinder, "Nezavisimaia," p. 284.
15. "K istorii Zubatovshchiny," p. 92.
16. *Revoliutsionnaia Rossiia*, no. 31 (Sept. 1, 1903); see also Bukhbinder, "Nezavisimaia," pp. 225, 236; "Dva dokumenta," p. 262; Sauvaire to Delcassé, Aug. 12, 1903, n. s.

Lopukhin for timely concessions. In fairness to Plehve it should be observed that his impression of events in Odessa was based on Arsen'ev's dispatches, which were more pessimistic about the threat of violence than Vasil'ev's reports to Lopukhin. Plehve, moreover, could not examine the Odessa general strike as an isolated phenomenon, for during July the ministry was flooded with reports of large-scale strikes in other southern industrial centers and port cities. An end to street disorders and the restoration of administrative authority were of the highest priority to Plehve, on whose shoulders lay ultimate responsibility for maintaining order throughout the empire. Working-class demands therefore were not to be considered while constituted authority was defied. Thus Plehve scolded city officials for negotiating with striking tram workers: "Your talks with the streetcar strikers, I consider a mistaken action, for with the presence of excesses by the crowd, one must show concern not about the workers but for the maintenance of order. In general I continue to find that the proper energy is not manifested. I approve in advance all drastic measures."[17]

Lopukhin's approach to events in Odessa differed radically. He was convinced that the situation in Odessa was not so desperate as Plehve was led to believe and as concerned with the frame of mind in which the strikers would resume work as with the re-establishment of order. "The most prompt satisfaction of the workers' just demands is desirable," he telegraphed Vasil'ev on July 15. Two days later, at the peak of the general strike, he telegraphed the mayor in the same vein: "In view of the presentation by the strikers of economic demands for the most part reasonable, their examination and the satisfaction of those which are just is desirable."[18] Almost at the same moment that Arsen'ev received Plehve's telegram pressing for decisive measures, a telegram arrived from Lopukhin suggesting a totally different course of action. Lopukhin's proposal was the only one offered that sought to conciliate the workers and end the strike without a legacy of bitterness against the government.

It would be desirable at once to print in a huge quantity and distribute among the strikers a declaration in the name of your excellency with a call for order and with an authorization to the strikers to discuss their needs by

17. Bukhbinder, "Nezavisimaia," pp. 233–34, and Shlosberg, p. 66; see also Sauvaire to Delcassé, Aug. 14, 1903, n. s.
18. Bukhbinder, "Nezavisimaia," p. 234.

occupational groupings, with an indication of the meeting places [and] the places for presenting declarations, with an indication of the administrative measures already taken for the satisfaction of the strikers' just demands. This will give those who are submitting to the regulation of the authorities an outlet from the violence of the masses and break them into small groups. It is urgently necessary to isolate the political agitators without delay.[19]

Arsen'ev chose Plehve's method of resolving the general strike; replying to Lopukhin, he held it was impossible to put the latter's proposal into effect since most strikers had left work without presenting demands "and the overwhelming majority of them were compelled to cease work by threats and compulsion."[20]

Little information is available on Zubatov's role during the July days. Evidently he had no authority to intervene and was restricted to the position of a passive observer as policy was made by Plehve and Lopukhin, his superiors. On July 12 he telegraphed Vasil'ev, requesting information on the activity of the Independents and proposing that the workers be urged to renew work if the Independents had initiated the Odessa strikes. The evidence available supports the conclusion that Zubatov for some time had been out of sympathy with the strike campaign conducted by the Independents. In an interview with Plehve in August 1903, he denied having advocated strikes and told of arguing with the leaders of the Independent Party over this issue. Once, in Gapon's presence, Zubatov burst out in anger upon receiving a telegram bearing news of the Odessa general strike, exclaiming: "Kill them all, the scoundrels!"[21] Zubatov nevertheless felt responsible for Shaevich's welfare; in October 1903, in forced retirement and awaiting the disposition of his own case, he petitioned the Department of Police to return Shaevich from banishment in Eastern Siberia.[22]

## The Balance Sheet: Strikers and Employers

Odessa had weathered the general strike without visible signs of destruction. What consequences, then, did the strike have for the Odessa working class which had exhibited extraordinary restraint

19. Shlosberg, p. 68; "Dva dokumenta," p. 260.
20. "Dva dokumenta," p. 260.
21. *Zapiski Georgiia Gapona*, p. 39; see also Bukhbinder, "Nezavisimaia," p. 234; Shlosberg and Shul'man, p. 129; "K istorii Zubatovshchiny," p. 95. For Zubatov's view of the general strike see Zubatov, "Zubatovshchina," p. 168.
22. "K istorii Zubatovshchiny," p. 98.

during its occupation of the city? For one thing, few were punished for their part in the strike as the city administration continued its lenient policy. On the basis of article 15 of the Statute on Reinforced Protection, 300 strikers were arrested and sentenced to three months or less in prison. Many were released shortly after their arrest on petition of their employers; the remainder were set free before the end of a month's imprisonment. Arsen'ev asked the chief of police for a list of individuals to be banished from Odessa for inciting the strike, but there is little indication that the order was executed.[23] According to an *Iskra* correspondent, however, a number of workers, most of whom had shunned or opposed political struggle, were banished to eastern Siberia. "It seemed that the government aimed at destroying the last spark of the workers' faith in the possibility of peaceful economic struggle," he commented.[24]

Shaevich in his last public appearance had suggested that workers at each factory immediately draw up their individual demands. On Saturday, July 19, and Monday, July 21, the workers presented petitions to Arsen'ev and the management of each enterprise. Improvements in hours and wages and more respectful treatment of employees were the predominant demands. There were a very few requests for profit sharing and for the work force to be consulted in the dismissal of employees, but even these demands bore no political overtones.

The manufacturers, gathering together several days after the conclusion of the general strike, expressed the opinion that their workers had been satisfied all along and had no demands to make; the demands before them thus were allegedly inspired by outsiders and therefore not subject to discussion.[25] Work at most Odessa factories and shops was renewed for the most part under the previous contractual conditions. In a few instances the workday was shortened and a small increase in wages was granted. Worst off were those workers whose employers took advantage of the law to

23. *Vseobshchaia stachka*, p. 105; "Dva dokumenta," p. 260; *Osvobozhdenie*, supplement to no. 4 (28) (Aug. 2, 1903); "Zapiska Lopukhina," p. 392; *Times*, Aug. 13 and 20, 1903; *Novoe vremia*, July 25, 1903; *Odesskii listok*, July 20, 22, 25, 27, 1903; S. A. Ratova [K. I. Zakharova-Tsederbaum], "Vseobshchaia stachka v 1903 godu na Kavkaze i Chernomorskom poberezh'e," *Byloe*, June 1907, p. 115.

24. Emel'ian [Iaroslavskii] to the editors of *Iskra*, Oct. 14, 1903, reprinted in "K 40-letiiu 'Iskry,'" *Krasnyi arkhiv*, 1940, no. 6(103), p. 34.

25. "Dva dokumenta," p. 260.

discharge them after an unauthorized absence for three days. The financial loss in wages to the Odessa workers during the strike was estimated at between 40,000 and 80,000 rubles.

The average worker thus gained little or nothing from the general strike.[26] The Independent Party's promise of material benefits from economic struggle was not fulfilled. The Independents blamed the socialists for the negligible results of the strike and its suppression; the working class had kept the strike within economic bounds until the socialists interfered, interjected politics, and compelled the authorities to intervene.[27]

The strike was costly to the factory owners and commercial interests. Popov estimated the loss of production at 600,000 rubles, without taking into consideration the spoilage of materials. Some entrepreneurs, already in a tight financial position, were forced to the verge of bankruptcy by the strike. The total loss to the city as a commercial and industrial center was estimated at two million rubles.[28]

Official dissatisfaction with the Odessa administration's handling of the strike led to the dismissal of General Arsen'ev and Golovin. Arsen'ev's dismissal undoubtedly stemmed from Lopukhin's report to Plehve of August 10. The report was based on extensive interviews in the last part of July with streetcar, railway, and factory workers and with local officials. The report was generally quite sympathetic to the interests and demands of the working class, whose extremely poor living and working conditions, Lopukhin concluded, drove them to participate in the strike. Summaries of his conversations with Odessa workers in the émigré socialist press

26. *Ibid.*, p. 261; Bortnikov, p. 116; *Posledniia izvestiia*, no. 141 (Aug. 14, 1903); *Times*, Aug. 13, 1903; "K 40-letiiu 'Iskry,'" pp. 33–35; Sauvaire to Delcassé, Aug. 3, 1903, n. s. The report of the Odessa Committee of Trade and Manufacture, citing information from the senior factory inspector, stated that 4,148 workers at 38 plants took a more or less active part in the general strike. "At 15 of these factories with 3,195 workers, work was renewed on the old basis; at 18 with 1,077 workers some minor concessions were made—the workday was shortened by a half hour to an hour [and] the pay of some workers was increased by 10 to 20 kopeks a day. During the disorders work was stopped by the crowd at 247 factories with 12,778 workers. At 230 of these factories having 11,645 workers, work was renewed in one to three days under the old conditions, and at 17 factories with 1,133 workers, partly in imitation of others, the workday was shortened by one-quarter to one-half hour, and wages of some workers were increased by 3 to 15 kopeks a day" (*Otchet odesskago komiteta*, pp. 129–30).

27. *Revoliutsionnaia Rossiia*, no. 29 (Aug. 5, 1903); Sushkin, p. 40; *Iskra*, no. 45 (Aug. 1, 1903); *Otchet odesskago komiteta*, p. 130.

28. "Dva dokumenta," p. 261; *Vseobshchaia stachka*, p. 5; *Times*, Aug. 15, 1903.

revealed that Lopukhin was primarily desirous of maintaining the workers' confidence in the benevolence of the autocracy toward them, for he promised groups of workers he would champion their case for economic improvements when he returned to Petersburg.[29]

The socialists claimed to be beneficiaries of the general strike. The local committee of the Party of Socialist Revolutionaries and the Odessa Committee of the R.S.D.R.P. had distributed leaflets among the strikers and sent speakers to address the mass rallies. Odessa correspondents for the émigré press agreed that the strike had raised the self-consciousness of the Odessa working class and made it more susceptible to the political approach of the revolutionary parties. *Iskra's* correspondent summed up the results of the strike as follows:

This strike showed the entire immense force of the workers. It relieved tension and revealed the mood and outlook of the laboring masses; it did very little in the sense of improving the economic life of the workers and very much for understanding those active forces in the masses, which, if not entirely concealed, were very vaguely visible. The strike brought the laboring masses in contact with various trends: it exposed the "Independents" to them, it showed them the autocratic government in all its bareness and thus drew them to an understanding of their true needs and tasks, having compelled the most inert to think about the position of the workers as a class in a country with autocratic oppression and violence.[30]

The Odessa Committee even more strongly emphasized the impact of the strike on the political maturation of the workers, who came to understand the inefficacy of economic strikes to change their lot. The strike, the committee concluded, "played a great role in regard to developing the self-consciousness of the Odessa proletariat. It brought the broad laboring masses together face to face with the sworn enemy of the Russian proletariat—the tsarist autocracy; it clearly showed that economic struggle cannot give anything except petty concessions, which we can retain [only] by means of hard, tireless struggle."[31]

The optimism of the socialists notwithstanding, the general strike

29. "Zapiska Lopukhina," pp. 385–92; *Iskra,* no. 46 (Aug. 15, 1903).

30. *Iskra,* no. 46; see also no. 48 (Sept. 15, 1903); *Osvobozhdenie,* no. 4(28) (Aug. 2, 1903); *Posledniia izvestiia,* no. 140 (Aug. 4, 1903); *Revoliutsionnaia Rossiia,* no. 34 (Oct. 15, 1903). On the role of the Odessa Socialist Revolutionaries see *Revoliutsionnaia Rossiia,* no. 29 (Aug. 5, 1903); *Perepiska V. I. Lenina i rukovodimykh,* p. 371.

31. *Slavnye stranitsy bor'by i pobed* (Baku, 1965), p. 25. "You can try as you please, but it is now impossible to hold back the wave of the political trend among the ranks

did not politicize the laboring masses. For some the July events surely engendered a crisis in confidence; Shaevich and the Independents as apparent representatives of the government had deceived the workers into believing economic strikes had administrative approval. Others—and this included the vast majority —retained faith in the tsar. "Our little father the tsar had ordered an increase in wages and a decrease in working hours and then we went too far and he had to give a counterorder," is how the shrewd and informed French consul summed up the view of the average Odessa worker at the end of the general strike.[32]

## The Socialists Examine the General Strike

On July 17, as the Odessa workers roved through the streets of the city in the greatest labor demonstration Russia had yet known, representatives of the all-Russian Social Democratic Labor Party opened their now historic Second Congress in Brussels. Organizational and programmatic issues dominated the congress, which on July 29 moved to London.

No lengthy discussion of the labor unrest then sweeping southern Russia is recorded in the congress protocols, although the Independents, the Zubatovshchina, and the general strike were central to two resolutions put forward by Martov and adopted by the congress. The first, "On Demonstrations," placed the party on record as supporting political demonstrations as "the best means of systematically disorganizing the governmental mechanism" and politically educating the masses. As demonstrations increased and broadened there would eventuate "a series of armed clashes between the people and governmental authorities, thus preparing the masses for an all-Russian uprising against the existing structure." In defending his resolution from criticism that it gave too little weight to armed opposition, Martov cited the Odessa events, exaggerating the actual influence of the Social Democrats over the Odessa masses: "It is said that the time of 'peaceful' demonstrations has passed. No! Events in Odessa have shown that when tens

of our workers," the *Osvobozhdenie* correspondent reported from Odessa in the supplement to no. 4(28) (Aug. 2, 1903).
32. Sauvaire to Delcassé, Aug. 12, 1903, n.s. An *Iskra* correspondent reported with irritation that the Odessa workers believed that the Independents, not the Social Democrats, had led the Odessa strike (*Perepiska V. I. Lenina i rukovodimykh*, p. 374).

of thousands are on our side, one can do a great deal even by means of peaceful demonstrations."[33]

The second half of the resolution criticized the party's past deficiencies in executing its position on demostrations and rec-ommended that local committees "take advantage of oppor-tunities for the organization of political demonstrations." Broad agitation was a necessary preliminary to securing the sym-pathy of the masses; demonstrations were to be organized only at those moments when the masses were in the right mood; the core of active demonstrators "had to be sufficiently numerous, well-organized and prepared for its role,"[34] and prepared also for armed resistance; if troops intervened, efforts should be made to win them over to the goals and purposes of the demonstration.

Judged by the tactical standards of the party resolution the actions of the Odessa Committee during the general strike reveal many shortcomings. Editorials and correspondence from Odessa in the émigré press called the revolutionary groups to task for not taking sufficient advantage of labor unrest, insufficient planning, yielding before the greater aggressiveness of the Independents, and moving too quickly in the direction of a political demonstration before be-ing certain of mass support.[35] An *Iskra* editorial on the strikes in southern Russia openly professed dissatisfaction "that the leadership of the 'general strikes' belonged to our committees to an extent far less than is desirable and necessary," contending also that the Odessa general strike proved that the working class was not ready for conscious political action.[36]

The second resolution adopted by the congress, "Concerning Trade Union Struggle," expressed the party's stand on economic struggle and the tactical approach to strikes initiated by Zubatov's supporters. Martov introduced the resolution with the following considerations:

Special attention is devoted to the obligation of social-democracy not to remain neutral in those clashes between capital and labor, which arise as the result of various "Independents," even if against their will.... The

33. *Vtoroi s"ezd RSDRP,* pp. 408, 431.
34. *Ibid.,* p. 432.
35. *Iskra,* no. 46 (Aug. 15, 1903); *Osvobozhdenie,* supplement to no. 4 (28); no. 5 (29) (Aug. 19, 1903); *Posledniia izvestiia,* no. 140 (Aug. 4, 1903).
36. *Iskra,* no. 46.

latest events in Odessa have indicated what results the flirtation of the government with legalization can yield; we therefore must keep aloof no longer from purely economic struggle, even when it is conducted under the patronage of the "legalizers."[37]

The resolution emphasized the importance of economic struggle for the working class and placed before the party the task of "leadership in the daily struggle of the workers for improvement of labor conditions and agitation for removal of all those obstacles which the legislation of the Russian autocracy places before the trade union movement, in a word—to combine individual clashes of separate groups of workers into a single organized class struggle." The second half of the resolution dealt with the party's tactical approach to the Zubatovshchina and the general question of the legalization of the labor movement:

The congress recommends to all comrades an unending struggle against the Zubatovshchina in all its forms, to unmask before the workers the self-interested and treacherous character of the tactics of the Zubatov demagogues and to summon the workers to unity in a single class movement of struggle for political and economic liberation of the proletariat. In the interests of this task the congress recognizes as desirable that party organizations should support and direct strikes called by legal labor organizations, and make use of these clashes at the same time for unmasking the reactionary character of an alliance between the workers and the autocracy.[38]

The Odessa Committee had fulfilled the terms of the resolution during the general strike but, as we have seen, it failed to command the allegiance of the working class.

To the émigré social-democratic intelligentsia, cut off from direct contact with the labor movement at home and unable to boast of massive organized trade-union or party support comparable to that available to Western European socialists, the summer strikes were a shot in the arm. The size and breadth of the strikes gave them significance for all of Europe. "The proletariat of Russia now becomes one of the progressive forces of civilized Europe," boasted an *Iskra* editorial on the general strike. European public opinion, badly informed about Russia, could no longer ignore events there:

It often occurs that events of Russian life, hardly noticed and poorly evaluated abroad, prepare great changes in the correlation of forces, which

37. *Vtoroi s"ezd RSDRP,* p. 409.
38. *Ibid.,* pp. 432–33.

have great influence on the course of the social development of all Europe. To the number of such events undoubtedly belongs the recent strikes in our south. They have great political significance. They represent a new and extremely strong blow to Russian tsarism. And since Russian tsarism is—according to Engels' expression—the last bulwark of European reaction, then it is clear that we do not sin in the least against the truth in saying that the above-mentioned strikes, whatever small consideration Western Europe gave them, by their significance are important not only for us, but also for all of the European West.[39]

For Zubatov's critics within the government the Odessa general strike was simply the outgrowth of a risky policy against which they had given ample forewarning. Sheltered by the local authorities, who permitted it willfully to break the law, the Independent Party had proceeded to school the working class for militant action; led by the Independents the Odessa workers thus undertook strike after strike until the whole city lay at their mercy. Shaevich predictably was unable to retain control over the labor movements he had nurtured. The revolutionaries as expected reaped the benefits of the Independents' work; the growth of the labor movement and the experience of participation in strikes had imbued the masses "with the spirit of revolutionary principles."[40]

The liberal intelligentsia was likewise disturbed by the course of the July events. The failure of the strike was attributed to the

39. *Iskra*, no. 46. More than a modicum of chauvinism was evident in another *Iskra* editorial on the meaning of the general strike, written by Vera Zasulich: "In the countries of Western Europe, which have larger trade-union organizations and [where] for a long time socialist parties have existed, there still have not been strikes which have attained such universality as in our south" (*Iskra*, no. 53 [Nov. 25, 1903]). Lenin believed that the July days in Odessa had vindicated his oft-expressed optimism that the Zubatovshchina would eventually fail and that the Social Democrats would be the beneficiaries of that failure (Lenin, VII, 319). Soviet historiography has magnified the political significance of the general strikes, exaggerating the role of the social-democratic committees. The strikes in the summer of 1903 were allegedly the culminating point of the labor agitation of the previous decade and a prelude to the mass strikes during 1905 (*Proletariat Rossii na puti*, I, 116–17). In particular, Soviet historians have stressed that the Odessa general strike brought about the downfall of the Zubatovshchina and destroyed the last vestiges of Economism, while drawing the workers closer to social democracy: Baturin, p. 84; I. Kogan, *Vseobshchaia stachka 1903 goda* (Moscow, 1928), p. 33; O. Chaadaeva's introduction to "K istorii vseobshchei stachki," p. 76; O. Chaadaeva, "Vseobshchaia stachka na iuge Rossii," *Vseobshchaia stachka*, p. 7; *Slavnye stranitsy*, p. 266; V. Nevskii, "Letnie stachki 1903 g.—predvestniki 1905 goda," *Bor'ba klassov*, Aug.–Sept. 1933, p. 136.

40. "Zapiska gen. Novitskago," p. 96. Also see Kokovtsov's report to the tsar, Jan. 19, 1905 (*Rabochii vopros v komissii V. N. Kokovtsova*, p. 6).

revolutionaries who allegedly broke the common strike front and led the workers astray from their true interests. The perceptive Odessa observer who wrote anonymously for *Osvobozhdenie* echoed Zubatov's thoughts in dissecting the causes for the strike's failure:

It also seems to me one ought to manifest the purely political demands separately from economic ones [and] not in the list of strike [demands]; the merger is illogical by the fact that, for one thing, strike demands concern the owner and are satisfied or not satisfied by him; political demands must look for quite another addressee. By such a more logical division it would also be possible, one would think, to prevent a grievous civil war between the "pure economists" and the "politicians"; on an economic basis all would make common cause in complete solidarity against the owners; political dissatisfaction would be demonstrated only by those who actually were conscious and felt deeply about it, without imposing it on ignorant and timid persons to whom all the blame for the failure of comrade "politicians" is shifted.[41]

The problem caused by the intervention of the socialists in an undertaking with broad public support—a dilemma which the nonsocialist center and left faced during the remaining years of the monarchy—was acutely delineated by the same observer:

The appeal to society about supporting the strikers (issued, by the way, too late, when the strike had already ended), which concluded with the exclamation "long live socialism!,"... was hardly appropriate: one can be a good citizen and a person completely sympathetic with the present labor movement, and neither accept at all socialist doctrine nor contribute money in its name: it is necessary to find a common basis of sympathy for all, but one can hardly consider as such the ideas of socialism, which are vague to the majority of both society and the strikers.[42]

Summary

The Independent movement in Odessa was by far the most successful experiment of the Zubatovshchina. In less than a year, and from the most meager beginnings, a small band of Independent leaders achieved control over the Odessa working class. In a city where the revolutionaries long had roots among the masses and where racial barriers had inhibited working-class unity, the Independent Party acquired a large following among workers in the most varied professions. In the transfer from Minsk to Odessa the

41. *Osvobozhdenie*, supplement to 4(28).
42. *Ibid.* The views expressed in *Osvobozhdenie* came under strong attack in an editorial in *Iskra*, no. 46.

Independents shed their exclusively Jewish character and broadened the base of their unions to other than artisans.

The Odessa authorities placed no obstacle in the path of the Independents, although several city officials were critical of their aims and tactics. In general, until the July days, the Odessa Independents received greater support from Petersburg officialdom than had Zubatov's followers in Minsk and Moscow. At no time, however, was Zubatov able to manipulate at will the Odessa Independent Labor Committee, whose revered leader, Shaevich, pursued a semi-independent course. On Shaevich's initiative the Independent unions in Odessa began a series of strikes as a practical means of carrying out their promises to the workers. The Independents' role in fomenting the general strike is more difficult to assess. At times they opposed a strike call; at other times their unions appear to have taken the lead. At all times during the July days they stood ready to do battle against their socialist opponents; by their militant opposition to the socialists the Independents thwarted a political demonstration of major proportions.

The Odessa general strike was the supreme practical test of the validity of Zubatov's labor program. Although socialist agitators were relatively free during the strike to address a massive audience of potential followers, they failed to gain significant support. The Independents were more attuned to the outlook and aims of the workers. The working class, as Zubatov had argued, was basically loyal to the autocracy but unwilling to accept its depressed economic position, regardless of the terms of the law.[43]

The supreme test of the Zubatovshchina, coming at an untimely moment when the autocracy was faced with other large-scale outbursts of labor unrest, could not be dispassionately examined in isolation. Fearful of the consequences of street disorders and spreading unrest the autocracy reacted in its habitual manner on critical occasions: restore order forcibly and examine the merits of the case later. The immediate losers were the masses, who gained next to nothing for their loyalty and rejection of the revolutionaries. In the long run it was the autocracy that suffered, having weathered the first of several crises in confidence among the industrial masses.

---

43. "The strikers have given proof of a very great force of resistance and an indifference with regard to punishment and sufferings of all sorts which awaits them" (Sauvaire to Delcassé, Aug. 12, 1903, n. s.).

# CHAPTER 14

# Epilogue

A month after the Odessa general strike Zubatov was uncere-moniously discharged from office. At Plehve's request Zubatov appeared at the minister's *dacha* on Aptekar Island on the afternoon of August 19, 1903, where he was greeted coldly by Plehve and Lieutenant General von Wahl, the Assistant Minister of Interior. Von Wahl's presence was necessary, Plehve remarked candidly, since he never spoke alone with anyone he did not trust. Momentarily disconcerted, Zubatov composed himself and under questioning by Plehve summarized his relations with the Jewish labor movement and the Independent Party. Everything he had described, Zubatov added, was well known to the authorities and could be verified by available documents signed by the late Minister of Interior, D. S. Sipiagin, and the former director of the Department of Police, S. E. Zvolianskii. Under interrogation Zubatov denied he had promoted strikes as a working-class weapon; he admitted providing Shaevich with money from his own account and from the funds of the Department of Police (with Lopukhin's knowledge).

The interrogation reached its climax when Plehve confronted Zubatov with a letter in which Zubatov had allegedly betrayed state secrets by repeating verbatim to Shaevich certain comments the tsar had made on the Jewish question.[1] Plehve thereupon angrily terminated the conversation, ordering Zubatov's immediate dismissal from the Department of Police and his departure from St. Petersburg by the following evening; final action on his case would be reached after Lopukhin's return from abroad. When Plehve had finished Zubatov silently turned and left the room, slamming the

1. "K istorii Zubatovshchiny," p. 96.

door behind him. At the railway station the following day he parted with loyal colleagues in the Department of Police who braved the minister's wrath to see him off to Moscow. So ended fifteen years of state service.[2]

The drama in the *dacha* was carefully staged by Plehve. Although the causes for Zubatov's dismissal are still not entirely clear, Plehve's charges were felt to be mere pretext by all close to the case. Behind the scene lay ministerial intrigue and rivalry. Zubatov incautiously became involved in the interministerial struggle between Witte and Plehve which dominated Russian bureaucratic politics during the spring and summer of 1903; his dismissal is most likely attributable to his disloyalty to Plehve.

Evidence indicates that almost up to the moment of his dismissal Zubatov retained Plehve's confidence. Shortly after being appointed minister in 1902, Plehve had listened sympathetically to General Novitskii's vitriolic attacks against Zubatov's police methods and labor program; at a second interview with Novitskii early in 1903, however, Plehve showed great displeasure at similar criticism of Zubatov, and in June of that year Novitskii was compelled to resign.[3] Moreover, in a conversation with Witte in May 1903, Plehve expressed utmost confidence in Zubatov. Lopukhin was going abroad at the time and Plehve, preparing to spend some time in the country, willingly left the entire responsibility for safeguarding order in Zubatov's reliable hands.[4]

Zubatov attributed his breach with Plehve to the latter's demand for the suppression of the Independent Party (prior to its self-dissolution) along with the minister's increasing recourse to repression. According to Zubatov, the Independents hastened to liquidate their party when they learned of Plehve's opposition to their activities. Zubatov thereupon tendered his resignation, which Plehve allegedly refused to accept.

Plehve's handling of the Odessa general strike and the closing of the Odessa branch of the Independent Party were the final blows for Zubatov. Utterly disregarding his official position and the obedience

2. *Ibid.*, pp. 96–97; "Pis'ma Mednikova Spiridovichu," p. 203; Spiridovich, "Pri tsarskom rezhime," p. 153; Alekseev, *Provokator,* p. 136; "Dnevnik A. N. Kuropatkina," p. 82.
3. Novitskii, *Iz vospominanii zhandarma,* pp. 221–22, 224. Novitskii maintained his dismissal was due to Zubatov's influence.
4. Witte, *Vospominaniia,* II, 218; "Dnevnik A. N. Kuropatkina," p. 82.

due a superior, Zubatov openly called for Plehve's removal from office for the good of the empire: "I could not refrain from uttering aloud my opinion about the domestic policy of my patron, finding that his activity had not justified the hopes which had been placed in him; to expect anything new from him was no longer warranted (the matter relates to the summer of 1903), and the sooner he would leave or be dismissed the better it would be for the tsar, and for Russia, and for him personally."[5]

Disenchanted with Plehve and apparently believing that the Minister of Finance had become more sympathetic to his program, Zubatov turned to Witte, who, according to rumors, was plotting with Prince Meshcherskii to have Plehve dismissed.[6] Serebriakova, in testimony in 1926, quoted Zubatov bitterly complaining: "Plehve does not sympathize with my policy at all; he considers that it only promotes the spread of the revolutionary movement. . . . I wish to break with the Department of Police and cross over to serve Witte. He must accept the working-class cause close to his heart and take my policy under his protection."[7]

Witte had known of Zubatov ever since factory inspectors' reports had reached him complaining of the high-handed interference by the Moscow administration in labor matters; he had been Zubatov's most powerful adversary within the bureaucracy and the chief stumbling block to the adoption of the Zubatovshchina throughout the empire. Nevertheless, the two did not meet until early February 1903, at the home of Prince Meshcherskii, the influential editor of *Grazhdanin*, a confidant of several tsars, and a master intriguer. Plehve was also present on that occasion, when both ministers allegedly sang Zubatov's praises.[8]

The only account of a meeting between Witte and Zubatov at the beginning of July is found in Witte's memoirs, which are often

5. Zubatov, "Iz nedavniago proshlago," p. 436.

6. Evidence of a plot to remove Plehve, involving Witte, E. V. Bogdanovich, and Prince Meshcherskii, is found in the entry for May 21, 1903, in A. V. Bogdanovich's diary (*Tri poslednikh samoderzhtsa*, p. 284) and in Lopukhin's memoirs (*Otryvki iz vospominanii* [Moscow-Leningrad, 1923], p. 71).

7. Alekseev, *Provokator*, p. 136.

8. "Pis'ma Mednikova Spiridovichu," p. 199. Spiridovich maintained that it was Meshcherskii's idea to bring Zubatov and Witte together and that at their meeting Witte led Zubatov to believe that there would be broad legalization of his program should he, Witte, be named Minister of Interior ( *Mladorosskaia iskra*, April 22, 1935). On Meshcherskii, see Zakharova, pp. 128–29.

inaccurate and highly colored by Witte's prejudices. Witte maintains that he had never met Zubatov until the latter's unexpected visit in early July. At that meeting Zubatov confided that intelligence reports indicated all Russia was seething with discontent and complained that police measures prescribed by Plehve would worsen matters and not prevent the revolution that was brewing. Suspicious of the purpose of the visit, Witte asked Zubatov why he had not discussed these matters with Plehve. Zubatov responded that he had done so but in vain; after obtaining Witte's promise that the substance of their conversation would not be made known to Plehve, Zubatov departed for Prince Meshcherskii's residence to further his case against Plehve.[9] Although the prince had been influential in obtaining Plehve's appointment as minister, his home had become the center of a conspiracy seeking Plehve's dismissal.[10] Nevertheless, after Zubatov's visit, Meshcherskii for no clear reason went straight to Plehve and informed him that Zubatov had spoken ill both of Plehve and his archrival, Witte.[11]

Evidently, then, Plehve was intent on dismissing Zubatov for personal insubordination and needed a pretext.[12] He admitted as much to Lopukhin upon the latter's return from abroad, although Plehve's version of the plot against him differed from Witte's account. Zubatov had composed a letter to the tsar, Lopukhin was told, censuring Plehve's policies and recommending he be removed and Witte installed in his place. Prince Meshcherskii was to transmit the letter and urge the sovereign to follow Zubatov's advice. Plehve, however, was able to foil the plot in time. Mikhail Ivanovich Gurevich, a secret agent of the Department of Police to whom Zubatov had negligently recounted details of the plot, at once informed Plehve, who revealed the plot to the tsar. To avoid public scandal the intrigue was kept secret and Zubatov's discharge made out to be in connection with the failure of his labor policies.[13]

The Odessa general strike furnished Plehve with a convenient pretext to dismiss Zubatov and also appease those who had

9. Witte, II, 218; "Dnevnik A. N. Kuropatkina," p. 82.

10. Lopukhin, p. 71; Gurko, p. 120.

11. "Dnevnik A. N. Kuropatkina," p. 82; Witte, II, 219, 286.

12. "Dnevnik A. N. Kuropatkina," p. 82.

13. Lopukhin, pp. 74–75. A third version holds that it was I. F. Manuilov who informed Plehve of the plot (" Prikliuchenie I. F. Manuilova," *Byloe,* Nov.–Dec. 1917, p. 270). An anonymous source maintains that Zubatov's relations with Witte were the cause of his dismissal (A. P., "Departament politsii v 1892–1898 gg.," *ibid.,* p. 21).

vociferously criticized the Zubatovshchina as detrimental to the interests of both the business community and the autocracy. The July days had confirmed the worst fears of Zubatov's critics that the government-sponsored labor unions would eventually fall into the hands of the radicals; some now went so far as to accuse Zubatov of being a revolutionary. Plehve, as Zubatov's superior, was open to criticism for having permitted the Zubatovshchina to spread to Vilna and Odessa after having initially opposed Zubatov's labor program on becoming minister. To a deputation of Odessa Jews with whom he met in late July, Plehve declared that the workmen's league, that is, the Independent unions, were an embarrassment to the government; the embarrassment in reality was his own.[14] Zubatov was thus jettisoned by Plehve to appease the critics of the Zubatovshchina and to free Plehve from association with Zubatov's labor program as well as any responsibility for the July days.

The intervention of the Grand Duke Aleksandr Mikhailovich was apparently crucial to Zubatov's dismissal. As director of the merchant marine the grand duke had received regular reports from the Odessa city administration on the port strikes, reports which, according to Witte, branded the Independents as instigators of the strikes. To strengthen the case against Zubatov, Witte forwarded factory inspectors reports on the Zubatovshchina to the grand duke along with his own comments on its detrimental effect on the interests of the autocracy. At first the grand duke was unconvinced by Witte since Zubatov had the confidence of the Grand Duke Sergei Aleksandrovich; later, however, he changed his mind, for he reportedly told the tsar that Zubatov had personally organized the Odessa general strike.[15] Plehve, desirous of removing Zubatov for his treachery, made a similar allegation to Nicholas, adding that Zubatov was intriguing to have him removed as minister.[16] No official of importance lifted a finger to defend Zubatov from these charges; the tsar thus readily agreed with Plehve, and Zubatov was hastily discharged from office.[17]

Zubatov's dismissal and the dissolution of the Independent Party did not end the Zubatovshchina, nor did they end the government's involvement with the labor movement. In Moscow the

14. *Times*, Aug. 5, 1903; Liubimov, p. 27.
15. Liubimov, p. 29; Spiridovich, "Pri tsarskom rezhime," p. 153; Witte, II, 219–20.
16. Spiridovich, *ibid.*
17. Spiridovich's account conforms with the tsar's alleged statement to the Grand

labor societies initiated by Zubatov survived until the revolution of 1905 and, in some cases, even beyond. New mutual-aid societies with aims, structures, and statutes similar to those associated with the Zubatovshchina were secretly subsidized by the Department of Police even after the disorders of Bloody Sunday.[18] Evidently the government feared that the autonomous growth of the labor movement could only lead to economic and political strife, especially after the vast wave of labor disorders in 1905.

Witte in later years never ceased to criticize the Zubatovshchina for having been harmful to state interests. In testimony before the Committee of Ministers in January 1905, he maintained that Zubatov's program of administratively guided labor unions had hindered the government's peaceful resolution of the labor question and instilled in the workers hostility toward the capitalist class. The Zubatovshchina had endangered the autocracy by nurturing a separately organized class trained to act outside the prescribed legal limits. These unions, Witte charged, were to blame for the strikes and labor unrest in Moscow in 1902 and the disorders in Odessa and the southern industrial centers the following year.[19] In an appearance before the State Council in April 1912, Witte ascribed the unduly slow enactment of factory legislation during the years he was at the helm of the Ministry of Finance to the prevalence of Zubatov's approach to the labor question in the Ministry of Interior. Obliquely attacking that Ministry, Witte spoke of obstacles placed in his way "by one of the departments which held the fashionable view that in order to safeguard the workers from pernicious influences a broadening of the workers' rights is necessary not by a legislative procedure, as the Ministry of Finance insisted, but by an administrative one."[20]

Yet Witte was not above secretly drawing on Ministry of Finance funds to subsidize labor unions organized in the Zubatov manner,

---

Duke Aleksandr Mikhailovich: "But you know, Witte is right, it appeared that Zubatov organized this whole strike and established all the labor organizations; he [Witte] is wrong only in . . . that he says that Plehve knew all about this. Plehve knew nothing, only now all is disclosed and presented to me about Zubatov's discharge" (Witte, II, 220).

18. See the case of the Smesovshchina: F. Semenov-Bulkin, "Smesovshchina," *Trud v Rossii,* 1925, no. 1, pp. 153–70; Semenov-Bulkin, *Soiuz metallistov,* pp. 36–46.

19. *Rabochii vopros v komissii V. N. Kokovtsova,* p. 23.

20. *Gosudarstvennyi Sovet, 1911–12 gody,* p. 3402. Witte also attacked the Zubatovshchina in a session of the State Council on May 5, 1910 (*Gosudarstvennyi Sovet, 1909–10 gody,* pp. 2645–46).

as archival material later disclosed. The St. Petersburg Society of
Mutual Help of Workers in Mechanical Factories led by M. A.
Ushakov, a former follower of Zubatov, had been founded with the
assistance of Witte and officials of the Ministry of Finance.[21] During
October 1905, when a general strike brought the autocracy to its
knees, Witte allegedly ordered that state subsidies be used to
reopen Gapon's labor societies. Their revival would be of benefit
to the government, a report to the tsar declared, for they would
be restricted exclusively to trade-unionist goals while serving
"as a counterweight to the criminal social-revolutionary organizations."[22] Witte sent agents abroad to seek out Gapon and convince him to return to Russia to resume the leadership of the
labor societies he had led. With Witte's acquiescence Gapon was
granted funds from the treasury upon his return to Petersburg.
Zubatov had initiated Gapon into the government-sponsored labor
movement; Witte inherited both Zubatov's protégé and labor policy
while never ceasing to criticize the Zubatovshchina.[23]

Plehve's involvement in labor affairs likewise did not terminate
with Zubatov's dismissal. As minister he continued to sanction the
use of administrative pressure against factory managements as
an effective means of preventing strikes and other disorders.[24]
Once the summer strikes in southern Russia had ended, however,
Plehve believed that the labor question was no longer pressing;
in December 1903 he told V. A. Gringmut, the editor of the
conservative *Moskovskiia vedomosti*, that the labor question was still
unresolved but of less immediacy than the peasant problem and the
Jewish and student questions.[25] The solution of the labor problem

21. *Rus'*, Oct. 4 and 11, 1904; Sablinsky, p. 177; P. Vasil'ev, "Ushakovshchina," *Trud
v Rossii*, 1925, no. 1, pp. 145, 152–53; Semenov-Bulkin, *Soiuz metallistov*, pp. 29–36.
Zubatov in a letter to Shaevich, April 28, 1903, wrote that the Ministry of Finance was
supporting a labor organization in St. Petersburg in competition with the one he was
organizing (Vovchik, p. 145).
22. Vovchik, p. 146.
23. "Prikliuchenie I. F. Manuilova," pp. 268–69. On the relations between Witte
and Gapon, see Sablinsky, pp. 745–62. In a letter to P. N. Durnovo on February 2,
1906, Witte presented no opposition to the opening of another branch of the
Assembly of Russian Factory and Mill Workers of the City of St. Petersburg
(Bukhbinder, "K istorii 'Sobraniia,'" p. 302).
24. On August 6, 1903, on Plehve's order, the Petersburg city-governor told factory
inspectors that factory managements were to obey orders from government officials
for preventing disorders under threat of banishment to Enisei *guberniia* (Ozerov,
*Politika*, p. 38).
25. Bogdanovich, p. 290.

lay in the transfer of jurisdiction over the working class to a proposed Department of Labor within the Ministry of Interior combined with a broadening of workers' rights and satisfaction of their just demands, he remarked in an interview with Ianzhul.[26] Plehve obtained provisional approval from the tsar for the transfer of the factory inspectorate to the jurisdiction of the Ministry of Interior, but determined opposition from V. N. Kokovtsov, Witte's successor as Minister of Finance, prevented the change.[27]

Although he never reconsidered his decision to dismiss Zubatov, Plehve had second thoughts regarding the utility of the Zubatovshchina for the maintenance of order. On February 15, 1904, without consulting the Ministry of Finance, he approved the statutes of Gapon's Assembly of Russian Factory and Mill Workers of the City of St. Petersburg, a labor organization having its roots in the circle of workers Zubatov had gathered in the capital.[28] Plehve discussed the question of the Zubatovshchina and its influence on the general course of the Russian labor movement in conversation with A. V. Pogozhev on July 12 of that year. Pogozhev on that occasion criticized the Zubatovshchina for intensifying labor strife. After a moment's reflection Plehve voiced agreement: "Yes you are right... I myself now see that it was premature to have called forth such a movement among the Russian workers."[29] This was Plehve's last recorded remark on the subject; three days later he lay dead from an assassin's bomb.

Zubatov's high-placed colleagues and benefactors did not abandon him even though he was discharged under a cloud of disloyalty. Lopukhin, on vacation in Paris, was surprised when Witte brought him news of Zubatov's discharge. Told that Zubatov was discharged because of the activities of his labor organizations,

26. Ianzhul, "Vospominaniia," *Russkaia starina*, no. 144 (Oct.–Dec. 1910), pp. 497–98.

27. Kokovtsov, pp. 27–29; Ozerov, *Politika*, pp. 170, 172–73; *Rabochii vopros v komissii V. N. Kokovtsova*, pp. 9–10.

28. Bukhbinder, "K istorii 'Sobraniia,'" pp. 297–98; report of V. N. Kokovtsov, Minister of Finance, to Nicholas II, Jan. 5, 1905, in *Revoliutsiia 1905–1907 gg. v Rossii*, ed. N. S. Trusova (Moscow, 1955), p. 16. On relations between Plehve and Gapon, see Sablinsky, p. 284. In a letter to the editors of *Vestnik Evropy*, in February 1906, Zubatov wrote: "It is curious that after my departure, V. K. Plehve and his associates carried on the cause which I had begun, but apparently without my faith in the matter, and not with the proper intimacy with it, by which I also explain its strange outcome" (Zubatov, "Iz nedavniago proshlago," p. 436).

29. Pogozhev, "Iz vospominanii o V. K. von-Pleve," p. 268.

Lopukhin replied in bewilderment that "all the organizations were formed with the knowledge and approval of Plehve; I possess official resolutions on this subject."[30] Lopukhin, a long-time friend and admirer of Zubatov, hoped that his report to Plehve on the Odessa general strike would change matters. Nothing could be done to assuage Plehve, however, and after a two-month sojourn in Moscow, Zubatov retired to Vladimir, prohibited from residing in either Moscow or Petersburg.[31]

Trepov and the Grand Duke Sergei Aleksandrovich stood by Zubatov. The grand duke used his influence at court to have Zubatov granted a state pension.[32] At the end of 1904 he resigned as Moscow governor-general and soon thereafter was killed by a Socialist Revolutionary assassin. Trepov played an active part in shaping labor policy in 1905, the year in which his political star reached its zenith. Two days after Bloody Sunday Trepov was entrusted with the crucial post of St. Petersburg governor-general, with almost dictatorial powers. In May he was appointed Assistant Minister of Interior and director of the Department of Police.

During this period of continual labor unrest Trepov remained a defender of the labor program associated with Zubatov's name. In reports to the tsar he rebutted Kokovtsov's criticism of the Ministry of Interior's intervention in labor matters and, in turn, attacked the Ministry of Finance for legislative inactivity and the factory inspectorate for failing to fulfill its prescribed duties. "Directly after Trepov was appointed governor-general of St. Petersburg he employed a method to pacify the workers of that city which was virtually [the same as the] Zubatovshchina," an official of the Ministry of Interior, recalled.[33] Trepov convinced the tsar, who had refused to receive a petition from the St. Petersburg working class on January 9 (Bloody Sunday), to hold an audience shortly thereafter with a deputation of St. Petersburg factory workmen; moreover, he drafted the tsar's speech to the workmen. In this manner Trepov hoped to reconcile tsar and nation, reassuring the working class that the autocracy had its interests at heart.[34]

30. Witte, II, 286; see also Lopukhin, pp. 69–72.

31. Zubatov, p. 436; Koz'min, pp. 38–39; "Pis'ma Mednikova Spiridovichu," p. 204; "K istorii Zubatovshchiny," pp. 93–99.

32. It was rumored that the grand duke wished to take Zubatov into his service ("Dnevnik A. N. Kuropatkina," p. 82).

33. Gurko, p. 364; see also Tatarov, pp. 109–23.

34. Gurko, pp. 364–65; Kokovtsov, pp. 38–40; Sablinsky, pp. 697–700; "Trepovskii

Trepov also actively interfered in labor conflicts as he had done earlier in Moscow, applying administrative pressure and threatening factory owners in order to wrest economic concessions for the workers. For his high-handed military despotism Trepov became hated by society; workers as well as employers were terrorized into accepting orders from the Ministry of Interior during labor disputes.[35] After the promulgation of the October Manifesto Trepov was appointed commandant of the Imperial Court, a position from which he continued as influential confidant and trusted adviser of the tsar until his death in 1906.

Zubatov lived out his remaining years in retirement, unshaken in his ideological conviction as a monarchist, yet bitter that his dismissal had been unjust. He never doubted the rectitude of his labor program. To Father Gapon, who was present at the railway station on that day in August 1903 when he left the capital in disgrace, Zubatov gave advice on how best to continue the labor societies he had initiated and named the officials who would support the project. In Moscow, awaiting final disposition of his case, Zubatov continued to seek new recruits among the factory workers. To these workers he distributed literature on the labor movement and spoke about how the working class could attain self-consciousness and economic well-being through evolutionary means and state support.[36]

After Prince Sviatopolk-Mirskii replaced Plehve as Minister of Interior the limitations on Zubatov's residence were removed and a larger state pension granted him.[37] Zubatov's enemies, Generals von Wahl and Novitskii, warned Sviatopolk-Mirskii that Zubatov was a revolutionary and had sheltered other revolutionaries in his labor societies and thus should not be restored to state service. Little heed was given to these accusations and Zubatov, respected in government circles for mastery in infiltrating the revolutionary parties, was invited to re-enter the Department of Police in turn by

proekt rechi Nikolaia II k rabochim posle 9 ianvaria 1905 g.," *Krasnyi arkhiv,* 1927, no. 1(20), pp. 240–42.

35. Kokovtsov, p. 34.

36. Varnashev, pp. 190, 193; Zubatov, "Zubatovshchina," pp. 169–70; Prudnikov, "Stranichka iz vospominanii o Zubatove," *Put' k Oktiabriu,* no. 1 (1923), pp. 122–25.

37. Zubatov, "Iz nedavniago proshlago," p. 436; entry of Jan. 3, 1904, in Lev Tikhomirov's diary ("25 let nazad," p. 24); "Pis'ma Mednikova Spiridovichu," pp. 210, 212.

Sviatopolk-Mirskii, Trepov, and Witte.[38] Zubatov rejected these offers and never again held an official position.[39]

Apparently, however, the stain on Zubatov's record was not completely erased, nor was trust in him fully restored. The Department of Police would not allow him to publish a lengthy defense of the Zubatovshchina replete with information on the interministerial dispute between Plehve and Witte.[40] His letters were regularly opened and inspected; from the Okhrana came a warning to cease corresponding with Vladimir Burtsev, the well-known editor of *Byloe* and an assiduous exposer of the Okhrana's counterrevolutionary activities.[41]

For the remainder of his life Zubatov was a forgotten figure. Now and then he appeared in print in defense of his policies or to discuss the post-1905 political structure, for which he had little sympathy.[42] On Prince Meshcherskii's invitation, Zubatov wrote several letters in 1906 and 1907 devoted to the new constitutional order for publication in *Grazhdanin*. Defense of monarchic absolutism was the recurrent theme. The unity of tsar and people, the uniqueness of the path of Russian history and its essential divergence from that of Western Europe, time-worn conservative themes out of tune with the post-1905 political order, were stressed in the letters.[43]

As time passed Zubatov increasingly became gloomy over the fate of the autocracy, foreseeing the coming of a revolution which would

38. Zubatov to Burtsev, Dec. 12, 1906 (Koz'min, p. 63; also found in *Byloe*, no. 14, 1912, p. 77); Bogdanovich, p. 312; "Pis'ma Mednikova Spiridovichu," p. 210. For Witte's high estimation of Zubatov's abilities in counterrevolutionary police work see his conversation with Kuropatkin, "Dnevnik A. N. Kuropatkina," p. 82. On von Wahl's opposition to Zubatov see Bogdanovich, pp. 301, 312, 415.

39. Koz'min, p. 43, 49; testimony of Zubatov at Lopukhin's trial (*Delo A. A. Lopukhina*, p. 141). For Zubatov's reason for not returning to state service, see his letter to Burtsev, Dec. 12, 1906 (Koz'min, pp. 63, 65).

40. The manuscript was discovered in the files of the Department of Police after the February revolution and published in October 1917 under the title "Zubatovshchina."

41. Koz'min published their intermittent correspondence between 1906 and 1908. On Zubatov's warning from the Okhrana, see his letter to Burtsev, Jan. 21, 1907 (Koz'min, p. 77). When Burtsev phoned Zubatov in 1916, Zubatov said that he could not see him because "it is dangerous both for me and for you" (V1. Burtsev, *Bor'ba za svobodnuiu Rossiiu* [Berlin, 1923], I, 179).

42. A letter to the editor of *Vestnik Evropy* was published under the title "Iz nedavniago proshlago: g. Zubatov o 'Zubatovshchine,'" in March 1906.

43. Zubatov to Burtsev, Dec. 12, 1906 (Koz'min, p. 65); *Grazhdanin*, Jan. 12, March 12, Nov. 2 and 19, 1906; May 3, Aug. 16, Sept. 16 and 27, 1907.

mean the death of the Russia he loved.[44] In a letter dated March 21, 1908, he declared himself to be a deeply sincere believer in monarchy, prepared "to disappear along with it."[45] When in 1917 Zubatov learned in Moscow that the tsar had abdicated, he left his family at the supper table, entered his study, locked the door, and shot himself.[46] The monarchy and its devoted utopist fittingly expired as one.

44. Conversation with P. P. Zavarzin in 1912 (Zavarzin, *Zhandarmy,* p. 59).
45. Koz'min, p. 90.
46. Zavarzin, p. 59; Liubimov, p. 25; *Mladorosskaia iskra,* April 22, 1935.

CHAPTER 15

# Conclusion

Russia entered the twentieth century with an unprecedented number of challenging and pressing problems. The totality of forces dissatisfied with the status quo had become frighteningly large and endangered the autocracy's survival. Early recognition and attentive study of problems with a view to resolving them before they reached significant proportions, however, were not distinguishing features of the tsarist autocracy.

The labor question emerged in the 1890's at a time when the monarchy believed it faced more serious problems in the form of the revolutionary movement and a revival of the peasant problem. The significance of the working-class question was therefore underestimated. A clearly defined and effective labor policy was needed; instead, piecemeal, stopgap measures were effected.

The government, moreover, was ill prepared by traditional outlook to meet the limited demands of the relatively small but vociferous working class created by the industrial revolution of the 1890's. Throughout the nineteenth century and into the early years of the twentieth century responsible officials held that Russia could progress without the attendant evils of industrialization all too evident in Western Europe—that is, without a working-class movement and class conflict. Yet by the turn of the century working-class protest in the form of strikes challenged these assumptions. In the government's favor was the traditional loyalty of its working-class subjects. In striking, the workers braved financial distress, Cossack whips, and imprisonment, not to alter or overthrow the political order but simply as a desperate means of exerting pressure for more tolerable working and living conditions.

Essentially the autocracy was in a quandary how best to resolve the labor problem. As the working class grew larger with each passing year the government had increasing difficulty coping effectively with labor agitation through repression alone. Yet large-scale strikes appeared to be the only means available to the workers to induce the government to enact labor legislation. The government was aware of the methods Bismarck and Disraeli had used to mitigate the labor problem. In Russia, however, the working class was not sufficiently large, organized, or militant to be considered an imminent threat demanding radical solutions. The autocracy, moreover, was inflexible, believing that concessions to the working class would generate demands for rights from other sectors of the population and eventually undermine its power.

The inadequacy of the government's response to their problems made the workers receptive to socialist propaganda. The tsarist government acted harshly toward strikers, not as a defender of the interests of the capitalist class, as the socialists claimed, but out of its own overly self-protective need for order and exaggerated fears that any collective activity was politically dangerous. The government did not possess sufficient psychological understanding of the worker and knowledge of his problems to realize that an outlet from the tensions and burdens of factory life was necessary. By treating economic strikes as criminal the government unwittingly tended to confirm the predictions of those socialists who maintained that economic struggle would eventually bring the workers into conflict with the police arm of the state and lead them to understand the need for political action. Zubatov's program, on the other hand, was aimed at preventing the workers from becoming politically "conscious" in a Marxist sense.

Zubatov wanted the autocracy to utilize the reservoir of faith the overwhelming mass of the tsar's subjects had in the existing order. Among tsarist officials of the time he was notable for his sensitivity to the mind and outlook of the factory workers. Zubatov realized that intolerable working conditions drove the workers to strike; his purpose was to channel their discontent within bounds acceptable and advantageous to both the working class and the autocracy. Zubatov was confident that if the working class were organized under its own leadership it would rebuff the efforts of the revolutionary intelligentsia to control it. In this respect he was a monarchic revisionist and stood alone among tsarist officials. In order to pacify his superiors and conservative critics, he had to provide evidence that the labor organizations he initiated were tightly supervised, led by hand-picked agents, and completely controlled by the police. The result was administratively-guided labor unions.

The socialist challenge to the autocracy had both a theoretical and a practical side. In the struggle for the loyalty of the working class, then emerging from peasant darkness, Zubatov believed the autocracy had to propagate a more relevant ideology, emphasizing the benefits of monarchic rule for the workers. The demands of the time also required that the autocracy trust its loyal followers more fully by permitting a degree of labor association: demonstrative loyalty to the throne had to supersede passive loyalty, or the field of action would be left open solely to the small, vigorous minority inimical to the monarchy.

The struggle between Zubatov and social democracy for the leadership of the labor movement thus was fought out on the grounds of ideology and practical achievement. Socialist ideology, with its promise of a glorious future brought about by the revolutionary proletariat, was countered with a vision of a progressive, supraclass autocracy sympathetic and responsive to working-class interests. Both contenders realized the significance of the support of the worker-intelligentsia and through them the broad mass of workers. Basically each fought for the worker's allegiance with a similar line of argument: that the other party did not have the worker's true interest at heart, pursued selfish goals, and would not deliver anything of appreciable benefit to the masses. The socialists branded the government as defender of the factory owners' interests and oppressor of the working class; Zubatov, endeavoring to widen the breach between the intelligentsia and the workers, emphasized that the socialist intelligentsia had little concern for the economic interests of the laboring masses but needed their assistance to attain its selfish goal of political power. In the battle for the loyalty of the working class the government was the harder pressed of the rivals to prove its case, for its actions could be closely scrutinized in relation to its promises.

Zubatov above all was a monarchist by conviction, opposed to any limitations on the autocracy's powers. His labor policies as well as his counterintelligence activities were directed at preserving the autocratic regime. Yet the Zubatovshchina was not a mere tactical device to divert the labor movement from a revolutionary course, as critics have charged. Zubatov truly believed that the working class and the autocracy were compatible. The workers had unique needs which could be satisfied only by the supraclass autocracy which justly mediated class interests; tangible assurances that the government was responsive to their interests, in turn, would reinforce the workers' faith in the monarchy. Zubatov reversed the socialist dictum "the worse, the better" to "the better [the labor conditions under the autocracy], the worse [for the socialists]."

Conservatives and socialists opposed the Zubatovshchina. Both believed that an organized working class could not be restrained and would seek a revolutionary path. The conservatives, drawing lessons from the recent history of Western Europe, distrusted the working class, believing it to be a turbulent, disruptive force, socialist by inclination, a potential enemy of the autocracy. The Social Democrats looked upon the Zubatovshchina with mixed feelings: hostility to government control of the labor movement and appreciation for the development of labor organization. The proletariat, they believed, would emerge from the experience with police guidance more conscious of the need for unity and ready to accept socialist ideology and leadership. The socialists and conservatives rightfully believed the working class would demand more than limited self-government; they erred in maintaining that the workers would naturally seek guidance from the socialist intelligentsia and become a revolutionary force.

Zubatov's assessment of the state of mind of the working class was closer to the mark than that of his opponents; he realistically accepted the new social force created by the industrial revolution and refused to believe it was a natural threat to order. Zubatov's policies were designed to give the working class a secure place in the structure of an industrialized Russia under the rule of a benevolent autocracy. His program was well tailored to fit the needs and interests of a Russian working class then in an early stage of development, indifferent to politics, loyal to the throne, and desirous, above all, of securing tangible improvements in living and working conditions. In general the Zubatovshchina during its short life attained its goals: the working class was drawn into the movement in large numbers, economic benefits were brought to the workers, and the labor movement was diverted from the revolutionary parties.

Zubatov's program, however, possessed internal contradictions and faced formidable external obstacles to its successful application to Russia's labor problem. Zubatov persuaded his followers to share his utopian vision of an ideal monarchy equitably dispensing social justice to all regardless of class or rank, without any assurances from the monarchy that it shared his outlook. In promising the working class a better life if it would forego political activity, he made a commitment he did not have the power to fulfill; should the monarchy fail to carry out Zubatov's pledge it stood to lose the confidence of the masses. It was not opposition from the monarchy, however, that destroyed Zubatov's dream, but the amorphous bureaucratic structure that blurred formal lines of authority and permitted contrary policies to exist simultaneously. The tsarist government therefore never formulated and executed a coherent labor policy. Zubatov, moreover, was never given free reign to test his program; opposition from Witte and the industrial estate was constant and largely accounts for the termination of the Zubatovshchina.

Zubatov's official station and reputation impeded the advance of his program. His positon as chief of political counterintelligence appeared to lend credence to the charge that the labor organizations associated with the Zubatovshchina were a police trap and served only the purposes of the Okhrana. In truth the charge disturbed the intelligentsia a good deal more than the workers, whose prime concerns were with the economic, organizational, and educational advancements the Zubatovshchina offered.

The artificial geographic wall that separated the Russian and Jewish nationalities permitted Zubatov to introduce an adapted program successfully among the Jewish workers without revealing its basic ideological incompatibility with the Moscow movement. The ideological conservatism of Official Nationality, stressed in the latter phase of the Moscow Zubatovshchina, with its appeal to the national-religious feelings of the Russian workers, would have alienated Zubatov's Jewish following. Moreover the Grand Duke

Sergei Aleksandrovich, Zubatov's most influential protector, and Fedor Slepov, the secretary of the Moscow Society of Machine Workers, were reputed anti-Semites. The viability of Zubatov's program among the Jewish artisans of the Pale was dependent on the government's nationality policy toward the Jews.

Zubatov's labor program demanded more than a dynamic adjustment by the autocracy; as liberal and social critics reiterated, an organized labor movement was inherently incompatible with the existence of the autocracy of Nicholas II. As it gained organizational experience the working class would realize the need for civil rights and freedoms and, without revolutionary intent, demand free speech, freedom of assembly, and a free press; these liberties could be provided and guaranteed by a constitutional monarchy, not an autocracy.

Socialist writers both before and after the Bolshevik revolution have emphasized the positive benefits brought to the proletariat, from their point of view, by the Zubatovshchina. The workers were awakened to importance of organization and made more conscious politically by having bitterly experienced what the socialists had long predicted: the government would desert them and support their enemy, the capitalists. Undoubtedly the Zubatov societies, with their funds, lectures, and assemblies, educated the workers regarding labor unions and the labor movement abroad. However, as the July days in Odessa illustrated, when Zubatov left the scene the struggle for the loyalty of the working class was unresolved, with the scales still tipped in favor of the monarchy. Time, however, was running out; without a positive and coherent labor program, matters drifted until the revolutionary events of 1905 brought the labor question dramatically to the forefront, ending once and for all the dream of a Russia free of labor strife.

# Bibliography

## Bibliographic and Reference Guides

"Bibliografiia," *Istoriia Rossii v XIX veke.* St. Petersburg: Granat, 1907–1909. VII, 273–86.

*Bibliografiia periodicheskikh izdanii Rossii, 1901–1916.* 4 vols. Leningrad, 1958–1961.

*Bibliografiia po istorii proletariata v epoku tsarizma: Feodal'no-krepostnoi period.* Edited by M. V. Nechkina. Moscow-Leningrad, 1935.

*Bibliografiia revoliutsionnoho rukhu v Odesi (1820–1920).* Odessa, 1933.

Borovskii, A. *1905 god-i: Khronika sobytii, bibliografiia.* Moscow, 1925.

Bourgina, Anna. *Russian Social Democracy: The Menshevik Movement. A Bibliography.* Stanford, 1968.

Golikov, K. I. *Pervaia russkaia revoliutsiia 1905–1907 gg.: Ukazatel' literatury, vyshedshei v 1954–1957 v sviazi s 50-letiem revoliutsii.* Moscow, 1957.

*Istoriia SSSR.* 2 vols.: *Ukazatel' sovetskoi literatury za 1917–1952 gg.; Istoriia SSSR v period kapitalizma (1861–1917).* Moscow, 1958.

Lesure, M. "Aperçu sur les fonds russe dans les Archives du Ministère des Affaires Etrangères français." *Cahiers du Monde Russe et Soviétique,* 4 (1963), 312–30.

Masanov, I. F. *Slovar' psevdonimov russkikh pisatelei, uchenykh i obshche-stvennykh deiatelei.* 4 vols. Moscow, 1956–1960.

*Materialy k bibliografii revoliutsionnogo dvizheniia v Odesse.* 2 vols. Odessa, 1927–1929.

Morley, Charles. *Guide to Research in Russian History.* Syracuse, 1951.

*Pervaia russkaia revoliutsiia: Ukazatel' literatury.* Edited by G. K. Derman. Moscow, 1930.

*Russkaia periodicheskaia pechat' (1702–1894): Spravochnik.* Edited by A. G. Dement'ev, A. V. Zapadov and M. S. Cherepakhov. Moscow, 1959.

*Russkaia periodicheskaia pechat' (1895–oktiabr' 1917): Spravochnik.* Edited by M. S. Cherepakhov and E. M. Fingerit. Moscow, 1957.

V., N. (V. I. Nevskii). "Bibliografiia o zubatovskikh soiuzakh, 'legal'-nom rabochem dvizhenii,'Gapone i 9-om ianvaria." *Krasnaia letopis',* 1922, no. 1, pp. 75–80.

Vol'tsenburg, O. E. *Bibliograficheskii putevoditel' po revoliutsii 1905 goda: Sistematicheskii obzor knig i zhurnal'nykh statei o pervoi russkoi revoliutsii.* Leningrad, 1925.

Zaleski, Eugène. *Mouvements ouvriers et socialistes (Chronologie et bibliographie): La Russie.* 2 vols. Paris, 1956.

## Unpublished Materials

Burch, Robert Jean. "Social Unrest in Imperial Russia: The Student Movement at Moscow University 1887–1905." Ph.D dissertation, Department of History, University of Washington, 1972.

France, Ministère des Affaires Etrangères, Paris (Quai d'Orsay). Archives Russie. Poltique intérieure, n.s. 12: Questions sociales, Agitation révolutionnaire, Anarchie, 1880–1904. Correspondance Consulaire et Commercial, 1793 à 1901: vol. 7: Moscow, 1897–1901; vol. 15: Odessa, October 1899–1901; vol. 55: St. Petersburg, October 1900–1901.

Johnson, Richard Jerome. "The Okhrana Abroad, 1885–1917: A Study in International Police Cooperation." Ph.D. dissertation, Faculty of Political Science, Columbia University, 1970.

Liubimov, D. N. "Russkaia smuta nachala deviatisotykh godov 1902–1906: Po vospominaniiam, lichnym zapiskam i dokumentam." Manuscript in the Archive of Russian and East European History and Culture, Columbia University, n.d.

"Protokol-bukh fun ferayn fun di stoliares, Minsk, dets. 1902–2 yuli 1903." Bund Archives, New York.

Sablinsky, Walter. "The Road to Bloody Sunday: Father Gapon, His Labor Organization, and the Massacre of Bloody Sunday." Ph.D. dissertation, Department of History, University of California, Berkeley, 1968.

Shmeleva, I. A. "Bor'ba moskovskikh rabochikh protiv zubatovshchiny." Candidate of Historical Science dissertation, Moskovskii gosudarstvennyi pedagogicheskii institut imeni V. I. Lenina, Moscow, 1962.

Spiridovich, A. I. Aleksandr Ivanovich Spiridovich Papers, Yale University Library.

U. S. Department of State. Consular Dispatches, Odessa. 1831–1906. National Archives.

Zuckerman, Frederic Scott. "The Russian Political Police at Home and Abroad (1880–1917): Its Structure, Functions, and Methods, and its Struggle with the Organized Opposition." Ph.D. dissertation, Department of History, New York University, 1973.

## Books and Pamphlets

Agafonov, V. K. *Zagranichnaia okhranka.* Petrograd, 1918.

Agurskii, S. *Ocherki po istorii revoliutsionnogo dvizheniia v Belorussii (1863–1917).* Minsk, 1928.

Ainzaft, S. *Istoriia rabochego i professional'nogo dvizheniia derevoobdelochnikov do revoliutsii 1917 goda*. Moscow, 1928.

———. *Pervyi etap professional'nogo dvizheniia v Rossii (1905–1907 gg.)*. 2 vols. Moscow-Gomel', 1924–1925.

———. *Zubatovshchina i gaponovshchina*. 4th ed. Moscow, 1925.

Alekseev, I. V. *Istoriia odnogo provokatora: Obvinitel'noe zakliuchenie i materialy k protsessu A. E. Serebriakovoi*. Moscow, 1925.

———. *Provokator Anna Serebriakova*. Moscow, 1932.

*Al'manakh sovremennykh russkikh gosudarstvennykh deiatelei*. St. Petersburg, 1897.

Almedingen, E. M. *An Unbroken Unity: A Memoir of Grand-Duchess Serge of Russia, 1864–1918*. London, 1964.

Angarskii, N. (ed.). *Doklady sots.-demokraticheskikh komitetov Vtoromu s"ezdu RSDRP*. Moscow-Leningrad, 1930.

Avchinnikov, A. G. *Velikii kniaz' Sergei Aleksandrovich: illiustrirovannyi biograficheskii ocherk, 1905–1915 g*. Ekaterinoslav, 1915.

Baron, Salo W. *The Russian Jews under Tsars and Soviets*. New York and London, 1964.

Baturin, N. [N. N. Zamiatin]. *Ocherki istorii sotsial-demokratii v Rossii*. 11th ed. Lenigrad, 1926.

Bauman, Nikolai Ernestovich. *Sbornik statei, vospominanii i dokumentov*. Moscow, 1937.

Bazylow, Ludwik. *Polityka wewnętrzna caratu i ruchy spoleczne w Rosji na początku XX wieku*. Warsaw, 1966.

Bendix, Reinhard. *Work and Authority in Industry: Ideologies of Management in the Course of Industrialization*. New York and London, 1956.

Berlin, P. A. *Russkaia burzhuaziia v staroe i novoe vremia*. Moscow, 1922.

Bill, Valentine T. *The Forgotten Class: The Russian Bourgeoisie from the Earliest Beginnings to 1900*. New York, 1959.

Black, Cyril E. (ed.). *The Transformation of Russian Society: Aspects of Social Change since 1861*. Cambridge, Mass., 1960.

Blackwell, William L. *The Beginnings of Russian Industrialization, 1800–1860*. Princeton, 1968.

Bogdanovich, A. V. *Tri poslednikh samoderzhtsa: Dnevnik A. V. Bogdanovich*. Moscow-Leningrad, 1924.

*Bol'shaia sovetskaia entsiklopediia*. 65 vols. Moscow, 1926–1947.

———. 2d ed. 51 vols. Moscow, 1950–1958.

Bortnikov, I. [V.]. *Iiul'skie dni 1903 goda na iuge Rossii*. Odessa, 1953.

Bukhbinder, N. A. *Istoriia evreiskogo rabochego dvizheniia v Rossii*. Leningrad, 1925.

———. *Zubatovshchina i rabochee dvizhenie v Rossii*. Moscow, 1926.

Burtsev, Vl. *Bor'ba za svobodnuiu Rossiiu: Moi vospominaniia (1882–1922 gg.)*. Vol. I. Berlin, 1923.

Buryshkin, P. A. *Moskva kupecheskaia*. New York, 1954.

Chernomordik, S. (P. Larionov). *1905 god v Moskve*. Moscow, 1925.

Chernov, Viktor. *Zapiski sotsialista-revoliutsionera*. Vol. I. Letopis' revoliutsii, no. 5. Berlin-Petersburg-Moscow, 1922.

Cohn, Norman. *Warrant for Genocide: The Myth of the Jewish World-Conspiracy and the Protocols of the Elders of Zion*. New York and Evanston, 1969.

[Dan, Fedor Il'ich]. *Doklad delegatsii Rossiiskoi Sots.-Dem. Rabochei Partii Amsterdamskomu Mezhdunarodnomu Sotsialisticheskomu Kongressu (14–20 avgusta 1904 g.)*. Geneva, 1904.

_____. *Iz istorii rabochago dvizheniia i sotsialdemokratii v Rossii 1900–1904 gg.* N. p., n. d.

*Deiatel'nost' Bunda za poslednie 2 goda (Ot IV-go do V-go s"ezda)*. London, 1903.

*Delo A. A. Lopukhina v osobom prisutsvii pravitel'stvuiushchago senata: Stenograficheskii otchet*. St. Petersburg, 1910.

Dillon, E. J. *The Eclipse of Russia*. New York, 1918.

*Doklad o russkom sotsial'demokraticheskom dvizhenii mezhdunarodnomu sotsialisticheskomu kongressu v Parizhe 1900 g.* Geneva, 1901.

Dubnov, S. M. *Kniga zhizni: Vospominaniia i razmyshleniia*. Vol. I *(do 1903 goda)*. Riga, 1934.

Dubnow, S. M. *History of the Jews in Russia and Poland: From the Earliest Times until the Present Day*. Translated by I. Friedlaender. 3 vols. Philadelphia, 1916–1920.

El'iashevich, V. B., A. A. Kizevetter, and M. M. Novikov (eds.). *Moskovskii universitet, 1755–1930: Iubileinii sbornik*. Paris, 1930.

*Encyclopedia of Zionism and Israel*. Edited by Raphael Patai. 2 vols. New York, 1971.

*Entsiklopedicheskii slovar' Russkogo bibliograficheskogo instituta Granat*. 7th rev. ed. Moscow, n.d. Articles: "Ozerov, Ivan Khristoforovich"; "Sergei Aleksandrovich, Velikii Kniaz'"; "Meshcheriakov, Nikolai Leonidovich"; "Mitskevich, Sergei Ivanovich"; "Sedoi (Litvin), Zinovii Iakovlevich."

Evsenin, Ev. *Ot fabrikanta k Krasnomu Oktiabriu: Iz istorii odnoi fabriki*. Moscow, 1927.

Fraenekl, J. *Dubnow, Herzl and Ahad Ha-Am*. London, 1963.

Galai, Shmuel. *The Liberation Movement in Russia, 1900–1905*. Cambridge, 1973.

Garvi, P. A. *Vospominaniia sotsialdemokrata*. New York, 1946.

Gerasimov, A. V. *Tsarisme et terrorisme: Souvenirs du général Guérassimov*. Paris, 1934.

Gerts, Ia. Sh., and S. M. Shvarts. *Zubatovshchina v Minske*. New York, 1962.

Gitelman, Zvi Y. *Jewish Nationality and Soviet Politics: The Jewish Sections of the CPSU, 1917–1930*. Princeton, 1972.

Golodets, M. G. (ed.). *Podpol'e: Iz istorii revoliutsionnogo dvizheniia v Sokol'nikakh*. Moscow-Leningrad, 1926.

Gordon, Manya. *Workers before and after Lenin.* New York, 1941.

Gorkii, M. *Zhizn' Klima Samgina (Sorok let) Povest'.* 3 vols. Moscow, 1934.

*Gosudarstvennyi Sovet. Stenograficheskie otchety. 1909–10 gody. Sessiia Piataia. Zasedaniia 1–64 (10 oktiabria 1909 g.–17 iiunia 1910 g.).* St. Petersburg, 1910.

_____. *1911–12 gody. Sessiia Sed'maia. Zasedaniia 1–81 (15 oktiabria 1911 g.–25 iiunia 1912 g.).* St. Petersburg, 1912.

Greenberg, Louis. *The Jews in Russia.* 2 vols. New Haven, 1944–1951.

Grigor'evskii, M. [M. G. Lunts]. *Politseiskii sotsializm v Rossii: Chto takoe Zubatovshchina?* St. Petersburg, 1906.

Grinevich, V. [M. G. Kogan]. *Professional'noe dvizhenie rabochikh v Rossii.* St. Petersburg, 1908.

*Gruppa "Osvobozhdenie truda": Iz arkhivov G. V. Plekhanova, V. I. Zasulicha i L. G. Deicha.* Edited by L. G. Deich. Vol. VI. Moscow-Leningrad, 1928.

Gurko, V. I. *Features and Figures of the Past: Government and Opinion in the Reign of Nicholas II.* Edited by J. E. Wallace Sterling, Xenia Joukoff Eudin, and H. H. Fisher. Translated by Laura Matveev. Stanford and London, 1939.

Gvozdev, S. *Zapiski fabrichnogo inspektora: Iz nabliudenii i praktiki v period 1894–1908 gg.* 2d ed. Moscow-Leningrad, 1925.

Hammond, Thomas Taylor. *Lenin on Trade Unions and Revolution, 1893–1917.* New York, 1957.

Harcave, Sidney. *First Blood: The Russian Revolution of 1905.* New York and London, 1964.

Hertzberg, Arthur (ed.). *The Zionist Idea: A Historical Analysis and Reader.* New York, 1970.

Ianzhul, I. I. *Iz vospominanii i perepiski fabrichnago inspektora pervago prizyva: Materialy dlia istorii russkago rabochago voprosa i fabrichnago zakonodatel'stva.* St. Petersburg, 1907.

Ignat'ev, V. *Bor'ba protiv zubatovshchiny v Moskve.* Moscow, 1939.

*Iskrovskie organizatsii na Ukraine: Sbornik dokumentov i materialov.* Kiev, 1950.

*Iskrovskii period v Moskve.* Edited by O. Piatnitskii, Ts. Borovskoi, and M. Vladimirskii. Moscow-Leningrad, 1928.

*Istoriia Kommunisticheskoi Partii Sovetskogo Soiuza.* 6 vols. Moscow, 1965–1970.

*Istoriia rabochego klassa Rossii, 1861–1900 gg.* Moscow, 1972.

*Istoriia Rossii v XIX veke.* 9 vols. St. Petersburg, 1907–1911.

*The Jewish People Past and Present.* 4 vols. New York, 1946–1955.

Johnpoll, Bernard K. *The Politics of Futility: The General Jewish Workers Bund of Poland, 1917–1943.* Ithaca, 1967.

Kanatchikov, S. *Iz istorii moego bytiia.* 2 vols. Moscow-Leningrad, 1929–1934.

Karataev, N. K. *Ekonomicheskie nauki v moskovskom universitete (1755–1955).* Moscow, 1956.

Kats, A., and Iu. Milonov (eds.). *1905: Professional'noe dvizhenie.* Moscow-Leningrad, 1926.

Katzenelson-Rubashow, Rachel (ed.). *The Plough Woman: Records of the Pioneer Women of Palestine.* Translated by Maurice Samuel. New York, 1932.

Keep, J. L. H. *The Rise of Social Democracy in Russia.* Oxford, 1963.

Kizevetter, A. A. *Na rubezhe dvukh stoletii (Vospominaniia 1881–1914).* Prague, 1929.

*Kniga o russkom evreistve ot 1860-kh godov do revoliutsii 1917 g.: Sbornik statei.* New York, 1960.

Kochan, Lionel (ed.). *The Jews in Soviet Russia since 1917.* London, 1970.

Kogan, I. *Vseobshchaia zabastovka 1903 goda.* Moscow, 1928.

Kokovtsov, V. N. *Out of My Past: The Memoirs of Count Kokovtsov.* Edited by H. H. Fisher. Translated by Laura Matveev. Stanford and London, 1935.

Kolesnikov, B. *Profsoiuzy v Rossii.* Kharkov, 1926.

Kolokol'nikov, P., and S. Rapoport (eds.). *1905–1907 gg. v professional'nom dvizhenii.* Moscow, 1925.

Koni, A. F. *Na zhiznennom puti.* Vol. V. Leningrad, 1929.

Koz'min, B. P. (ed.). *S. V. Zubatov i ego korrespondenty: Sredi okhrannikov, zhandarmov i provokatorov.* Moscow-Leningrad, 1928.

*Kratkaia istoriia rabochego dvizheniia v Rossii (1861–1917 gody).* Moscow, 1962.

Kulstein, David I. *Napoleon III and the Working Class: A Study of Government Propaganda under the Second Empire.* N. p., 1969.

Kurlov, P. G. *Gibel' imperatorskoi Rossii.* Berlin, 1923.

Kuz'mich, A. *Moskovskaia organizatsiia na II s"ezde RSDRP.* Moscow, 1963.

Lane, David. *The Roots of Russian Communism: A Social and Historical Study of Russian Social-Democracy, 1891–1907.* Assen, 1969.

Lapitskaia, S. *Byt rabochikh Trekhgornoi manufaktury.* Moscow, 1935.

Laporte, Maurice. *Historie de l'Okhrana: La Police secrète des Tsars, 1880–1917.* Paris, 1935.

Laqueur, Walter. *Russia and Germany: A Century of Conflict.* Boston and Toronto, 1965.

_____, and George L. Mosse (eds.). *International Fascism, 1920–1945.* New York, 1966.

Laverychev, V. Ia. *Tsarizm i rabochii vopros v Rossii (1861–1917 gg.).* Moscow, 1972.

*Legal'nye soiuzy i russkoe rabochee dvizhenie.* Munich, 1902.

Lenin, V. I. *Polnoe sobranie sochinenii.* 5th ed. 55 vols. Moscow, 1959–1965.

*Leninskaia "Iskra" i mestnye partiinye organizatsii Rossii (1900–1903 gg.).* Perm, 1971.

*Leninskii Sbornik.* 36 vols. Moscow, 1924–1959.

Liadov, M. N. [M. Mandel'shtam]. *Kak nachal skladyvat'sia rossiiskaia kommunisticheskaia partiia.* 2d ed. Moscow, 1925.

*Listovki peterburgskikh bol'shevikov, 1902–1917.* Vol. I: *1902–1907.* Leningrad, 1939.

*Listovki revoliutsionnykh sotsial-demokraticheskikh organizatsii Ukrainy 1896–1904.* Kiev, 1963.

Lopukhin, A. A. *Nastoiashchee i budushchee russkoi politsii.* Moscow, 1907.

_____. *Otryvki iz vospominanii (Po povodu "Vospominanii" gr. S. Iu. Vitte).* Moscow-Petrograd, 1923.

Los', F. E. *Formirovanie rabochego klassa na Ukraine i ego revoliutsionnaia bor'ba v kontse XIX i v nachale XX st. (konets XIX st.–1904 g.).* Kiev, 1955.

Lunts, M. G. *Sbornik statei: Iz istorii fabrichnago zakonodatel'stva, fabrichnoi inspektsii i rabochago dvizheniia v Rossii.* Moscow, 1909.

Lyashchenko, Peter I. *History of the National Economy of Russia to the 1917 Revolution.* Translated by L. M. Herman. New York, 1949.

Martov, L. *Istoriia rossiiskoi sotsial-demokratii.* 3rd ed. Petrograd-Moscow, 1923.

*Martov i ego blizkie: Sbornik.* New York, 1959.

*Materialy k istorii evreiskago rabochago dvizheniia.* St. Petersburg, 1906.

Mavor, James. *An Economic History of Russia.* 2 vols. London and Toronto, 1914.

McKay, John P. *Pioneers for Profit: Foreign Entrepreneurship and Russian Industrialization, 1885–1913.* Chicago and London, 1970.

Mehlinger, Howard D., and John M. Thompson. *Count Witte and the Tsarist Government in the 1905 Revolution.* Bloomington and London, 1972.

Mel'nik, S. V. I. *Lenin i odesskaia partiinaia organizatsiia.* Odessa, 1960.

Mendelsohn, Ezra. *Class Struggle in the Pale: The Formative Years of the Jewish Workers' Movement in Tsarist Russia.* Cambridge, 1970.

Men'shchikov, L. P. *Okhrana i revoliutsiia: K istorii tainykh politicheskikh organizatsii, sushchestvovavshikh vo vremena samoderzhaviia.* 3 vols. Moscow, 1925–1932.

_____. *Otkrytoe pis'mo P. A. Stolypinu russkomu prem'erministru.* Paris, 1911.

Meyer, Alfred G. *Leninism.* Cambridge, Mass., 1957.

Miliukov, P. *Ocherki po istorii russkoi kul'tury.* 6th ed. 3 vols. St. Petersburg, 1909.

_____. *Russia and its Crisis.* New York, 1962.

Miliutina, N. *Nakanune pervoi revoliutsii v Moskve.* Moscow-Leningrad, 1926.

Milonov, Iu., and M. Rakovskii. *Istoria moskovskogo professional'nogo soiuza rabochikh-derevoobdelochnikov.* Vol. I: *Ot pervykh stachek (90-e gody) do razgroma soiuza (1907 god).* Moscow, 1928.

Ministerstvo Finansov. Otdel promyshlennosti. *Materialy po izdaniiu zakona 2 iiunia 1897 goda ob ogranichenii i raspredelenii rabochago vremeni v zavedeniiakh fabrichno-zavodskoi promyshlennosti.* St. Petersburg, 1905.

_____. *Spisok fabrik i zavodov Evropeiskoi Rossii.* St. Petersburg, 1903.

_____. *Svod otchetov fabrichnykh inspektorov za 1901, 1902.* St. Petersburg, 1903–1904.

Ministerstvo Torgovli i Promyshlennosti. Otdel promyshlennosti. *Svod otchetov fabrichnykh inspektorov za 1903 god*. St. Petersburg, 1906.

Ministerstvo Vnutrennikh Del. Departament Politsii. *Sbornik sekretnykh tsirkuliarov obrashchennykh k Nachal'nikam gubernskikh zhandarmskikh upravlenii, gubernatoram i pr. v techenie 1902–1907 g.g.* [New York, 1929].

_____. *Sionizm: Istoricheskii ocherk ego razvitiia. Zapiska, sostavlennaia v departamente politsii*. St. Petersburg, 1903.

Mitskevich, S. *K 25-letiiu Moskovskoi organizatsii*. Moscow, 1918.

_____. *Ot narodnichestva k marksizmu: Memuarnaia zapis'*. Moscow, 1937.

_____. *Revoliutsionnaia Moskva, 1885–1905*. Moscow, 1940.

_____ (ed.). *Na zare rabochego dvizheniia v Moskve: Vospominaniia uchastnikov moskovskogo rabochego soiuza (1893–1895 gg.) i dokumenty*. Moscow, 1932.

Monas, Sidney. *The Third Section: Police and Society in Russia under Nicholad I.* Cambridge, Mass., 1961.

Morozov-Vorontsov, N. (ed.). *Zamoskvorech'e v 1905 g.: Sbornik vospominanii, dokumentov i fotografii*. Moscow, 1925.

Morskoi, A. [Vladimir von Shtein]. *Zubatovshchina: Stranichka iz istorii rabochago voprosa v Rossii*. Moscow, 1913.

Nedasek, N. *Bol'shevizm v revoliutsionnom dvizhenii Belorussii: Vvedenie v istoriiu bol'shevizma v Belorussii*. Munich, 1956.

Nesterenko, A. A. *Ocherki istorii promyshlennosti i polozheniia proletariata Ukrainy v kontse XIX i nachale XX v.* Moscow, 1954.

Nikolajewsky, Boris. *Aseff the Spy: Russian Terrorist and Political Stool.* Translated by George Reavy. Garden City, N. Y., 1934.

Normano, J. F. *The Spirit of Russian Economics*. London, 1950.

Novitskii, V. D. *Iz vospominanii zhandarma*. Edited by P. E. Shchegolev. Leningrad, 1929.

*Obshchestvennoe dvizhenie v Rossii v nachale XX-go veka*. Edited by L. Martov, P. Maslov, and A. Potresov. 4 vols. St. Petersburg, 1909–1914.

*Ocherki istorii moskovskoi organizatsii KPSS 1883–1965*. Moscow, 1966.

*Ocherki po istorii revoliutsionnogo dvizheniia i bol'shevistkoi organizatsii v Baumanskom raione*. Moscow-Leningrad, 1928.

Ol'denburg, S. S. *Tsarstvovanie imperatora Nikolaia II*. 2 vols. Belgrade, 1939.

*Otchet odesskago komiteta torgovli i manufaktur za 1903–1905 gody*. Odessa, 1906.

*Otchet po deloproizvodstvu gosudarstvennago soveta za sessiiu 1896–1897 g.g.; 1899–1900, vol. II; 1902–1903, vol. II; 1904–1905; 1905–1906*. St. Petersburg, 1897–1906.

Ovsiannikov, N. (ed.). *Na zare rabochego dvizheniia v Moskve*. Materialy po istorii proletarskoi revoliutsii, no. 2. Moscow, 1919.

Ozerov, I. Kh. *Iz zhizni truda: Sbornik statei*. Moscow, 1904.

_____. *Nuzhdy rabochago klassa v Rossii*. Moscow, 1906.

_____. *Politika po rabochemu voprosu v Rossii za poslednie gody*. Moscow, 1906.

*Pamiati Viacheslava Konstantinovich Pleve (Sbornik)*. St. Petersburg, 1904.

Pankratova, A. *Fabzavkomy Rossii v bor'be za sotsialisticheskuiu fabriku.* Moscow, 1923.

Patkin, A. L. *The Origins of the Russian-Jewish Labour Movement.* Melbourne and London, 1947.

*Perepis' Moskvy 1902 goda.* Vol. I, nos. 1 and 2: *Naselenie.* Moscow, 1904–1906.

*Perepiska V. I. Lenina i redaktsii gazety "Iskra" s sotsial-demokraticheskimi organizatsiiami v Rossii 1900–1903 gg.* 3 vols. Moscow, 1969–1970.

*Perepiska V. I. Lenina i rukovodimykh im zagranichnykh partiinykh organov s sotsial-demokraticheskimi organizatsiiami Ukrainy (1901–1905 gg.): Sbornik dokumentov i materialov.* Kiev, 1964.

Pintner, Walter McKenzie. *Russian Economic Policy under Nicholas I.* Ithaca, 1967.

Pipes, Richard. *Social Democracy and the St. Petersburg Labor Movement, 1885–1897.* Cambridge, Mass., 1963.

*Pis'ma P. B. Aksel'roda i Iu. O. Martova.* Edited by F. Dan, B. Nikolaevskii, and L. Tsederbaum-Dan. Berlin, 1924.

Pletnev, V. F. (ed.). *Instsenirovka: Sud nad Zubatovym i Gaponom 9 ianvaria 1905 g.* Moscow, 1925.

*Pochemu russkim rabochim nuzhna politicheskaia svoboda?* Geneva, 1902.

Pogogeff, Alexandre, and Pavel Natanovich Apostol. *L'économie sociale à la section Russe (Exposition Universelle International de 1900).* Paris, 1900.

Pogozhev, A. V. *Uchet chislennosti i sostava rabochikh v Rossii: Materialy po statistike truda.* St. Petersburg, 1906.

Polevoi, Iu. *Iz istorii moskovskoi organizatsii VKP (b.) (1894–1904 gg.).* Moscow, 1947.

Popova, E. (ed.). *1905 v Moskovskoi gubernii.* Moscow, 1926.

Portal, R. *La Russie industrielle de 1880 à 1914: Etudes régionales.* Paris, 1966.

Pospielovsky, Dimitry. *Russian Police Trade Unionism: Experiment or Provocation?* London, 1971.

Potresov, A. N., and B. I. Nikolaevskii (eds.). *Sotsial-demokraticheskoe dvizhenie v Rossii: Materialy.* Vol. I. Moscow-Leningrad, 1928.

*Prechistenskie rabochie kursy: Pervyi rabochii universitet v Moskve. Sbornik statei i vospominanii.* Moscow, 1948.

Premysler, I. *Revoliutsiinii rukh na Ukraini na pochatku XX stolittia (1900–1903 gg.).* Kiev, 1958.

*Proletariat Rossii na puti k Oktiabriu 1917 goda (oblik, bor'ba, gegemoniia): Materialy k nauchnoi sessii po istorii proletariata, posviashchennoi 50-letiiu Velikogo Oktiabria, 14–17 noiabria 1967 goda.* Parts I and II. Odessa, 1967.

*Rabochee dvizhenie v Rossii v XIX veke: Sbornik dokumentov i materialov.* Vol. IV, 1895–1900. Part 1, 1895–1897; Part 2, 1898–1900. Edited by L. M. Ivanov. Moscow-Leningrad, 1961–1963.

*Rabochie Trekhgornoi manufaktury v 1905 godu: Russkii rabochii v revoliutsionnom dvizhenii.* Vol. I. Moscow, 1930.

*Rabochii klass i rabochee dvizhenie v Rossii 1861–1917.* Moscow, 1966.

*Rabochii vopros v komissii V. N. Kokovtsova v 1905 g.* Moscow, 1926.

*Rabochii zavod "Serp i molot" (b. Guzhon) v 1905 gody: Russkii rabochii v revoliutsionnom dvizhenii.* Vol. II. Moscow, 1931.

Rafes, M. G. *Ocherki istorii evreiskogo rabochego dvizheniia.* Moscow-Leningrad, 1929.

———. *Ocherki po istorii "Bunda."* Moscow, 1923.

Rashin, A. G. *Formirovanie rabochego klassa Rossii: Istoriko-ekonomicheskie ocherki.* Moscow, 1958.

———. *Naselenie Rossii za 100 let (1811–1913 gg.): Statisticheskie ocherki.* Moscow, 1956.

*Revoliutsiia 1905–1907 gg. v Rossii: Dokumenty i materialy. Nachalo pervoi russkoi revoliutsii: Ianvar'-mart 1905 goda.* Edited by N. S. Trusova. Moscow, 1955.

*Revoliutsionnoe dvizhenie sredi evreev.* Vol. I. Moscow, 1930.

Riasanovsky, Nicholas V. *Nicholas I and Official Nationality in Russia, 1825–1855.* Berkeley and Los Angeles, 1959.

———. *Russia and the West in the Teaching of the Slavophiles: A Study of Romantic Ideology.* Cambridge, Mass., 1952.

Rogger, Hans, and Eugen Weber (eds.). *The European Right: A Historic Profile.* Berkeley and Los Angeles, 1965.

*Rossiiskii proletariat: Oblik, bor'ba, gegemoniia.* Moscow, 1970.

Rozhkov, N. A., and A. Sokolov. *O 1905 gode: Vospominaniia.* Moscow, 1925.

*Russkii zakon i rabochii.* Materialy po rabochemu voprosu, Vol. I. Stuttgart, 1902.

*Samoderzhavie i stachki: Zapiska Ministerstva Finansov o razreshenii stachek, s prilozheniem statii: "Novaia pobeda russkikh rabochikh" L. Martova.* Geneva, 1902.

*Sbornik statei Antonova (i dr.).* Moscow, 1908.

Schapiro, Leonard. *The Communist Party of the Soviet Union.* New York, 1959.

Schwarz, Solomon M. *The Jews in the Soviet Union.* Syracuse, 1951.

———. *Lénine et le mouvement syndical.* Paris, 1935.

———. *Men'shevizm i bol'shevizm v ikh otnoshenii k massovomu rabochemu dvizheniiu.* New York: Inter-University Project on the History of the Menshevik Movement, n.d.

———. *The Russian Revolution of 1905: The Workers' Movement and the Formation of Bolshevism and Menshevism.* Chicago and London, 1967.

Semenov-Bulkin, F. *Soiuz metallistov i departament politsii.* Leningrad, 1926.

Shchap, Z. *Moskovskie metallisty v professional'nom dvizhenii: Ocherki po istorii Moskovskogo soiuza metallistov.* Moscow, 1927.

Shelymagin, I. I. *Zakonodatel'stvo o fabrichno-zavodskom trude v Rossii, 1900–1917.* Moscow, 1952.

Sher, V. V. *Istoriia professional'nago dvizheniia rabochikh pechatnago dela v Moskve: Materialy k istorii professional'nago dvizheniia v Rossii.* Moscow, 1911.

Shestakov, P. M. *Rabochie na manufakture T-va "Emil' Tsindel" v Moskve.* Moscow, 1900.

Simmons, Ernest J. (ed.). *Continuity and Change in Russian and Soviet Thought.* Cambridge, Mass., 1955.

Simonenko, V. V., and G. D. Kostomarov (eds.). *Iz istorii revoliutsii 1905 goda v Moskve i Moskovskoi gubernii: Materialy i dokumenty.* Moscow, 1931.

Skarzhinskii, L. B. *Zabastovki i rabochiia sotovarishchestva.* St. Petersburg, 1905.

*Slavnye stranitsy bor'by i pobed: Materialy nauchnoi sessii, posviashchennoi 60-letiiu II s"ezda RSDRP i vseobshchikh zabastovok v Baku i na Iuge Rossii letom 1903 g. Baku, 17–20 sentiabria 1963 g.* Baku, 1965.

Sliozberg, G. B. *Dela minuvshikh dnei: Zapiski russkago evreia.* 3 vols. Paris, 1933–1934.

*Soiuz metallistov v Odesse (Po vospominaniiam veteranov) 1898–1925.* Odessa, 1925.

Solov'ev, Iu. B. *Samoderzhavie i dvorianstvo v kontse XIX veka.* Leningrad, 1973.

*Sovetskaia istoricheskaia entsiklopediia.* 14 vols. to date. Moscow, 1961–.

Spiridovich, A. I. *Pri tsarskom rezhime: Zapiski nachal'nika okhrannogo otdeleniia.* Moscow, 1926.

_____. *Zapiski zhandarma.* Kharkov, 1927 (?).

[Steklov, Iu. M., and N. Trotskii] *Iz rabochago dvizheniia v Odesse i Nikolaeve.* Geneva, 1900.

Sushkin, G. G. *Pod krovavym znamenem: 1903-iiul'–1933.* Moscow, 1933.

Suvorin, A. S. *Dnevnik A. S. Suvorina.* Edited by M. Krichevskii. Moscow-Petrograd, 1923.

Sviatlovskii, V. *Professional'noe dvizhenie v Rossii.* St. Petersburg, 1907.

*Svod vysochaishikh otmetok po vsepoddanneishim otchetam za 1895–1901 gg. general-gubernatorov, gubernatorov, voennykh gubernatorov i gradonachal'nikov.* St. Petersburg, 1897–1904.

Syrkin, Marie. *Nachman Syrkin, Socialist Zionist: A Biographical Memoir. Selected Essays.* New York, 1961.

*Tainye dokumenty otnosiashchiesia k zakonu 2-go iiunia 1897 goda.* Geneva, 1898.

*"Tekushchii moment": Sbornik.* Moscow, 1906.

Tereshkovich, K. *Moskovskaia revoliutsionnaia molodezh' 80-kh godov i S. V. Zubatov.* Moscow, 1928.

Tikhomirov, Lev. *Rabochii vopros i russkie idealy.* Moscow, 1902.

Titov, A. A. *Iz vospominanii o studencheskom dvizhenii 1901 g. Moskva.* Moscow, 1906 or 1907.

Tobias, Henry J. *The Jewish Bund in Russia: From Its Origins to 1905*. Stanford, 1972.

Treadgold, Donald W. *Lenin and His Rivals: The Struggle for Russia's Future, 1898–1906*. New York, 1955.

*Trudy vysochaishe uchrezhdennago vserossiiskago torgovo-promyshlennago s"ezda 1896 g. v Nizhnem Novgorode*. 3 vols. St. Petersburg, 1897.

Tugan-Baranovskii, M. *Russkaia fabrika v proshlom i nastoiashchem: Istoriko-ekonomicheskoe izsledovanie*. 2d ed. St. Petersburg, 1900.

Turin, S. P. *From Peter the Great to Lenin: A History of the Russian Labour Movement with Special Reference to Trade Unionism*. London, 1935.

Urussov, Prince Serge Dmitriyevich. *Memoirs of a Russian Governor*. Translated and edited by Herman Rosenthal. London and New York, 1908.

*V staroi Moskve: Kak khozianichali kuptsi i fabrikanty. Materialy i dokumenty*. Edited by L. Nikulin and G. Ryklin. Moscow, 1939.

Varzar, V. E. (ed.). *Statisticheskiia svedeniia o stachkakh rabochikh na fabrikakh i zavodakh za desiatiletie 1895–1904 goda*. St. Petersburg, 1905.

Vasin, I. *Sotsial-demokraticheskoe dvizhenie v Moskve, 1883–1901 gg*. Moscow, 1955.

Vassilyev, A. T. *The Ochrana: The Russian Secret Police*. Philadelphia and London, 1930.

Venturi, Franco. *Roots of Revolution: A History of the Populist and Socialist Movements in Nineteenth-Century Russia*. London, 1960.

*Vladimirskaia okruzhnaia organizatsiia R.S.-D.R.P. (Materialy k istorii sotsial-demokraticheskoi bol'shevistskoi raboty vo Vladimirskoi gubernii), 1892–1914*. Vladimir, 1927.

Von Laue, Theodore H. *Sergei Witte and the Industrialization of Russia*. New York and London, 1963.

Vovchik, A. F. *Politika tsarizma po rabochemu voprosu v predrevoliutsionnyi period (1895–1904)*. Lvov, 1964.

*Vseobshchaia stachka na iuge Rossii v 1903 godu: Sbornik dokumentov*. Moscow, 1938.

*Vtoroi s"ezd RSDRP, iiul'-avgust 1903 goda: Protokoly*. Moscow, 1959.

Walkin, Jacob. *The Rise of Democracy in Pre-Revolutionary Russia: Political and Social Institutions under the Last Three Czars*. New York, 1962.

Wildman, Allan K. *The Making of a Workers' Revolution: Russian Social Democracy, 1891–1903*. Chicago and London, 1967.

Witte, S. Iu. *Konspekt lektsii o narodnom i gosudarstvennom khoziaistve, chitannykh Ego Imperatorskomu Vysochestvu Velikomu Kniaziu Mikhailu Aleksandrovichu v 1900–1902 gg*. 2d ed. St. Petersburg, 1912.

———. *Vospominaniia*. 3 vols. Moscow, 1960.

Wolfe, Bertram D. *Three Who Made a Revolution: A Biographical History*. Boston, 1948.

*Zakonodatel'nye materialy k zakonu o starostakh v promyshlennykh predpriiatiiakh.* Materialy po rabochemu voprosu, vol. II. Stuttgart, 1903.

*Zapiski Georgiia Gapona (Ocherk rabochago dvizheniia v Rossii 1900-kh godov).* Moscow, 1918.

Zaslavskii, D. *Zubatov i Mania Vil'bushevich.* Moscow, 1923.

Zavarzin, P. P. *Rabota tainoi politsii.* Paris, 1924.

————. *Zhandarmy i revoliutsionery: Vospominaniia.* Paris, 1930.

Zelnik, Reginald E. *Labor and Society in Tsarist Russia: The Factory Workers of St. Petersburg, 1855–1870.* Stanford, 1971.

## ARTICLES

Abramsky, Chimen. "The Jewish Labour Movement: Some Historiographical Problems," *Soviet Jewish Affairs*, no. 1 (June 1971), pp. 45–51.

Achkanov, F. "Zamety pamiati," *Kommunist* (Odessa), March 1923, pp. 61–69.

Afenogenov, P. "Zubatovshchina," *Malaia sovetskaia entsiklopediia*, 2d ed., vol. IV (1935).

Ainzaft, S. "Zubatov i studenchestvo," *Katorga i ssylka*, 1927, no. 5 (34), pp. 65–69.

————. "Zubatovshchina v Moskve: (Po neizdannym arkhivnym materialam)," *Katorga i ssylka*, 1928, no. 2 (39), pp. 53–75.

Aizenberg, L. M. "Velikii kniaz' Sergei Aleksandrovich, Vitte i evreimoskovskie kuptsy (Iz istorii izgnaniia evreev iz Moskvy)," *Evreiskaia starina*, 13 (1930), 80–99.

Antoshkin, D. V. "Rabochee dvizhenie na trekhgornoi manufakture do 1918 goda," *Istoriia proletariata SSSR*, no. 5 (1931), 154–58.

Arbekov, P. "Ochag zubatovshchiny: Kizil-Arvatskoe remeslennoe sobranie," *Turkmenovedenie*, Dec. 1930, pp. 24–29.

Ascher, A. "The Coming Storm: The Austro-Hungarian Embassy on Russia's Internal Crisis, 1902–06," *Survey*, Oct. 1964, pp. 148–64.

B———skii, V. [V. Bogucharskii]. "Zubatovshchina," *Novyi entsiklopedicheskii slovar'*, vol. XVIII (n.d.).

Bailey, Sidney D. "Police Socialism in Tsarist Russia," *Review of Politics*, 19 (1957), 462–71.

Belen'kii, Ef. (Sergei). "Vospominaniia o bol'shevistskoi organizatsii v g. Minske v 1903 g.," *Proletarskaia revoliutsiia*, Nov. 1924, pp. 196–202.

Bleklov, S. "Obrazovatel'nyia uchrezhdeniia dlia rabochikh g. Moskvy," *Russkaia mysl'*, 1904, no. 5, pp. 121–45.

Bogdanov, D. "Zubatovshchina i gaponovshchina. (Politseiskii sotsializm)," *Bol'shevistskaia mysl'*, Dec. 1938, pp. 59–63.

Bortnikov, I. V. "Vseobshchaia stachka 1903 goda rabochikh g. Odessy," Odes'kii derzhavnii pedagogichnii institut im. K. D. Ushins'kogo, *Naukovi zapiski*, 8 (1947), 55–87.

Bukhbinder, N. A. "Dobavlenie k stat'e 'Evreiskoe rabochee dvizhenie v Gomele,'" *Krasnaia letopis'*, 1922, no. 2-3, pp. 391–418.

——. "Evreiskoe rabochee dvizhenie v Gomele (1890–1905 gg.): Po neizdannym arkhivnym materialam," *Krasnaia letopis'*, 1922, no. 2-3, pp. 38–102.

——. "Evreiskoe rabochee dvizhenie v Minske (1893–1905 gg.): Po neizdannym arkhivnym materialam," *Krasnaia letopis'*, 1923, no. 5, pp. 122–68.

——. "Iz istorii revoliutsionnoi propagandy sredi evreev v Rossii v 70-kh gg.," *Istoriko-revoliutsionnyi sbornik*, 1 (1924), 37–66.

——. "K istorii zubatovshchiny v Moskve (Po neizdannym protokolam zubatovskikh soveshchanii)," *Istoriia proletariata SSSR*, no. 2 (1930), 169–98.

——. "Nezavisimaia evreiskaia rabochaia partiia: Po neizdannym arkhivnym dokumentam," *Krasnaia letopis'*, 1922, no. 2-3, pp. 208–84.

——. "O zubatovshchine," *Krasnaia letopis'*, 1922, no. 4, pp. 289–335.

——. "I s"ezd 'Vseobshchego evreiskogo rabochego soiuza' 'Bunda,'" *Proletarskaia revoliutsiia*, Nov. 1924, pp. 203–8.

——. "Razgrom evreiskogo rabochego dvizheniia v 1898 g. (Po neizdannym arkhivnym materialam)," *Krasnaia letopis'*, 1922, no. 4, pp. 147–97.

——. "Zubatovshchina v Moskve (Neizdannye materialy)," *Katorga i ssylka*, 1925, no. 1, pp. 96–133.

——(ed.). "K istorii 'Sobraniia russkikh fabrichno-zavodskikh rabochikh g. S. Peterburga': Arkhivnye dokumenty," *Krasnaia letopis'*, 1922, no. 1, pp. 288–329.

Burtsev, V. "Police Provocation in Russia: I. Azef, The Tsarist Spy," *Slavonic Review*, 6 (1927), 247–60.

Cherniavskii, I. "Promyshlennyi kapitalizm v Belorussii i Litve i obrazovanie evreiskogo proletariata," *Istoriia proletariata SSSR*, no. 7 (1931), 86–118.

Chernomordik, S. [P. Larionov]. "Dvadtsat' let tomu nazad (Otryvki vospominanii)," *Put' k Oktiabriu*, no. 3 (1923), pp. 44–50.

——. "Vybory delegatov na 2-i s"ezd R.S.-D.R.P. ot moskovskoi organizatsii," *Proletarskaia revoliutsiia*, 1923, no. 2, pp. 601–5.

Crisp, Olga. "Some Problems of French Investment in Russian Joint-Stock Companies, 1894–1914," *Slavonic and East European Review*, 35 (1956), 223–40.

Degot', V. "Odesskie pechatniki v revoliutsionnom dvizhenii (Iz lichnykh vospominanii)," *Materialy po istorii professional'nogo dvizheniia v Rossii*, 3 (1925), 236–45.

"Dokumenty o I s"ezde R.S.D.R.P.," *Krasnaia letopis'*, 1923, no. 7, pp. 389–409.

"Dva dokumenta iz istorii zubatovshchiny," *Krasnyi arkhiv,* 1926, no. 6 (19), pp. 210–11.

"Dva dokumenta (K istorii zubatovskogo dvizheniia v g. Odesse, Iiul' 1903 g.)," *Materialy po istorii professional'nogo dvizheniia v Rossii,* 3 (1925), 246–73.

Dzhervis, M. "K istorii professional'nogo dvizheniia v Odesse," *Materialy po istorii professional'nogo dvizheniia v SSSR,* 5 (1927), 5–44.

_____. "Stachka tramvaishchikov (Iz istorii vseobshchei zabastovki 1903 g.)," *Professional'naia zhizn'* (Odessa), Dec. 1923, pp. 48–51.

Egorov, I. I. "V riadakh peterburgskikh sotsial-demokratov nakanune vtorogo s''ezda," *Krasnaia letopis',* 1928, no. 2 (26), pp. 33–44.

Evseev, E. S. "Iz istorii sionizma v tsarskoi Rossii," *Voprosy istorii,* May 1973, pp. 59–78.

Filatov, N. N. "Iz istorii sotsial-demokraticheskogo i rabochego dvizheniia v Odesse v nachale XX veka (1901–1903 gg.)," Odesskaia vyshaia partiinaia shkola, *Sbornik statei i soobshchenii,* 1958, pp. 49–67.

Frankel, Jonathan. "Economism: A Heresy Exploited," *Slavic Review,* 22 (1963), 263–84.

Frumkin, B. M. "Zubatovshchina i evreiskoe rabochee dvizhenie," *Perezhitoe,* 3 (1911), 199–230.

Gaisinovich, A. "Pervyi etap rabochego dvizheniia na zavode 'Serp i molot,'" *Istoriia proletariata SSSR,* no. 6 (1931), 156–65.

Gerschenkron, Alexander. "The Rate of Industrial Growth in Russia since 1885," *Journal of Economic History,* supplement 7 (1947), "The Tasks of Economic History," pp. 144–74.

Gershuni, G. "Zaiavlenie Grigoriia Gershuni Zubatovu: Iz arkhiva Zubatova," *Byloe,* March 1918, pp. 129–31.

Ginzburg, S. "Poezdka Teodora Gertslia v Peterburg," *Evreiskii mir,* 2 (1944), 197–209.

"Girsh Lekert i ego pokushenie," *Krasnyi arkhiv,* 1926, no. 2(15), pp. 86–103.

Godlevskii. "Kishinev, Odessa, Nikolaev. (Iz istorii s.-d. dvizheniia 1895–1903 gg.) Vospominaniia," *Letopis' revoliutsii,* 1924, no. 2(7), pp. 113–35.

Gol'dman, An. "Dve popravki," *Krasnaia letopis',* 1923, no. 8, pp. 250–51.

Goldsmith, Raymond W. "The Economic Growth of Tsarist Russia, 1860–1913," *Economic Development and Cultural Change,* 9 (1961), 441–75.

Gol'tsev, V. "Pervyi arest: Znakomstvo s g. Zubatovym (Iz vospominanii i perepiski)," *Russkaia mysl',* 1906, no. 11, pp. 113–17.

Gorev, B. I. [B. I. Gol'dman]. "Leonid Men'shchikov: Iz istorii politicheskoi politsii i provokatsii (Po lichnym vospominaniiam)," *Katorga i ssylka,* 1924, no. 10, pp. 130–40.

_____. "Pered vtorym s''ezdom (Vospominaniia)," *Katorga i ssylka,* 1924, no. 8, pp. 42–65.

Gotz, M. R. "S. V. Zubatov (Stranichka iz perezhitago)," *Byloe*, Sept. 1906, pp. 63–68.

Grigor'evskii, M. [M. G. Lunts]. "Politseiskii sotsializm v Rossii (Zubatovshchina)," *Obrazovanie*, 15 (1906), 187–227.

Haimson, Leopold. "The Problem of Social Stability in Urban Russia, 1905–1917," *Slavic Review*. 23 (1964), 619–42; 24 (1965), 1–22.

Hammond, Thomas T. "Lenin on Russian Trade Unions under Capitalism, 1894–1904," *American Slavic and East European Review*, 8 (1949), 275–88.

Hourwich, Isaac A. "The Political Situation in Russia," *Forum*, 34 (1902), 298–309.

Ianzhul, Ivan. "Vospominaniia I. I. Ianzhula o perezhitom i vidennom," *Russkaia starina*, no. 144 (Oct.-Dec. 1910), pp. 258–72, 485–500; no. 146 (June 1911), pp. 488–506.

Ivanov, L. M. "Samoderzhavie, burzhuaziia i rabochie (K voprosu ob ideologicheskom vliianii na proletariat)," *Voprosy istorii*, January 1971, pp. 81–96.

———. "Samoderzhavie i rabochii klass: Nekotorye voprosy politiki tsarizma," *Voprosy istorii*, June 1968, pp. 38–53.

"Iz istorii bor'by samoderzhaviia s rabochim dvizheniem," *Krasnyi arkhiv*, 1935, no. 1(68), pp. 154–57.

"Iz istorii rabochego dvizheniia kontsa 90-kh godov i 'Soiuzy bor'by za osvobozhdenie rabochego klassa,'" *Krasnyi arkhiv*, 1939, no. 2(93), pp. 119–89.

"Iz nedalekago proshlago," *Byloe*, February 1907, pp. 142–43.

"Iz perepiski 'Iskry' s mestnymi organizatsiiami," *Proletarskaia revoliutsiia*, June-July 1928, pp. 93–178.

"Iz perepiski redaktsii 'Iskry' s I. V. Babushkinym i N. E. Baumanom," *Proletarskaia revoliutsiia*, 1939, no. 1, pp. 222–28.

Johnson, Richard J. "Zagranichnaia Agentura: The Tsarist Police in Europe," *Journal of Contemporary History*, 7, no. 1-2 (Jan.-Apr. 1972), pp. 221–42.

"K 40-letiiu 'Iskry,'" *Krasnyi arkhiv*, 1940, no. 6(103), pp. 3–44.

"K istorii rabochego dvizheniia 90-kh g.g. (Zapiska pom. shefa korpusa zhandarmov gen.-ad'iut. Panteleeva)," *Ivanovo-Voznesenskii gubernskii ezhegodnik na 1921 god*, pp. 109–14.

"K istorii vseobshchei stachki na iuge Rossii v 1903 g.," *Krasnyi arkhiv*, 1938, no. 3(88), pp. 76–122.

"K istorii Zubatovshchiny," *Byloe*, July 1917, pp. 86–99.

K. and R. "Iz vrazheskogo lageria (1905–1907 god) (Arkhivnye materialy Moskovskogo metallicheskogo zavoda, byvshego Guzhona, nyne, 'Serp Molot,' v Moskve)," *Materialy po istorii professional'nogo dvizheniia v Rossii*, 3 (1925), 293–311.

K-tsyi. "Politseiskii sotsializm i sotsialdemokratiia," *Zhizn'*, May 1902, pp. 331–56.

Kheraskov, Ivan. "Reminiscences of the Moscow Students' Movement," *Russian Review*, 11 (1952), 223–32.

Khokhlov, A. "D. F. Trepov v bor'be s obshchestvennost'iu," *Russkoe proshloe*, 1923, no. 4, pp. 42–54.

"Khronika vnutrennei zhizni," IV, "Odesskii pogrom," *Russkoe bogatstvo*, Aug. 1900, pp. 159–62.

Kolokol'nikov, P. [K. Dmitriev]. "Otryvki iz vospominanii (Glava III)," *Materialy po istorii professional'nogo dvizheniia v Rossii*, 3 (1925), 215–35.

Kolpenskii, V. "Rabochee dvizhenie 90-kh gg. i mery pravitel'stvennoi bor'by s nim (Po arkhivnym dokumentam i materialam)," *Krasnaia letopis'*, 1922, no. 2-3, pp. 197–207.

Koniaev, A. "Guzhon," *Istoriia zavodov*, no. 3 (1932), pp. 68–76.

Korchmar', Ia. I. "K istorii stachki 1903 g. v Kieve," Kievskii gosudarstvennyi universitet, *Trudy istoricheskogo fakul'teta*, 1 (1939 or 1940), 175–208.

Korelin, A. P. "Krakh ideologii 'politseiskogo sotsializma' v tsarskoi Rossii," *Istoricheskie zapiski*, 92 (1973), 109–52.

_____. "Russkii 'politseiskii sotsializm' (Zubatovshchina)," *Voprosy istorii*, Oct. 1968, pp. 41–58.

Kristalovskii, Iosif. "Iz istorii zarozhdeniia i razvitiia bol'shevizma v Odesse (Vospominaniia)," *Letopis' revoliutsii*, 1924, no. 2(7), pp. 136–55.

Kuropatkin, A. N. "Dnevnik A. N. Kuropatkina," *Krasnyi arkhiv*, 1922, no. 2, pp. 5–112.

Lavrov, Z. L. "Zhizn' rabochego-revoliutsionera (Avtobiografiia)," *Katorga i ssylka*, 1925, no. 1(14), pp. 156–68.

Lebedev, M. "Politseiskii sotsializm v Rossii," *Propaganda i agitatsiia*, December 1938, pp. 41–47.

Lelevich, G. "D-r. Shaevich v tiur'me," *Krasnaia letopis'*, 1922, no. 5, pp. 392–93.

Levitskaia, Evg. "Iz zhizni odesskogo podpol'ia (Iz vospominanii 1901–1907 gg.)" *Proletarskaia revoliutsiia*, 1922, no. 6, pp. 135–57.

*Malaia sovetskaia entsiklopediia*, 2d ed., vol. IV (1935). Article, "Zubatov."

Meller, V. "Iz istorii zavoda 'Serp i molot': Ot podpol'nykh kruzhkov k bor'be za vlast' sovetov," *Bor'ba klassov*, 1931, no. 6-7, pp. 123–33.

Mendelsohn, Ezra. "The Russian Jewish Labor Movement and Others," *Yivo Annual of Jewish Social Science*, 14 (1969), 87–98.

_____. "Worker Opposition in the Russian Jewish Socialist Movement, from the 1890's to 1903," *International Review of Social History*, 10 (1965), 268–82.

Miliutina, M. "Kratkii ocherk istorii moskovskoi organizatsii," *Put' k Oktiabriu*, no. 2 (1923), pp. 7–25.

Mishkinsky, Moshe. "Ha-sotsializm ha-mishtari u-megamot ba-mediniut ha-shilton ha-tsari legabay ha-yehudim," *Zion* (Jerusalem), 25 (1960), 238–49.

Moshinskii, I. N. [Iuz. Konarskii]. "Do i posle I s"ezda R.S.-D.R.P. (Poiski iuzhnoi tipografii i razgrom s. -d. organizatsii)," *Katorga i ssylka*, 1928, no. 3(40), pp. 41–54.

N. "Tri dnia (Iz lichnykh vospominanii)," *Vestnik russkoi revoliutsii*, March 1905, pp. 299–314.

Nevskii, V. "Letnie stachki 1903 g.—predvestniki 1905 goda," *Bor'ba klassov*, Aug.-Sept. 1933, pp. 130–43.

Nogin, V. P. "Vospominaniia V. P. Nogina o moskovskoi organizatsii," *Proletarskaia revoliutsiia*, Feb. 1925, pp. 204–12.

Novikov, V. I. "Leninskaia 'Iskra' v bor'be s zubatovshchinoi," *Voprosy istorii*, Aug. 1974, pp. 24–35.

"Novoe o zubatovshchine," *Krasnyi arkhiv*, 1922, no. 1, pp. 289–328.

Novomirskii, D. "Iz istorii odesskogo podpol'ia (Iuzhnaia revoliutsionnaia gruppa sotsial-demokratov v 1901 g.)," *Proletarskaia revoliutsiia*, April 1927, pp. 181–202.

Novopolin, G. "Iz istorii rabochego dvizheniia (1880–1903 gg.)," *Letopis' revoliutsii*, 1923, no. 2, pp. 16–28.

———. "Zubatovshchina v Ekaterinoslave," *Istoriia proletariata SSSR*, no. 2 (1930), 233–49.

"Ocherk anarkhicheskago dvizheniia v Odesse," *Buntar'*, Dec. 1, 1906, pp. 30–32.

"O dvizhenii sredi moskovskikh rabochikh metallistov," *Materialy po istorii professional'nogo dvizheniia v Rossii*, 1(1924), 133–52.

Osipovich, N. "Rasskazy o sekretnykh sotrudnikakh," *Kandal'nyi zvon* (Odessa), no. 1 (1925), 115–34.

P., A. "Departament politsii v 1892–1908 gg. (Iz vospominanii chinovnika)," *Byloe*, November-December 1917, pp. 17–24.

Paialin, N. P. "Zavod byvsh. Semiannikova," *Krasnaia letopis'*, 1930, no. 6(39), pp. 231–49.

"Peterburgskoe dukhovenstvo i 9 ianvaria," *Krasnyi arkhiv*, 1929, no. 5(36), pp. 192–99.

Pintner, Walter M. "Government and Industry during the Ministry of Count Kankrin, 1823–1844," *Slavic Review*, 23 (1964), 45–62.

Piontkovskii, S. (ed.). "Zubatovshchina i sotsial-demokratiia (Arkhivnye materialy)," *Katorga i ssylka*, 1924, no. 8, pp. 66–101.

Pipes, Richard. "Russian Conservatism in the Second Half of the Nineteenth Century," *Slavic Review*, 30 (1971), 121–28.

"Pis'ma Mednikova Spiridovichu," *Krasnyi arkhiv*, 1926, no. 4(17), pp. 192–219.

Pogozhev, A. "Iz vospominanii o V. K. von-Pleve," *Vestnik Evropy*, July 1911, pp. 259–80.

Pokrovskii, M. Review of *Zubatovshchina i gaponovshchina* by S. Ainzaft, *Vestnik Sotsialisticheskoi akademii*, no. 2 (Jan. 1923), pp. 262–68.

Polovtsev, A. A. "Dnevnik A. A. Polovtseva," *Krasnyi arkhiv,* 1923, no. 3, pp. 75–172.

Portal, R. "Industriels moscouvites: Le secteur cotonnier (1861–1914)," *Cahiers du Monde Russe et Soviétique,* 4 (1963), 5–46.

Pototskii, N. "Vernye slugi Tsaria i Rossii," *Znamia Rossii,* June 1960, pp. 2–5.

"Prikliuchenie I. F. Manuilova: Po arkhivnym materialam," *Byloe,* Nov.-Dec. 1917, pp. 236–86.

Prudnikov. "Stranichka iz vospominanii o Zubatove," *Put' k Oktiabriu,* no. 1 (1923), pp. 122–25.

R., D. "Odessa," *Novyi entsiklopedicheskii slovar',* vol. XXIX (1916).

"Rabochee dvizhenie na zavodakh Peterburga v mae 1901 g.," *Krasnyi arkhiv,* 1936, no. 3(76), pp. 49–66.

Rakovskii, M. "Zubatov i moskovskie gravery (1898–1899 gg.)," *Istoriia proletariata SSSR,* no. 2 (1930), 199–232.

Rataev, L. A. "Evno Azef: Istoriia ego predatel'stva," *Byloe,* Aug. 1917, pp. 187–210.

———. "Iz perepiski okhrannikov: Pis'ma L. A. Rataeva–S. V. Zubatovu," *Golos minuvshago,* June 1922, pp. 51–59.

Ratova, S. A. [K. I. Zakharova-Tsederbaum]. "Vseobshchaia stachka v 1903 godu na Kavkaze i Chernomorskom poberezh'e (K istorii rabochago dvizheniia v Rossii)," *Byloe,* June 1907, pp. 97–117.

Riabushinskii, P. L. "Kupechestvo Moskovskoe," *Den' russkago rebenka,* April 1951, pp. 168–89.

Rimlinger, Gaston V. "Autocracy and the Factory Order in Early Russian Industrialization," *Journal of Economic History,* 20 (1960), 67–92.

———. "The Management of Labor Protest in Tsarist Russia: 1870–1905," *International Review of Social History,* 5 (1960), 226–48.

Rogger, Hans. "The Formation of the Russian Right, 1900–1906," *California Slavic Studies,* 3 (1964), 66–94.

———."Reflections on Russian Conservatism: 1861–1905," *Jahrbücher für Geschichte Osteuropas,* 14 (1966), 195–212.

———. "Was There a Russian Fascism? The Union of Russian People," *Journal of Modern History,* 36 (1964), 398–415.

Rozhkova, M. K. "Sostav rabochikh Trekhgornoi manufaktury nakanune imperialisticheskoi voiny," *Istoriia proletariata SSSR,* no. 5 (1931), 169–80.

Rybakov, I. F. "Dinamika gorodskogo naseleniia Rossii vo vtoroi polovine XIX veka," Leningradskii ordena Lenina gosudarstvennyi universitet imeni A. A. Zhdanova, *Uchenye zapiski,* no. 288, Seriia ekonomicheskikh nauk, pt. 2 (1959), pp. 181–210.

Schneiderman, Jeremiah, trans. "From the Files of the Moscow Gendarme Corps: A Lecture on Combatting Revolution," *Canadian Slavic Studies,* 2 (1968), 86–99.

Semenov-Bulkin, F. "Smesovshchina," *Trud v Rossii*, 1925, no. 1, pp. 153–70.

Shatz, Marshall. "Jan Waclaw Machajski: The 'Conspiracy' of the Intellectuals," *Survey,* Jan. 1967, pp. 45–57.

_____. "The Makhaevists and the Russian Revolutionary Movement," *International Review of Social History,* 15 (1970), 235–65.

Sheimin, P. "Politsiia," *Entsiklopedicheskii slovar'*, vol. xxiv (1898).

Shestakov, A. V. (Nikodim). "V tsikle 25 let," *Put' k Oktiabriu*, no. 3 (1923), pp. 5–43.

Shidlovskii, Georgii. "Chelovek revoliutsionnoi energii: O V. P. Nogine (Materialy)," *Krasnaia letopis'*, 1924, no. 2(11), pp. 165–80.

Shlosberg, D. "Vseobshchaia stachka 1903 g. na Ukraine," *Istoriia proletariata SSSR*, no. 7 (1931), 52–85.

_____, and B. Shul'man, "Vseobshchaia zabastovka v Odesse v 1903 gody i 'nezavisimtsy,'" *Litopis revoliutsii*, 1929, no. 1(34), pp. 102–144.

Shmeleva, I. A. "Bor'ba moskovskikh rabochikh protiv zubatovshchiny," Moskovskii gosudarstvennyi pedagogicheskii institut imeni V. I. Lenina, *Uchenye zapiski*, vol. 110, Kafedra istorii SSSR, pt. 4 (1957), pp. 31–70.

_____. "Bor'ba protiv zubatovshchiny v Moskve po vospominaniiam rabochikh," Shuiskii gosudarstvennyi pedagogicheskii institut, *Uchenye zapiski*, pt. 9 (1960), pp. 56–74.

_____. "Bor'ba sotsial-demokraticheskikh organizatsii Moskvy s zubatovshchinoi," Shuiskii gosudarstvennyi pedagogicheskii institut, *Uchenye zapiski,* pt. 8 (1959), pp. 126–54.

"Shochat, Mania Wilbushewitch," *Encyclopaedia Judaica*, vol. XIV(1971), pp. 1441–42.

Shtein, V. I. "Neudachnyi opyt (Zubatovshchina),"*Istoricheskii vestnik*, no. 129 (July 1912), pp. 223–55.

Sliozberg, G. B. "Baron G. O. Gintsburg i pravovoe polozhenie evreev," *Perezhitoe*, 2 (1910), 94–115.

Spiridovich, A. I. "Pri tsarskom rezhime," *Arkhiv russkoi revoliutsii*, 15 (1924), 85–206.

"Stachka rabochikh zavoda br. Bromlei v 1903 g.," *Krasnyi arkhiv*, 1933, no. 1(56), pp. 138–44.

"Studencheskie volneniia v 1901–1902 gg.," *Krasnyi arkhiv*, 1938, no. 4-5 (85–90), pp. 258–308.

"Studencheskoe dvizhenie v 1901 g.," *Krasnyi arkhiv*, 1936, no. 2(75), pp. 83–112.

Szeftel, Marc. "Personal Inviolability in the Legislation of the Russian Absolute Monarchy," *American Slavic and East European Review*, 17 (1958), 1–24.

Tatarov, I. "K istorii 'politseiskogo sotsializma,'" *Proletarskaia revoliutsiia*, May 1927, pp. 109–123.

Tereshkovich, K. "Moskovskaia molodezh' 80-kh godov i Sergei Zubatov (Iz vospominanii)," *Minuvshie gody,* 1908, no. 5-6, pp. 207–215.

Tidmarsh, Kyril. "The Zubatov Idea," *American Slavic and East European Review,* 19 (1960), 335–46.

Tikhomirov, L. "25 let nazad: Iz dnevnikov L. Tikhomirova," *Krasnyi arkhiv,* 1930, no. 1(38), pp. 20–69; 1933, no. 6(61), pp. 82–128.

Tompkins, Stuart R. "Witte as Minister of Finance, 1892–1903," *Slavonic and East European Review,* 11 (1933), 590–606.

"Trepovskii proekt rechi Nikolaia II k rabochim posle 9 ianvaria 1905 g.," *Krasnyi arkhiv,* 1927, no. 1(20), pp. 240–42.

Tseitlin, L. S. "V Moskve pered II s"ezdom RSDRP," *Katorga i ssylka,* 1934, no. 5-6, pp. 89–126.

Ugarov, I. F. "V. I. Lenin i obrazovanie iskrovskoi organizatsii v Moskve," *Istoricheskie zapiski,* 84 (1969), 275–94.

Ushakov, A. V. "Rabochee dvizhenie v Moskve nakanune pervoi russkoi revoliutsii," Karelo-finskii pedagogicheskii institut, Petrozavodsk, *Uchenye zapiski,* 2, pt. 1 (1955), Seriia obshchestvennykh nauk, pp. 54–81.

V-ich, A. "Zubatovskiia obshchestva i professional'nye soiuzy," *Rabochii soiuz,* Oct. 3, 1906, pp. 4–6.

Varnashev, N. M. "Ot nachala do kontsa s gaponovskoi organizatsiei v S.-Peterburge (Vospominaniia)," *Istoriko-revoliutsionnyi sbornik,* 1(1924), 177–208.

Vasil'ev, P. "Ushakovshchina," *Trud v Rossii,* 1925, no. 1, pp. 143–52.

"Vecher vospominanii: Stenogramma," *Materialy po istorii professional'nogo dvizheniia v Rossii,* 4 (1925), 5–63.

Vol'shtein, Liza. "Zapiski fabrichnoi rabotnitsy," *Proletarskaia revoliutsiia,* Sept. 1922, pp. 160–81.

Von Laue, Theodore H. "The Chances for Liberal Constitutionalism," *Slavic Review,* 24 (1965), 34–46.

———. "Factory Inspection under the Witte System: 1892–1903," *American Slavic and East European Review,* 19 (1960), 347–62.

———. "The Industrialization of Russia in the Writings of Sergej Witte," *American Slavic and East European Review,* 10 (1951), 177–90.

———. "Russian Labor between Field and Factory, 1892–1903," *California Slavic Studies,* 3 (1964), 33–65.

———. "Russian Peasants in the Factory, 1892–1904," *Journal of Economic History,* 21 (1961), 61–80.

———. "Tsarist Labor Policy, 1895-1903," *Journal of Modern History,* 34 (1962), 135–45.

Vostokov, L. "Antinarodnaia deiatel'nost' sionistov v Rossii," *Voprosy istorii,* March 1973, pp. 23–35.

Walkin, Jacob. "The Attitude of the Tsarist Government toward the Labor Problem," *American Slavic and East European Review,* 13 (1954), 163–84.

Wildman, Allan K. "Lenin's Battle with Kustarnichestvo: The Iskra Organization in Russia," *Slavic Review,* 23 (1964), 479–503.

_____. "The Russian Intelligentsia of the 1890's," *American Slavic and East European Review,* 19 (1960), 157–79.

Wischnitzler, Mark. "Minsk," *Universal Jewish Encyclopedia,* vol. VII (1942?).

Wolfe, Bertram D. "Gapon and Zubatov: An Experiment in 'Police Socialism,'" *Russian Review,* 7 (1948), 53–61.

Zaiats, M. "Zachatki professional'nogo dvizheniia tekstil'shchikov Tsentral'nogo Promyshlennogo Raiona," *Materialy po istorii professional'nogo dvizheniia v Rossii,* 2 (1924), 103–117.

Zakharova, L. G. "Krizis samoderzhaviia nakanune revoliutsii 1905 goda," *Voprosy istorii,* August 1972, pp. 119–40.

"Zapiska direktora depart. pol. Lopukhina o stachkakh v iiule 1903 g. v Odesse, Kieve, Nikolaeve," *Krasnaia letopis',* 1922, no. 4, pp. 382–95.

"Zapiska gen. Novitskago, podannaia na vysochaishee imia cherez kn. Sviatopolka-Mirskago," *Sotsialist-revoliutsioner,* no. 2 (1910), pp. 53–113.

"Zasedanie Soveta 'Russkago Sobraniia' (10 dekabria)," *Izvestiia russkago sobraniia,* 1, no. 1 (1903), pp. 46–60.

Zaslavskii, D. "Zubatov i Mania Vil'bushevich," *Byloe,* March 1918, pp. 99–128.

Zelnik, Reginald E. "The Sunday-School Movement in Russia, 1859–1862," *Journal of Modern History,* 37 (1965), 151–70.

Zel'tser, V. "Moskva XIX-XX vv.," *Bor'ba klassov,* July-Aug. 1934, pp. 56–69.

_____. "Promyshlennaia revoliutsiia v Rossii," *Bor'ba klassov,* Sept. 1934, pp. 80–88.

Zhilinskii, V. "Organizatsiia i zhizn' okhrannago otdeleniia vo vremena tsarskoi vlasti," *Golos minuvshago,* Sept.-Oct. 1917, pp. 247–306.

"Znachenie 19 fevralia 1902 g. dlia moskovskikh rabochikh," *Byloe,* no. 14, 1912, pp. 81–88.

Zubatov, S. V. "Iz nedavniago proshlago: G. Zubatov o 'Zubatovshchine,'" *Vestnik Evropy,* March 1906, pp. 432–36.

_____. "Pis'mo S. V. Zubatova [ot 7 avgusta 1916 g.] A. I. Spiridovichu po povodu vykhoda v svet ego knigi 'Partiia s.-r. i ee predshestvenniki,'" *Krasnyi arkhiv,* 1922, no. 2, pp. 281–83.

_____. "Zubatovshchina," *Byloe,* Oct. 1917, pp. 157–78.

"Zubatovshchina ('Politseiskii sotsializm')," *Istoricheskii zhurnal,* 9, no. 1 (1939), pp. 113–15.

## Newspapers and Emigré Publications

*Birzhevye vedomosti*
*Biulleteni Muzeia sodeistviia trudu*
*Budushchnost'*
*Grazhdanin*

Iskra
Listok "Rabochago dela"
Listok "Rabotnika"
Mladorosskaia iskra
Moskovskiia vedomosti
Nasha zhizn'
Novoe vremia
Obshchee delo
Odesskii listok
Osvobozhdenie
Posledniia izvestiia
Pravda
Professional'nyi soiuz
Rabochaia gazeta
Rabochaia mysl'
Rabochee delo
Rabochii soiuz
Rabotnik
Revoliutsionnaia Rossiia
Rodnaia rech'
Russkiia vedomosti
Russkoe delo
Russkoe slovo
Russkoe znamia
Rus'
S.-Peterburgskiia vedomosti
The Times (London)
Torgovo-promyshlennaia gazeta
Vestnik Bunda
Vestnik russkoi revoliutsii
Vozrozhdenie
Zhizn'

# Index

Sergei Zubatov and
Revolutionary Marxism

Designed by R. E. Rosenbaum.
Composed by Utica Typesetting Company, Inc.,
in 10 point VIP Palatino, 2 points leaded,
with display lines in VIP Palatino.
Printed offset by LithoCrafters, Inc.
on Warren's Number 66 text, 50 pound basis.
Bound by LithoCrafters, Inc.
in Joanna book cloth
and stamped in All Purpose foil.

Library of Congress Cataloging in Publication Data
Schneiderman, Jeremiah.
    Sergei Zubatov and revolutionary Marxism.

    Bibliography: p.
    Includes index.
    1. Labor policy--Russia--History. 2. Zubatov,
Sergei Vasil'evich, 1864-1917. I. Title.
HD8526.S32        331'.0947        75-27881
ISBN 0-8014-0876-8